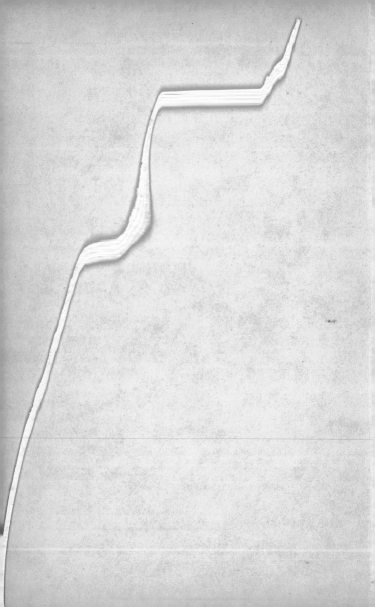

Charles Lamb

A BOOK OF
ENGLISH ESSAYS

SELECTED AND EDITED BY

C. T. WINCHESTER

**PROFESSOR OF ENGLISH LITERATURE IN
WESLEYAN UNIVERSITY**

NEW YORK

HENRY HOLT AND COMPANY

CONTENTS

The figures in the second column indicate the pages of the Biographical Sketches and Notes.

THE ESSAY

The Essay, as a distinct literary form, may be defined as a prose composition of moderate length, dealing with one subject, and in such a way as to give free expression to the personality of the writer. The term has, indeed, been loosely applied to a wide variety of prose works, such as the philosophical treatise, the historical or biographical monograph, and the brief anonymous article of the newspaper. But the essay, in the stricter sense in which the word is employed in this volume, is always personal, always in some degree autobiographical. The essayist is, in some special sense, writing of himself. The essay thus, in this respect, corresponds in prose with the lyric in verse.

The essay as thus defined did not originate in England. The form and the name were both invented by that most entertaining French egoist, Michael de Montaigne. Montaigne's *Essais*, of which the first two volumes were published in 1580 and the third in 1588, are the first specimens of this kind of composition in European literature, and they have been models of the essay ever since. They are the frank comment of a shrewd, half-stoical man upon the varied circumstances and experiences of life. Easy, sometimes almost garrulous in manner, they are collected into books without any discoverable principle of arrangement; it is not improbable that they may have grown out of such detached observations and memoranda as a reflective man might write

down to please himself in a common-place book. Sometimes the subject is a personal quality or habit, as "Idleness" or "Envy"; sometimes it is a principle of morals
or society, as "That our Actions are judged by our
Intentions"; sometimes it is merely trivial or humorous,
as "On Smells," "On Thumbs." It makes little difference what is the subject—— Montaigne can write
charmingly about his dog or his cat; in any case, it is
the shrewd, racy personality of the man, humorist,
philosopher, skeptic, that interests us. As he said truly
in a prefatory note, "It is myself that I portray."

Montaigne's Essays were immediately admired and
imitated in England. In 1597, only five years after the
death of Montaigne, Francis Bacon gave to his first thin
volume of English papers the title "Essays." This is
the first known use of the word in English, and was undoubtedly borrowed from Montaigne. Six years later,
in 1603, appeared the first English translation of the
Essais, by that eccentric Elizabethan scholar and dic-
tionary-maker, John Florio. The popularity of the translation is attested by the fact that other editions were
called for in 1613 and 1632. This is the translation
through which Montaigne became known in English
to the men of Shakespeare's generation. For fifty years
probably no French book was more familiar or more
widely read in England, or had more influence upon the
development of English prose. Florio's translation is
not always accurate; but in spirit and vivacity it has
never been surpassed, and it is still probably the best
version for the general reader.

Bacon's Essays have too little ease and fluency to be
good examples of the Montaigne type. They are over
sententious, packed too full of thought, and have little
of Montaigne's leisurely and familiar manner. Yet on

that very account they are all the more faithful expressions of the mind of Bacon, who was deficient in the more genial forms of emotion, and saw all things in the cold, dry light of the intellect. The Essays certainly bear traces in every line of the personality of their author.

Much of the writing of those delightful early seventeenth century men, Thomas Fuller, Sir Thomas Browne, Isaac Walton, is of the familiar personal sort well fitted for the essay. Excellent essays, one thinks, could be shaped out of their books; but they did not adopt the essay form. It is in the prose of Abraham Cowley that we first see in English, essays precisely after the model of Montaigne's. His *Discourses by Way of Essays* were written late in his life, and printed in 1668, the year after his death. In unity of subject combined with ease and lucidity of style, in felicity of illustration and example, and in their tone of complacent personal revelation, Cowley's essays are almost equal to Montaigne's. Indeed, such papers as those *Of Myself* and *Of Solitude* one could imagine written by Montaigne himself.

Before the close of the seventeenth century the term essay came to be applied sometimes to treatises philosophical like Locke's *Essay on the Human Understanding*, or critical like Dryden's *Essay of Dramatic Poesy*, or religious like Clarendon's *Reflections upon Christian Doctrine by Way of Essays;* but there is only one other writer of any eminence in the century whose work was cast in the strict form of the essay. Sir William Temple had been prominent in English politics and diplomacy before the Revolution of 1688; but he retired early from public life and spent his later years as a superannuated statesman, in learned and elegant leisure, playing at Greek and gardening on his estate at Moor Park.

Temple is principally remembered as the patron of Swift and a party in the quarrel out of which grew Swift's *Battle of the Books;* but in the years of his retirement he wrote a number of pleasing papers that in subject and manner are genuine essays.   The best of these are those entitled *Of Gardens, Of Poetry,* and *Of Health and Long Life.*   Temple's writing has a kind of dignified ease, reflecting a courtly, self-satisfied personality; but the reader of to-day is likely to find his reflections a little superficial and his manner a little pompous.   The limits of this volume do not allow any selections from his work.

Both Cowley and Temple mention Montaigne with admiration; both show unmistakably his influence in the general form of their essays; and both, in some instances, have borrowed from him titles and subject matter.   The *Essais* continued to be popular in England throughout the century.   In 1685 an entirely new translation of them was made by Charles Cotton, which is somewhat more accurate than Florio's and more temperate in style.   Through all the centuries, indeed, many of the masters of English prose, Dryden, Addison, Hazlitt, Lamb, Thackeray, Emerson, Lowell, Stevenson have borne emphatic testimony to the wisdom and the charm of the father of the essay.

After the beginning of the eighteenth century, the essay received considerable modification at the hands of Steele and Addison.   The paper of the *Tatler* and *Spectator* is quite a different thing from the essay of Cowley or Temple.   The familiar personal quality of the older essay, indeed, is retained and increased.   It is Mr. Bickerstaff or Mr. Spectator who is talking with us; and certainly no writers ever revealed themselves more frankly than they, or put themselves into more cordial relations with their readers.   But in their treatment the older essay was made simpler in structure and was very much shortened. A daily essay, to be read in the coffee-house, must of necessity be brief. Furthermore, the tone of this essay was different in some respects from that of the older. In the Queen Anne age, literature, like philosophy, descended into the street. The readers of the *Tatler* and *Spectator* were not interested in the meditations of the study, but in the conversation of the club and the drawing-room. The periodical literature of such an age must reflect the charm of manners and society; it may be wise, but it cannot be abstract or profound; it must be witty and urbane. If it touch upon serious matters, it must do so with brevity and grace. It is the special praise of Steele and Addison that they perfected a form of the essay exactly satisfying these conditions. Addison, in particular, perceived that it was possible to give to writing colloquial in manner and familiar even to commonplace in subject, an exquisite literary form and finish. The *Spectator* papers were accounted for nearly a century, correct models of the essay form. A multitude of periodicals in imitation of the *Spectator* were set up during the course of the century— nearly two hundred in all—but most of them were very short lived. A few papers of pleasing humor by Goldsmith and of sound sense by Johnson may be found in these volumes now mostly forgotten or lost; but nobody ever succeeded in writing the Addisonian essay with the charm of Addison.

At the opening of the nineteenth century, a further change in the form of the essay brought it back more nearly to the original type. The two great English reviews, the *Edinburgh* founded in 1802, and the *Quarterly* in 1807, must be credited with introducing a new variety of prose—the extended discussion, in careful literary manner, of topics of current interest, literary, philosophical, and especially political. But the articles in these reviews are hardly to be called essays. They are impersonal and objective in subject, expressly avoiding individual quality, and quite properly, therefore, always anonymous. They are, moreover, critical in plan, and take the shape of a review of some book or books. And it must be said that, dealing in this impersonal manner with questions of the hour, they are seldom of permanent literary interest. It is in another kind of periodical, the Magazine, that we shall find the essay in its developed, modern form. There had been several "magazines" in the eighteenth century; but they had been for the most part, as their name was meant to imply, mere receptacles for fugitive facts supposed to be valuable or curious, literary dust-bins. But early in the new century several magazines were started of a very different character from their predecessors of that name. The *New Monthly Magazine*, 1810, the more famous *Blackwood*, 1817, and the *London Magazine*, 1821, aimed to maintain the high standard of periodical writing set by the Reviews, but to include a wider range of subjects treated in a more popular and entertaining manner. They welcomed writing that was original and imaginative, and encouraged every pronounced expression of personality. Under the stimulus of such an opportunity the latest and best form of the essay was speedily developed. It was for these magazines and one other—*Tait's Edinburgh Magazine*—that most of the best work of Hazlitt, Lamb and DeQuincey was done. Indeed it has been in the pages of the magazine, English and American, that the essay for the last hundred years has found its most congenial place of publication.

No other literary form affords opportunity for a greater

variety of excellence than the personal essay. It is not fitted to express the most intense emotion, pathetic or sublime; such emotion is too reticent for familiar or colloquial utterance. But with this exception the whole range of experience is open to the essayist. The only requirement upon him is that he shall be sincere. Any suspicion of affectation or pretence alienates our sympathies at once. His rhetorical manner, if he be sincere, will be decided by his temperament. We may find, therefore, all varieties of style in the work of different essayists. There could hardly be greater diversity in vocabulary, structure, imagery, rhythm, and general tone of utterance than may be seen, for example, by a comparison of the writing of Lamb, DeQuincey, Hazlitt, Emerson, and Stevenson, each in his own way a master.

Ease and familiarity are, however, almost always virtues of the personal essay. The essayist must not talk too much like a book. Yet his ease must not for a moment degenerate into slackness, nor his familiarity into coarseness or vulgarity. He must know how to combine with his ease, precision of phrase and a certain distinction of manner. Nothing is more difficult in writing than this combination; it is a hall-mark of good style. And nowhere is it more imperative than in the essay.

The essay must, of course, have some unity of theme, but its plan need not be rigidly methodical. The essayist often writes as the good talker talks, in a flowing, continuous manner. He does not always see the end clearly from the beginning. He allows himself some natural digressions, without ever losing his way in them. He follows his thought or his narrative as that spontaneously develops, and the plan of his essay thus seems to shape itself while he is writing. But at the end he will be found to have had a plan, and his essay will be neither formless nor incoherent.

Finally, it should be said that no other literary form affords a better test of genius than the personal essay. None reveals more surely whatever in the character of the writer is forcible or original; and, on the other hand, more readily betrays him into amiable platitude and egotism. Mediocre work in the essay, although it may perhaps be pleasant reading, rarely survives beyond a single generation. It is not surprising, therefore, that the list of English writers who have attained permanent fame in this form of work should be very short.

ENGLISH ESSAYS

FRANCIS BACON

OF RICHES

I CANNOT call riches better than the baggage of virtue. The Roman word is better, *impedimenta*. For as the baggage is to an army, so is riches to virtue. It cannot be spared nor left behind, but it hindreth the march; yea, and the care of it sometimes loseth or disturb- 5 eth the victory. Of great riches there is no real use, except it be in the distribution; the rest is but conceit. So saith Salomon: *Where much is, there are many to consume it; and what hath the owner but the sight of it with his eyes?* The personal fruition in any man cannot reach 10 to feel great riches: there is a custody of them; or a power of dole and donative of them; or a fame of them; but no solid use to the owner. Do you not see what feigned prices are set upon little stones and rarities? and what works of ostentation are undertaken, because there 15 might seem to be some use of great riches? But then you will say, they may be of use to buy men out of dangers or trouble. As Salomon saith: *Riches are as a strong hold, in the imagination of the rich man.* But this is excellently expressed, that it is in imagination, and 20 not always in fact. For certainly great riches have sold more men than they have brought out. Seek not proud riches, but such as thou mayest get justly, use soberly,

distribute cheerfully, and leave contentedly. Yet have
no abstract nor friarly contempt of them. But distinguish, as Cicero saith well of Rabirius Posthumus: *In
studio rei amplificandæ apparebat non avaritiæ prædam*
5 *sed instrumentum bonitati quæri.* Hearken also to
Salomon, and beware of hasty gathering of riches: *Qui
festinat ad divitias non erit insons.* The poets feign that
when Plutus (which is Riches) is sent from Jupiter, he
limps and goes slowly; but when he is sent from Pluto,
10 he runs and is swift of foot: meaning, that riches gotten
by good means and just labor pace slowly; but when
they come by the death of others (as by the course
of inheritance, testaments, and the like), they come
tumbling upon a man. But it might be applied like-
15 wise to Pluto, taking him for the devil. For when riches
come from the devil (as by fraud and oppression and
unjust means), they come upon speed. The ways to
enrich are many, and most of them foul. Parsimony is
one of the best, and yet is not innocent; for it with-
20 holdeth men from works of liberality and charity. The
improvement of the ground is the most natural obtaining
of riches; for it is our great mother's blessing, the
earth's; but it is slow. And yet, where men of great
wealth do stoop to husbandry, it multiplieth riches
25 exceedingly. I knew a nobleman in England that had
the greatest audits of any man in my time: a great
grazier, a great sheep-master, a great timber man, a great
collier, a great corn-master, a great lead-man, and so of
iron, and a number of the like points of husbandry: so
30 as the earth seemed a sea to him, in respect of the
perpetual importation. It was truly observed by one,
that himself came very hardly to a little riches, and very
easily to great riches. For when a man's stock is come
to that, that he can expect the prime of markets, and

overcome those bargains which for their greatness are
few men's money, and be partner in the industries of
younger men, he cannot but increase mainly. The gains
of ordinary trades and vocations are honest, and furthered
by two things chiefly: by diligence, and by a good name 5
for good and fair dealing. But the gains of bargains are
of a more doubtful nature; when men shall wait upon
others' necessity, broke by servants and instruments to
draw them on, put off others cunningly that would be
better chapmen, and the like practices, which are crafty 10
and naught. As for the chopping of bargains, when a
man buys, not to hold, but to sell over again, that commonly grindeth double, both upon the seller and upon
the buyer. Sharings do greatly enrich, if the hands be
well chosen that are trusted. Usury is the certainest 15
means of gain, though one of the worst; as that whereby
a man doth eat his bread *in sudore vultûs alieni*, and
besides, doth plow upon Sundays. But yet, certain
though it be, it hath flaws; for that the scriveners and
brokers do value unsound men, to serve their own turn. 20
The fortune in being the first in an invention, or in a
privilege, doth cause sometimes a wonderful overgrowth
in riches; as it was with the first sugar man in the
Canaries: therefore if a man can play the true logician,
to have as well judgment as invention, he may do great 25
matters; especially if the times be fit. He that resteth
upon gains certain, shall hardly grow to great riches:
and he that puts all upon adventures, doth oftentimes
break and come to poverty: it is good therefore to guard
adventures with certainties that may uphold losses. 30
Monopolies, and coemption of wares for re-sale, where
they are not restrained, are great means to enrich;
especially if the party have intelligence what things are
like to come into request, and so store himself before-

hand. Riches gotten by service, though it be of the best rise, yet when they are gotten by flattery, feeding humors, and other servile conditions, they may be placed amongst the worst. As for fishing for testaments
5 and executorships (as Tacitus saith of Seneca, *testamenta et orbos tanquam indagine capi*) it is yet worse; by how much men submit themselves to meaner persons than in service. Believe not much them that seem to despise riches; for they despise them that despair of them; and
10 none worse, when they come to them. Be not penny-wise; riches have wings, and sometimes they fly away of themselves, sometimes they must be set flying to bring in more. Men leave their riches either to their kindred, or to the public; and moderate portions pros-
15 per best in both. A great state left to an heir, is as a lure to all the birds of prey round about to seize on him, if he be not the better stablished in years and judgment. Likewise glorious gifts and foundations are like *sacrifices without salt;* and but the painted sepulchers
20 of alms, which soon will putrefy and corrupt inwardly. Therefore measure not thine advancements by quantity, but frame them by measure: and defer not charities till death; for certainly, if a man weigh it rightly, he that doth so is rather liberal of another man's than of his own.

OF STUDIES

25 STUDIES serve for delight, for ornament, and for ability. Their chief use for delight is in privateness and retiring; for ornament, is in discourse; and for ability, is in the judgment and disposition of business. For expert men can execute, and perhaps judge of
30 particulars, one by one; but the general counsels, and the plots and marshaling of affairs, come best from

those that are learned. To spend too much time in studies is sloth; to use them too much for ornament is affectation; to make judgment wholly by their rules is the humor of a scholar. They perfect nature, and are perfected by experience; for natural abilities are like natural plants, that need proyning by study; and studies themselves do give forth directions too much at large, except they be bounded in by experience. Crafty men contemn studies; simple men admire them; and wise men use them: for they teach not their own use; but that is a wisdom without them and above them, won by observation. Read not to contradict and confute; nor to believe and take for granted; nor to find talk and discourse; but to weigh and consider. Some books are to be tasted, others to be swallowed, and some few to be chewed and digested: that is, some books are to be read only in parts; others to be read, but not curiously; and some few to be read wholly, and with diligence and attention. Some books also may be read by deputy, and extracts made of them by others; but that would be only in the less important arguments, and the meaner sort of books; else distilled books are like common distilled waters, flashy things. Reading maketh a full man; conference a ready man; and writing an exact man. And therefore, if a man write little, he had need have a great memory; if he confer little, he had need have a present wit; and if he read little, he had need have much cunning, to seem to know that he doth not. Histories make men wise; poets witty; the mathematics subtle; natural philosophy deep; moral grave; logic and rhetoric able to contend. *Abeunt studia in mores*. Nay, there is no stond or impediment in the wit, but may be wrought out by fit studies: like as diseases of the body may have appropriate exercises.

Bowling is good for the stone and reins; shooting for
the lungs and breast; gentle walking for the stomach;
riding for the head; and the like. So if a man's wit
be wandering, let him study the mathematics; for in
5 demonstrations, if his wit be called away never so little,
he must begin again: if his wit be not apt to distinguish
or find differences, let him study the schoolmen; for
they are *cymini sectores:* if he be not apt to beat over
matters, and to call one thing to prove and illustrate
10 another, let him study the lawyers' cases: so every
defect of the mind may have a special receipt.

OF ATHEISM

I HAD rather believe all the fables in the Legend and
the Talmud and the Alcoran, than that this universal
frame is without a mind. And therefore God never
15 wrought miracle to convince atheism, because his
ordinary works convince it. It is true that a little
philosophy inclineth man's mind to atheism; but depth
in philosophy bringeth men's minds about to religion:
for while the mind of man looketh upon second causes
20 scattered, it may sometimes rest in them, and go no
further; but when it beholdeth the chain of them,
confederate and linked together, it must needs fly to
Providence and Deity. Nay, even that school which is
most accused of atheism doth most demonstrate religion;
25 that is, the school of Leucippus and Democritus and
Epicurus. For it is a thousand times more credible
that four mutable elements and one immutable fifth
essence, duly and eternally placed, need no God, than
that an army of infinite small portions or seeds unplaced
30 should have produced this order and beauty without a
divine marshal. The Scripture saith, *The fool hath said*

in his heart, there is no God: it is not said, *The fool hath thought in his heart:* so as he rather saith it by rote to himself, as that he would have, than that he can throughly believe it, or be persuaded of it. For none deny there is a God but those for whom it maketh that there were no God. It appeareth in nothing more, that atheism is rather in the lip than in the heart of man, than by this; that atheists will ever be talking of that their opinion, as if they fainted in it within themselves, and would be glad to be strengthened by the consent of others: nay more, you shall have atheists strive to get disciples, as it fareth with other sects: and, which is most of all, you shall have of them that will suffer for atheism, and not recant; whereas, if they did truly think that there were no such thing as God, why should they trouble themselves? Epicurus is charged that he did but dissemble for his credit's sake, when he affirmed there were blessed natures, but such as enjoyed themselves without having respect to the government of the world. Wherein they say he did temporize, though in secret he thought there was no God. But certainly he is traduced; for his words are noble and divine: *Non deos vulgi negare profanum, sed vulgi opiniones diis applicare profanum.* Plato could have said no more. And although he had the confidence to deny the administration, he had not the power to deny the nature. The Indians of the West have names for their particular gods, though they have no name for God: as if the heathens should have had the names Jupiter, Apollo, Mars, etc., but not the word *Deus:* which shews that even those barbarous people have the notion, though they have not the latitude and extent of it. So that against atheists the very savages take part with the very subtlest philosophers. The contemplative atheist is

rare; a Diagoras, a Bion, a Lucian perhaps, and some
others; and yet they seem to be more than they are; for
that all that impugn a received religion, or superstition,
are, by the adverse part, branded with the name of
5 atheists. But the great atheists indeed are hypocrites;
which are ever handling holy things, but without feeling;
so as they must needs be cauterized in the end. The
causes of atheism are: divisions in religion, if they be
many; for any one main division addeth zeal to both
10 sides, but many divisions introduce atheism. Another
is, scandal of priests; when it is come to that which St.
Bernard saith: *Non est jam dicere, ut populus, sic
sacerdos; quia nec sic populus, ut sacerdos.* A third is,
custom of profane scoffing in holy matters, which doth
15 by little and little deface the reverence of religion. And
lastly, learned times, specially with peace and prosperity;
for troubles and adversities do more bow men's minds
to religion. They that deny a God destroy man's
nobility; for certainly man is of kin to the beasts by his
20 body; and if he be not of kin to God by his spirit, he
is a base and ignoble creature. It destroys likewise
magnanimity, and the raising of human nature; for take
an example of a dog, and mark what a generosity and
courage he will put on when he finds himself maintained
25 by a man, who to him is in stead of a god, or *melior
natura;* which courage is manifestly such as that
creature, without that confidence of a better nature than
his own, could never attain. So man, when he resteth
and assureth himself upon divine protection and favor,
30 gathereth a force and faith which human nature in itself
could not obtain. Therefore, as atheism is in all
respects hateful, so in this, that it depriveth human
nature of the means to exalt itself above human frailty.
As it is in particular persons, so it is in nations: never

was there such a state for magnanimity as Rome: of
this state hear what Cicero saith: *Quam volumus licet,*
patres conscripti, nos amemus, tamen nec numero Hispanos,
nec robore Gallos, nec calliditate Pœnos, necartibus Græcos,
nec denique hoc ipso hujus gentis et terræ domestico nativo- 5
que sensu Italos ipsos et Latinos; sed pietate, ac religione,
atque hâc unâ sapientiâ, quod Deorum immortalium
numine omnia regi gubernarique perspeximus, omnes
gentes nationesque superavimus.

ABRAHAM COWLEY

OF SOLITUDE

"Nunquam minus solus, quam cum solus," is now
become a very vulgar saying. Every man, and almost
every boy, for these seventeen hundred years, has had
it in his mouth. But it was at first spoken by the excel-
5 lent Scipio, who was without question a most eloquent
and witty person, as well as the most wise, most worthy,
most happy, and the greatest of all mankind. His
meaning, no doubt, was this, that he found more satisfaction to his mind, and more improvement of it, by solitude
10 than by company; and, to show that he spoke not this
loosely, or out of vanity, after he had made Rome mistress of almost the whole world, he retired himself from
it by a voluntary exile, and at a private house in the
middle of a wood near Linternum, passed the remainder
15 of his glorious life no less gloriously. This house Seneca
went to see so long after with great veneration; and,
among other things, describes his baths to have been of
so mean a structure, that now, says he, the basest of the
people would despise them, and cry out, "Poor Scipio
20 understood not how to live." What an authority is here
for the credit of retreat! and happy had it been for
Hannibal, if adversity could have taught him as much
wisdom as was learnt by Scipio from the highest pros-
25 perities. This would be no wonder, if it were as truly
as it is colorably and wittily said by Monsieur de Mon-

taigne, "that ambition itself might teach us to love solitude; there is nothing does so much hate to have companions." It is true, it loves to have its elbows free, it detests to have company on either side; but it delights above all things in a train behind, aye, and ushers too 5 before it. But the greatest part of men are so far from the opinion of that noble Roman, that, if they chance at any time to be without company, they are like a becalmed ship; they never move but by the wind of other men's breath, and have no oars of their own to 10 steer withal. It is very fantastical and contradictory in human nature, that men should love themselves above all the rest of the world, and yet never endure to be with themselves. When they are in love with a mistress, all other persons are importunate and burden- 15 some to them. "Tecum vivere amem, tecum obeam lubens," they would live and die with her alone.

> "Sic ego secretis possum bene vivere sylvis,
>   Qua nulla humano sit via trita pede.
> Tu mihi curarum requies, tu nocte vel atra   20
>   Lumen, et in solis tu mihi turba locis."

> With thee for ever I in woods could rest,
> Where never human foot the ground has prest.
> Thou from all shades the darkness canst exclude,
> And from a desert banish solitude.   25

And yet our dear self is so wearisome to us, that we can scarcely support its conversation for an hour together. This is such an odd temper of mind, as Catullus expresses toward one of his mistresses, whom we may suppose to have been of a very unsociable humor.   30

> "Odi, et amo: quare id faciam fortasse requiris.
>   Nescio; sed fieri sentio, et excrucior."

> I hate, and yet I love thee too;
> How can that be? I know not how;
> Only that so it is I know,
> And feel with torment that 'tis so.

5   It is a deplorable condition, this, and drives a man sometimes to pitiful shifts, in seeking how to avoid himself.

The truth of the matter is, that neither he who is a fop in the world, is a fit man to be alone; nor he who 10 has set his heart much upon the world, though he have never so much understanding; so that solitude can be well fitted and sit right, but upon a very few persons. They must have enough knowledge of the world to see the vanity of it, and enough virtue to despise all vanity; 15 if the mind be possessed with any lust or passions, a man had better be in a fair, than in a wood alone. They may, like petty thieves, cheat us perhaps, and pick our pockets, in the midst of company; but, like robbers, they use to strip and bind, or murder us, when they catch 20 us alone. This is but to retreat from men, and to fall into the hands of devils. It is like the punishment of parricides among the Romans, to be sewed into a bag, with an ape, a dog, and a serpent.

The first work, therefore, that a man must do, to 25 make himself capable of the good of solitude, is the very eradication of all lusts; for how is it possible for a man to enjoy himself while his affections are tied to things without himself? In the second place, he must learn the art and get the habit of thinking; for this, too, no 30 less than well speaking, depends upon much practice; and cogitation is the thing which distinguishes the solitude of a God from a wild beast. Now, because the soul of man is not, by its own nature or observation, furnished with sufficient materials to work upon, it is

necessary for it to have continual recourse to learning
and books for fresh supplies, so that the solitary life
will grow indigent, and be ready to starve, without
them; but if once we be thoroughly engaged in the love
of letters, instead of being wearied with the length of 5
any day, we shall only complain of the shortness of our
whole life.

> "O vita, stulto longa, sapienti brevis!"
> O life, long to the fool, short to the wise!

The first minister of state has not so much business 10
in public as a wise man has in private: if the one have
little leisure to be alone, the other has less leisure to be
in company; the one has but part of the affairs of one
nation, the other all the works of God and nature,
under his consideration. There is no saying shocks 15
me so much as that which I hear very often, "That a man
does not know how to pass his time." It would have
been but ill spoken by Methuselah in the nine hundred
and sixty-ninth year of his life; so far it is from us,
who have not time enough to attain to the utmost per- 20
fection of any part of any science, to have cause to complain that we are forced to be idle for want of work. But
this, you will say, is work only for the learned; others
are not capable either of the employments or divertise-
ments that arrive from letters. I know they are not; 25
and, therefore, cannot much recommend solitude to a man
totally illiterate. But, if any man be so unlearned, as
to want entertainment of the little intervals of accidental
solitude, which frequently occur in almost all conditions
(except the very meanest of the people, who have 30
business enough in the necessary provisions for life),
it is truly a great shame both to his parents and himself;
for a very small portion of any ingenious art will stop

up all those gaps of our time; either music, or painting,
or designing, or chemistry, or history, or gardening, or
twenty other things, will do it usefully and pleasantly;
and, if he happen to set his affections upon poetry (which
5 I do not advise him too immoderately), that will over-do
it; no wood will be thick enough to hide him from the
importunities of company or business, which would
abstract him from his beloved.

> "———O qui me gelidis in vallibus Haemi
10 Sistat, et ingenti ramorum protegat umbra?"

1

Hail, old patrician trees, so great and good!
    Hail, ye plebeian under-wood!
    Where the poetic birds rejoice,
And for their quiet nests and plenteous food
15   Pay, with their grateful voice.

2

Hail, the poor Muses' richest manor-seat!
    Ye country houses and retreat,
    Which all the happy gods so love,
That for you oft they quit their bright and great
20   Metropolis above.

3

Here Nature does a house for me erect,
    Nature, the wisest architect,
    Who those fond artists does despise
That can the fair and living trees neglect;
25   Yet the dead timber prize.

4

Here, let me, careless and unthoughtful lying,
    Hear the soft winds, above me flying,
    With all their wanton boughs dispute,
And the more tuneful birds to both replying,
30   Nor be myself, too, mute.

5

A silver stream shall roll his waters near,
    Gilt with the sun-beams here and there,
    On whose enamel'd bank I'll walk,
And see how prettily they smile, and hear
    How prettily they talk.   5

6

Ah wretched, and too solitary he,
    Who loves not his own company!
    He'll feel the weight oft many a day,
Unless he call in sin or vanity
    To help to bear't away.   10

7

Oh Solitude, first state of human-kind!
    Which blest remain'd till man did find
    Ev'n his own helper's company.
As soon as two (alas!) together join'd,
    The serpent made up three.   15

8

Tho' God himself, through countless ages, thee
    His sole companion chose to be,
    Thee, sacred Solitude, alone,
Before the branchy head of number's tree
    Sprang from the trunk of one.   20

9

Thou (tho' men think mine an unactive part)
    Dost break and tame th' unruly heart,
    Which else would know no settled pace,
Making it move, well manag'd by thy art,
    With swiftness and with grace.   25

10

Thou the faint beams of reason's scatter'd light
 Dost, like a burning glass, unite,
 Dost multiply the feeble heat,
And fortify the strength, till thou dost bright
  And noble fires beget.

11

Whilst this hard truth I teach, methinks I see
 The monster London laugh at me;
 I should at thee too, foolish city,
If it were fit to laugh at misery;
  But thy estate I pity.

12

Let but thy wicked men from out thee go,
 And all the fools that crowd thee so,
 Even thou, who dost thy millions boast,
A village less than Islington wilt grow,
  A solitude almost.

OF MYSELF

It is a hard and nice subject for a man to write of himself; it grates his own heart to say anything of disparagement, and the reader's ears to hear anything of praise from him. There is no danger from me of offending him in this kind; neither my mind, nor my body, nor my fortune, allow me my materials for that vanity. It is sufficient for my own contentment, that they have preserved me from being scandalous, or remarkable on the defective side. But besides that, I shall here speak of myself, only in relation to the subject of these precedent discourses, and shall be likelier thereby to fall into the contempt, than rise up to the estimation, of most people.

As far as my memory can return back into my past life, before I knew, or was capable of guessing, what the world, or the glories or business of it were, the natural affections of my soul gave me a secret bent of aversion from them, as some plants are said to turn away from others, by an antipathy imperceptible to themselves, and inscrutable to man's understanding. Even when I was a very young boy at school instead of running about on holidays and playing with my fellows, I was wont to steal from them, and walk into the fields, either alone with a book, or with some one companion, if I could find any of the same temper. I was then, too, so much an enemy to all constraint, that my masters could never prevail on me, by any persuasions or encouragements, to learn without book the common rules of grammar; in which they dispensed with me alone, because they found I made a shift to do the usual exercise out of my own reading and observation. That I was then of the same mind as I am now (which, I confess, I wonder at, myself) may appear by the latter end of an ode, which I made when I was but thirteen years old, and which was then printed with many other verses. The beginning of it is boyish; but of this part, which I here set down (if a very little were corrected), I should hardly now be much ashamed.

9

This only grant me, that my means may lie
Too low for envy, for contempt too high.
　　Some honor I would have,
Not from great deeds, but good alone;
The unknown are better, than ill-known:
　　Rumor can ope the grave.
Acquaintance I would have, but when't depends
Not on the number, but the choice of friends.

10

Books should, not business, entertain the light,
And sleep, as undisturb'd as death, the night.
    My house a cottage more
    Than palace; and should fitting be
5   For all my use, no luxury.
    My garden painted o'er
With Nature's hand, not art's; and pleasures yield,
Horace might envy in his Sabine field.

11

Thus would I double my life's fading space;
10 For he, that runs it well, twice runs his race.
    And in this true delight,
    These unbought sports, this happy state,
    I would not fear, nor wish, my fate;
    But boldly say each night,
15 To-morrow let my sun his beams display,
Or, in clouds hide them; I have liv'd, to-day.

You may see by it, I was even then acquainted with
the poets (for the conclusion is taken out of Horace);
and perhaps it was the immature and immoderate love
20 of them, which stamped first, or rather engraved, these
characters in me: they were like letters cut into the bark
of a young tree, which with the tree still grow proportion-
ably. But how this love came to be produced in me so
early, is a hard question. I believe I can tell the particu-
25 lar little chance that filled my head first with such chimes
of verse as have never since left ringing there: for I
remember, when I began to read, and to take some
pleasure in it, there was wont to lie in my mother's
parlor (I know not by what accident, for she herself
30 never in her life read any book but of devotion) but
there was wont to lie Spenser's works: this I happened
to fall upon, and was infinitely delighted with the stories

of the knights, and giants, and monsters, and brave houses, which I found everywhere there (though my understanding had little to do with all this); and, by degrees, with the tinkling of the rime and dance of the numbers; so that, I think, I had read him all over before I was twelve years old, and was thus made a poet as immediately as a child is made an eunuch.

With these affections of mind, and my heart wholly set upon letters, I went to the university; but was soon torn from thence by that violent public storm, which would suffer nothing to stand where it did, but rooted up every plant, even from the princely cedars to me the hyssop. Yet I had as good fortune as could have befallen me in such a tempest; for I was cast by it into the family of one of the best persons, and into the court of one of the best princesses, of the world. Now, though I was here engaged in ways most contrary to the original design of my life, that is, into much company, and no small business, and into a daily sight of greatness, both militant and triumphant (for that was the state then of the English and French courts); yet all this was so far from altering my opinion, that it only added the confirmation of reason to that which was before but natural inclination. I saw plainly all the paint of that kind of life, the nearer I came to it; and that beauty, which I did not fall in love with, when, for aught I knew, it was real, was not like to bewitch or entice me, when I saw that it was adulterate. I met with several great persons, whom I liked very well; but could not perceive that any part of their greatness was to be liked or desired, no more than I would be glad or content to be in a storm, though I saw many ships which rid safely and bravely in it. A storm would not agree with my stomach, if it did with my courage. Though I was in a crowd of as

good company as could be found anywhere, though I
was in business of great and honorable trust, though I
ate at the best table, and enjoyed the best conveniences
for present subsistence that ought to be desired by a
5 man of my condition in banishment and public distresses;
yet I could not abstain from renewing my old school-
boy's wish, in a copy of verses to the same effect:

> Well then; I now do plainly see
> This busy world and I shall ne'er agree, etc.

10   And I never then proposed to myself any other advantage from his majesty's happy Restoration, but the getting into some moderately convenient retreat in the
country; which I thought, in that case, I might easily
have compassed, as well as some others, who with no
15 greater probabilities or pretences, have arrived to extraordinary fortune: but I had before written a shrewd
prophecy against myself; and I think Apollo inspired
me in the truth, though not in the elegance, of it:

> "Thou neither great at court, nor in the war,
> 20   Nor at th' exchange shalt be, nor at the wrangling bar.
> Content thyself with the small barren praise,
>   Which neglected voice does raise."
> She spake; and all my years to come
>   Took their unlucky doom.
> 25   Their several ways of life let others choose,
>   Their several pleasures let them use;
> But I was born for Love, and for a Muse.

> 4

> With Fate what boots it to contend?
> Such I'began, such am, and so must end.
> 30   The star, that did my being frame,
>   Was but a lambent flame,

And some small light it did dispense,
But neither heat nor influence.
No matter, Cowley; let proud Fortune see,
That thou canst her despise no less than she does thee.
  Let all her gifts the portion be   5
  Of folly, lust, and flattery,
  Fraud, extortion, calumny,
  Murder, infidelity,
  Rebellion and hypocrisy.
  Do thou nor grieve nor blush to be,   10
  As all th' inspired tuneful men,
And all thy great forefathers were, from Homer down to Ben·

However, by the failing of the forces which I had
expected, I did not quit the design which I had resolved
on; I cast myself into it a *corps perdu*, without making 15
capitulations, or taking counsel of fortune. But God
laughs at a man, who says to his soul, Take thy ease.
I met presently not only with many little incumbrances
and impediments, but with so much sickness (a new
misfortune to me) as would have spoiled the happiness 20
of an emperor as well as mine; yet I do neither repent,
nor alter my course. "Non ego perfidum dixi sacramentum;" nothing shall separate me from a mistress, which
I have loved so long, and have now at last married;
though she neither has brought me a rich portion, nor 25
lived yet so quietly with me as I hoped from her:

  ——"Nec vos, dulcissima mundi
Nomina, vos Musæ, Libertas, Otia, Libri,
Hortique Sylvæque, anima remanente, relinquam."

   Nor by me e'er shall you,   30
You, of all names the sweetest, and the best,
You, Muses, books, and liberty, and rest;
You, gardens, fields, and woods, forsaken be,
As long as life itself forsakes not me.

But this is a very pretty ejaculation; because I have
concluded all the other chapters with a copy of verses,
I will maintain the humor to the last.

MARTIAL, LIB. X. EPIGR. XLV

5
"Vitam quae faciunt beatiorem,
Jucundissime Martialis, haec sunt:
Res non parta labore, sed relicta;
Non ingratus ager, focus perennis,
Lis nunquam; toga rara; mens quieta;

10
Vires ingenuæ; salubre corpus;
Prudens simplicitas; pares amici;
Convictus facilis; sine arte mensa;
Nox non ebria, sed soluta curis;
Non tristis torus, et tamen pudicus;

15
Somnus, qui faciat breves tenebras;
Quod sis, esse velis, nihilque malis:
Summum nec metuas diem, nec optes."

Since, dearest friend, 'tis you desire to see
A true receipt of happiness from me;

20
These are the chief ingredients, if not all:
Take an estate neither too great nor small,
Which *quantum sufficit* the doctors call.
Let this estate from parents' care descend;
The getting it too much of life does spend.

25
Take such a ground, whose gratitude may be
A fair encouragement for industry.
Let constant fires the winter's fury tame;
And let thy kitchen's be a vestal flame.
Thee to the town let never suit at law,

30
And rarely, very rarely, business draw.
Thy active mind in equal temper keep,
In undisturbed peace, yet not in sleep.
Let exercise a vigorous health maintain,
Without which all the composition's vain.

35
In the same weight prudence and innocence take.
Ana of each does the just mixture make.

But a few friendships wear, and let them be
By nature and by fortune fit for thee.
Instead of art and luxury in food,
Let mirth and freedom make thy table good.
If any cares into thy day-time creep,   5
At night, without wine's opium, let them sleep.
Let rest, which nature does to darkness wed,
And not lust, recommend to thee thy bed.
Be satisfied, and pleased with what thou art,
Act cheerfully and well th' allotted part;   10
Enjoy the present hour, be thankful for the past,
And neither fear, nor wish, th' approaches of the last.

MARTIAL, LIB. X. EPIGR. LXXXVII

"Saepe loquar nimium gentes quod, avite, remotas,
Miraris, Latia factus in urbe senex;   15
Auriferumque Tagum sitiam, patriumque Salonem,
Et repetam saturæ sordida rura casæ.
Illa placet tellus, in qua res parva beatum
Me facit, et tenues luxuriantur opes.
Pascitur hic; ibi pascit ager: tepet igne maligno   20
Hic focus, ingenti lumine lucet ibi.
Hic pretiosa fames, conturbatorque macellus,
Mensa ibi divitiis ruris operta sui.
Quatuor hic æstate togæ, pluresve teruntur;
Autumnis ibi me quatuor una tegit.   25
I, cole nunc reges: quicquid non præstat amicus
Cum praestare tibi possit, avite, locus."

Me, who have liv'd so long among the great,
You wonder to hear talk of a retreat:
And a retreat so distant, as may show   30
No thoughts of a return, when once I go.
Give me a country, how remote so e'er,
Where happiness a mod'rate rate does bear,
Where poverty itself in plenty flows,
And all the solid use of riches knows.   35

The ground about the house maintains it there,
The house maintains the ground about it here.
Here even hunger's dear; and a full board
Devours the vital substance of the lord.
5   The land itself does there the feast bestow,
The land itself must here to market go.
Three or four suits one winter here does waste,
One suit does there three or four winters last.
Here every frugal man must oft be cold,
10   And little lukewarm fires are to you sold.
There fire's an element, as cheap and free,
Almost as any of the other three.
Stay you then here, and live among the great,
Attend their sports, and at their tables eat.
15   When all the bounties here of men you score,
The place's bounty there shall give me more.

EPITAPHIUM VIVI AUCTORIS

"Hic, o viator, sub lare parvulo
Couleius hic est conditus, hic jacet;
        Defunctus humani laboris
20   Sorte, supervacuaque vita.

Non indecora pauperie nitens,
Et non inerti nobilis otio,
        Vanoque dilectis popello
25   Divitiis animosus hostis.

Possis ut illum dicere mortuum;
En terra jam nunc quantula sufficit;
        Exempta sit curis, viator,
           Terra sit illa levis, precare.

30   Hic sparge flores, sparge breves rosas,
Nam vita gaudet mortua floribus,
        Herbisque odoratis corona
           Vatis adhuc cinerem calentem."

EPITAPH ON THE LIVING AUTHOR

1

Here, stranger, in this humble nest,
    Here, Cowley sleeps; here lies,
Scap'd all the toils, that life molest,
    And its superfluous joys.

2

Here, in no sordid poverty,
    And no inglorious ease,
He braves the world, and can defy
    Its frowns and flatteries.

3

The little earth, he asks, survey:
    Is he not dead, indeed?
"Light lye that earth," good stranger, pray,
    "Nor thorn upon it breed!"

4

With flow'rs, fit emblem of his fame,
    Compass your poet round;
With flow'rs of ev'ry fragrant name
    Be his warm ashes crown'd!

SIR RICHARD STEELE

RECOLLECTIONS OF CHILDHOOD

Dies, ni fallor, adest, quem semper acerbum,
Semper honoratum, sic dii voluistis, habebo.

Virg. Æn. v. 49.

And now the rising day renews the year,
5   A day for ever sad, for ever dear.—Dryden.

THERE are those among mankind, who can enjoy no
relish of their being, except the world is made acquainted
with all that relates to them, and think every thing lost
that passes unobserved; but others find a solid delight
10 in stealing by the crowd, and modeling their life after
such a manner as is as much above the approbation as
the practice of the vulgar. Life being too short to give
instances great enough of true friendship or good will,
some sages have thought it pious to preserve a certain
15 reverence for the manes of their deceased friends; and
have withdrawn themselves from the rest of the world
at certain seasons, to commemorate in their own thoughts
such of their acquaintance who have gone before them
out of this life. And indeed, when we are advanced in
20 years, there is not a more pleasing entertainment than
to recollect in a gloomy moment the many we have
parted with, that have been dear and agreeable to us,
and to cast a melancholy thought or two after those with
whom, perhaps, we have indulged ourselves in whole
25 nights of mirth and jollity. With such inclinations in

my heart I went to my <u>closet</u> yesterday in the evening,
and resolved to be sorrowful; upon which occasion I
could not but look with disdain upon myself, that
though all the reasons which I had to lament the loss
of many of my friends are now as forcible as at the 5
moment of their departure, yet did not my heart swell
with the same sorrow which I felt at the time; but I
could, without tears, reflect upon many pleasing adventures I have had with some who have long been
blended with common earth.   Though it is by the benefit 10
of nature, that length of time thus blots out the violence
of afflictions; yet, with tempers too much given to pleasure, it is almost necessary to revive the old places of
grief in our memory; and ponder step by step on past
life, to lead the mind into that sobriety of thought which 15
poises the heart, and makes it beat with due time, without being quickened with desire or retarded with despair,
from its proper and equal motion.   When we wind up
a clock that is out of order, to make it go well for the
future, we do not immediately set the hand to the pres- 20
ent instant, but we make it strike the round of all its
hours, before it can recover the regularity of its time.
Such, thought I, shall be my method this evening; and
since it is that day of the year which I dedicate to the
memory of such in another life as I much delighted in 25
when living, an hour or two shall be sacred to sorrow and
their memory, while I run over all the melancholy circumstances of this kind which have occurred to me in my
whole life.

The first sense of sorrow I ever knew was upon the 30
death of my father, at which time I was not quite five
years of age; but was rather amazed at what all the house
meant, than possessed with a real understanding why
nobody was willing to play with me.   I remember I

went into the room where his body lay, and my mother
sat weeping alone by it. I had my battledore in my
hand, and fell a beating the coffin, and calling Papa; for,
I know not how, I had some slight idea that he was
5 locked up there. My mother catched me in her arms,
and, transported beyond all patience of the silent grief
she was before in, she almost smothered me in her
embraces; and told me in a flood of tears, "Papa could
not hear me, and would play with me no more, for they
10 were going to put him under ground, whence he could
never come to us again." She was a very beautiful
woman, of a noble spirit, and there was dignity in her
grief amidst all the wildness of her transport; which,
methought, struck me with an instinct of sorrow, that,
15 before I was sensible of what it was to grieve, seized my
very soul, and has made pity the weakness of my heart
ever since. The mind in infancy is, methinks, like the
body in embryo; and receives impressions so forcible
that they are as hard to be removed by reason, as any
20 mark with which a child is born is to be taken away by
any future application. Hence it is that good-nature
in me is no merit; but having been so frequently over-
whelmed with her tears before I knew the cause of any
affliction, or could draw defences from my own judgment,
25 I imbibed commiseration, remorse, and an unmanly
gentleness of mind, which has since insnared me into
ten thousand calamities; and from whence I can reap no
advantage, except it be, that, in such a humor as I am
now in, I can the better indulge myself in the softness of
30 humanity, and enjoy that sweet anxiety which arises
from the memory of past afflictions.

We that are very old are better able to remember things
which befell us in our distant youth, than the passages of
later days. For this reason it is that the companions of

my strong and vigorous years present themselves more immediately to me in this office of sorrow. Untimely and unhappy deaths are what we are most apt to lament; so little are we able to make it indifferent when a thing happens, though we know it must happen. Thus we 5 groan under life and bewail those who are relieved from it. Every object that returns to our imagination raises different passions, according to the circumstances of their departure. Who can have lived in an army, and in a serious hour reflect upon the many gay and agreeable 10 men that might long have flourished in the arts of peace, and not join with the imprecations of the fatherless and widow on the tyrant to whose ambition they fell sacrifices? But gallant men who are cut off by the sword, move rather our veneration than our pity; and we gather relief 15 enough from their own contempt of death, to make that no evil, which was approached with so much cheerfulness and attended with so much honor. But when we turn our thoughts from the great parts of life on such occasions, and instead of lamenting those who stood 20 ready to give death to those from whom they had the fortune to receive it; I say, when we let our thoughts wander from such noble objects and consider the havoc which is made among the tender and the innocent, pity enters with an unmixed softness and possesses all our souls at 25 once.

Here (were there words to express such sentiments with proper tenderness) I should record the beauty, innocence, and untimely death of the first object my eyes ever beheld with love. The beauteous virgin! how 30 ignorantly did she charm, how carelessly excel! Oh death! thou hast right to the bold, to the ambitious, to the high, and to the haughty; but why this cruelty to the humble, to the meek, to the undiscerning, to the

thoughtless? Nor age, nor business, nor distress can
erase the dear image from my imagination. In the
same week, I saw her dressed for a ball, and in a shroud.
How ill did the habit of death become the pretty trifler?
5 I still behold the smiling earth——A large train of dis-
asters were coming on to my memory, when my servant
knocked at my closet-door and interrupted me with a
letter, attended with a hamper of wine, of the same sort
with that which is to be put to sale on Thursday next
10 at Garraway's coffee-house. Upon the receipt of it, I
sent for three of my friends. We are so intimate that we
can be company in whatever state of mind we meet,
and can entertain each other without expecting always
to rejoice. The wine we found to be generous and warm-
15 ing, but with such a heat as moved us rather to be cheerful than frolicsome. It revived the spirits, without
firing the blood. We commended it until two of the
clock this morning; and having to-day met a little
before dinner, we found, that though we drank two
20 bottles a man, we had much more reason to recollect
than forget what had passed the night before.

A VISIT TO A FRIEND

Interea dulces pendent circum oscula nati,
Casta pudicitiam servat domus.——

Virg. *Georg.* ii. 523.

25   His cares are eas'd with intervals of bliss;
        His little children, climbing for a kiss,
        Welcome their father's late return at night.

THERE are several persons who have many pleasures
and entertainments in their possession, which they do
30 not enjoy. It is, therefore, a kind and good office to
acquaint them with their own happiness and turn their

attention to such instances of their good fortune as they
are apt to overlook. Persons in the married state often
want such a monitor; and pine away their days, by
looking upon the same condition in anguish and murmur,
which carries with it in the opinion of others a complica- 5
tion of all the pleasures of life, and a retreat from its
inquietudes.

I am led into this thought by a visit I made an old
friend, who was formerly my schoolfellow. He came to
town last week with his family for the winter, and yester- 10
day morning sent me word his wife expected me to dinner.
I am, as it were, at home at that house, and every member of it knows me for their well-wisher. I cannot indeed express the pleasure it is, to be met by the children
with so much joy as I am when I go thither. The boys 15
and girls strive who shall come first, when they think it
is I that am knocking at the door; and that child which
loses the race to me runs back again to tell the father it
is Mr. Bickerstaff. This day I was led in by a pretty
girl that we all thought must have forgot me; for the 20
family has been out of town these two years. Her
knowing me again was a mighty subject with us, and
took up our discourse at the first entrance. After which,
they began to rally me upon a thousand little stories they
heard in the country, about my marriage to one of my 25
neighbor's daughters. Upon which the gentleman, my
friend, said, "Nay, if Mr. Bickerstaff marries a child of
any of his old companions, I hope mine shall have the
preference; there is Mrs. Mary is now sixteen and would
make him as fine a widow as the best of them. But I 30
know him too well; he is so enamored with the very
memory of those who flourished in our youth, that he
will not so much as look upon the modern beauties. I
remember, old gentleman, how often you went home in

a day to refresh your countenance and dress when Tera-
minta reigned in your heart. As we came up in the
coach, I repeated to my wife some of your verses on her."
With such reflections on little passages which happened
5 long ago, we passed our time, during a cheerful and
elegant meal. After dinner his lady left the room, as
did also the children. As soon as we were alone, he took
me by the hand: "Well, my good friend," says he, "I
am heartily glad to see thee; I was afraid you would
10 never have seen all the company that dined with you
to-day again. Do not you think the good woman of
the house a little altered since you followed her from
the playhouse, to find out who she was, for me?" I
perceived a tear fall down his cheek as he spoke, which
15 moved me not a little. But, to turn the discourse, I
said, "She is not indeed quite that creature she was,
when she returned me the letter I carried from you; and
told me, 'she hoped, as I was a gentleman, I would be
employed no more to trouble her, who had never offended
20 me; but would be so much the gentleman's friend, as to
dissuade him from a pursuit which he could never succeed
in.' You may remember, I thought her in earnest; and
you were forced to employ your cousin Will, who made
his sister get acquainted with her for you. You cannot
25 expect her to be for ever fifteen." "Fifteen!" replied
my good friend: "Ah! you little understand, you that
have lived a bachelor, how great, how exquisite a pleasure there is in being really beloved! It is impossible
that the most beauteous face in nature should raise in
30 me such pleasing ideas as when I look upon that excellent
woman. That fading in her countenance is chiefly
caused by her watching with me in my fever. This was
followed by a fit of sickness, which had like to have
carried her off last winter. I tell you sincerely, I have

so many obligations to her that I cannot, with any sort
of moderation, think of her present state of health.
But as to what you say of fifteen, she gives me every day
pleasures beyond what I ever knew in the possession of
her beauty, when I· was in the vigor of youth. Every 5
moment of her· life brings me fresh instances of her
complacency to my inclinations and her prudence in
regard to my fortune. Her face is to me much more
beautiful than when I first saw it; there is no decay in
any feature which I cannot trace from the very instant 10
it was occasioned' by some anxious concern for my
welfare and interests. Thus, at the same time, methinks,
the love I conceived toward her for what she was, is
heightened by my gratitude for what she is. The love
of a wife is as much above the idle passion commonly 15
called by that name as the loud laughter of buffoons is
inferior to the elegant mirth of gentlemen. Oh! she is
an inestimable jewel. In her examination of her household affairs, she shows a certain fearfulness to find a
fault, which makes her servants obey her like children; 2c
and the meanest we have has an ingenuous shame for
an offence, not always to be seen in children in other
families. I speak freely to you, my old friend; ever
since her sickness, things that gave me the quickest joy
before, turn now to a certain anxiety. As the children 25
play in the next room, I know the poor things by their
steps, and am considering what they must do, should
they lose their mother in their tender years. The pleasure I used to take in telling my boy stories of battles, and
asking my girl questions about the disposal of her baby, 30
and the gossiping of it, is turned into inward reflection
and melancholy."

He would have gone on in this tender way, when the
good lady entered, and with an inexpressible sweetness

in her countenance told us she had been searching her
closet for something very good, to treat such an old
friend as I was. Her husband's eyes sparkled with
pleasure at the cheerfulness of her countenance; and I
5 saw all his fears vanish in an instant.. The lady, observing something in our looks which showed we had been
more serious than ordinary, and seeing her husband
receive her with great concern under a forced cheerfulness, immediately guessed at what we had been talking
10 of; and applying herself to me, said, with a smile, "Mr.
Bickerstaff, do not believe a word of what he tells you,
I shall still live to have you for my second, as I have
often promised you, unless he takes more care of himself than he has done since his coming to town. You
15 must know, he tells me that he finds London is a much
more healthy place than the country; for he sees several
of his old acquaintance and schoolfellows are here young
fellows with fair full-bottomed periwigs. I could scarce
keep him in this morning from going out open-breasted."
20 My friend, who is always extremely delighted with her
agreeable humor, made her sit down with us. She did
it with that easiness which is peculiar to women of sense;
and to keep up the good humor she had brought in with
her, turned her raillery upon me. "Mr. Bickerstaff,
25 you remember you followed me one night from the
playhouse; suppose you should carry me thither to-
morrow night and lead me into the front box." This
put us into a long field of discourse about the beauties
who were mothers to the present and shined in the boxes
30 twenty years ago. I told her, "I was glad she had transferred so many of her charms, and I did not question
but her eldest daughter was within half a year of being a
toast."

We were pleasing ourselves with this fantastical preferment of the young lady, when on a sudden we were alarmed with the noise of a drum, and immediately entered my little godson to give me a point of war. His mother, between laughing and chiding, would have put him out of the room; but I would not part with him so. 5 I found, upon conversation with him, though he was a little noisy in his mirth, that the child had excellent parts, and was a great master of all the learning on the other side eight years old. I perceived him a very great historian in Æsop's Fables: but he frankly declared to 10 me his mind, "that he did not delight in that learning, because he did not believe they were true"; for which reason I found he had very much turned his studies, for about a twelvemonth past, into the lives and adventures of Don Belianis of Greece, Guy of Warwick, the Seven 15 Champions, and other historians of that age. I could not but observe the satisfaction the father took in the forwardness of his son; and that these diversions might turn to some profit, I found the boy had made remarks which might be of service to him during the course of his 20 whole life. He would tell you the mismanagements of John Hickerthrift, find fault with the passionate temper in Bevis of Southampton, and loved Saint George for being the champion of England; and by this means had his thoughts insensibly molded into the notions of 25 discretion, virtue, and honor. I was extolling his accomplishments, when the mother told me that the little girl who led me in this morning was in her way a better scholar than he. "Betty," said she, "deals chiefly in fairies and sprites; and sometimes in a winter night will 30 terrify the maids with her accounts, until they are afraid to go up to bed."

I sat with them until it was very late, sometimes in merry, sometimes in serious discourse, with this particu-

lar pleasure, which gives the only true relish to all conversation, a sense that every one of us liked each other.
I went home, considering the different conditions of a
married life and that of a bachelor; and I must confess it
5 struck me with a secret concern, to reflect that whenever
I go off I shall leave no traces behind me. In this pensive
mood I returned to my family; that is to say, to my maid,
my dog, and my cat, who only can be the better or
worse for what happens to me.

MR. BICKERSTAFF'S THREE NEPHEWS

10   THE vigilance, the anxiety, the tenderness, which I
have for the good people of England, I am persuaded,
will in time be much commended; but I doubt whether
they will be ever rewarded. However, I must go on
cheerfully in my work of reformation: that being my
15 great design, I am studious to prevent my labor's increasing upon me; therefore am particularly observant
of the temper and inclinations of childhood and youth,
that we may not give vice and folly supplies from the
growing generation. It is hardly to be imagined how
20 useful this study is, and what great evils or benefits arise
from putting us in our tender years to what we are fit
and unfit: therefore, on Tuesday last (with a design to
sound their inclinations) I took three lads, who are under
my guardianship, a-rambling in a hackney-coach, to
25 show them the town; as the lions, the tombs, Bedlam,
and the other places which are entertainments to raw
minds, because they strike forcibly on the fancy. The
boys are brothers, one of sixteen, the other of fourteen
the other of twelve. The first was his father's darling,
30 the second his mother's and the third mine, who am
their uncle. Mr. William is a lad of true genius; but,

being at the upper end of a great school, and having all the boys below him, his arrogance is insupportable. If I begin to show a little of my Latin, he immediately interrupts: "Uncle, under favor, that which you say, is not understood in that manner." "Brother," says my boy Jack, "you do not show your manners much in contradicting my uncle Isaac!" "You queer cur," says Mr. William, "do you think my uncle takes any notice of such a dull rogue as you are?" Mr. William goes on, "He is the most stupid of all my mother's children: he knows nothing of his book: when he should mind that, he is hiding or hoarding his taws and marbles, or laying up farthings. His way of thinking is, four-and-twenty farthings make sixpence, and two sixpences a shilling; two shillings and sixpence half-a-crown, and two half-crowns five shillings. So within these two months the close hunks has scraped up twenty shillings, and we will make him spend it all before he comes home." Jack immediately claps his hands into both pockets, and turns as pale as ashes. There is nothing touches a parent (and such I am to Jack) so nearly as a provident conduct. This lad has in him the true temper for a good husband, a kind father, and an honest executor.

All the great people you see make considerable figures on the exchange, in court, and sometimes in senates, are such as in reality have no greater faculty than what may be called human instinct, which is a natural tendency to their own preservation, and that of their friends, without being capable of striking out the road for adventurers. There is Sir William Scrip was of this sort of capacity from his childhood; he has bought the country round him, and makes a bargain better than Sir Harry Wildfire, with all his wit and humor. Sir Harry never wants money but he comes to Scrip, laughs at him half

an hour, and then gives bond for the other thousand.
The close men are incapable of placing merit anywhere
but in their pence, and therefore gain it; while others
who have larger capacities, are diverted from the pur-
5 suit by enjoyments which can be supported only by
that cash which they despise; and, therefore, are in the
end slaves to their inferiors both in fortune and understanding. I once heard a man of excellent sense observe
that more affairs in the world failed by being in the hands
10 of men of too large capacities for their business than by
being in the conduct of such as wanted abilities to execute them. Jack, therefore, being of a plodding make,
shall be a citizen: and I design him to be the refuge of
his family in their distress, as well as their jest in pros-
15 perity. His brother Will shall go to Oxford with all
speed, where, if he does not arrive at being a man of
sense, he will soon be informed wherein he is a coxcomb.
There is in that place such a true spirit of raillery and
humor, that if they cannot make you a wise man, they
20 will certainly let you know you are a fool; which is all
my cousin wants, to cease to be so. Thus, having
taken these two out of the way, I have leisure to look
at my third lad. I observe in the young rogue a natural
subtility of mind, which discovers itself rather in for-
25 bearing to declare his thoughts on any occasion, than in
any visible way of exerting himself in discourse. For
which reason I will place him, where, if he commits no
faults, he may go farther than those in other stations,
though they excel in virtues. The boy is well-fashioned
30 and will easily fall into a graceful manner; wherefore,
I have a design to make him a page to a great lady of
my acquaintance; by which means he will be well skilled
in the common modes of life, and make a greater progress
in the world by that knowledge, than with the

greatest qualities without it. A good mien in a court will carry a man greater lengths than a good understanding in any other place. We see a world of pains taken and the best years of life spent in collecting a set of thoughts in a college for the conduct of life, and, 5 after all, the man so qualified shall hesitate in a speech to a good suit of clothes, and want common sense before an agreeable woman. Hence it is that wisdom, valor, justice, and learning cannot keep a man in countenance that is possessed with these excellencies, if he wants 10 that inferior art of life and behavior called good-breeding. A man endowed with great perfections, without this, is like one who has his pockets full of gold but always wants change for his ordinary occasions.

Will Courtly is a living instance of this truth, and has 15 had the same education which I am giving my nephew. He never spoke a thing but what was said before, and yet can converse with the wittiest men without being ridiculous. Among the learned, he does not appear ignorant; nor with the wise, indiscreet. Living in con- 20 versation from his infancy, makes him no where at a loss; and a long familiarity with the persons of men is, in a manner, of the same service to him as if he knew their arts. As ceremony is the invention of wise men to keep fools at a distance, so good-breeding is an expedient 25 to make fools and wise men equals.

JOSEPH ADDISON

NED SOFTLY

"Idem inficeto est inficetior rure
Simul poemata attigit; neque idem unquam
Æquè est beatus, ac poema cum scribit:
Tam gaudet in se, tamque se ipse miratur.
5 Nimirum idem omnes fallimur; neque est quisquam
Quem non in aliqua re videre Suffenum
Possis"——

—CATUL. *de Suffeno*, 20.14.
Will's Coffee-house, April 24 [1710].

10 I yesterday came hither about two hours before the
company generally make their appearance, with a design
to read over all the newspapers; but upon my sitting
down I was accosted by Ned Softly, who saw me from a
corner in the other end of the room, where I found he
15 had been writing something. "Mr. Bickerstaff," says
he, "I observe by a late paper of yours that you and I
are just of a humor; for you must know, of all imperti-
nences there is nothing which I so much hate as news. I
never read a gazette in my life; and never trouble my
20 head about our armies, whether they win or lose, or in
what part of the world they lie encamped." Without
giving me time to reply he drew a paper of verses out of
his pocket, telling me that he had something which would
entertain me more agreeably, and that he would desire
25 my judgment upon every line, for that we had time
enough before us until the company came in.

Ned Softly is a very pretty poet and a great admirer
of easy lines. Waller is his favorite: and as that admirable writer has the best and worst verses of any
among our great English poets, Ned Softly has got all
the bad ones without book, which he repeats upon occa- 5
sion, to show his reading and garnish his conversation.
Ned is indeed a true English reader, incapable of relish-
ing the great and masterly strokes of this art; but wonderfully pleased with the little gothic ornaments of epi-
grammatical conceits, turns, points, and quibbles, which 10
are so frequent in the most admired of our English
poets, and practised by those who want genius and
strength to represent, after the manner of the ancients,
simplicity in its natural beauty and perfection.

Finding myself unavoidably engaged in such a con- 15
versation, I was resolved to turn my pain into a pleasure
and to divert myself as well as I could with so very odd
a fellow. "You must understand," says Ned, "that the
sonnet I am going to read to you was written upon a
lady, who showed me some verses of her own making, 20
and is perhaps the best poet of our age. But you shall
hear it." Upon which he begun to read as follows:

"TO MIRA, ON HER INCOMPARABLE POEMS

1

"When dressed in laurel wreaths you shine,
    And tune your soft melodious notes, 25
  You seem a sister of the Nine,
    Or Phœbus' self in petticoats.

2

"I fancy, when your song you sing
    (Your song you sing with so much art),
  Your pen was plucked from Cupid's wing; 30
    For ah! it wounds me like his dart."

"Why," says I, "this is a little nosegay of conceits, a
very lump of salt: every verse hath something in it
that piques; and then the dart in the last line is certainly
as pretty a sting in the tail of an epigram (for so I
5 think your critics call it) as ever entered into the thought
of a poet." "Dear Mr. Bickerstaff," says he, shaking
me by the hand, "everybody knows you to be a judge
of these things; and to tell you truly, I read over Roscommon's translation of Horace's *Art of Poetry* three
10 several times before I sat down to write the sonnet which
I have shown you. But you shall hear it again, and pray
observe every line of it, for not one of them shall pass
without your approbation.

"When dressed in laurel wreaths you shine.

15 "That is," says he, "when you have your garland on;
when you are writing verses." To which I replied, "I
know your meaning: a metaphor!" "The same," said
he, and went on:

"And tune your soft melodious notes.

20 "Pray observe the gliding of that verse; there is scarce
a consonant in it: I took care to make it run upon
liquids. Give me your opinion of it." "Truly," said
I, "I think it as good as the former." "I am very glad
to hear you say so," says he; "but mind the next:

25   "You seem a sister of the Nine.

"That is," says he, "you seem a sister of the Muses;
for if you look into ancient authors, you will find it was
their opinion that there were nine of them." "I remember it very well," said I; "but pray proceed."

30   "Or Phœbus' self in petticoats.

"Phœbus," says he, "was the god of poetry. These little instances, Mr. Bickerstaff, show a gentleman's reading. Then, to take off from the air of learning which Phœbus and the Muses have given to this first stanza, you may observe how it falls all of a sudden 5 into the familiar: 'in petticoats!'

> "Or Phœbus' self in petticoats."

"Let us now," says I, "enter upon the second stanza I find the first line is still a continuation of the metaphor:

> "I fancy when your song you sing."   10

"It is very right," says he; "but pray observe the turn of words in those two lines. I was a whole hour in adjusting of them, and have still a doubt upon me whether in the second line it should be, 'Your song you sing'; or, 'You sing your song.' You shall hear them both: 15

> "I fancy, when your song you sing,
> (Your song you sing with so much art),

"or,

> "I fancy, when your song you sing,
> (You sing your song with so much art). 20

"Truly," said I, "the turn is so natural either way that you have made me almost giddy with it." "Dear sir," said he, grasping me by the hand, "you have a great deal of patience; but pray what do you think of the next verse?

> "Your pen was plucked from Cupid's wing." 25

"Think!" says I, "I think you have made Cupid look like a little goose." "That was my meaning," says he; "I think the ridicule is well enough hit off. But we come now to the last, which sums up the whole matter.

> "For ah! it wounds me like his dart. 30

"Pray how do you like that 'ah'? Doth it not make a pretty figure in that place? 'Ah!'—it looks as if I felt the dart and cried out at being pricked with it.

"For ah! it wounds me like his dart.

5   "My friend, Dick Easy," continued he, "assured me he would rather have written that 'ah!' than to have been the author of the *Æneid*. He indeed objected that I made Mira's pen like a quill in one of the lines, and like a dart in the other. But as to that——" "Oh, as 10 to that," says I, "it is but supposing Cupid to be like a porcupine, and his quills and darts will be the same thing." He was going to embrace me for the hint; but half a dozen critics coming into the room, whose faces he did not like, he conveyed the sonnet into his pocket, 15 and whispered me in the ear he would show it me again as soon as his man had written it over fair.

SIR ROGER DE COVERLEY IN WESTMINSTER ABBEY

Ire tamen restat Numa quo devenit et Ancus.

HOR.

My friend Sir Roger de Coverley told me t'other night 20 that he had been reading my paper upon Westminster Abbey, "in which," says he, "there are a great many ingenious fancies." He told me, at the same time, that be observed I had promised another paper upon the tombs, and that he should be glad to go and see them with 25 me, not having visited them since he had read history. I could not at first imagine how this came into the knight's head, till I recollected that he had been very busy all last summer upon Baker's *Chronicle*, which he has quoted several times in his disputes with Sir Andrew Freeport since his last coming to town. Accordingly, I promised to call upon him the next morning, that we might go together to the Abbey.

I found the knight under his butler's hands, who always shaves him. He was no sooner dressed than he called for a glass of the Widow Trueby's water, which he told me he always drank before he went abroad. He recommended me to a dram of it at the same time with so much heartiness that I could not forbear drinking it. As soon as I had got it down, I found it very unpalatable; upon which the knight, observing that I had made several wry faces, told me that he knew I should not like it at first, but that it was the best thing in the world against the stone or gravel. I could have wished, indeed, that he had acquainted me with the virtues of it sooner; but it was too late to complain, and I knew what he had done was out of good-will. Sir Roger told me, further, that he looked upon it to be very good for a man, whilst he stayed in town, to keep off infection; and that he got together a quantity of it upon the first news of the sickness being at Dantzic. When, of a sudden, turning short to one of his servants, who stood behind him, he bid him call a hackney-coach, and take care it was an elderly man that drove it.

He then resumed his discourse upon Mrs. Trueby's water, telling me that the Widow Trueby was one who did more good than all the doctors and apothecaries in the county; that she distilled every poppy that grew within five miles of her; that she distributed her water gratis among all sorts of people. To which the knight added that she had a very great jointure, and that the whole country would fain have it a match between him and her. "And truly," said Sir Roger, "if I had not been engaged, perhaps I could not have done better."

His discourse was broken off by his man's telling him he had called a coach. Upon our going to it, after having cast his eye upon the wheels, he asked the coachman if his axle-tree was good; upon the fellow's telling him
5 he would warrant it, the knight turned to me, told me he looked like an honest man, and went in without further ceremony.

We had not gone far when Sir Roger, popping out his head, called the coachman down from his box, and upon
10 his presenting himself at the window, asked him if he smoked. As I was considering what 'this would end in, he bid him stop by the way at any good tobacconist's, and take in a roll of their best Virginia. Nothing material happened in the remaining part of our journey till
15 we were set down at the west end of the Abbey.

As we went up the body of the church, the knight pointed at the trophies upon one of the new monuments, and cried out, "A brave man, I warrant him!" Passing afterward by Sir Cloudesley Shovel, he flung his hand
20 that way, and cried, "Sir Cloudesley Shovel! a very gallant man!" As we stood before Busby's tomb, the knight uttered himself again after the same manner: "Dr. Busby—a great man! he whipped my grandfather —a very great man! I should have gone to him myself
25 if I had not been a blockhead—a very great man!"

We were immediately conducted into the little chapel on the right hand. Sir Roger, planting himself at our historian's elbow, was very attentive to everything he said, particularly to the account he gave us of the lord
30 who had cut off the King of Morocco's head. Among several other figures, he was very well pleased to see the statesman Cecil upon his knees; and, concluding them all to be great men, was conducted to the figure which represents that martyr to good housewifery who died by

the prick of a needle.   Upon our interpreter's telling us
that she was a maid of honor to Queen Elizabeth, the
knight was very inquisitive into her name and family; and
after having regarded her finger for some time, "I wonder," says he, "that Sir Richard Baker has said nothing 5
of her in his *Chronicle*."

We were then conveyed to the two coronation chairs,
where my old friend, after having heard that the stone
underneath the most ancient of them, which was brought
from Scotland, was called Jacob's Pillar, sat himself down 10
in the chair, and looking like the figure of an old Gothic
king, asked our interpreter what authority they had to
say that Jacob had ever been in Scotland.   The fellow,
instead of returning him an answer, told him that he
hoped his honor would pay his forfeit.   I could observe 15
Sir Roger a little ruffled upon being thus trepanned; but,
our guide not insisting upon his demand, the knight soon
recovered his good humor, and whispered in my ear that
if Will Wimble were with us, and saw those two chairs,
it would go hard but he would get a tobacco-stopper out 20
of one or t'other of them.

Sir Roger, in the next place, laid his hand upon Edward the Third's sword, and leaning upon the pommel
of it, gave us the whole history of the Black Prince;
concluding that, in Sir Richard Baker's opinion, Edward 25
the Third was one of the greatest princes that ever sat
upon the English throne.

We were then shown Edward the Confessor's tomb,
upon which Sir Roger acquainted us that he was the first
who touched for the evil; and afterward Henry the 30
Fourth's, upon which he shook his head and told us there
was fine reading in the casualties of that reign.

Our conductor then pointed to that monument where
there is a figure of one of our English kings without a

head; and upon giving us to know that the head, which was of beaten silver, had been stolen away several years since—"Some Whig, I'll warrant you," says Sir Roger; "you ought to lock up your kings better; they will carry 5 off the body too, if you don't take care."

The glorious names of Henry the Fifth and Queen Elizabeth gave the knight great opportunities of shining and of doing justice to Sir Richard Baker, who, as our knight observed with some surprise, had a great many 10 kings in him whose monuments he had not seen in the Abbey.

For my own part, I could not but be pleased to see the knight show such an honest passion for the glory of his country, and such a respectful gratitude to the memory 15 of its princes.

I must not omit that the benevolence of my good old friend, which flows out toward every one he converses with, made him very kind to our interpreter, whom he looked upon as an extraordinary man; for which reason 20 he shook him by the hand at parting, telling him that he should be very glad to see him at his lodgings in Norfolk Buildings, and talk over these matters with him more at leisure.

REFLECTIONS IN WESTMINSTER ABBEY

Pallida mors æquo pulsat pede pauperum tabernas
25   Regumque turres. O beate Sesti,
Vitæ summa brevis spem nos vetat incohare longam.
          Jam te premet nox, fabulæque manes,
          Et domus exilis Plutonia——HOR.

WHEN I am in a serious humor, I very often walk by 30 myself in Westminster Abbey; where the gloominess of the place and the use to which it is applied, with the solemnity of the building and the condition of the people who lie in it, are apt to fill the mind with a kind of melancholy, or rather thoughtfulness, that is not disagreeable. I yesterday passed a whole afternoon in the churchyard, the cloisters, and the church, amusing myself with the tombstones and inscriptions that I met with in those several regions of the dead. Most of them recorded nothing else of the buried person but that he was born upon one day and died upon another; the whole history of his life being comprehended in those two circumstances that are common to all mankind. I could not but look upon these registers of existence, whether of brass or marble, as a kind of satire upon the departed persons who had left no other memorial of them but that they were born and that they died. They put me in mind of several persons mentioned in the battles of heroic poems, who have sounding names given them for no other reason but that they may be killed, and are celebrated for nothing but being knocked on the head. The life of these men is finely described in Holy Writ by "the Path of an Arrow," which is immediately closed up and lost.

Upon my going into the church, I entertained myself with the digging of a grave; and saw in every shovelfull of it that was thrown up the fragment of a bone or skull intermixed with a kind of fresh mouldering earth that some time or other had a place in the Composition of a human body. Upon this, I began to consider with myself what innumerable multitudes of people lay confused together under the pavement of that ancient cathedral; how men and women, friends and enemies, priests and soldiers, monks and prebendaries, were crumbled amongst one another and blended together in the same common mass; how beauty, strength, and youth, with old age, weakness, and deformity, lay undistinguished in the same promiscuous heap of matter.

After having thus surveyed this great magazine of mortality, as it were, in the lump, I examined it more particularly by the accounts which I found on several of the monuments which are raised in every quarter of that ancient fabric. Some of them were covered with such extravagant epitaphs that, if it were possible for the dead person to be acquainted with them, he would blush at the praises which his friends have bestowed upon him. There are others so excessively modest, that they deliver the character of the person departed in Greek or Hebrew, and by that means are not understood once in a twelvemonth. In the poetical quarter, I found there were poets who had no monuments, and monuments which had no poets. I observed indeed that the present war had filled the church with many of these uninhabited monuments, which had been erected to the memory of persons whose bodies were perhaps buried in the plains of Blenheim, or in the bosom of the ocean.

I could not but be very much delighted with several modern epitaphs, which are written with great elegance of expression and justness of thought, and therefore do honor to the living as well as to the dead. As a foreigner is very apt to conceive an idea of the ignorance or politeness of a nation from the turn of their public monuments and inscriptions, they should be submitted to the perusal of men of learning and genius before they are put in execution. Sir Cloudesley Shovel's monument has very often given me great offence. Instead of the brave rough English admiral, which was the distinguishing character of that plain gallant man, he is represented on his tomb by the figure of a beau, dressed in a long perriwig, and reposing himself upon velvet cushions under a canopy of state. The inscription is answerable to the monument; for instead of celebrating the many remarkable actions he had performed in the service of his country, it acquaints us only with the manner of his death, in which it was impossible for him to reap any honor. The Dutch, whom we are apt to despise for want of genius, shew an infinitely greater taste of antiquity and politeness in their buildings and works of this nature, than what we meet with in those of our own country. The monuments of their admirals, which have been erected at the public expense, represent them like themselves; and are adorned with rostral crowns and naval ornaments, with beautiful festoons of seaweed, shells, and coral.

But to return to our subject. I have left the repository of our English kings for the contemplation of another day, when I shall find my mind disposed for so serious an amusement. I know that entertainments of this nature are apt to raise dark and dismal thoughts in timorous minds and gloomy imaginations; but for my own part, though I am always serious, I do not know what it is to be melancholy, and can therefore take a view of nature in her deep and solemn scenes, with the same pleasure as in her most gay and delightful ones. By this means I can improve myself with those objects which others consider with terror. When I look upon the tombs of the great, every emotion of envy dies in me; when I read the epitaphs of the beautiful, every inordinate desire goes out; when I meet with the grief of parents upon a tombstone, my heart melts with compassion; when I see the tomb of the parents themselves, I consider the vanity of grieving for those whom we must quickly follow. When I see kings lying by those who deposed them, when I consider rival wits placed side by side, or the holy men that divided the world with their contests and disputes, I reflect with sorrow and astonishment on the little competitions, factions, and debates of mankind. When I read the several dates of the tombs, of some that died yesterday, and some six hundred years ago, I consider that great day when we shall all of us be contemporaries, and make our appearance together.

CHARLES LAMB

A QUAKERS' MEETING

"Still-born Silence? thou that art
Flood-gate of the deeper heart!
Offspring of a heavenly kind!
Frost o' the mouth, and thaw o' the mind!
Secrecy's confidant, and he   5
Who makes religion mystery!
Admiration's speaking'st tongue!
Leave, thy desert shades among,
Reverend hermits' hallowed cells,
Where retired devotion dwells!   10
With thy enthusiasms come,
Seize our tongues, and strike us dumb!"

READER, would'st thou know what true peace and
quiet mean: would'st thou find a refuge from the noises
and clamors of the multitude; would'st thou enjoy at 15
once solitude and society; would'st thou possess the
depth of thine own spirit in stillness, without being shut
out from the consolatory faces of thy species; would'st
thou be alone, and yet accompanied; solitary, yet not
desolate; singular, yet not without some to keep thee in 20
countenance;—a unit in aggregate; a simple in compos-
ite:—come with me into a Quakers' Meeting.

Dost thou love silence deep as that "before the winds
were made"? go not out into the wilderness, descend not

53

into the profundities of the earth; shut not up thy case-
ments; nor pour wax into the little cells of thy ears,
with little-faith'd self-mistrusting Ulysses.—Retire with
me into a Quakers' Meeting.

5   For a man to refrain even from good words, and to
hold his peace, it is commendable; but for a multitude,
it is great mastery.

What is the stillness of the desert, compared with this
place? what the uncommunicating muteness of fishes?—
10 here the goddess reigns and revels.—"Boreas, and Cesias,
and Argestes loud," do not with their inter-confounding
uproars more augment the brawl—nor the waves of the
blown Baltic with their clubbed sounds—than their opposite (Silence her sacred self) is multiplied and rendered
15 more intense by numbers, and by sympathy. She too
hath her deeps, that call unto deeps. Negation itself
hath a positive more or less; and closed eyes would seem
to obscure the great obscurity of midnight.

There are wounds, which an imperfect solitude can-
20 not heal. By imperfect I mean that which a man en-
joyeth by himself. The perfect is that which he can
sometimes attain in crowds, but nowhere so absolutely
as in a Quakers' Meeting.—Those first hermits did certainly understand this principle, when they retired into
25 Egyptian solitudes, not singly, but in shoals, to enjoy
one another's want of conversation. The Carthusian is
bound to his brethren by this agreeing spirit of incom-
municativeness. In secular occasions, what so pleasant as to be reading a book through a long winter evening,
30 with a friend sitting by—say, a wife—he, or she, too
(if that be probable), reading another, without interruption, or oral communication?—can there be no sympathy without the gabble of words?—away with this
inhuman, shy, single, shade-and-cavern-haunting soli-

tariness. Give me, Master Zimmerman, a sympathetic solitude.

To pace alone in the cloisters, or side aisles of some cathedral, time-stricken:

> Or under hanging mountains,
> Or by the fall of fountains;

is but a vulgar luxury, compared with that which those enjoy, who come together for the purposes of more complete, abstracted solitude. This is the loneliness "to be felt."—The Abbey Church of Westminster hath nothing so solemn, so spirit-soothing, as the naked walls and benches of a Quakers' Meeting. Here are no tombs, no inscriptions,

> —— sands, ignoble things,
> Dropt from the ruined sides of kings—

but here is something, which throws Antiquity herself into the foreground—SILENCE—eldest of things—language of old Night—primitive Discourser—to which the insolent decays of mouldering grandeur have but arrived by a violent, and, as we may say, unnatural progression.

> How reverend is the view of these hushed heads,
> Looking tranquility!

Nothing-plotting, nought-caballing, unmischievous synod! convocation without intrigue! parliament without debate! what a lesson dost thou read to council, and to consistory! if my pen treat of you lightly—as haply it will wander—yet my spirit hath gravely felt the wisdom of your custom, when sitting among you in deepest peace, which some out-welling tears would rather confirm than disturb, I have reverted the times of your beginnings, and the sowings of the seed by Fox and

Dewsbury.—I have witnessed that, which brought before my eyes your heroic tranquillity, inflexible to the rude jests and serious violences of the insolent soldiery, republican or royalist, sent to molest you—for ye sate 5 betwixt the fires of two persecutions, the outcast and off-scowering of church and presbytery.—I have seen the reeling sea-ruffian, who had wandered into your receptacle, with the avowed intention of disturbing your quiet, from the very spirit of the place receive in a moment 10 a new heart, and presently sit among ye as a lamb amidst lambs. And I remembered Penn before his accusers, and Fox in the bail-dock, where he was lifted up in spirit, as he tells us, and "the judge and the jury became as dead men under his feet."

15 Reader, if you are not acquainted with it, I would recommend to you, above all church-narratives, to read Sewel's *History of the Quakers*. It is in folio, and is the abstract of the journals of Fox, and the primitive Friends. It is far more edifying than anything you will read of 20 Wesley and his colleagues. Here is nothing to stagger you, nothing to make you mistrust, no suspicion of alloy, no drop or dreg of the worldly or ambitious spirit. You will here read the true story of that much-injured, ridiculed man (who perhaps hath been a by-word in your 25 mouth)—James Naylor: what dreadful sufferings, with what patience, he endured even to the boring through of his tongue with red-hot irons without a murmur; and with what strength of mind, when the delusion he had fallen into, which they stigmatized for blasphemy, had 30 given way to clearer thoughts, he could renounce his error, in a strain of the beautifullest humility, yet keep his first grounds, and be a Quaker still!—so different from the practice of your common converts from enthusiasm, who, when they apostatize, *apostatize all*, and think

they can never get far enough from the society of their former errors, even to the renunciation of some saving truths, with which they had been mingled, not implicated.

Get the writings of John Woolman by heart; and love the early Quakers.

How far the followers of these good men in our days have kept to the primitive spirit, or in what proportion they have substituted formality for it, the Judge of Spirits can alone determine. I have seen faces in their assemblies, upon which the dove sate visibly brooding. Others again I have watched, when my thoughts should have been better engaged, in which I could possibly detect nothing but a blank inanity. But quiet was in all, and the disposition to unanimity, and the absence of the fierce controversial workings.—If the spiritual pretensions of the Quakers have abated, at least they make few pretences. Hypocrites they certainly are not, in their preaching. It is seldom indeed that you shall see one get up amongst them to hold forth. Only now and then a trembling female, generally *ancient*, voice is heard—you cannot guess from what part of the meeting it proceeds—with a low, buzzing, musical sound, laying out a few words which "she thought might suit the condition of some present," with a quaking diffidence, which leaves no possibility of supposing that any thing of female vanity was mixed up, where the tones were so full of tenderness, and a restraining modesty.—The men, for what I have observed, speak seldomer.

Once only, and it was some years ago, I witnessed a sample of the old Foxian orgasm. It was a man of giant stature, who, as Wordsworth phrases it, might have danced "from head to foot equipt in iron mail." His frame was of iron too. But *he* was malleable. I saw him shake all over with the spirit—I dare not say, of

delusion. The strivings of the outer man were unutterable—he seemed not to speak, but to be spoken from. I saw the strong man bowed down, and his knees to fail—his joints all seemed loosening—it was a figure to set off
5 against Paul Preaching—the words he uttered were few, and sound—he was evidently resisting his will—keeping down his own word-wisdom with more mighty effort, than the world's orators strain for theirs. "He had been a WIT in his youth," he told us, with expressions of a
10 sober remorse. And it was not till long after the impression had begun to wear away, that I was enabled, with something like a smile, to recall the striking incongruity of the confession—understanding the term in its worldly acceptation—with the frame and physiognomy of the
15 person before me. His brow would have scared away the Levites—the *Jocos Risus-que*—faster than the Loves fled the face of Dis at Enna. By *wit*, even in his youth, I will be sworn he understood something far within the limits of an allowable liberty.
20   More frequently the Meeting is broken up without a word having been spoken. But the mind has been fed. You go away with a sermon, not made with hands. You have been in the milder caverns of Trophonius; or as in some den, where that fiercest and savagest of all wild
25 creatures, the TONGUE, that unruly member, has strangely lain tied up and captive. You have bathed with stillness.—O when the spirit is sore fettered, even tired to sickness of the janglings, and nonsense noises of the world, what a balm and a solace it is, to go and seat
30 yourself for a quiet half hour, upon some undisputed corner of a bench, among the gentle Quakers!
    Their garb and stillness conjoined, present a uniformity, tranquil and herd-like—as in the pasture—"forty feeding like one."—

The very garments of a Quaker seem incapable of receiving a soil; and cleanliness in them to be something more than the absence of its contrary. Every Quakeress is a lily; and when they come up in bands to their Whitsun-conferences, whitening the easterly streets of the metropolis, from all parts of the United Kingdom, they show like troops of the Shining Ones.

A DISSERTATION UPON ROAST PIG

MANKIND, says a Chinese manuscript, which my friend M. was obliging enough to read and explain to me, for the first seventy thousand ages ate their meat raw, clawing or biting it from the living animal, just as they do in Abyssinia to this day. This period is not obscurely hinted at by their great Confucius in the second chapter of his Mundane Mutations, where he designates a kind of golden age by the term Cho-fang, literally "the Cook's holiday." The manuscript goes on to say, that the art of roasting, or rather broiling (which I take to be the elder brother) was accidentally discovered in the manner following. The swine-herd, Ho-ti, having gone out into the woods one morning, as his manner was, to collect mast for his hogs, left his cottage in the care of his eldest son Bo-bo, a great lubberly boy, who being fond of playing with fire, as younkers of his age commonly are, let some sparks escape into a bundle of straw, which kindling quickly, spread the conflagration over every part of their poor mansion, till it was reduced to ashes. Together with the cottage (a sorry antediluvian make-shift of a building, you may think it), what was of much more importance, a fine litter of new-farrowed pigs, no less than nine in number, perished. China pigs have been esteemed a luxury all over the East from the remotest

periods that we read of. Bo-bo was in utmost consternation, as you may think, not so much for the sake of the
tenement, which his father and he could easily build up
again with a few dry branches, and the labor of an hour
5 or two, at any time, as for the loss of the pigs. While he
was thinking what he should say to his father, and wring-
ing his hands over the smoking remnants of one of those
untimely sufferers, an odor assailed his nostrils, unlike
any scent which he had before experienced. What could
10 it proceed from?—not from the burnt cottage—he had
smelt that smell before—indeed this was by no means
the first accident of the kind which had occurred through
the negligence of this unlucky young fire-brand. Much
less did it resemble that of any known herb, weed, or
15 flower. A premonitory moistening at the same time
overflowed his nether lip. He knew not what to think. He
next stooped down to feel the pig, if there were any signs
of life in it. He burnt his fingers, and to cool them he
applied them in his booby fashion to his mouth. Some of
20 the crumbs of the scorched skin had come away with his
fingers, and for the first time in his life (in the world's
life indeed, for before him no man had known it) he tasted
—*crackling!* Again he felt and fumbled at the pig. It
did not burn him so much now, still he licked his fingers
25 from a sort of habit. The truth at length broke into his
slow understanding, that it was the pig that smelt so,
and the pig that tasted so delicious; and, surrendering
himself up to the newborn pleasure, he fell to tearing
up whole handfuls of the scorched skin with the flesh
30 next it, and was cramming it down his throat in his
beastly fashion, when his sire entered amid the smoking
rafters, armed with retributory cudgel, and finding how
affairs stood, began to rain blows upon the young rogue's
shoulders, as thick as hailstones, which Bo-bo heeded not

any more than if they had been flies. The tickling pleasure, which he experienced in his lower regions, had rendered him quite callous to any inconveniences he might feel in those remote quarters. His father might lay on, but he could not beat him from his pig, till he had 5 fairly made an end of it, when, becoming a little more sensible of his situation, something like the following dialogue ensued.

"You graceless whelp, what have you got there devouring? Is it not enough that you have burnt me down 10 three houses with your dog's tricks, and be hanged to you, but you must be eating fire, and I know not what—what have you got there, I say?"

"O, father, the pig, the pig, do come and taste how nice the burnt pig eats." 15

The ears of Ho-ti tingled with horror. He cursed his son, and he cursed himself that ever he should beget a son that should eat burnt pig.

Bo-bo, whose scent was wonderfully sharpened since morning, soon raked out another pig, and fairly rending 20 it asunder, thrust the lesser half by main force into the fists of Ho-ti, still shouting out "Eat, eat, eat the burnt pig, father, only taste—O Lord,"—with such-like barbarous ejaculations, cramming all the while as if he would choke. 25

Ho-ti trembled every joint while he grasped the abominable thing, wavering whether he should not put his son to death for an unnatural young monster, when the crackling scorching his fingers, as it had done his son's, and applying the same remedy to them, he in his turn 30 tasted some of its flavor, which, make what sour mouths he would for a pretence, proved not altogether displeasing to him. In conclusion (for the manuscript here is a little tedious) both father and son fairly sat down to the mess,

and never left off till they had dispatched all that
remained of the litter.

Bo-bo was strictly enjoined not to let the secret escape,
for the neighbors would certainly have stoned them for a
5 couple of abominable wretches, who could think of im-
proving upon the good meat which God had sent them.
Nevertheless, strange stories got about. It was observed
that Ho-ti's cottage was burnt down now more frequently
than ever. Nothing but fires from this time forward.
10 Some would break out in broad day, others in the night-
time. As often as the sow farrowed, so sure was the house
of Ho-ti to be in a blaze; and Ho-ti himself, which was
the more remarkable, instead of chastising his son, seemed
to grow more indulgent to him than ever. At length
15 they were watched, the terrible mystery discovered, and
father and son summoned to take their trial at Pekin,
then an inconsiderable assize town. Evidence was given,
the obnoxious food itself produced in court, and verdict
about to be pronounced, when the foreman of the jury
20 begged that some of the burnt pig, of which the culprits
stood accused, might be handed into the box. He handled it, and they all handled it, and burning their fingers,
as Bo-bo and his father had done before them, and nature
prompting to each of them the same remedy, against the
25 face of all the facts, and the clearest charge which judge
had ever given—to the surprise of the whole court,
townsfolk, strangers, reporters, and all present—without
leaving the box, or any manner of consultation whatever,
they brought in a simultaneous verdict of Not Guilty.

30   The judge, who was a shrewd fellow, winked at the
manifest iniquity of the decision; and, when the court was
dismissed, went privily, and bought up all the pigs that
could be had for love or money. In a few days his Lordship's town house was observed to be on fire. The thing

took wing, and now there was nothing to be seen but fires
in every direction.   Fuel and pigs grew enormously dear
all over the district.   The insurance offices one and all
shut up shop.   People built slighter and slighter every
day, until it was feared that the very science of architec-   5
ture would in no long time be lost to the world.   Thus
this custom of firing houses continued, till in process of
time, says my manuscript, a sage arose, like our Locke,
who made a discovery, that the flesh of swine, or indeed
of any other animal, might be cooked (*burnt*, as they   10
called it) without the necessity of consuming a whole
house to dress it.   Then first began the rude form of a
gridiron.   Roasting by the string, or spit, came in a
century or two later, I forget in whose dynasty.   By
such slow degrees, concludes the manuscript, do the   15
most useful, and seemingly the most obvious arts, make
their way among mankind.——

Without placing too implicit faith in the account above
given, it must be agreed, that if a worthy pretext for so
dangerous an experiment as setting houses on fire (espe-   20
cially in these days) could be assigned in favor of any
culinary object, that pretext and excuse might be found
in ROAST PIG.

Of all the delicacies in the whole *mundus edibilis*, I will
maintain it to be the most delicate—*princeps obsoniorum*.   25

I speak not of your grown porkers—things between pig
and pork—those hobbydehoys—but a young and tender
suckling—under a moon old—guiltless as yet of the sty—
with no original speck of the *amor immunditiæ*, the hereditary failing of the first parent, yet manifest—his voice   30
as yet not broken, but something between a childish
treble, and a grumble—the mild forerunner, or *præludium*, of a grunt.

He must be roasted.   I am not ignorant that our ances-

tors ate them seethed, or boiled—but what a sacrifice
of the exterior tegument!

There is no flavor comparable, I will contend, to that
of the crisp, tawny, well-watched, not over-roasted, *crack-*
5 *ling*, as it is well called—the very teeth are invited to
their share of the pleasure at this banquet in overcom-
ing the coy, brittle resistance—with the adhesive oleagi-
nous—O call it not fat—but an indefinable sweetness
growing up to it—the tender blossoming of fat—fat
10 cropped in the bud—taken in the shoot—in the first
innocence—the cream and quintessence of the child-
pig's yet pure food——the lean, no lean, but a kind
of animal manna—or, rather, fat and lean (if it must be
so) so blended and running into each other, that both
15 together make but one ambrosian result, or common
substance.

Behold him, while he is doing—it seemeth rather a
refreshing warmth, than a scorching heat, that he is so
passive to.　How equably he twirleth round the string!—
20 Now he is just done.　To see the extreme sensibility of
that tender age, he hath wept out his pretty eyes—
radiant jellies—shooting stars—

See him in the dish, his second cradle, how meek he
lieth!—wouldst thou have had this innocent grow up to
25 the grossness and indocility which too often accompany
maturer swinehood?　Ten to one he would have proved
a glutton, a sloven, an obstinate, disagreeable animal—
wallowing in all manner of filthy conversation—from
these sins he is happily snatched away—

30　　　　　　Ere sin could blight, or sorrow fade,
　　　　　　　Death came with timely care—

his memory is odoriferous—no clown curseth, while his
stomach half rejecteth, the rank bacon—no coalheaver

bolteth him in reeking sausages—he hath a fair sepulcher in the grateful stomach of the judicious epicure—and for such a tomb might be content to die.

He is the best of Sapors. Pine-apple is great. She is indeed almost too transcendent—a delight, if not sinful, yet so like to sinning, that really a tender-conscienced person would do well to pause—too ravishing for mortal taste, she woundeth and excoriateth the lips that approach her—like lovers' kisses, she biteth—she is a pleasure bordering on pain from the fierceness and insanity of her relish—but she stoppeth at the palate—she meddleth not with the appetite—and the coarsest hunger might barter her consistently for a mutton chop.

Pig—let me speak his praise—is no less provocative of the appetite, than he is satisfactory to the criticalness of the censorious palate. The strong man may batten on him, and weakling refuseth not his mild juices.

Unlike to mankind's mixed characters, a bundle of virtues and vices, inexplicably intertwisted, and not to be unraveled without hazard, he is—good throughout. No part of him is better or worse than another. He helpeth, as far as his little means extend, all around. He is the least envious of banquets. He is all neighbors' fare.

I am one of those, who freely and ungrudgingly impart a share of the good things of this life which fall to their lot (few as mine are in this kind) to a friend. I protest I take as great an interest in my friend's pleasures, his relishes, and proper satisfactions, as in mine own. "Presents," I often say, "endear Absents." Hares, pheasants, partridges, snipes, barn-door chickens (those "tame villatic fowl"), capons, plovers, brawn, barrels of oysters, I dispense as freely as I receive them.

I love to taste them, as it were, upon the tongue of
my friend. But a stop must be put somewhere.
One would not, like Lear, "give everything." I make
my stand upon pig. Methinks it is an ingratitude to the
5 Giver of all good flavors, to extra-domiciliate, or send
out of the house, slightingly (under pretext of friendship, or I know not what) a blessing so particularly
adapted, predestined, I may say, to my individual
palate—It argues an insensibility.
10 I remember a touch of conscience in this kind at
school. My good old aunt, who never parted from me
at the end of a holiday without stuffing a sweetmeat, or
some nice thing, into my pocket, had dismissed me one
evening with a smoking plum-cake, fresh from the oven.
15 In my way to school (it was over London Bridge) a
grey-headed old beggar saluted me (I have no doubt at
this time of day that he was a counterfeit). I had no
pence to console him with, and in the vanity of self-
denial, and the very coxcombry of charity, school-boy-
20 like, I made him a present of—the whole cake! I walked
on a little, buoyed up, as one is on such occasions, with
a sweet soothing of self-satisfaction; but before I had
got to the end of the bridge, my better feelings returned,
and I burst into tears, thinking how ungrateful I had
25 been to my good aunt, to go and give her good gift away
to a stranger, that I had never seen before, and who
might be a bad man for aught I knew; and then I thought
of the pleasure my aunt would be taking in thinking that
I—I myself, and not another—would eat her nice cake—
30 and what should I say to her the next time I saw her—
how naughty I was to part with her pretty present—
and the odor of that spicy cake came back upon my
recollection, and the pleasure and the curiosity I had
taken in seeing her make it, and her joy when she sent it

to the oven, and how disappointed she would feel that I had never had a bit of it in my mouth at last—and I blamed my impertinent spirit of alms-giving, and out-of-place hypocrisy of goodness, and above all I wished never to see the face again of that insidious, good-for-nothing, old grey impostor.

Our ancestors were nice in their method of sacrificing these tender victims. We read of pigs whipt to death with something of a shock, as we hear of any other obsolete custom. The age of discipline is gone by, or it would be curious to inquire (in a philosophical light merely) what effect this process might have toward intenerating and dulcifying a substance, naturally so mild and dulcet as the flesh of young pigs. It looks like refining a violet. Yet we should be cautious, while we condemn the inhumanity, how we censure the wisdom of the practice. It might impart a gusto—

I remember an hypothesis, argued upon by the young students, when I was at St. Omer's, and maintained with much learning and pleasantry on both sides, "Whether, supposing that the flavor of a pig who obtained his death by whipping (*per flagellationem extremam*) superadded a pleasure upon the palate of a man more intense than any possible suffering we can conceive in the animal, is man justified in using that method of putting the animal to death?" I forget the decision.

His sauce should be considered. Decidedly, a few bread crumbs, done up with his liver and brains, and a dash of mild sage. But, banish, dear Mrs. Cook, I beseech you, the whole onion tribe. Barbecue your whole hogs to your palate, steep them in shalots, stuff them out with plantations of the rank and guilty garlic; you cannot poison them, or make them stronger than they are—but consider, he is a weakling—a flower.

DREAM CHILDREN

CHILDREN love to listen to stories about their elders,
when *they* were children; to stretch their imagination to
the conception of a traditionary great-uncle or grandame,
whom they never saw. It was in this spirit that my little
5 ones crept about me the other evening to hear about their
great-grandmother Field, who lived in a great house in
Norfolk (a hundred times bigger than that in which they
and papa lived) which had been the scene—so at least it
was generally believed in that part of the country—of the
10 tragic incidents which they had lately become familiar
with from the ballad of the Children in the Wood. Certain it is that the whole story of the children and their
cruel uncle was to be seen fairly carved out in wood upon
the chimney-piece of the great hall, the whole story down
15 to the Robin Redbreasts, till a foolish rich person pulled
it down to set up a marble one of modern invention in its
stead, with no story upon it. Here Alice put out one of
her dear mother's looks, too tender to be called upbraid-
ing. Then I went on to say, how religious and how good
20 their great-grandmother Field was, how beloved and
respected by everybody, though she was not indeed the
mistress of this great house, but had only the charge of it
(and yet in some respects she might be said to be the
mistress of it too) committed to her by the owner, who
25 preferred living in a newer and more fashionable mansion
which he had purchased somewhere in the adjoining
county; but still she lived in it in a manner as if it had
been her own, and kept up the dignity of the great house
in a sort while she lived, which afterward came to decay,
30 and was nearly pulled down, and all its old ornaments
stripped and carried away to the owner's other house,
where they were set up, and looked as awkward as if

some one were to carry away the old tombs they had seen lately at the Abbey, and stick them up in Lady C.'s tawdry gilt drawing-room. Here John smiled, as much as to say, "that would be foolish indeed." And then I told how, when she came to die, her funeral was attended 5 by a concourse of all the poor, and some of the gentry too, of the neighborhood for many miles round, to show their respect for her memory, because she had been such a good and religious woman; so good indeed that she knew all the Psaltery by heart, ay, and a great part of the Testa- 10 ment besides. Here little Alice spread her hands. Then I told what a tall, upright, graceful person their great-grandmother Field once was; and how in her youth she was esteemed the best dancer—here Alice's little right foot played an involuntary movement, till upon my look- 15 ing grave, it desisted—the best dancer, I was saying, in the county, till a cruel disease, called a cancer, came, and bowed her down with pain; but it could never bend her good spirits, or make them stoop, but they were still upright, because she was so good and religious. Then I 20 told how she was used to sleep by herself in a lone chamber of the great lone house; and how she believed that an apparition of two infants was to be seen at midnight gliding up and down the great staircase near where she slept, but she said "those innocents would do her no 25 harm"; and how frightened I used to be, though in those days I had my maid to sleep with me, because I was never half so good or religious as she—and yet I never saw the infants. Here John expanded all his eyebrows and tried to look courageous. Then I told how good she was to all 30 her grand-children, having us to the great house in the holydays, where I in particular used to spend many hours by myself, in gazing upon the old busts of the Twelve Cæsars, that had been Emperors of Rome, till the old

marble heads would seem to live again, or I to be turned
into marble with them; how I never could be tired with
roaming about that huge mansion, with its vast empty
rooms, with their worn-out hangings, fluttering tapestry,
5 and carved oaken panels, with the gilding almost rubbed
out—sometimes in the spacious old-fashioned gardens,
which I had almost to myself, unless when now and then a
solitary gardening man would cross me—and how the
nectarines and peaches hung upon the walls, without my
10 ever offering to pluck them, because they were forbidden
fruit, unless now and then—and because I had more
pleasure in strolling about among the old melancholy-
looking yew trees, or the firs, and picking up the red
berries, and the fir apples, which were good for nothing
15 but to look at—or in lying about upon the fresh grass,
with all the fine garden smells around me—or basking in
the orangery, till I could almost fancy myself ripening too
along with the oranges and the limes in that grateful
warmth—or in watching the dace that darted to and fro
20 in the fish-pond, at the bottom of the garden, with here
and there a great sulky pike hanging midway down the
water in silent state, as if it mocked at their impertinent
friskings—I had more pleasure in these busy-idle diversions than in all the sweet flavors of peaches, nectarines,
25 oranges, and such like common baits of children. Here
John slily deposited back upon the plate a bunch of
grapes, which, not unobserved by Alice, he had meditated
dividing with her, and both seemed willing to relinquish
them for the present as irrelevant. Then in somewhat
30 a more heightened tone, I told how, though their great-
grandmother Field loved all her grand-children, yet in an
especial manner she might be said to love their uncle,
John L——, because he was so handsome and spirited a
youth, and a king to the rest of us; and, instead of moping

about in solitary corners, like some of us, he would mount
the most mettlesome horse he could get, when but an imp
no bigger than themselves, and make it carry him half
over the county in a morning, and join the hunters when
there were any out—and yet he loved the old great house   5
and gardens too, but had too much spirit to be always
pent up within their boundaries—and how their uncle
grew up to man's estate as brave as he was handsome, to
the admiration of everybody, but of their great-grandmother Field most especially; and how he used to carry   10
me upon his back when I was a lame-footed boy—for he
was a good bit older than me—many a mile when I could
not walk for pain;—and how in after life he became lame-
footed too, and I did not always (I fear) make allowances
enough for him when he was impatient, and in pain, nor   15
remember sufficiently how considerate he had been to
me when I was lame-footed; and how when he died,
though he had not been dead an hour, it seemed as if he
had died a great while ago, such a distance there is
betwixt life and death; and how I bore his death as I   20
thought pretty well at first, but afterward it haunted and
haunted me; and though I did not cry or take it to heart
as some do, and as I think he would have done if I had
died, yet I missed him all day long, and knew not till then
how much I had loved him.   I missed his kindness, and   25
I missed his crossness, and wished him to be alive again,
to be quarreling with him (for we quarreled sometimes),
rather than not have him again, and was as uneasy
without him, as he their poor uncle must have been when
the doctor took off his limb.   Here the children fell a   30
crying, and asked if their little mourning which they had
on was not for uncle John, and they looked up, and prayed
me not to go on about their uncle, but to tell them some
stories about their pretty dead mother.   Then I told how

for seven long years, in hope sometimes, sometimes in despair, yet persisting ever, I courted the fair Alice W——n; and, as much as children could understand, I explained to them what coyness, and difficulty, and denial
5 meant in maidens—when suddenly, turning to Alice, the soul of the first Alice looked out at her eyes with such a reality of re-presentment, that I became in doubt which of them stood there before me, or whose that bright hair was; and while I stood gazing, both the children gradu-
10 ally grew fainter to my view, receding, and still receding till nothing at last but two mournful features were seen in the uttermost distance, which, without speech, strangely impressed upon me the effects of speech: "We are not of Alice, nor of thee, nor are we children at all. The
15 children of Alice call Bartrum father. We are nothing; less than nothing, and dreams. We are only what might have been, and must wait upon the tedious shores of Lethe millions of ages before we have existence, and a name"—and immediately awaking, I found myself
20 quietly seated in my bachelor armchair, where I had fallen asleep, with the faithful Bridget unchanged by my side—but John L. (or James Elia) was gone forever.

quiet, cheerful endurance,
   almost heroic

WILLIAM HAZLITT

MY FIRST ACQUAINTANCE WITH POETS

My father was a Dissenting minister, at Wem, in
Shropshire; and in the year 1798 (the figures that compose the date are to me like the "dreaded name of Demogorgon") Mr. Coleridge came to Shrewsbury, to succeed Mr. Rowe in the spiritual charge of a Unitarian   5
congregation there. He did not come till late on the
Saturday afternoon before he was to preach; and Mr.
Rowe, who himself went down to the coach, in a state
of anxiety and expectation, to look for the arrival of
his successor, could find no one at all answering the de- 10
scription but a round-faced man, in a short black coat
(like a shooting jacket) which hardly seemed to have
been made for him, but who seemed to be talking at a
great rate to his fellow passengers. Mr. Rowe had
scarce returned to give an account of his disappointment 15
when the round-faced man in black entered, and dissi-
pated all doubts on the subject by beginning to talk.
He did not cease while he stayed; nor has he since, that
I know of. He held the good town of Shrewsbury in
delightful suspense for three weeks that he remained 20
there, "fluttering the *proud Salopians*, like an eagle in
a dove-cote"; and the Welsh mountains that skirt the
horizon with their tempestuous confusion, agree to have
heard no such mystic sounds since the days of

"High-born Hoel's harp or soft Llewellyn's lay."   25

73

As we passed along between Wem and Shrewsbury, and I eyed their blue tops seen through the wintry branches, or the red rustling leaves of the sturdy oak trees by the road-side, a sound was in my ears as of a Syren's song; I was stunned, startled with it, as from deep sleep; but I had no notion then that I should ever be able to express my admiration to others in motley imagery or quaint allusion, till the light of his genius shone into my soul like the sun's rays glittering in the puddles of the road. I was at that time dumb, inarticulate, helpless, like a worm by the wayside, crushed, bleeding, lifeless; but now, bursting the deadly bands that "bound them,

"With Styx nine times round them,"

my ideas float on winged words, and as they expand their plumes, catch the golden light of other years. My soul has indeed remained in its original bondage, dark, obscure, with longings infinite and unsatisfied; my heart, shut up in the prison-house of this rude clay, has never found, nor will it ever find, a heart to speak to; but that my understanding also did not remain dumb and brutish, or at length found a language to express itself, I owe to Coleridge. But this is not to my purpose.

My father lived ten miles from Shrewsbury, and was in the habit of exchanging visits with Mr. Rowe, and with Mr. Jenkins of Whitchurch (nine miles farther on), according to the custom of Dissenting ministers in each other's neighborhood. A line of communication is thus established, by which the flame of civil and religious liberty is kept alive, and nourishes its smouldering fire unquenchable, like the fires in the *Agamemnon* of Æschylus, placed at different stations, that waited for ten long years to announce with their blazing pyramids the destruction of Troy. Coleridge had agreed to come over and see my father, according to the courtesy of the country, as Mr. Rowe's probable successor; but in the meantime, I had gone to hear him preach the Sunday after his arrival. A poet and a philosopher getting up into a Unitarian pulpit to preach the gospel, was a romance in these degenerate days, a sort of revival of the primitive spirit of Christianity, which was not to be resisted.

It was in January of 1798, that I rose one morning before daylight, to walk ten miles in the mud, to hear this celebrated person preach. Never, the longest day I have to live, shall I have such another walk as this cold, raw, comfortless one, in the winter of the year 1798. *Il y a des impressions que ni le temps ni les circonstances peuvent effacer. Dusse-je vivre des siecles entiers, le doux temps de ma jeunesse ne peut renaître pour moi, ni s'effacer jamais dans ma mémoire.* When I got there, the organ was playing the hundredth Psalm, and when it was done, Mr. Coleridge rose and gave out his text, "And he went up into the mountain to pray, *himself, alone.*" As he gave out this text, his voice "rose like a steam of rich distilled perfumes," and when he came to the two last words, which he pronounced loud, deep, and distinct, it seemed to me, who was then young, as if the sounds had echoed from the bottom of the human heart, and as if that prayer might have floated in solemn silence through the universe. The idea of St. John came into my mind, "of one crying in the wilderness, who had his loins girt about, and whose food was locusts and wild honey." The preacher then launched into his subject, like an eagle dallying with the wind. The sermon was upon peace and war; upon church and state—not their alliance but their separation—on the spirit of the world and

the spirit of Christianity, not as the same, but as opposed
to one another. He talked of those who had "inscribed
the cross of Christ on banners dripping with human
gore." He made a poetical and pastoral excursion—
5 and to show the fatal effects of war, drew a striking contrast between the simple shepherd-boy, driving his team
afield, or sitting under the hawthorn, piping to his flock,
"as though he should never be old," and the same poor
country lad, crimped, kidnapped, brought into town,
10 made drunk at an alehouse, turned into a wretched
drummer-boy, with his hair sticking on end with powder
and pomatum, a long cue at his back, and tricked out
in the loathsome finery of the profession of blood:

"Such were the notes our once-loved poet sung."

15 And for myself, I could not have been more delighted if
I had heard the music of the spheres. Poetry and Philosophy had met together. Truth and Genius had em-
braced, under the eye and with the sanction of Religion.
This was even beyond my hopes. I returned home well
20 satisfied. The sun that was still laboring pale and wan
through the sky, obscured by thick mists, seemed an
emblem of the *good cause;* and the cold dank drops of
dew, that hung half melted on the beard of the thistle,
had something genial and refreshing in them; for there
25 was a spirit of hope and youth in all nature, that turned
everything into good. The face of nature had not then
the brand of *Jus Divinum* on it:

"Like to that sanguine flower inscrib'd with woe."

On the Tuesday following, the half-inspired speaker
30 came. I was called down into the room where he was,
and went half-hoping, half-afraid. He received me very

graciously, and I listened for a long time without utter-
ing a word. I did not suffer in his opinion by my silence. "For those two hours," he afterward was pleased
to say, "he was conversing with William Hazlitt's forehead"! His appearance was different from what I had
anticipated from seeing him before. At a distance, and
in the dim light of the chapel, there was to me a strange
wildness in his aspect, a dusky obscurity, and I thought
him pitted with the smallpox. His complexion was at
that time clear, and even bright—   10

> "As are the children of yon azure sheen."

His forehead was broad and high, light as if built of
ivory, with large projecting eyebrows, and his eyes rolling beneath them, like a sea with darkened luster. "A
certain tender bloom his face o'erspread," a purple tinge 15
as we see it in the pale thoughtful complexions of the
Spanish portrait painters, Murillo and Valasquez. His
mouth was gross, voluptuous, open, eloquent; his chin
good-humored and round; but his nose, the rudder of
the face, the index of the will, was small, feeble, nothing 20
—like what he has done. It might seem that the genius
of his face as from a height surveyed and projected
him (with sufficient capacity and huge aspiration)
into the world unknown of thought and imagination,
with nothing to support or guide his veering purpose, 25
as if Columbus had launched his adventurous course for
the New World in a scallop, without oars or compass.
So, at least, I comment on it after the event. Coleridge, in his person, was rather above the common size,
inclining to the corpulent, or like Lord Hamlet, "some- 30
what fat and pursy." His hair (now, alas! gray) was
then black and glossy as the raven's, and fell in smooth
masses over his forehead. This long pendulous hair is

peculiar to enthusiasts, to those whose minds tend
heavenward; and is traditionally inseparable (though of
a different color) from the pictures of Christ. It ought
to belong, as a character, to all who preach *Christ cruci-*
5 *fied*, and Coleridge was at that time one of those!

It was curious to observe the contrast between him and
my father, who was a veteran in the cause, and then declining into the vale of years. He had been a poor Irish
lad, carefully brought up by his parents, and sent to the
10 University of Glasgow (where he studied under Adam
Smith) to prepare him for his future destination. It was
his mother's proudest wish to see her son a Dissenting
minister. So, if we look back to past generations (as
far as eye can reach), we see the same hopes, fears, wishes,
15 followed by the same disappointments, throbbing in the
human heart; and so we may see them (if we look forward) rising up forever, and disappearing, like vaporish
bubbles, in the human breast! After being tossed about
from congregation to congregation in the heats of the
20 Unitarian controversy, and squabbles about the American war, he had been relegated to an obscure village,
where he was to spend the last thirty years of his life,
far from the only converse that he loved, the talk about
disputed texts of Scripture, and the cause of civil and
25 religious liberty. Here he passed his days, repining,
but resigned, in the study of the Bible, and the perusal
of the commentators—huge folios, not easily got through,
one of which would outlast a winter! Why did he pore
on these from morn to night (with the exception of a
30 walk in the fields or a turn in the garden to gather
broccoli-plants or kidney beans of his own rearing, with
no small degree of pride and pleasure)? Here were "no
figures nor no fantasies"—neither poetry nor philosophy
—nothing to dazzle, nothing to excite modern curiosity;

but to his lack-luster eyes there appeared within the pages of the ponderous, unwieldy, neglected tomes, the sacred name of JEHOVAH in Hebrew capitals: pressed down by the weight of the style, worn to the last fading thinness of the understanding, there were glimpses, glimmering notions of the patriarchal wanderings, with palm trees hovering in the horizon, and processions of camels at the distance of three thousand years; there was Moses with the Burning Bush, the number of the Twelve Tribes, types, shadows, glosses on the law and the prophets; there were discussions (dull enough) on the age of Methuselah, a mighty speculation! there were outlines, rude guesses at the shape of Noah's Ark and of the riches of Solomon's Temple; questions as to the date of the creation, predictions of the end of all things; the great lapses of time, the strange mutations of the globe were unfolded with the voluminous leaf, as it turned over; and though the soul might slumber with an hiero-glyphic veil of inscrutable mysteries drawn over it, yet it was in a slumber ill-exchanged for all the sharp-ened realities of sense, wit, fancy, or reason. My father's life was comparatively a dream; but it was a dream of infinity and eternity, of death, the resurrection, and a judgment to come!

No two individuals were ever more unlike than were the host and his guest. A poet was to my father a sort of nondescript; yet whatever added grace to the Unitarian cause was to him welcome. He could hardly have been more surprised or pleased, if our visitor had worn wings. Indeed, his thoughts had wings: and as the silken sounds rustled round our little wainscoted parlor, my father threw back his spectacles over his forehead, his white hairs mixing with its sanguine hue; and a smile of delight beamed across his rugged, cordial face, to think that

Truth had found a new ally in Fancy![1] Besides, Coleridge seemed to take considerable notice of me, and that of itself was enough. He talked very familiarly, but agreeably, and glanced over a variety of subjects. At dinner time he grew more animated, and dilated in a very edifying manner on Mary Wollstonecraft and Mackintosh. The last, he said, he considered (on my father's speaking of his *Vindiciæ Gallicæ* as a capital performance) as a clever, scholastic man—a master of the topics—or, as the ready warehouseman of letters, who knew exactly where to lay his hand on what he wanted, though the goods were not his own. He thought him no match for Burke, either in style or matter. Burke was a metaphysician, Mackintosh a mere logician. Burke was an orator (almost a poet) who reasoned in figures, because he had an eye for nature: Mackintosh, on the other hand, was a rhetorician, who had only an eye to commonplaces. On this I ventured to say that I had always entertained a great opinion of Burke, and that (as far as I could find) the speaking of him with contempt might be made the test of a vulgar, democratical mind. This was the first observation I ever made to Coleridge, and he said it was a very just and striking one. I remember the leg of Welsh mutton and the turnips on the table that day had the finest flavor imaginable. Coleridge added that Mackintosh and Tom Wedgwood (of whom, however, he spoke highly) had expressed a very indifferent opinion of his friend Mr. Wordsworth, on which he remarked to them—"He strides on so far before you, that he dwindles in the distance!" Godwin had once boasted to him of having carried on an

[1] My father was one of those who mistook his talent, after all. He used to be very much dissatisfied that I preferred his *Letters* to his *Sermons*. The last were forced and dry; the first came naturally from him. For ease, half-plays on words, and a supine, monkish, indolent pleasantry, I have never seen them equalled.

argument with Mackintosh for three hours with dubious success; Coleridge told him—"If there had been a man of genius in the room he would have settled the question in five minutes." He asked me if I had ever seen Mary Wollstonecraft, and I said, I had once for a few moments, and that she seemed to me to turn off Godwin's objections to something she advanced with quite a playful, easy air. He replied, that "this was only one instance of the ascendency which people of imagination exercised over those of mere intellect." He did not rate Godwin very high[1] (this was caprice or prejudice, real or affected), but he had a great idea of Mrs. Wollstonecraft's powers of conversation; none at all of her talent for book-making. We talked a little about Holcroft. He had been asked if he was not much struck *with* him, and he said, he thought himself in more danger of being struck *by* him. I complained that he would not let me get on at all, for he required a definition of every the commonest word, exclaiming, "What do you mean by a *sensation*, Sir? What do you mean by an *idea?*" This, Coleridge said, was barricading the road to truth; it was setting up a turnpike-gate at every step we took. I forget a great number of things, many more than I remember; but the day passed off pleasantly, and the next morning Mr. Coleridge was to return to Shrewsbury.

When I came down to breakfast, I found that he had just received a letter from his friend, T. Wedgwood, making him an offer of 150*l.* a year if he chose to waive his present pursuit, and devote himself entirely to the study of poetry and philosophy. Coleridge seemed to

---

[1] He complained in particular of the presumption of his attempting to establish the future immortality of man, "without" (as he said) "knowing what Death was or what Life was"—and the tone in which he pronounced these two words seemed to convey a complete image of both.

make up his mind to close with this proposal in the act
of tying on one of his shoes. It threw an additional damp
on his departure. It took the wayward enthusiast quite
from us to cast him into Deva's winding vales, or by the
5 shores of old romance. Instead of living at ten miles'
distance, of being the pastor of a Dissenting congregation
at Shrewsbury, he was henceforth to inhabit the Hill of
Parnassus, to be a Shepherd on the Delectable Mountains. Alas! I knew not the way thither, and felt very
10 little gratitude for Mr. Wedgwood's bounty. I was
presently relieved from this dilemma; for Mr. Coleridge,
asking for a pen and ink, and going to a table to write
something on a bit of card, advanced toward me with
undulating step, and giving me the precious document,
15 said that that was his address, *Mr. Coleridge, Nether
Stowey, Somersetshire;* and that he should be glad to see
me there in a few weeks' time, and, if I chose, would come
half-way to meet me. I was not less surprised than the
shepherd-boy (this simile is to be found in *Cassandra*),
20 when he sees a thunderbolt fall close at his feet. I
stammered out my acknowledgements and acceptance
of this offer (I thought Mr. Wedgwood's annuity a trifle
to it) as well as I could; and this mighty business being
settled, the poet-preacher took leave, and I accompanied
25 him six miles on the road.

It was a fine morning in the middle of winter, and he
talked the whole way. The scholar in Chaucer is
described as going

——"sounding on his way."

30 So Coleridge went on his. In digressing, in dilating, in
passing from subject to subject, he appeared to me to
float in air, to slide on ice. He told me in confidence
(going along) that he should have preached two sermons

before he accepted the situation at Shrewsbury, one on Infant Baptism, the other on the Lord's Supper, showing that he could not administer either, which would have effectually disqualified him for the object in view. I observed that he continually crossed me on the way by shifting from one side of the footpath to the other. This struck me as an odd movement; but I did not at that time connect it with any instability of purpose or involuntary change of principle, as I have done since. He seemed unable to keep on in a straight line. He spoke slightingly of Hume (whose *Essay on Miracles* he said was stolen from an objection started in one of South's sermons—*Credat Judæus Appella!*). I was not very much pleased at this account of Hume, for I had just been reading, with infinite relish, that completest of all metaphysical *chokepears*, his *Treatise on Human Nature*, to which the *Essays* in point of scholastic subtlety and close reasoning, are mere elegant trifling, light summer reading. Coleridge even denied the excellence of Hume's general style, which I think betrayed a want of taste or candor. He however made me amends by the manner in which he spoke of Berkeley. He dwelt particularly on his *Essay on Vision* as a masterpiece of analytical reasoning. So it undoubtedly is. He was exceedingly angry with Dr. Johnson for striking the stone with his foot, in allusion to this author's theory of matter and spirit, and saying, "Thus I confute him, Sir." Coleridge drew a parallel (I don't know how he brought about the connection) between Bishop Berkeley and Tom Paine. He said the one was an instance of a subtle, the other of an acute mind, than which no two things could be more distinct. The one was a shop-boy's quality, the other the characteristic of a philosopher. He considered Bishop Butler as a true philosopher, a profound and conscientious thinker, a

genuine reader of nature and his own mind. He did not
speak of his *Analogy*, but of his *Sermons at the Rolls'
Chapel*, of which I had never heard. Coleridge somehow
always contrived to prefer the *unknown* to the *known*. In
5 this instance he was right. The *Analogy* is a tissue of
sophistry, of wire-drawn, theological special-pleading;
the *Sermons* (with the preface to them) are in a fine vein
of deep, matured reflection, a candid appeal to our observation of human nature, without pedantry and with-
10 out bias. I told Coleridge I had written a few remarks,
and was sometimes foolish enough to believe that I had
made a discovery on the same subject (the *Natural
disinterestedness of the Human Mind*)—and I tried to
explain my view of it to Coleridge, who listened with
15 great willingness, but I did not succeed in making myself
understood. I sat down to the task shortly afterward
for the twentieth time, got new pens and paper, determined to make clear work of it, wrote a few meager
sentences in the skeleton style of a mathematical demon-
20 stration, stopped half-way down the second page; and,
after trying in vain to pump up any words, images,
notions, apprehensions, facts, or observations, from that
gulf of abstraction in which I had plunged myself for
four or five years preceding, gave up the attempt as
25 labor in vain, and shed tears of helpless despondency on
the blank, unfinished paper. I can write fast enough
now. Am I better than I was then? Oh no! One
truth discovered, one pang of regret at not being able to
express it, is better than all the fluency and flippancy in
30 the world. Would that I could go back to what I then
was! Why can we not revive past times as we can revisit
old places? If I had the quaint Muse of Sir Philip Sidney
to assist me, I would write a *Sonnet to the Road between
Wem and Shrewsbury*, and immortalize every step of it

by some fond enigmatical conceit. I would swear that the very milestones had ears, and that Harmer-hill stooped with all its pines, to listen to a poet, as he passed! I remember but one other topic of discourse in this walk. He mentioned Paley, praised the naturalness and clearness of his style, but condemned his sentiments, thought him a mere time-serving casuist, and said that "the fact of his work on Moral and Political Philosophy being made a text-book in our universities was a disgrace to the national character."

We parted at the six-mile stone; and I returned homeward, pensive, but much pleased. I had met with unexpected notice from a person whom I believed to have been prejudiced against me. "Kind and affable to me had been his condescension, and should be honored ever with suitable regard." He was the first poet I had known, and he certainly answered to that inspired name. I had heard a great deal of his powers of conversation and was not disappointed. In fact, I never met with anything at all like them, either before or since. I could easily credit the accounts which were circulated of his holding forth to a large party of ladies and gentlemen, an evening or two before, on the Berkeleian Theory, when he made the whole material universe look like a transparency of fine words; and another story (which I believe he has somewhere told himself) of his being asked to a party at Birmingham, of his smoking tobacco and going to sleep after dinner on a sofa, where the company found him, to their no small surprise, which was increased to wonder when he started up of a sudden, and rubbing his eyes, looked about him, and launched into a three-hours' description of the third heaven, of which he had had a dream, very different from Mr. Southey's *Vision of Judgment*, and also from that other *Vision of Judgment*,

which Mr. Murray, the Secretary of the Bridge-street
Junta, took into his especial keeping.

On my way back I had a sound in my ears—it was the
voice of Fancy; I had a light before me—it was the face
of Poetry. The one still lingers there, the other has not
quitted my side! Coleridge, in truth, met me half-way
on the ground of philosophy, or I should not have been
won over to his imaginative creed. I had an uneasy,
pleasurable sensation all the time, till I was to visit
him. During those months the chill breath of winter
gave me a welcoming; the vernal air was balm and inspiration to me. The golden sunsets, the silver star of
evening, lighted me on my way to new hopes and prospects. *I was to visit Coleridge in the spring*. This circumstance was never absent from my thoughts, and
mingled with all my feelings. I wrote to him at the
time proposed, and received an answer postponing my
intended visit for a week or two, but very cordially urging me to complete my promise then. This delay did
not damp, but rather increased my ardor. In the meantime, I went to Llangollen Vale, by way of initiating
myself in the mysteries of natural scenery; and I must
say I was enchanted with it. I had been reading Coleridge's description of England in his fine *Ode on the
Departing Year*, and I applied it, *con amore*, to the objects
before me. That valley was to me (in a manner) the
cradle of a new existence: in the river that winds through
it, my spirit was baptized in the waters of Helicon!

I returned home, and soon after set out on my journey
with unworn heart, and untired feet. My way lay
through Worcester and Gloucester, and by Upton, where
I thought of Tom Jones and the adventure of the muff.
I remember getting completely wet through one day,
and stopping at an inn (I think it was at Tewkesbury)

where I sat up all night to read *Paul and Virginia*. Sweet were the showers in early youth that drenched my body, and sweet the drops of pity that fell upon the books I read! I recollect a remark of Coleridge's upon this very book that nothing could show the gross in- 5 delicacy of French manners and the entire corruption of their imagination more strongly than the behavior of the heroine in the last fatal scene, who turns away from a person on board the sinking vessel, that offers to save her life, because he has thrown off his clothes to assist 10 him in swimming. Was this a time to think of such a circumstance? I once hinted to Wordsworth, as we were sailing in his boat on Grasmere lake, that I thought he had borrowed the idea of his *Poems on the Naming of Places* from the local inscriptions of the same kind in 15 *Paul and Virginia*. He did not own the obligation, and stated some distinction without a difference in defence to his claim to originality. Any, the slightest varia- tion, would be sufficient for this purpose in his mind; for whatever *he* added or altered would inevitably be 20 worth all that any one else had done, and contain the marrow of the sentiment. I was still two days before the time fixed for my arrival, for I had taken care to set out early enough. I stopped these two days at Bridgewater; and when I was tired of sauntering on the banks of its 25 muddy river, returned to the inn and read *Camilla*. So have I loitered my life away, reading books, looking at pictures, going to plays, hearing, thinking, writing on what pleased me best. I have wanted only one thing to make me happy; but wanting that have wanted 30 everything!

I arrived, and was well received. The country about Nether Stowey is beautiful, green and hilly, and near the sea-shore. I saw it but the other day, after an interval

of twenty years, from a hill near Taunton. How was
the map of my life spread out before me, as the map of
the country lay at my feet! In the afternoon, Coleridge
took me over to Alfoxden, a romantic old family mansion
5 of the St. Aubins, where Wordsworth lived. It was then
in the possession of a friend of the poet's, who gave him
the free use of it. Somehow, that period (the time just
after the French Revolution) was not a time when *nothing was given for nothing*. The mind opened and a soft-
10 ness might be perceived coming over the heart of individuals, beneath "the scales that fence" our self-interest.
Wordsworth himself was from home, but his sister kept
house, and set before us a frugal repast; and we had free
access to her brother's poems, the *Lyrical Ballads*,
15 which were still in manuscript, or in the form of *Sybilline
Leaves*. I dipped into a few of these with great satisfaction, and with the faith of a novice. I slept that
night in an old room with blue hangings, and covered
with the round-faced family portraits of the age of George
20 I. and II., and from the wooded declivity of the adjoining park that overlooked my window, at the dawn of
day, could

———"hear the loud stag speak."

In the outset of life (and particularly at this time I
25 felt it so) our imagination has a body to it. We are in a
state between sleeping and waking, and have indistinct
but glorious glimpses of strange shapes, and there is
always something to come better than what we see. As
in our dreams the fulness of the blood gives warmth and
30 reality to the coinage of the brain, so in youth our ideas
are clothed, and fed, and pampered with our good spirits;
we breathe thick with thoughtless happiness, the weight
of future years presses on the strong pulses of the heart,

and we repose with undisturbed faith in truth and good.
As we advance, we exhaust our fund of enjoyment and
of hope. We are no longer wrapped in *lamb's-wool*,
lulled in Elysium. As we taste the pleasures of life,
their spirit evaporates, the sense palls; and nothing is 5
left but the phantoms, the lifeless shadows of what *has
been!*

That morning, as soon as breakfast was over, we
strolled out into the park, and seating ourselves on the
trunk of an old ash-tree that stretched along the ground, 10
Coleridge read aloud with a sonorous and musical voice,
the ballad of *Betty Foy*. I was not critically or skeptic-
ally inclined. I saw touches of truth and nature, and
took the rest for granted. But in the *Thorn*, the *Mad
Mother*, and the *Complaint of a Poor Indian Woman*, I 15
felt that deeper power and pathos which have been since
acknowledged,

> "In spite of pride, in erring reason's spite,"

as the characteristics of this author; and the sense of a
new style and a new spirit in poetry came over me. It 20
had to me something of the effect that arises from the
turning up of the fresh soil, or of the first welcome breath
of Spring:

> "While yet the trembling year is unconfirmed."

Coleridge and myself walked back to Stowey that even- 25
ing, and his voice sounded high

> "Of Providence, foreknowledge, will, and fate,
> Fix'd fate, free-will, foreknowledge absolute,"

as we passed through echoing grove, by fairy stream
or waterfall, gleaming in the summer moonlight! He 30
lamented that Wordsworth was not prone enough to

believe in the traditional superstitions of the place, and that there was a something corporeal, a *matter-of-factness*, a clinging to the palpable, or often to the petty, in his poetry, in consequence. His genius was not a spirit that descended to him through the air; it sprung out of the ground like a flower, or unfolded itself from a green spray, on which the goldfinch sang. He said, however (if I remember right), that this objection must be confined to his descriptive pieces, that his philosophic poetry had a grand and comprehensive spirit in it, so that his soul seemed to inhabit the universe like a palace, and to discover truth by intuition, rather than by deduction.

The next day Wordsworth arrived from Bristol at Coleridge's cottage. I think I see him now. He answered in some degree to his friend's description of him, but was more gaunt and Don Quixote-like. He was quaintly dressed (according to the costume of that unconstrained period) in a brown fustian jacket and striped pantaloons. There was something of a roll, a lounge in his gait, not unlike his own *Peter Bell*. There was a severe, worn pressure of thought about his temples, a fire in his eye (as if he saw something in objects more than the outward appearance), an intense, high, narrow forehead, a Roman nose, cheeks furrowed by strong purpose and feeling, and a convulsive inclination to laughter about the mouth, a good deal at variance with the solemn, stately expression of the rest of his face. Chantrey's bust wants the marking traits; but he was teased into making it regular and heavy: Haydon's head of him, introduced into the *Entrance of Christ into Jerusalem*, is the most like his drooping weight of thought and expression. He sat down and talked very naturally and freely, with a mixture of clear, gushing accents in his voice, a deep guttural intonation, and a

strong tincture of the northern *burr*, like the crust on
wine.   He instantly began to make havoc of the half of a
Cheshire cheese on the table, and said, triumphantly,
that "his marriage with experience had not been so productive as Mr. Southey's in teaching him a knowledge 5
of the good things of this life."   He had been to see the
Castle Specter by Monk Lewis, while at Bristol, and
described it very well.   He said "it fitted the taste of
the audience like a glove."   This *ad captandum* merit
was however by no means a recommendation of it, 10
according to the severe principles of the new school,
which reject rather than court popular effect.   Wordsworth, looking out of the low, latticed window, said
"How beautifully the sun sets on that yellow bank!"
I thought within myself, "With what eyes these poets 15
see nature!" and ever after, when I saw the sun-set
stream upon the objects facing it, conceived I had made
a discovery, or thanked Mr. Wordsworth for having
made one for me!

We went over to Alfoxden again the day following, 20
and Wordsworth read us the story of *Peter Bell* in the
open air; and the comment upon it by his face and voice
was very different from that of some later critics!   Whatever might be thought of the poem, "his face was as a
book where men might read strange matters," and he 25
announced the fate of his hero in prophetic tones.   There
is a *chaunt* in the recitation both of Coleridge and Wordsworth, which acts as a spell upon the hearer, and disarms
the judgment.   Perhaps they have deceived themselves
by making habitual use of this ambiguous accompani- 30
ment.   Coleridge's manner is more full, animated, and
varied; Wordsworth's more equable, sustained, and in-
ternal.   The one might be termed more *dramatic*, the
other more *lyrical*.   Coleridge has told me that he him-

self liked to compose in walking over uneven ground,
or breaking through the straggling branches of a copse
wood; whereas Wordsworth always wrote (if he could)
walking up and down a straight gravel walk, or in some
5 spot where the continuity of his verse met with no col-
lateral interruption. Returning that same evening, I
got into a metaphysical argument with Wordsworth,
while Coleridge was explaining the different notes of the
nightingale to his sister, in which we neither of us suc-
10 ceeded in making ourselves perfectly clear and intelligible.
Thus I passed three weeks at Nether Stowey and in the
neighborhood, generally devoting the afternoons to a
delightful chat in an arbor made of bark by the poet's
friend Tom Poole, sitting under two fine elm-trees, and
15 listening to the bees humming round us while we quaffed
our *flip*.

It was agreed, among other things, that we should
make a jaunt down the Bristol Channel, as far as Linton.
We set off together on foot, Coleridge, John Chester, and
20 I. This Chester was a native of Nether Stowey, one of
those who were attracted to Coleridge's discourse as
flies are to honey, or bees in swarming-time to the sound
of a brass pan. He "followed in the chase like a dog who
hunts, not like one that made up the cry." He had on
25 a brown cloth coat, boots, and corduroy breeches, was low
in stature, bow-legged, had a drag in his walk like a drover,
which he assisted by a hazel switch, and kept on a sort of
trot by the side of Coleridge, like a running footman by a
state coach, that he might not lose a syllable or sound that
30 fell from Coleridge's lips. He told me his private opinion, that Coleridge was a wonderful man. He scarcely
opened his lips, much less offered an opinion the whole
way: yet of the three, had I to choose during that journey,
I would be John Chester. He afterward followed Cole-

ridge into Germany, where the Kantean philosophers were puzzled how to bring him under any of their categories. When he sat down at table with his idol, John's felicity was complete; Sir Walter Scott's, or Mr. Blackwood's, when they sat down at the same table with the king, was not more so. We passed Dunster on our right, a small town between the brow of a hill and the sea. I remember eyeing it wistfully as it lay below us: contrasted with the woody scene around, it looked as clear, as pure, as *embrowned* and ideal as any landscape I have seen since, of Gaspar Poussin's or Domenichino's. We had a long day's march (our feet kept time to the echoes of Coleridge's tongue) through Minehead and by the Blue Anchor, and on to Linton, which we did not reach till near midnight, and where we had some difficulty in making a lodgment. We, however, knocked the people of the house up at last, and we were repaid for our apprehensions and fatigue by some excellent rashers of fried bacon and eggs. The view in coming along had been splendid. We walked for miles and miles on dark brown heaths overlooking the Channel, with the Welsh hills beyond, and at times descended into little sheltered valleys close by the sea-side, with a smuggler's face scowling by us, and then had to ascend conical hills with a path winding up through a coppice to a barren top, like a monk's shaven crown, from one of which I pointed out to Coleridge's notice the bare masts of a vessel on the very edge of the horizon, and within the red-orbed disk of the setting sun, like his own specter-ship in the *Ancient Mariner*.

At Linton the character of the sea-coast becomes more marked and rugged. There is a place called the *Valley of Rocks* (I suspect this was only the poetical name for it), bedded among precipices overhanging the sea, with rocky caverns beneath. into which the waves dash, and where

the sea-gull for ever wheels its screaming flight. On
the tops of these are huge stones thrown transverse,
as if an earthquake had tossed them there, and behind
these is a fretwork of perpendicular rocks, something like
5 the Giant's Causeway. A thunder-storm came on while
we were at the inn, and Coleridge was running out bare-
headed to enjoy the commotion of the elements in the
Valley of Rocks, but as if in spite, the clouds only mut-
tered a few angry sounds, and let fall a few refreshing
10 drops. Coleridge told me that he and Wordsworth were
to have made this place the scene of a prose-tale, which
was to have been in the manner of, but far superior to,
the *Death of Abel*, but they had relinquished the design.
In the morning of the second day, we breakfasted luxu-
15 riously in an old-fashioned parlor on tea, toast, eggs,
and honey, in the very sight of the bee-hives from which
it had been taken, and a garden full of thyme and wild
flowers that had produced it.

On this occasion Coleridge spoke of Virgil's *Georgics*,
20 but not well. I do not think he had much feeling for the
classical or elegant.[1] It was in this room that we found
a little worn-out copy of the *Seasons*, lying in a window-
seat, on which Coleridge exclaimed, "*That* is true fame!"
He said Thomson was a great poet, rather than a good
25 one; his style was as meretricious as his thoughts were
natural. He spoke of Cowper as the best modern poet.
He said the *Lyrical Ballads* were an experiment about to

---

[1] He had no idea of pictures, of Claude or Raphael, and at this
time I had as little as he. He sometimes gives a striking account
at present of the Cartoons at Pisa by Buffamalco and others; of one
in particular, where Death is seen in the air brandishing his scythe,
and the great and mighty of the earth shudder at his approach,
while the beggars and the wretched kneel to him as their deliverer.
He would, of course, understand so broad and fine a moral as this at
any time.

be tried by him and Wordsworth, to see how far the
public taste would endure poetry written in a more natural and simple style than had hitherto been attempted;
totally discarding the artifices of poetical diction, and
making use only of such words as had probably been 5
common in the most ordinary language since the days of
Henry II. Some comparison was introduced between
Shakespeare and Milton. He said "he hardly knew
which to prefer. Shakespeare appeared to him a mere
stripling in the art; he was as tall and as strong, with 10
infinitely more activity than Milton, but he never
appeared to have come to man's estate; or if he had, he
would not have been a man, but a monster." He
spoke with contempt of Gray, and with intolerance of
Pope. He did not like the versification of the latter. 15
He observed that "the ears of these couplet-writers might
be charged with having short memories, that could not
retain the harmony of whole passages." He thought
little of Junius as a writer; he had a dislike of Dr. Johnson; and a much higher opinion of Burke as an orator 20
and politician, than of Fox or Pitt. He, however,
thought him very inferior in richness of style and imagery
to some of our elder prose-writers, particularly Jeremy
Taylor. He liked Richardson, but not Fielding; nor
could I get him to enter into the merits of *Caleb Williams*. 25
In short, he was profound and discriminating with respect
to those authors whom he liked, and where he gave his
judgment fair play; capricious, perverse, and prejudiced
in his antipathies and distastes.

We loitered on the "ribbed sea sands," in such talk as 30
this a whole morning, and, I recollect, met with a curious seaweed, of which John Chester told us the country
name! A fisherman gave Coleridge an account of a boy
that had been drowned the day before, and that they had

tried to save him at the risk of their own lives. He said "he did not know how it was that they ventured, but, Sir, we have a *nature* toward one another." This expression, Coleridge remarked to me, was a fine illustration of that theory of disinterestedness which I (in common with Butler) had adopted. I broached to him an argument of mine to prove that *likeness* was not mere association of ideas. I said that the mark in the sand put one in mind of a man's foot, not because it was part of a former impression of a man's foot (for it was quite new), but because it was like the shape of a man's foot. He assented to the justness of this distinction (which I have explained at length elsewhere, for the benefit of the curious) and John Chester listened; not from any interest in the subject, but because he was astonished that I should be able to suggest anything to Coleridge that he did not already know. We returned on the third morning, and Coleridge remarked the silent cottage-smoke curling up the valleys where, a few evenings before, we had seen the lights gleaming through the dark.

In a day or two after we arrived at Stowey, we set out, I on my return home, and he for Germany. It was a Sunday morning, and he was to preach that day for Dr. Toulmin of Taunton. I asked him if he had prepared anything for the occasion? He said he had not even thought of the text, but should as soon as we parted. I did not go to hear him—this was a fault—but we met in the evening at Bridgewater. The next day we had a long day's walk to Bristol, and sat down, I recollect, by a well-side on the road, to cool ourselves and satisfy our thirst, when Coleridge repeated to me some descriptive lines of his tragedy of *Remorse;* which I must say became his mouth and that occasion better than they, some years after, did Mr. Elliston's and the Drury-lane boards—

> "Oh memory; shield me from the world's poor strife,
> And give those scenes thine everlasting life."

I saw no more of him for a year or two, during which period he had been wandering in the Hartz Forest, in Germany; and his return was cometary, meteorous, unlike his setting out. It was not till some time after that I knew his friends Lamb and Southey. The last always appears to me (as I first saw him) with a commonplace book under his arm, and the first with a *bon-mot* in his mouth. It was at Godwin's that I met him with Holcroft and Coleridge, where they were disputing fiercely which was the best—*Man as he was, or man as he is to be.* "Give me," says Lamb, "man as he is *not* to be." This saying was the beginning of a friendship between us which I believe still continues. Enough of this for the present.

> "But there is matter for another rime,
> And I to this may add a second tale."

ON GOING A JOURNEY

ONE of the pleasantest things in the world is going a journey; but I like to go by myself. I can enjoy society in a room; but out of doors, nature is company enough for me. I am then never less alone than when alone.

> "The fields his study, nature was his book."

I cannot see the wit of walking and talking at the same time. When I am in the country, I wish to vegetate like the country. I am not for criticising hedge-rows and black cattle. I go out of town in order to forget the town and all that is in it. There are those who for this purpose go to watering-places, and carry the metropolis with them. I like more elbow-room, and fewer incumbrances.

I like solitude, when I give myself up to it, for the sake of solitude; nor do I ask for

> ——"a friend in my retreat,
> Whom I may whisper solitude is sweet."

5 The soul of a journey is liberty, perfect liberty, to think, feel, do just as one pleases. We go a journey chiefly to be free of all impediments and of all inconveniences; to leave ourselves behind, much more to get rid of others. It is because I want a little breathing-space to muse on indiffer-
10 ent matters, where Contemplation

> "May plume her feathers and let grow her wings,
> That in the various bustle of resort
> Were all too ruffled, and sometimes impair'd,"

that I absent myself from the town for awhile, without
15 feeling at a loss the moment I am left by myself. Instead of a friend in a postchaise or in a Tilbury, to exchange good things with, and vary the same stale topics over again, for once let me have a truce with impertinence. Give me the clear blue sky over my head, and the green
20 turf beneath my feet, a winding road before me, and a three hours' march to dinner—and then to thinking! It is hard if I cannot start some game on these lone heaths. I laugh, I run, I leap, I sing for joy. From the point of yonder rolling cloud, I plunge into my past being, and
25 revel there, as the sun-burnt Indian plunges headlong into the wave that wafts him to his native shore. Then long-forgotten things, like "sunken wrack and sumless treasuries," burst upon my eager sight, and I begin to feel, think, and be myself again. Instead of an awkward
30 silence, broken by attempts at wit or dull commonplaces, mine is that undisturbed silence of the heart which alone is perfect eloquence. No one likes puns, alliterations,

antitheses, argument, and analysis better than I do; but I sometimes had rather be without them. "Leave, oh, leave me to my repose!" I have just now other business in hand, which would seem idle to you, but is with me "very stuff of the conscience." Is not this wild rose 5 sweet without a comment? Does not this daisy leap to my heart set in its coat of emerald? Yet if I were to explain to you the circumstance that has so endeared it to me, you would only smile. Had I not better then keep it to myself, and let it serve me to brood over, from here to 10 yonder craggy point, and from thence onward to the far-distant horizon? I should be but bad company all that way, and therefore prefer being alone. I have heard it said that you may, when the moody fit comes on, walk or ride on by yourself, and indulge your reveries. But 15 this looks like a breach of manners, a neglect of others, and you are thinking all the time that you ought to rejoin your party. "Out upon such half-faced fellow-ship," say I. I like to be either entirely to myself, or entirely at the disposal of others; to talk or be silent, to 20 walk or sit still, to be sociable or solitary. I was pleased with an observation of Mr. Cobbett's, that "he thought it a bad French custom to drink our wine with our meals, and that an Englishman ought to do only one thing at a time." So I cannot talk and think, or indulge in melan- 25 choly musing and lively conversation by fits and starts. "Let me have a companion of my way," says Sterne, "were it but to remark how the shadows lengthen as the sun declines." It is beautifully said: but in my opinion, this continual comparing of notes interferes with the 30 involuntary impression of things upon the mind, and hurts the sentiment. If you only hint what you feel in a kind of dumb show, it is insipid: if you have to explain it, it is making a toil of a pleasure. You cannot read the book of nature, without being perpetually put to the trouble of translating it for the benefit of others.

I am for the synthetical method on a journey, in preference to the analytical. I am content to lay in a stock of ideas then, and to examine and anatomize them afterward. I want to see my vague notions float like the down of the thistle before the breeze, and not to have them entangled in the briars and thorns of controversy. For once, I like to have it all my own way; and this is impossible unless you are alone, or in such company as I do not covet. I have no objection to argue a point with any one for twenty miles of measured road, but not for pleasure. If you remark the scent of a beanfield crossing the road, perhaps your fellow-traveler has no smell. If you point to a distant object, perhaps he is short-sighted, and has to take out his glass to look at it. There is a feeling in the air, a tone in the color of a cloud which hits your fancy, but the effect of which you are unable to account for. There is then no sympathy, but an uneasy craving after it, and a dissatisfaction which pursues you on the way, and in the end probably produces ill humor. Now I never quarrel with myself, and take all my own conclusions for granted till I find it necessary to defend them against objections. It is not merely that you may not be of accord on the objects and circumstances that present themselves before you—these may recall a number of objects, and lead to associations too delicate and refined to be possibly communicated to others. Yet these I love to cherish, and sometimes still fondly clutch them, when I can escape from the throng to do so. To give way to our feelings before company, seems extravagance or affectation; and on the other hand, to have to unravel this mystery of our being at every turn, and to make others take an equal interest in it (otherwise the end is

not answered) is a task to which few are competent.   We
must "give it an understanding, but no tongue."   My
old friend C———, however, could do both.   He could
go on in the most delightful explanatory way over hill
and dale, a summer's day, and convert a landscape into a   5
didactic poem or a Pindaric ode.   "He talked far above
singing."   If I could so clothe my ideas in sounding and
flowing words, I might perhaps wish to have some one
with me to admire the swelling theme; or I could be more
content, were it possible for me still to hear his echoing   10
voice in the woods of Alfoxden.   They had "that fine
madness in them which our first poets had"; and if they
could have been caught by some rare instrument, would
have breathed such strains as the following:

> ———"Here be woods as green   15
> As any, air likewise as fresh and sweet
> As when smooth zephyrus plays on the fleet
> Face of the curled stream, with flow'rs as many
> As the young spring gives, and as choice as any;
> Here be all new delights, cool streams and wells,   20
> Arbors o'ergrown with woodbine, caves and dells;
> Choose where thou wilt, while I sit by and sing,
> Or gather rushes to make many a ring
> For thy long fingers; tell thee tales of love,
> How the pale Phœbe, hunting in a grove,   25
> First saw the boy Endymion, from whose eyes
> She took eternal fire that never dies;
> How she convey'd him softly in a sleep,
> His temples bound with poppy, to the steep
> Head of old Latmos, where she stoops each night,   30
> Gilding the mountain with her brother's light,
> To kiss her sweetest."———

FAITHFUL SHEPHERDESS.

Had I words and images at command like these, I would
attempt to wake the thoughts that lie slumbering on   35

golden ridges in the evening clouds: but at the sight of
nature my fancy, poor as it is, droops and closes up its
leaves, like flowers at sunset. I can make nothing out on
the spot:—I must have time to collect myself.—

5 In general, a good thing spoils out-of-door prospects:
it should be reserved for Table-talk. L—— is for this
reason, I take it, the worst company in the world out of
doors; because he is the best within. I grant, there is
one subject on which it is pleasant to talk on a journey;
10 and that is, what one shall have for supper when we get to
our inn at night. The open air improves this sort of
conversation or friendly altercation, by setting a keener
edge on appetite. Every mile of the road heightens the
flavor of the viands we expect at the end of it. How fine
15 it is to enter some old town, walled and turreted just at
the approach of nightfall, or to come to some straggling
village, with the lights streaming through the surrounding
gloom; and then after inquiring for the best entertainment that the place affords, to "take one's ease at one's
20 inn"! These eventful moments in our lives' history are
too precious, too full of solid, heartfelt happiness to be
frittered and dribbled away in imperfect sympathy. I
would have them all to myself, and drain them to the
last drop: they will do to talk of or to write about after-
25 ward. What a delicate speculation it is, after drinking
whole goblets of tea,

"The cups that cheer, but not inebriate,"

and letting the fumes ascend into the brain, to sit considering what we shall have for supper—eggs and a rasher,
30 a rabbit smothered in onions, or an excellent veal-cutlet!
Sancho in such a situation once fixed upon cow-heel; and
his choice, though he could not help it, is not to be
disparaged. Then in the intervals of pictured scenery

and Shandean contemplation, to catch the preparation
and the stir in the kitchen—*Procul, O procul este profani!*
These hours are sacred to silence and to musing, to be
treasured up in the memory, and to feed the source of
smiling thoughts hereafter. I would not waste them in 5
idle talk; or if I must have the integrity of fancy broken
in upon, I would rather it were by a stranger than a friend.
A stranger takes his hue and character from the time and
place; he is a part of the furniture and costume of an
inn. If he is a Quaker, or from the West Riding of York- 10
shire, so much the better. I do not even try to sympa-
thize with him, and he breaks no squares. I associate
nothing with my traveling companion but present objects
and passing events. In his ignorance of me and my
affairs, I in a manner forget myself. But a friend reminds 15
one of other things, rips up old grievances, and destroys
the abstraction of the scene. He comes in ungraciously
between us and our imaginary character. Something is
dropped in the course of conversation that gives a hint of
your profession and pursuits; or from having some one 20
with you that knows the less sublime portions of your
history, it seems that other people do. You are no longer
a citizen of the world: but your "unhoused free condition
is put into circumscription and confine."

The *incognito* of an inn is one of its striking privileges— 25
"lord of one's-self, uncumber'd with a name." Oh!
it is great to shake off the trammels of the world and of
public opinion—to lose our importunate, tormenting,
everlasting personal identity in the elements of nature,
and become the creature of the moment, clear of all ties— 30
to hold to the universe only by a dish of sweetbreads, and
to owe nothing but the score of the evening—and no
longer seeking for applause and meeting with contempt,
to be known by no other title than *the Gentleman in the*

Parlor! One may take one's choice of all characters in this romantic state of uncertainty as to one's real pretensions, and become indefinitely respectable and negatively right-worshipful. We baffle prejudice and disappoint conjecture; and from being so to others, begin to be objects of curiosity and wonder even to ourselves. We are no more those hackneyed commonplaces that we appear in the world: an inn restores us to the level of nature, and quits scores with society! I have certainly spent some enviable hours at inns—sometimes when I have been left entirely to myself, and have tried to solve some metaphysical problem, as once at Witham-common, where I found out the proof that likeness is not a case of the association of ideas—at other times, when there have been pictures in the room, as at St. Neot's (I think it was), where I first met with Gribelin's engravings of the Cartoons, into which I entered at once and at a little inn on the borders of Wales, where there happened to be hanging some of Westall's drawings, which I compared triumphantly (for a theory that I had, not for the admired artist) with the figure of a girl who had ferried me over the Severn, standing up in the boat between me and the twilight—at other times I might mention luxuriating in books, with a peculiar interest in this way, as I remember sitting up half the night to read *Paul and Virginia*, which I picked up at an inn at Bridgewater, after being drenched in the rain all day; and at the same place I got through two volumes of Madame D'Arblay's *Camilla*. It was on the tenth of April, 1798, that I sat down to a volume of the *New Eloïse*, at the inn at Llangollen, over a bottle of sherry and a cold chicken. The letter I chose was that in which St. Preux describes his feelings as he first caught a glimpse from the heights of the Jura of the Pays de Vaud, which I had brought with me as a *bon bouche* to crown the evening with. It was my birthday, and I had for the first time come from a place in the neighborhood to visit this delightful spot. The road to Llangollen turns off between Chirk and Wrexham; and on passing a certain point, you come all at once upon the valley, which opens 5 like an amphitheater, broad, barren hills rising in majestic state on either side, with "green upland swells that echo to the bleat of flocks" below, and the river Dee babbling over its stony bed in the midst of them. The valley at this time "glittered green with sunny showers," and a 10 budding ash-tree dipped its tender branches in the chiding stream. How proud, how glad I was to walk along the high road that overlooks the delicious prospect, repeating the lines which I have just quoted from Mr. Coleridge's poems! But besides the prospect which opened beneath 15 my feet, another also opened to my inward sight, a heavenly vision, on which were written, in letters large as Hope could make them, these four words, LIBERTY, GENIUS, LOVE, VIRTUE; which have since faded into the light of common day, or mock my idle gaze. 20

> "The beautiful is vanished, and returns not."

Still I would return some time or other to this enchanted spot; but I would return to it alone. What other self could I find to share that influx of thoughts, of regret, and delight, the fragments of which I could hardly conjure up 25 to myself, so much have they been broken and defaced! I could stand on some tall rock, and overlook the precipice of years that separates me from what I then was. I was at that time going shortly to visit the poet whom I have above named. Where is he now? Not only I 30 myself have changed; the world, which was then new to me, has become old and incorrigible. Yet will I turn to thee in thought, O sylvan Dee, in joy, in youth and

gladness as thou then wert; and thou shalt always be
to me the river of Paradise, where I will drink of the
waters of life freely!

There is hardly any thing that shows the short-sighted-
5 ness of capriciousness of the imagination more than traveling does. With change of place we change our ideas;
nay, our opinions and feelings. We can by an effort
indeed transport ourselves to old and long-forgotten
scenes, and then the picture of the mind revives again;
10 but we forget those that we have just left. It seems that
we can think but of one place at a time. The canvas of
the fancy is but of a certain extent, and if we paint one set
of objects upon it, they immediately efface every other.
We cannot enlarge our conceptions, we only shift our
15 point of view. The landscape bares its bosom to the
enraptured eye, we take our fill of it, and seem as if we
could form no other image of beauty or grandeur. We
pass on, and think no more of it: the horizon that shuts it
from our sight, also blots it from our memory like a
20 dream. In traveling through a wild barren country, I
can form no idea of a woody and cultivated one. It
appears to me that all the world must be barren, like what
I see of it. In the country we forget the town, and in
town we despise the country. "Beyond Hyde Park,"
25 says Sir Fopling Flutter, "all is a desert." All that part
of the map that we do not see before us is a blank. The
world in our conceit of it is not much bigger than a nutshell. It is not one prospect expanded into another,
county joined to county, kingdom to kingdom, lands to
30 seas, making an image voluminous and vast;—the mind
can form no larger idea of space than the eye can take in
at a single glance. The rest is a name written in a
map, a calculation of arithmetic. For instance, what is
the true signification of that immense mass of territory

and population known by the name of China to us? An inch of paste-board on a wooden globe, of no more account than a China orange! Things near us are seen of the size of life: things at a distance are diminished to the size of the understanding. We measure the universe by ourselves, and even comprehend the texture of our own being only piecemeal. In this way, however, we remember an infinity of things and places. The mind is like a mechanical instrument that plays a great variety of tunes, but it must play them in succession. One idea recalls another, but it at the same time excludes all others. In trying to renew old recollections, we cannot as it were unfold the whole web of our existence; we must pick out the single threads. So in coming to a place where we have formerly lived and with which we have intimate associations, every one must have found that the feeling grows more vivid the nearer we approach the spot, from the mere anticipation of the actual impression: we remember circumstances, feelings, persons, faces, names, that we had not thought of for years; but for the time all the rest of the world is forgotten!—To return to the question I have quitted above.

I have no objection to go to see ruins, aqueducts, pictures, in company with a friend or a party, but rather the contrary, for the former reason reversed. They are intelligible matters, and will bear talking about. The sentiment here is not tacit, but communicable and overt. Salisbury Plain is barren of criticism, but Stonehenge will bear a discussion antiquarian, picturesque, and philosophical. In setting out on a party of pleasure, the first consideration always is where we shall go to: in taking a solitary ramble, the question is what we shall meet with by the way. "The mind is its own place"; nor are we anxious to arrive at the end of our journey.

I can myself do the honors indifferently well to works of
art and curiosity. I once took a party to Oxford with
no mean *éclat*—shewed them that seat of the Muses at
a distance,

5   "With glistering spires and pinnacles adorn'd"—

descanted on the learned air that breathes from the grassy
quadrangles and stone walls of halls and colleges—was at
home in the Bodleian; and at Blenheim quite super-
seded the powdered Cicerone that attended us, and that
10 pointed in vain with his wand to commonplace beauties
in matchless pictures.—As another exception to the above
reasoning, I should not feel confident in venturing on a
journey in a foreign country without a companion. I
should want at intervals to hear the sound of my own
15 language. There is an involuntary antipathy in the
mind of an Englishman to foreign manners and notions
that requires the assistance of social sympathy to carry
it off. As the distance from home increases, this relief,
which was at first a luxury, becomes a passion and an
20 appetite. A person would almost feel stifled to find
himself in the deserts of Arabia without friends and
countrymen: there must be allowed to be something in
the view of Athens or old Rome that claims the utterance
of speech; and I own that the pyramids are too mighty
25 for any single contemplation. In such situations, so
opposite to all one's ordinary train of ideas, one seems a
species by one's-self, a limb torn off from society, unless
one can meet with instant fellowship and support.—Yet
I did not feel this want or craving very pressing once,
30 when I first set my foot on the laughing shores of France.
Calais was peopled with novelty and delight. The confused, busy murmur of the place was like oil and wine
poured into my ears; nor did the mariners' hymn, which

was sung from the top of an old crazy vessel in the harbor, as the sun went down, send an alien sound into my soul. I only breathed the air of general humanity. I walked over "the vine-covered hills and gay regions of France," erect and satisfied; for the image of man was not cast down and chained to the foot of arbitrary thrones: I was at no loss for language, for that of all the great schools of painting was open to me. The whole is vanished like a shade. Pictures, heroes, glory, freedom, all are fled: nothing remains but the Bourbons and the French people!—There is undoubtedly a sensation in traveling into foreign parts that is to be had nowhere else: but it is more pleasing at the time than lasting. It is too remote from our habitual associations to be a common topic of discourse or reference, and, like a dream or another state of existence, does not piece into our daily modes of life. It is an animated but a momentary hallucination. It demands an effort to exchange our actual for our ideal identity; and to feel the pulse of our old transports revive very keenly, we must "jump" all our present comforts and connections. Our romantic and itinerant character is not to be domesticated. Dr. Johnson remarked how little foreign travel added to the facilities of conversation in those who had been abroad. In fact, the time we have spent there is both delightful and in one sense instructive; but it appears to be cut out of our substantial, downright existence, and never to join kindly on to it. We are not the same, but another, and perhaps more enviable individual, all the time we are out of our own country. We are lost to ourselves, as well as our friends. So the poet somewhat quaintly sings,

"Out of my country and myself I go."

Those who wish to forget painful thoughts, do well to

absent themselves for a while from the ties and objects
that recall them: but we can be said only to fulfil our
destiny in the place that gave us birth. I should on
this account like well enough to spend the whole of my
5 life in traveling abroad, if I could anywhere borrow
another life to spend afterward at home!—

ON READING OLD BOOKS

I HATE to read new books. There are twenty or
thirty volumes that I have read over and over again,
and these are the only ones that I have any desire ever
10 to read at all. It was a long time before I could bring
myself to sit down to the *Tales of My Landlord*, but now
that author's works have made a considerable addition
to my scanty library. I am told that some of Lady
Morgan's are good, and have been recommended to look
15 into *Anastasius;* but I have not yet ventured upon that
task. A lady, the other day, could not refrain from expressing her surprise to a friend who said he had been
reading *Delphine:* she asked if it had not been published
some time back. Women judge of books as they do
20 of fashions or complexions, which are admired only "in
their newest gloss." That is not my way. I am not
one of those who trouble the circulating libraries much,
or pester the book-sellers for mail-coach copies of standard periodical publications. I cannot say that I am
25 greatly addicted to black-letter, but I profess myself
well versed in the marble bindings of Andrew Millar,
in the middle of the last century; nor does my taste revolt at Thurloe's *State Papers* in Russia leather, or an
ample impression of Sir William Temple's *Essays*, with
30 a portrait after Sir Godfrey Kneller in front. I do not
think altogether the worse of a book for having survived

the author a generation or two. I have more confidence in the dead than the living. Contemporary writers may generally be divided into two classes—one's friends or one's foes. Of the first we are compelled to think too well, and of the last we are disposed to think too ill, to 5 receive much genuine pleasure from the perusal or to judge fairly of the merits of either. One candidate for literary fame, who happens to be of our acquaintance, writes finely and like a man of genius, but unfortunately has a foolish face, which spoils a delicate passage; 10 another inspires us with the highest respect for his personal talents and character, but does not quite come up to our expectations in print. All these contradictions and petty details interrupt the calm current of our reflections. If you want to know what any of the authors 15 were who lived before our time and are still objects of anxious inquiry, you have only to look into their works. But the dust and smoke and noise of modern literature have nothing in common with the pure, silent air of immortality. 20

When I take up a work that I have read before (the oftener the better), I know what I have to expect. The satisfaction is not lessened by being anticipated. When the entertainment is altogether new, I sit down to it as I should to a strange dish—turn and pick out a bit here 25 and there, and am in doubt what to think of the composition. There is a want of confidence and security to second appetite. New-fangled books are also like made dishes in this respect, that they are generally little else than hashes and *rifaccimentos* of what has been served 30 up entire, and in a more natural state, at other times. Besides, in thus turning to a well-known author there is not only an assurance that my time will not be thrown away, or my palate nauseated with the most insipid

or vilest trash, but I shake hands with and look an old,
tried, and valued friend in the face, compare notes, and
chat the hours away. It is true we form dear friendships
with such ideal guests—dearer, alas, and more lasting
5 than those with our most intimate acquaintance. In
reading a book which is an old favorite with me (say the
first novel I ever read) I not only have the pleasure of
imagination and of a critical relish of the work, but the
pleasures of memory added to it. It recalls the same
10 feelings and associations which I had in first reading
it and which I can never have again in any other way.
Standard productions of this kind are links in the chain
of our conscious being. They bind together the different
scattered divisions of our personal identity. They are
15 landmarks and guides in our journey through life. They
are pegs and loops on which we can hang up, or from
which we can take down, at pleasure, the wardrobe of a
moral imagination, the relics of our best affections, the
tokens and records of our happiest hours. They are
20 "for thoughts and for remembrance." They are like
Fortunatus's wishing-cap—they give us the best riches,
those of fancy, and transport us, not over half the globe,
but (which is better) over half our lives, at a word's
notice.

25 My father Shandy solaced himself with *Bruscambille*.
Give me for this purpose a volume of *Peregrine Pickle* or
Tom Jones. Open either of them anywhere—at the
Memoirs of Lady Vane, or the adventures at the mas-
querade with Lady Bellaston, or the disputes between
30 Thwackum and Square, or the escape of Molly Seagrim,
or the incident of Sophia and her muff, or the edifying
prolixity of her aunt's lecture—and there I find the same
delightful, busy, bustling scene as ever, and feel myself
the same as when I was first introduced into the midst

of it. Nay, sometimes the sight of an odd volume of these good old English authors on a stall, or the name lettered on the back among others on the shelves of a library, answers the purpose, revives the whole train of ideas, and sets "the puppets dallying." Twenty years are struck off the list, and I am a child again. A sage philosopher, who was not a very wise man, said that he should like very well to be young again if he could take his experience along with him. This ingenious person did not seem to be aware, by the gravity of his remark, that the great advantage of being young is to be without this weight of experience, which he would fain place upon the shoulders of youth and which never comes too late with years. O what a privilege to be able to let this hump, like Christian's burden, drop from off one's back, and transport oneself, by the help of a little musty duodecimo, to the time when "ignorance was bliss," and when we first got a peep at the raree-show of the world through the glass of fiction, gazing at mankind, as we do at wild beasts in a menagerie, through the bars of their cages, or at curiosities in a museum, that we must not touch! For myself, not only are the old ideas of the contents of the work brought back to my mind in all their vividness, but the old associations of the faces and persons of those I then knew, as they were in their lifetime—the place where I sat to read the volume, the day when I got it, the feeling of the air, the fields, the sky—return, and all my early impressions with them. This is better to me—those places, those times, those persons, and those feelings that come across me as I retrace the story and devour the page, are to me better far than the wet sheets of the last new novel from the Ballantyne press, to say nothing of the Minerva press in Leadenhall Street. It is like visiting the scenes of

early youth. I think of the time "when I was in my
father's house, and my path ran down with butter and
honey"—when I was a little thoughtless child, and had
no other wish or care but to con my daily task and be
5 happy. *Tom Jones*, I remember, was the first work that
broke the spell. It came down in numbers once a fortnight, in Cooke's pocket-edition, embellished with cuts.
I had hitherto read only in school-books and a tiresome
ecclesiastical history (with the exception of Mrs. Rad-
10 cliffe's *Romance of the Forest*); but this had a different
relish with it—"sweet in the mouth," though not "bitter in the belly." It smacked of the world I lived in
and in which I was to live, and showed me groups,"gay
creatures" not "of the element" but of the earth, not
15 "living in the clouds" but traveling the same road that
I did—some that had passed on before me, and others
that might soon overtake me. My heart had palpitated
at the thoughts of a boarding-school ball, or gala-day at
midsummer or Christmas; but the world I had found out
20 in Cooke's edition of the *British Novelists* was to me a
dance through life, a perpetual gala-day. The sixpenny
numbers of this work regularly contrived to leave off
just in the middle of a sentence and in the nick of a
story. . . . With what eagerness I used to look for-
25 ward to the next number, and open the prints! Ah,
never again shall I feel the enthusiastic delight with
which I gazed at the figures, and anticipated the story
and adventures of Major Bath and Commodore Trunnion, of Trim and my Uncle Toby, of Don Quixote and
30 Sancho and Dapple, of Gil Blas and Dame Lorenza Sephora, of Laura and the fair Lucretia, whose lips open and
shut like buds of roses. To what nameless ideas did
they give rise, with what airy delights I filled up the
outlines, as I hung in silence over the page. Let me still

recall them, that they may breathe fresh life into me
and that I may live that birthday of thought and romantic pleasure over again! Talk of the ideal! This is
the only true ideal—the heavenly tints of fancy reflected
in the bubbles that float upon the spring-tide of human   5
life.

> "O Memory, shield me from the world's poor strife,
> And give those scenes thine everlasting life!"

The paradox with which I set out is, I hope, less startling than it was; the reader will, by this time, have been 10
let into my secret. Much about the same time, or I
believe rather earlier, I took a particular satisfaction in
reading Chubb's *Tracts*, and I often think I will get them
again to wade through. There is a high gusto of polem-
ical divinity in them; and you fancy that you hear a 15
club of shoemakers at Salisbury debating a disputable
text from one of St. Paul's epistles in a workmanlike
style, with equal shrewdness and pertinacity. I cannot say much for my metaphysical studies, into which
I launched shortly after with great ardor, so as to make 20
a toil of a pleasure. I was presently entangled in the
briers and thorns of subtle distinctions—of "fate, free-
will, fore-knowledge absolute," though I cannot add that
"in their wandering mazes I found no end," for I did
arrive at some very satisfactory and potent conclusions; 25
nor will I go so far, however ungrateful the subject
might seem, as to exclaim with Marlowe's Faustus,
"Would I had never seen Wittenberg, never read book"—
that is, never studied such authors as Hartley, Hume,
Berkeley, etc. Locke's *Essay on the Human Under-* 30
standing is, however, a work from which I never derived
either pleasure or profit; and Hobbes, dry and powerful
as he is, I did not read till long afterward. I read a

few poets, which did not much hit my taste—for I would
have the reader understand I am deficient in the faculty
of imagination; but I fell early upon French romances
and philosophy, and devoured them tooth-and-nail.
5 Many a dainty repast have I made of the *New Eloïse*—
the description of the kiss; the excursion on the water;
the letter of St. Preux, recalling the time of their first
loves; and the account of Julia's death: these I read over
and over again with unspeakable delight and wonder.
10 Some years after, when I met with this work again, I
found I had lost nearly my whole relish for it (except
some few parts), and was, I remember, very much mortified with the change in my taste, which I sought to
attribute to the smallness and gilt edges of the edition I
15 had bought, and its being perfumed with rose-leaves.
Nothing could exceed the gravity, the solemnity, with
which I carried home and read the dedication to the
Social Contract, with some other pieces of the same author,
which I had picked up at a stall in a coarse leathern
20 cover. Of the *Confessions* I have spoken elsewhere, and
may repeat what I have said: "Sweet is the dew of
their memory, and pleasant the balm of their recollection." Their beauties are not "scattered like stray gifts
o'er the earth," but sown thick on the page, rich and rare.
25 I wish I had never read the *Emilius*, or read it with less
implicit faith. I had no occasion to pamper my natural
aversion to affectation or pretence, by romantic and artificial means. I had better have formed myself on the
model of Sir Fopling Flutter. There is a class of persons
30 whose virtues and most shining qualities sink in, and
are concealed by, an absorbent ground of modesty and
reserve; and such a one I do, without vanity, profess
myself. Now, these are the very persons who are likely
to attach themselves to the character of Emilius, and of

whom it is sure to be the bane. This dull, phlegmatic, retiring humor is not in a fair way to be corrected, but confirmed and rendered desperate, by being in that work held up as an object of imitation, as an example of simplicity and magnanimity, by coming upon us with all the recommendations of novelty, surprise, and superiority to the prejudices of the world, by being stuck upon a pedestal, made amiable, dazzling, a *leurre de dupe*. The reliance on solid worth which it inculcates, the preference of sober truth to gaudy tinsel, hangs like a millstone round the neck of the imagination—"a load to sink a navy,"—impedes our progress, and blocks up every prospect in life. A man, to get on, to be successful, conspicuous, applauded, should not retire upon the center of his conscious resources, but be always at the circumference of appearances. He must envelop himself in a halo of mystery—he must ride in an equipage of opinion—he must walk with a train of self-conceit following him—he must not strip himself to a buff-jerkin, to the doublet and hose of his real merits, but must surround himself with a *cortège* of prejudices, like the signs of the Zodiac—he must seem anything but what he is, and then he may pass for anything he pleases. The world love to be amused by hollow professions, to be deceived by flattering appearances, to live in a state of hallucination, and can forgive everything but the plain, downright, simple, honest truth—such as we see it chalked out in the character of Emilius.—To return from this digression, which is a little out of place here.

Books have in a great measure lost their power over me, nor can I revive the same interest in them as formerly. I perceive when a thing is good, rather than feel it. It is true,

"Marcian Colonna is a dainty book";

and the reading of Mr. Keats's *Eve of St. Agnes* lately
made me regret that I was not young again. The beautiful and tender images there conjured up "come like
shadows—so depart." The "tiger-moth's wings," which
he has spread over his rich poetic blazonry, just flit
across my fancy; the gorgeous twilight window which he
has painted over again in his verse, to me "blushes"
almost in vain "with blood of queens and kings." I
know how I should have felt at one time in reading such
passages; and that is all. The sharp, luscious flavor, the
fine aroma, is fled, and nothing but the stalk, the bran,
the husk of literature is left. If anyone were to ask me
what I read now, I might answer with my Lord Hamlet in
the play, "Words, words, words." "What is the matter?" "Nothing"—they have scarce a meaning. But
it was not always so. There was a time when to my
thinking every word was a flower or a pearl, like those
which dropped from the mouth of the little peasant-girl
in the fairy tale, or like those that fall from the great
preacher in the Caledonian Chapel. I drank of the
stream of knowledge that tempted but did not mock my
lips, as of the river of life, freely. How eagerly I slaked
my thirst of German sentiment, "as the hart that panteth
for the water-springs"; how I bathed and revelled, and
added my floods of tears to Goethe's *Sorrows of Werter*
and to Schiller's *Robbers*.

"Giving my stock of more to that which had too much."

I read and assented with all my soul to Coleridge's fine
sonnet beginning,

"Schiller, that hour I would have wished to die,
If through the shuddering midnight I had sent,
From the dark dungeon of the tow'r, time-rent,
That fearful voice, a famish'd father's cry!"

I believe I may date my insight into the mysteries of poetry from the commencement of my acquaintance with the authors of the *Lyrical Ballads;* at least, my discrimination of the higher sorts, not my predilection for such writers as Goldsmith or Pope: nor do I imagine they will say I got my liking for the novelists or the comic writers, for the characters of Valentine, Tattle, or Miss Prue, from them. If so, I must have got from them what they never had themselves. In points where poetic diction and conception are concerned, I may be at a loss and liable to be imposed upon; but in forming an estimate of passages relating to common life and manners I cannot think I am a plagiarist from any man. I there "know my cue without a prompter." I may say of such studies, *"intus et in cute."* I am just able to admire those literal touches of observation and description which persons of loftier pretensions overlook and despise. I think I comprehend something of the characteristic part of Shakespeare; and in him, indeed, all is characteristic, even the nonsense and poetry. I believe it was the celebrated Sir Humphrey Davy who used to say that Shakespeare was rather a metaphysician than a poet. At any rate, it was not ill said. I wish that I had sooner known the dramatic writers contemporary with Shakespeare, for in looking them over, about a year ago, I almost revived my old passion for reading and my old delight in books, though they were very nearly new to me. The periodical essayists I read long ago. *The Spectator* I liked extremely, but *The Tatler* took my fancy most. I read the others soon after—*The Rambler, The Adventurer, The World, The Connoisseur;* I was not sorry to get to the end of them, and have no desire to go regularly through them again. I consider myself a thorough adept in Richardson. I like the longest of his novels best, and think no part of them tedious; nor should I ask to have anything better to do than to read them from beginning to end, to take them up when I chose and lay them down when I was tired, in some old family mansion in the country, till every 5 word and syllable relating to the bright Clarissa, the divine Clementina, the beautiful Pamela, "with every trick and line of their sweet favor," were once more "graven in my heart's table." I have a sneaking kindness for Mackenzie's *Julia de Roubigné*—for the deserted 10 mansion, and straggling gilliflowers on the mouldering garden wall; and still more for his *Man of Feeling*— not that it is better, nor so good, but at the time I read it I sometimes thought of the heroine, Miss Walton, and of Miss—— together, and "that ligament, fine as it was, 15 was never broken."—One of the poets that I have always read with most pleasure, and can wander about in forever with a sort of voluptuous indolence, is Spenser; and I like Chaucer even better. The only writer among the Italians I can pretend to any knowledge of is Boccaccio, 20 and of him I cannot express half my admiration. His story of the hawk I could read and think of from day to day, just as I would look at a picture of Titian's.

I remember, as long ago as the year 1798, going to a neighboring town (Shrewsbury, where Farquhar has laid 25 the plot of his *Recruiting Officer*) and bringing home with me, "at one proud swoop," a copy of Milton's *Paradise Lost* and another of Burke's *Reflections on the French Revolution*—both which I have still; and I still recollect, when I see the covers, the pleasure with which I dipped 30 into them as I returned with my double prize. I was set up for one while. That time is past, "with all its giddy raptures"; but I am still anxious to preserve its memory, "embalmed with odors." With respect to the first of these works, I would be permitted to remark here,

in passing, that it is a sufficient answer to the German
criticism which has since been started against the character of Satan (viz., that it is not one of disgusting
deformity, or pure, defeated malice) to say that Milton
has there drawn, not the abstract principle of evil, not a 5
devil incarnate, but a fallen angel. This is the Scriptural
account, and the poet has followed it. We may safely
retain such passages as that well-known one,

> "His form had not yet lost
> All her original brightness; nor appear'd 10
> Less than archangel ruin'd, and the excess
> Of glory obscur'd,"

for the theory which is opposed to them "falls flat upon
the grunsel edge and shames its worshippers." Let us
hear no more, then, of this monkish cant and bigoted 15
outcry, for the restoration of the horns and tail of the
devil.

Again, as to the other work, Burke's *Reflections*, I
took a particular pride and pleasure in it, and read it to
myself and others for months afterward. I had reason 20
for my prejudice in favor of this author. To understand
an adversary is some praise; to admire him is more. I
thought I did both; I knew I did one. From the first
time I ever cast my eyes on anything of Burke's (which
was an extract from his *Letter to a Noble Lord*, in a three- 25
times-a-week paper, *The St. James's Chronicle*, in 1796)
I said to myself, "This is true eloquence: this is a man
pouring out his mind on paper." All other style seemed
to me pedantic and impertinent. Dr. Johnson's was
walking on stilts; and even Junius's (who was at that time 30
a favorite with me), with all his terseness, shrunk up
into little antithetic points and well-trimmed sentences.
But Burke's style was forked and playful as the lightning,

crested like the serpent.   He delivered plain things on a
plain ground; but when he rose, there was no end of his
flights and circumgyrations—and in this very *Letter* "he,
like an eagle in a dove-cote, fluttered *his* Volscians"
5 (the Duke of Bedford and the Earl of Lauderdale) "in
Corioli."   I did not care for his doctrines.   I was then,
and am still, proof against their contagion; but I admired
the author, and was considered as not a very staunch
partisan of the opposite side, though I thought myself
10 that an abstract proposition was one thing, a masterly
transition, a brilliant metaphor, another.   I conceived,
too, that he might be wrong in his main argument, and
yet deliver fifty truths in arriving at a false conclusion.
I remember Coleridge assuring me, as a poetical and
15 political set-off to my skeptical admiration, that Wordsworth had written an *Essay on Marriage* which, for
manly thought and nervous expression, he deemed incomparably superior.   As I had not, at that time, seen
any specimens of Mr. Wordsworth's prose style, I could
20 not express my doubts on the subject.   If there are
greater prose-writers than Burke, they either lie out of
my course of study or are beyond my sphere of comprehension.   I am too old to be a convert to a new
mythology of genius.   The niches are occupied, the
25 tables are full.   If such is still my admiration of this
man's misapplied powers, what must it have been at a
time when I myself was in vain trying, year after year,
to write a single essay, nay, a single page or sentence;
when I regarded the wonders of his pen with the longing
30 eyes of one who was dumb and a changeling; and when to
be able to convey the slightest conception of my meaning
to others in words was the height of an almost hopeless
ambition.   But I never measured others' excellences
by my own defects, though a sense of my own incapacity

d of the steep, impassable ascent from me to them
ade me regard them with greater awe and fondness.

I have thus run through most of my early studies and
vorite authors, some of whom I have since criticised
ore at large. Whether those observations will survive 5
e I neither know nor do I much care; but to the works
emselves, "worthy of all acceptation," and to the feel-
gs they have always excited in me since I could dis-
nguish a meaning in language, nothing shall ever pre-
nt me from looking back with gratitude and triumph. 10
o have lived in the cultivation of an intimacy with
ch works, and to have familiarly relished such names,
not to have lived quite in vain.

There are other authors whom I have never read, and
t whom I have frequently had a great desire to read 15
om some circumstance relating to them. Among
ese is Lord Clarendon's *History of the Grand Re-
llion*, after which I have a hankering from hearing it
oken of by good judges, from my interest in the events
d knowledge of the characters from other sources, 20
d from having seen fine portraits of most of them.
like to read a well-penned character, and Clarendon
said to have been a master in this way. I should
e to read Froissart's *Chronicles*, Holinshed and Stowe,
d Fuller's *Worthies*. I intend, whenever I can, to 25
ad Beaumont and Fletcher all through. There are
ty-two of their plays, and I have only read a dozen
fourteen of them. *A Wife for a Month* and *Thierry*
d *Theodoret* are, I am told, delicious, and I can believe
. I should like to read the speeches in Thucydides, 30
d Guicciardini's *History of Florence*, and *Don Quixote*
the original. I have often thought of reading *The*
ves of Persiles and Sigismunda and the *Galatea* of the
me author. But I somehow reserve them, like "an-

other Yarrow." I should also like to read the last new
novel (if I could be sure it was so) of the author of
Waverley; no one would be more glad than I to find it
the best.

THOMAS DE QUINCEY

MEETING WITH COLERIDGE

It was, I think, in the month of August, but certainly
in the summer season, and certainly in the year 1807,
that I first saw this illustrious man. My knowledge of
him as a man of most original genius began about the
year 1799. A little before that time Wordsworth had   5
published the first edition (in a single volume) of the
Lyrical Ballads, and into this had been introduced Mr.
Coleridge's poem of the *Ancient Mariner,* as the contribution of an anonymous friend. It would be directing
the reader's attention too much to myself if I were to   10
linger upon this, the greatest event in the unfolding of
my own mind. Let me say, in one word, that, at a period when neither the one nor the other writer was valued
by the public—both having a long warfare to accomplish
of contumely and ridicule before they could rise into their   15
present estimation—I found in these poems "the ray of
a new morning," and an absolute revelation of untrodden
worlds teeming with power and beauty as yet unsuspected
amongst men. I may here mention that, precisely at the
same time, Professor Wilson, entirely unconnected with   20
myself, and not even known to me until ten years later,
received the same startling and profound impressions
from the same volume. With feelings of reverential interest, so early and so deep, pointing toward two contemporaries, it may be supposed that I inquired eagerly after   25

their names. But these inquiries were self-baffled; t
same deep feelings which prompted my curiosity causi
me to recoil from all casual opportunities of pushing t
inquiry, as too generally lying amongst those who ga
no sign of participating in my feelings; and, extravaga
as this may seem, I revolted with as much hatred fro
coupling the question with any occasion of insult to t
persons whom it respected as a primitive Christian fro
throwing frankincense upon the altars of Cæsar, or
lover from giving up the name of his beloved to the coar
license of a Bacchanalian party. It is laughable
record for how long a period my curiosity in this partic
lar was thus self-defeated. Two years passed before
ascertained the two names. Mr. Wordsworth publish
his in the second and enlarged edition of the poems; a
for Mr. Coleridge's I was "indebted" to a priva
source; but I discharged that debt ill, for I quarrel
with my informant for what I considered his profane w
of dealing with a subject so hallowed in my own though
After this I searched, east and west, north and south,
all known works or fragments of the same authors.
had read, therefore, as respects Mr. Coleridge, the Al
gory which he contributed to Mr. Southey's *Joan of A*
I had read his fine ode entitled *France*, his *Ode to*
Duchess of Devonshire, and various other contribution
more or less interesting, to the two volumes of t
Anthology published at Bristol, about 1799–1800, by N
Southey; and, finally, I had, of course, read the sm
volume of poems published under his own name. The
however, as a juvenile and immature collection, ma
expressly with a view to pecuniary profit, and theref
courting expansion at any cost of critical discretion, h
in general greatly disappointed me.

Meantime, it had crowned the interest which to

vested his name, that about the year 1804 or 1805 I had
en informed by a gentlemen from the English Lakes,
ho knew him as a neighbor, that he had for some time
plied his whole mind to metaphysics and psychology—
hich happened to be my own absorbing pursuit. From
03 to 1808, I was a student at Oxford; and, on the first
casion when I could conveniently have sought for a
rsonal knowledge of one whom I contemplated with so
uch admiration, I was met by a painful assurance that
had quitted England, and was then residing at Malta,
the quality of secretary to the Governor. I began to
quire about the best route to Malta; but, as any route
that time promised an inside place in a French prison, I
conciled myself to waiting; and at last, happening to
sit the Bristol Hot-wells in the summer of 1807, I had
e pleasure to hear that Coleridge was not only once
ore upon English ground, but within forty and odd miles
my own station. In that same hour I bent my way to
e south; and, before evening, reaching a ferry on the
er Bridgewater, at a village called, I think, Stogursey
e., Stoke de Courcy, by way of distinction from some
her Stoke), I crossed it, and a few miles farther attained
y object—viz., the little town of Nether Stowey,
ongst the Quantock Hills. Here I had been assured
at I should find Mr. Coleridge, at the house of his
d friend Mr. Poole. On presenting myself, however,
that gentleman, I found that Coleridge was absent
Lord Egmont's, an elder brother (by the father's
le) of Mr. Perceval, the Prime Minister, assassinated
e years later; and, as it was doubtful whether he might
t then be on the wing to another friend's in the town
Bridgewater, I consented willingly, until his motions
uld be ascertained, to stay a day or two with this
. Poole—a man on his own account well deserving

a separate notice; for, as Coleridge afterward remarked
to me, he was almost an ideal model for a useful member
of Parliament. I found him a stout, plain-looking
farmer, leading a bachelor life, in a rustic, old-fashioned
5 house; the house, however, upon further acquaintance,
proving to be amply furnished with modern luxuries,
and especially with a good library, superbly mounted in
all departments bearing at all upon political philosophy;
and the farmer turning out a polished and liberal English-
10 man, who had traveled extensively, and had so entirely
dedicated himself to the service of his humble fellow-
countrymen—the hewers of wood and drawers of water
in this southern part of Somersetshire—that for many
miles round he was the general arbiter of their disputes,
15 the guide and counselor of their difficulties; besides
being appointed executor and guardian to his children
by every third man who died in or about the town of
Nether Stowey.

The first morning of my visit, Mr. Poole was so kind
20 as to propose, knowing my admiration of Wordsworth,
that we should ride over to Alfoxden—a place of singular
interest to myself, as having been occupied in his unmarried days by that poet, during the minority of Mr.
St. Aubyn, its present youthful proprietor. At this
25 delightful spot, the ancient residence of an ancient
English family, and surrounded by those ferny Quantock
Hills which are so beautifully glanced at in the poem of
Ruth, Wordsworth, accompanied by his sister, had
passed a good deal of the interval between leaving the
30 university (Cambridge) and the period of his final settlement amongst his native lakes of Westmoreland: some
allowance, however, must be made—but how much I do
not accurately know—for a long residence in France, for
a short one in North Germany, for an intermitting one

in London, and for a regular domestication with his
sister at Race Down in Dorsetshire.

Returning late from this interesting survey, we found
ourselves without company at dinner; and, being thus
seated *tête-à-tête*, Mr. Poole propounded the following 5
question to me, which I mention because it furnished me
with the first hint of a singular infirmity besetting Coleridge's mind:—"Pray, my young friend, did you ever
form any opinion, or, rather, did it ever happen to you
to meet with any rational opinion or conjecture of others, 10
upon that most revolting dogma of Pythagoras about
beans? You know what I mean: that monstrous doctrine in which he asserts that a man might as well, for
the wickedness of the thing, eat his own grandmother
as meddle with beans." 15

"Yes," I replied; "the line is, I believe, in the Golden
Verses. I remember it well."

P.—"True: now, our dear excellent friend Coleridge,
than whom God never made a creature more divinely
endowed, yet, strange it is to say, sometimes steals from 20
other people, just as you or I might do; I beg your
pardon—just as a poor creature like myself might do,
that sometimes have not wherewithal to make a figure
from my own exchequer: and the other day, at a dinner
party, this question arising about Pythagoras and his 25
beans, Coleridge gave us an interpretation which, from
his manner, I suspect to have been not original. Think,
therefore, if you have anywhere read a plausible
solution."

"I have: and it was a German author. This German, 30
understand, is a poor stick of a man, not to be named
on the same day with Coleridge: so that, if Coleridge
should appear to have robbed him, be assured that he has
done the scamp too much honor."

P.—"Well: what says the German?"

"Why, you know the use made in Greece of bear
in voting and balloting? Well: the German says tha
Pythagoras speaks symbolically; meaning that electio
5 eering, or, more generally, all interference with politic.
intrigues, is fatal to a philosopher's pursuits and the
appropriate serenity. Therefore, says he, follower
mine, abstain from public affairs as you would fro.
parricide."

10 P.—"Well, then, Coleridge *has* done the scamp to
much honor: for, by Jove, that is the very explanatic
he gave us!"

Here was a trait of Coleridge's mind, to be first mac
known to me by his best friend, and first published
15 the world by me, the foremost of his admirers! B
both of us had sufficient reasons:—Mr. Poole knew tha
stumbled on by accident, such a discovery would
likely to impress upon a man as yet unacquainted wi
Coleridge a most injurious jealousy with regard to
20 he might write: whereas, frankly avowed by one wh
knew him best, the fact was disarmed of its sting; sin
it thus became evident that, where the case had be
best known and most investigated, it had not operate
to his serious disadvantage. On the same argument-
25 to forestall, that is to say, other discoverers, who wou
make a more unfriendly use of the discovery—and al
as matters of literary curiosity, I shall here point out
few others of Coleridge's unacknowledged obligatior
noticed by myself in a very wide course of reading.

30 1. The *Hymn to Chamouni* is an expansion of a sho
poem in stanzas, upon the same subject, by Frederi
Brun, a female poet of Germany, previously known
the world under her maiden name of Münter. The me
framework of the poem is exactly the same—an appe

to the most impressive features of the regal mountain
(Mont Blanc), adjuring them to proclaim their author:
the torrent, for instance, is required to say by whom it
had been arrested in its headlong raving, and stiffened,
as by the petrific touch of Death, into everlasting pillars
of ice; and the answer to these impassioned apostrophes
is made by the same choral burst of rapture. In mere
logic, therefore, and even as to the choice of circumstances, Coleridge's poem is a translation. On the other
hand, by a judicious amplification of some topics, and
by its far deeper tone of lyrical enthusiasm, the dry
bones of the German outline have been awakened by
Coleridge into the fulness of life. It is not, therefore, a
paraphrase, but a re-cast of the original. And how was
this calculated, if frankly avowed, to do Coleridge any
injury with the judicious?

2. A more singular case of Coleridge's infirmity is
this:—In a very noble passage of *France* a fine expression or two occur from *Samson Agonistes*. Now, to
take a phrase or an inspiriting line from the great fathers
of poetry, even though no marks of quotation should be
added, carries with it no charge of plagiarism. Milton
is justly presumed to be as familiar to the ear as nature
to the eye; and to steal from him as impossible as to
appropriate, or sequester to a private use, some "bright
particular star." And there is a good reason for reject-
ing the typographical marks of quotation: they break
the continuity of the passion, by reminding the reader of
a printed book; on which account Milton himself (to
give an instance) has not marked the sublime words,
"tormented all the air" as borrowed; nor has Wordsworth, in applying to an unprincipled woman of commanding beauty the memorable expression "a weed of
glorious feature," thought it necessary to acknowledge

it as originally belonging to Spenser. Some dozens of
similar cases might be adduced from Milton. But
Coleridge, when saying of republican France that,

> *"Insupportably advancing,*
> 5   Her arm made mockery of the warrior's tramp."

not satisfied with omitting the marks of acknowledgment, thought fit positively to deny that he was indebted
to Milton. Yet who could forget that semi-chorus in
the *Samson* where the "bold Ascalonite" is described
10 as having "fled from his lion ramp"? Or who, that was
not in this point liable to some hallucination of judgment, would have ventured on a public challenge
(for virtually it was that) to produce from the *Samson*
words so impossible to be overlooked as those of "in-
15 supportably advancing the foot"? The result was
that one of the critical journals placed the two passages
in juxtaposition and left the reader to his own conclusions with regard to the poet's veracity. But, in this
instance, it was common sense rather than veracity
20 which the facts impeach.

   3. In the year 1810 I happened to be amusing myself
by reading, in their chronological order, the great classical
circumnavigations of the earth; and, coming to Shelvocke,
I met with a passage to this effect:—That Hatley, his
25 second captain (*i.e.*, lieutenant), being a melancholy
man, was possessed by a fancy that some long season of
foul weather, in the solitary sea which they were then
traversing, was due to an albatross which had steadily
pursued the ship; upon which he shot the bird, but
30 without mending their condition. There at once I saw
the germ of the *Ancient Mariner;* and I put a question
to Coleridge accordingly. Could it have been imagined
that he would see cause utterly to disown so slight an

obligation to Shelvocke? Wordsworth, a man of stern veracity, on hearing of this, professed his inability to understand Coleridge's meaning; the fact being notorious, as he told me, that Coleridge had derived from the very passage I had cited the original hint for the action of the poem; though it is very possible, from something which Coleridge said on another occasion, that, before meeting a fable in which to embody his ideas, he had meditated a poem on delirium, confounding its own dream-scenery with external things, and connected with the imagery of high latitudes.

4. All these cases amount to nothing at all as cases of plagiarism, and for this reason expose the more conspicuously that obliquity of feeling which could seek to decline the very slight acknowledgments required. But now I come to a case of real and palpable plagiarism; yet that, too, of a nature to be quite unaccountable in a man of Coleridge's attainments. It is not very likely that this particular case will soon be detected; but others will. Yet who knows? Eight hundred or a thousand years hence, some reviewer may arise who, having read the *Biographia Literaria* of Coleridge, will afterward read the *Philosophical*——[1] of Schelling, the great Bavarian professor—a man in some respects worthy to be Coleridge's assessor; and he will then make a singular discovery. In the *Biographia Literaria* occurs a dissertation upon the reciprocal relations of the *esse* and the *cogitare*—that is, of the *objective* and the *subjective;* and an attempt is made, by inverting the postulates from which the argument starts, to show how each might arise as a product, by an intelligible genesis, from the

---

[1] I forget the exact title, not having seen the book since 1823, and then only for one day; but I believe it was Schelling's *Kleine Philosophische Werke.*

other. It is a subject which, since the time of Fichte, has much occupied the German metaphysicians; and many thousands of essays have been written on it, or indirectly so, of which many hundreds have been read 5 by many tens of persons. Coleridge's essay, in particular, is prefaced by a few words in which, aware of his coincidence with Schelling, he declares his willingness to acknowledge himself indebted to so great a man in any case where the truth would allow him to do so; but, in 10 this particular case, insisting on the impossibility that he could have borrowed arguments which he had first seen some years after he had thought out the whole hypothesis *proprio marte*. After this, what was my astonishment to find that the entire essay, from the 15 first word to the last, is a *verbatim* translation from Schelling, with no attempt in a single instance to appropriate the paper by developing the arguments or by diversifying the illustrations? Some other obligations to Schelling, of a slighter kind, I have met with in the 20 *Biographia Literaria;* but this was a barefaced plagiarism, which could in prudence have been risked only by relying too much upon the slight knowledge of German literature in this country, and especially of that section of the German literature. Had, then, Coleridge any need to 25 borrow from Schelling? Did he borrow *in forma pauperis?* Not at all: there lay the wonder. He spun daily, and at all hours, for mere amusement of his own activities, and from the loom of his own magical brain, theories more gorgeous by far, and supported by a pomp 30 and luxury of images such as neither Schelling—no, nor any German that ever breathed, not John Paul—could have emulated in his dreams. With the riches of El Dorado lying about him, he would condescend to filch a handful of gold from any man whose purse he fancied, and in fact reproduced in a new form, applying itself to intellectual wealth, that maniacal propensity which is sometimes well known to attack enormous proprietors and millionaires for acts of petty larceny. The last Duke of Anc—— could not abstain from exercising his furtive mania upon articles so humble as silver spoons; and it was the nightly care of a pious daughter, watching over the aberrations of her father, to have his pockets searched by a confidential valet, and the claimants of the purloined articles traced out.

Many cases have crossed me in life of people, otherwise not wanting in principle, who had habits, or at least hankerings, of the same kind. And the phrenologists, I believe, are well acquainted with the case, its signs, its progress, and its history. Dismissing, however, this subject, which I have at all noticed only that I might anticipate, and (in old English) that I might *prevent*, the uncandid interpreter of its meaning, I will assert finally that, after having read for thirty years in the same track as Coleridge—that track in which few of any age will ever follow us, such as German metaphysicians, Latin Schoolmen, thaumaturgic Platonists, religious Mystics— and having thus discovered a large variety of trivial thefts, I do, nevertheless, most heartily believe him to have been as entirely original in all his capital pretensions as any one man that ever has existed; as Archimedes in ancient days, or as Shakespeare in modern. Did the reader ever see Milton's account of the rubbish contained in the Greek and Latin Fathers? Or did he ever read a statement of the monstrous chaos with which an African Obeah man stuffs his enchanted scarecrows? Or, take a more common illustration, did he ever amuse himself by searching the pockets of a child—three years old, suppose—when buried in slumber after a long sum-

mer's day of out-o'-doors intense activity? I have done
this; and, for the amusement of the child's mother,
have analyzed the contents, and drawn up a formal
register of the whole. Philosophy is puzzled, conjecture
5 and hypothesis are confounded, in the attempt to explain
the law of selection which *can* have presided in the
child's labors; stones remarkable only for weight, old
rusty hinges, nails, crooked skewers stolen when the
cook had turned her back, rags, broken glass, tea-cups
10 having the bottom knocked out, and loads of similar
jewels, were the prevailing articles in this *procès-verbal*.
Yet, doubtless, much labor had been incurred, some
sense of danger perhaps had been faced, and the anxieties of a conscious robber endured, in order to amass this
15 splendid treasure. Such in value were the robberies
of Coleridge; such their usefulness to himself or anybody else; and such the circumstances of uneasiness
under which he had committed them. I return to my
narrative.
20   Two or three days slipped away in waiting for Coleridge's re-appearance at Nether Stowey, when suddenly
Lord Egmont called upon Mr. Poole, with a present for
Coleridge: it was a canister of peculiarly fine snuff, which
Coleridge now took profusely. Lord Egmont, on this
25 occasion, spoke of Coleridge in the terms of excessive
admiration, and urged Mr. Poole to put him upon
undertaking some great monumental work, that might
furnish a sufficient arena for the display of his various
and rare accomplishments; for his multiform erudition
30 on the one hand, for his splendid power of theorizing
and combining large and remote notices of facts on the
other. And he suggested, judiciously enough, as one
theme which offered a field at once large enough and
indefinite enough to suit a mind that could not show its

full compass of power unless upon very plastic materials —a History of Christianity, in its progress and in its chief divarications into Church and Sect, with a continual reference to the relations subsisting between Christianity and the current philosophy; their occasional connections or approaches, and their constant mutual repulsions. "But, at any rate, let him do something," said Lord Egmont; "for at present he talks very much like an angel, and does nothing at all." Lord Egmont I understood from everybody to be a truly good and benevolent man; and on this occasion he spoke with an earnestness which agreed with my previous impression. Coleridge, he said, was now in the prime of his powers—uniting something of youthful vigor with sufficient experience of life; having the benefit, beside, of vast meditation, and of reading unusually discursive. No man had ever been better qualified to revive the heroic period of literature in England, and to give a character of weight to the philosophic erudition of the country upon the Continent. "And what a pity," he added, "if this man were, after all, to vanish like an apparition, and you, I, and a few others, who have witnessed his grand *bravuras* of display, were to have the usual fortune of ghost-seers, in meeting no credit for any statements that we might vouch on his behalf!"

On this occasion we learned, for the first time, that Lord Egmont's carriage had, some days before, conveyed Coleridge to Bridgewater, with a purpose of staying one single day at that place, and then returning to Mr. Poole's. From the sort of laugh with which Lord Egmont taxed his own simplicity, in having confided at all in the stability of any Coleridgian plan, I now gathered that procrastination in excess was, or had become, a marking feature in Coleridge's daily life.

Nobody who knew him ever thought of depending on any appointment he might make: spite of his uniformly honorable intentions, nobody attached any weight to his assurances *in re futura:* those who asked him to 5 dinner or any other party, as a matter of course, sent a carriage for him, and went personally or by proxy to fetch him; and, as to letters, unless the address were in some female hand that commanded his affectionate esteem, he tossed them all into one general *dead-letter* 10 *bureau,* and rarely, I believe, opened them at all.   Bourrienne mentions a mode of abridging the trouble attached to a very extensive correspondence, by which infinite labor was saved to himself, and to Napoleon, when First Consul.   Nine out of ten letters, supposing them 15 letters of business with official applications of a special kind, he contends, answer themselves: in other words, time alone must soon produce events which virtually contain the answer.   On this principle the letters were opened periodically, after intervals, suppose, of six 20 weeks; and, at the end of that time, it was found that not many remained to require any further more particular answer.   Coleridge's plan, however, was shorter: he opened none, I understood, and answered none.   At least such was his habit at that time.   But, on that same 25 day, all this, which I heard now for the first time and with much concern, was fully explained; for already he was under the full dominion of opium, as he himself revealed to me, and with a deep expression of horror at the hideous bondage, in a private walk of some length 30 which I took with him about sunset.

Lord Egmont's information, and the knowledge now gained of Coleridge's habits, making it very uncertain when I might see him in my present hospitable quarters, I immediately took my leave of Mr. Poole and went over to Bridgewater. I had received directions for finding out the house where Coleridge was visiting; and, in riding down a main street of Bridgewater, I noticed a gateway corresponding to the description given me. Under this was standing, and gazing about him, a man whom I will describe. In height he might seem to be about five feet eight (he was, in reality, about an inch and a half taller, but his figure was of an order which drowns the height); his person was broad and full, and tended even to corpulence; his complexion was fair, though not what painters technically style fair, because it was associated with black hair; his eyes were large, and soft in their expression; and it was from the peculiar appearance of haze or dreaminess which mixed with their light that I recognized my object. This was Coleridge. I examined him steadfastly for a minute or more; and it struck me that he saw neither myself nor any other object in the street. He was in a deep reverie; for I had dismounted, made two or three trifling arrangements at an inn-door, and advanced close to him, before he had apparently become conscious of my presence. The sound of my voice, announcing my own name, first awoke him; he started, and for a moment seemed at a loss to understand my purpose or his own situation; for he repeated rapidly a number of words which had no relation to either of us. There was no *mauvaise honte* in his manner, but simple perplexity, and an apparent difficulty in recovering his position amongst daylight realities. This little scene over, he received me with a kindness of manner so marked that it might be called gracious. The hospitable family with whom he was domesticated were distinguished for their amiable manners and enlightened understandings: they were descendants from Chubb, the philosophic writer, and bore

the same name. For Coleridge they all testified deep
affection and esteem—sentiments in which the whole
town of Bridgewater seemed to share; for in the evening,
when the heat of the day had declined, I walked out with
5 him; and rarely, perhaps never, have I seen a person so
much interrupted in one hour's space as Coleridge, on this
occasion, by the courteous attentions of young and old.

All the people of station and weight in the place, and
apparently all the ladies, were abroad to enjoy the lovely
10 summer evening; and not a party passed without some
mark of smiling recognition, and the majority stopping
to make personal inquiries about his health, and to
express their anxiety that he should make a lengthened
stay amongst them. Certain I am, from the lively
15 esteem expressed toward Coleridge at this time by the
people of Bridgewater, that a very large subscription
might, in that town, have been raised to support him
amongst them, in the character of a lecturer, or philosophical professor. Especially I remarked that the
20 young men of the place manifested the most liberal
interest in all that concerned him; and I can add my
attestation to that of Mr. Coleridge himself, when describing an evening spent amongst the enlightened
tradesmen of Birmingham, that nowhere is more un-
25 affected good sense exhibited, and particularly nowhere
more elasticity and *freshness* of mind, than in the conversation of the reading men in manufacturing towns.
In Kendal, especially, in Bridgewater, and in Manchester, I have witnessed more interesting conversations,
30 as much information, and more natural eloquence in
conveying it, than usually in literary cities, or in places
professedly learned. One reason for this is that in
trading towns the time is more happily distributed; the
day given to business and active duties—the evening to

relaxation; on which account, books, conversation, and literary leisure are more cordially enjoyed: the same satiation never can take place which too frequently deadens the genial enjoyment of those who have a surfeit of books and a monotony of leisure. Another reason is that more simplicity of manner may be expected, and more natural picturesqueness of conversation, more open expression of character, in places where people have no previous name to support. Men in trading towns are not afraid to open their lips for fear they should disappoint your expectations, nor do they strain for showy sentiments that they may meet them. But, elsewhere, many are the men who stand in awe of their own reputation: not a word which is unstudied, not a movement in the spirit of natural freedom, dare they give way to, because it might happen that on review something would be seen to retract or to qualify—something not properly planed and chiseled to build into the general architecture of an artificial reputation. But to return:—

Coleridge led me to a drawing-room, rang the bell for refreshments, and omitted no point of a courteous reception. He told me that there would be a very large dinner party on that day, which, perhaps, might be disagreeable to a perfect stranger; but, if not, he could assure me of a most hospitable welcome from the family. I was too anxious to see him under all aspects to think of declining this invitation. That point being settled, Coleridge, like some great river, the Orellana, or the St. Lawrence, that, having been checked and fretted by rocks or thwarting islands, suddenly recovers its volume of waters and its mighty music, swept at once, as if returning to his natural business, into a continuous strain of eloquent dissertation, certainly the most novel, the most finely illustrated, and traversing the most spacious

fields of thought by transitions the most just and logical,
that it was possible to conceive.   What I mean by saying
that his transitions were "just" is by way of contra-
distinction to that mode of conversation which courts
5 variety through links of *verbal* connections.   Coleridge,
to many people, and often I have heard the complaint,
seemed to wander; and he seemed then to wander the
most when, in fact, his resistance to the wandering instinct was greatest—viz., when the compass and huge
10 circuit by which his illustrations moved traveled farthest
into remote regions before they began to revolve.   Long
before this coming round commenced most people had
lost him, and naturally enough supposed that he had lost
himself.   They continued to admire the separate beauty
15 of the thoughts, but did not see their relations to the
dominant theme.   Had the conversation been thrown
upon paper, it might have been easy to trace the continuity of the links; just as in Bishop Berkeley's
Siris,[1] from a pedestal so low and abject, so culinary,
20 as Tar Water, the method of preparing it, and its
medicinal effects, the dissertation ascends, like Jacob's
ladder, by just gradations, into the Heaven of Heavens
and the thrones of the Trinity.   But Heaven is there connected with earth by the Homeric chain of gold; and,
25 being subject to steady examination, it is easy to trace
the links; whereas, in conversation, the loss of a single
word may cause the whole cohesion to disappear from
view.   However, I can assert, upon my long and intimate knowledge of Coleridge's mind, that logic the most
30 severe was as inalienable from his modes of thinking as
grammar from his language.

[1] *Seiris* ought to have been the title—*i.e.*, Σειρις, a chain.   From
this defect in the orthography, I did not in my boyish days perceive,
nor could obtain any light upon its meaning.

On the present occasion, the original theme, started by myself, was Hartley and the Hartleian theory. I had carried as a little present to Coleridge a scarce Latin pamphlet, *De Ideis*, written by Hartley about 1746 —that is, about three years earlier than the publication of his great work. He had also preluded to this great work in a little English medical tract upon Joanna Stephens's medicine for the stone; for indeed Hartley was the person upon whose evidence the House of Commons had mainly relied in giving to that same Joanna a reward of £5000 for her idle medicines—an application of public money not without its use, in so far as it engaged men by selfish motives to cultivate the public service, and to attempt public problems of very difficult solution; but else, in that particular instance, perfectly idle, as the groans of three generations since Joanna's era have too feelingly established. It is known to most literary people that Coleridge was, in early life, so passionate an admirer of the Hartleian philosophy that "Hartley" was the sole baptismal name which he gave to his eldest child; and in an early poem, entitled *Religious Musings*, he has characterized Hartley as

> "Him of mortal kind
> Wisest, him first who mark'd the ideal tribes
> Up the fine fibers through the sentient brain
> Pass in fine surges."

But at present (August 1807) all this was a forgotten thing. Coleridge was so profoundly ashamed of the shallow Unitarianism of Hartley, and so disgusted to think that he could at any time have countenanced that creed, that he would scarcely allow to Hartley the reverence which is undoubtedly his due; for I must contend that, waiving all question of the extent to which Hartley would have pushed it (as though the law of association accounted not only for our complex pleasures and pains, but also might be made to explain the act of ratiocination)—waiving also the physical substratum of nervous vibrations and miniature vibrations to which he has chosen to marry his theory of association;—all this apart, I must contend that the *Essay on Man, his Frame, his Duty, and his Expectations* stands forward as a specimen almost unique of elaborate theorizing, and a monument of absolute beauty in the impression left of its architectural grace. In this respect it has, to my mind, the spotless beauty and the ideal proportions of some Grecian statue. However, I confess that, being myself, from my earliest years, a reverential believer in the doctrine of the Trinity, simply because I never attempted to bring all things within the mechanic understanding, and because, like Sir Thomas Browne, my mind almost demanded mysteries in so mysterious a system of relations as those which connect us with another world, and also because the farther my understanding opened the more I perceived of dim analogies to strengthen my creed, and because nature herself, mere physical nature, has mysteries no less profound; for these, and for many other "*becauses,*" I could not reconcile with my general reverence for Mr. Coleridge the fact, so often reported to me, that he was a Unitarian. But, said some Bristol people to me, not only is he a Unitarian—he is also a Socinian. In that case, I replied, I cannot hold him a Christian. I am a liberal man, and have no bigotry or hostile feelings toward a Socinian; but I can never think that man a Christian who has blotted out of his scheme the very powers by which only the great offices and functions of Christianity can be sustained; neither can I think that any man, though he make himself a marvelously clever disputant, ever could tower upward into a very great philosopher unless he should begin or should end with Christianity. Kant is a dubious exception. Not that I mean to question his august pretensions, so far as they went, and in his proper line. Within his own circle none durst tread but he. But that circle was limited. He was called, by one who weighed him well, the *alles-zermalmender*, the world-shattering Kant. He could destroy—his intellect was essentially destructive. He was the Gog and he was the Magog of Hunnish desolation to the existing schemes of Philosophy. He probed them; he showed the vanity of vanities which besieged their foundations—the rottenness below, the hollowness above. But he had no instincts of creation or restoration within his Apollyon mind; for he had no love, no faith, no self-distrust, no humility, no childlike docility; all which qualities belonged essentially to Coleridge's mind, and waited only for manhood and sorrow to bring them forward.

Who can read without indignation of Kant that, at his own table, in social sincerity and confidential talk, let him say what he would in his books, he exulted in the prospect of absolute and ultimate annihilation; that he planted his glory in the grave, and was ambitious of rotting for ever? The King of Prussia, though a personal friend of Kant's, found himself obliged to level his state thunders at some of his doctrines, and terrified him in his advance; else I am persuaded that Kant would have formally delivered atheism from the professor's chair, and would have enthroned the horrid ghoulish creed (which privately he professed) in the University of Königsberg. It required the artillery of a great king to make him pause; his menacing or warning letter to Kant is extant. The general notion is, that the royal

logic applied so austerely to the public conduct of Kant in his professor's chair was of that kind which rests its strength "upon thirty legions." My own belief is that the king had private information of Kant's ultimate
5 tendencies as revealed in his table-talk. The fact is that, as the stomach has been known, by means of its own potent acid secretion, to attack not only whatsoever alien body is introduced within it, but also (as John Hunter first showed) sometimes to attack itself and its own
10 organic structure, so, and with the same preternatural extension of instinct, did Kant carry forward his destroying functions, until he turned them upon his own hopes and the pledges of his own superiority to the dog, the ape, the worm. But *"exoriare aliquis"*—and some
15 philosopher, I am persuaded, *will* arise; and "one sling of some victorious arm" will yet destroy the destroyer, in so far as he has applied himself to the destruction of Christian hope. For my faith is that, though a great man may, by a rare possibility, be an infidel, an intellect
20 of the highest order must build upon Christianity. A very clever architect may choose to show his power by building with insufficient materials; but the supreme architect must require the very best, because the perfection of the forms cannot be shown but in the perfection of
25 the matter.

On these accounts I took the liberty of doubting, as often as I heard the reports I have mentioned of Coleridge; and I now found that he disowned most solemnly (and I may say penitentially) whatever had been true in
30 these reports. Coleridge told me that it had cost him a painful effort, but not a moment's hesitation, to abjure his Unitarianism, from the circumstance that he had amongst the Unitarians many friends, to some of whom he was greatly indebted for great kindness. In par-

ticular, he mentioned Mr. Estlin of Bristol, a distinguished Dissenting clergyman, as one whom it grieved him to grieve. But he would not dissemble his altered views. I will add, at the risk of appearing to dwell too long on religious topics, that, on this my first introduction to Coleridge, he reverted with strong compunction to a sentiment which he had expressed in earlier days upon prayer. In one of his youthful poems, speaking of God, he had said—

> "Of whose omniscient and all-spreading love
> Aught to implore were impotence of mind."

This sentiment he now so utterly condemned that, on the contrary, he told me, as his own peculiar opinion, that the act of praying was the very highest energy of which the human heart was capable; praying, that is, with the total concentration of the faculties; and the great mass of worldly men, and of learned men, he pronounced absolutely incapable of prayer.

For about three hours he had continued to talk, and in the course of this performance he had delivered many most striking aphorisms, embalming more weight of truth, and separately more deserving to be themselves embalmed, than would easily be found in a month's course of select reading. In the midst of our conversation, if that can be called conversation which I so seldom sought to interrupt, and which did not often leave openings for contribution, the door opened, and a lady entered. She was in person full and rather below the common height; whilst her face showed to my eye some prettiness of rather a commonplace order. Coleridge paused upon her entrance; his features, however, announced no particular complacency, and did not relax into a smile. In a frigid tone he said, whilst turning to

me, "Mrs. Coleridge"; in some slight way he then
presented me to her: I bowed; and the lady almost
immediately retired. From this short but ungenial
scene, I gathered, what I afterward learned redund-
antly, that Coleridge's marriage had not been a very
happy one. But let not the reader misunderstand me.
Never was there a baser insinuation, viler in the motive,
or more ignoble in the manner, than that passage in
some lampoon of Lord Byron's, where, by way of ven-
geance on Mr. Southey (who was the sole delinquent),
he described both him and Coleridge as having married
"two milliners from Bath." Everybody knows what is
meant to be conveyed in that expression, though it
would be hard, indeed, if, even at Bath, there should
be any class under such a fatal curse, condemned so
irretrievably, and so hopelessly prejudged, that ignominy
must, at any rate, attach, in virtue of a mere name or
designation, to the mode by which they gained their
daily bread, or possibly supported the declining year
of a parent. However, in this case, the whole sting of
the libel was a pure falsehood of Lord Byron's. Bath
was not the native city, nor at any time the residence
of the ladies in question, but Bristol. As to the other
word, "*milliners*," that is not worth inquiring about.
Whether they, or any one of their family, ever *did* exer
cise this profession, I do not know; they were, at all
events, too young, when removed by marriage from
Bristol, to have been much tainted by the worldly feel
ings which may beset such a mode of life. But, what
is more to the purpose, I heard, at this time, in Bristol
from Mr. Cottle, the author, a man of high principle
as also from his accomplished sisters—from the ladies
again, who had succeeded Mrs. Hannah More in her
school, and who enjoyed her entire confidence—that

the whole family of four or five sisters had maintained an irreproachable character, though naturally exposed, by their personal attractions, to some peril and to the malevolence of envy. This declaration, which I could strengthen by other testimony equally disinterested, if it were at all necessary, I owe to truth; and I must also add, upon a knowledge more personal, that Mrs. Coleridge was, in all circumstances of her married life, a virtuous wife and a conscientious mother; and, as a mother, she showed at times a most meritorious energy. In particular, I remember that, wishing her daughter to acquire the Italian language, and having in her retirement at Keswick no means of obtaining a master, she set to work resolutely, under Mr. Southey's guidance, to learn the language herself, at a time of life when such attainments are not made with ease or pleasure. She became mistress of the language in a very respectable extent, and then communicated her new accomplishment to her most interesting daughter.

I go on, therefore, to say, that Coleridge afterward made me, as doubtless some others, a confidant in this particular. What he had to complain of was simply incompatibility of temper and disposition. Wanting all cordial admiration, or indeed comprehension, of her husband's intellectual powers, Mrs. Coleridge wanted the original basis for affectionate patience and candor. Hearing from everybody that Coleridge was a man of most extraordinary endowments, and attaching little weight, perhaps, to the distinction between popular talents and such as by their very nature are doomed to a slower progress in the public esteem, she naturally looked to see, at least, an extraordinary measure of worldly consequence attend upon their exercise. Now, had Coleridge been as persevering and punctual as the

great mass of professional men, and had he given no
reason to throw the *onus* of the different result upon his
own different habits, in that case this result might, possibly and eventually, have been set down to the peculiar
5 constitution of his powers, and their essential mal-
adaptation to the English market. But, this trial having
never fairly been made, it was natural to impute his non-
success exclusively to his own irregular application, and
to his carelessness in forming judicious connections. In
10 circumstances such as these, however, no matter how
caused or how palliated, was laid a sure ground of discontent and fretfulness in any woman's mind, not unusually indulgent or unusually magnanimous. Coleridge, besides, assured me that his marriage was not his
15 own deliberate act, but was in a manner forced upon his
sense of honor by the scrupulous Southey, who insisted
that he had gone too far in his attentions to Miss Fricker
for any honorable retreat. On the other hand, a neutral
spectator of the parties protested to me, that, if ever in
20 his life he had seen a man under deep fascination, and
what he would have called desperately in love, Coleridge,
in relation to Miss F., was that man. Be that as it
might, circumstances occurred soon after the marriage
which placed all the parties in a trying situation for their
25 candor and good temper. I had a full outline of the
situation from two of those who were chiefly interested,
and a partial one from a third: nor can it be denied that
all the parties offended in point of prudence. A young
lady became a neighbor, and a daily companion of Cole-
30 ridge's walks, whom I will not describe more particularly
than by saying that intellectually she was very much
superior to Mrs. Coleridge. That superiority alone, when
made conspicuous by its effects in winning Coleridge's
regard and society, could not but be deeply mortifying

to a young wife. However, it was moderated to her feelings by two considerations:—1. That the young lady was much too kind-hearted to have designed any annoyance in this triumph, or to express any exultation. 2. That no shadow of suspicion settled upon the moral conduct or motives of either party: the young lady was always attended by her brother; she had no personal charms; and it was manifest that mere intellectual sympathies, in reference to literature and natural scenery, had associated them in their daily walks.

Still, it is a bitter trial to a young married woman to sustain any sort of competition with a female of her own age for any part of her husband's regard, or any share of his company. Mrs. Coleridge, not having the same relish for long walks or rural scenery, and their residence being, at this time, in a very sequestered village, was condemned to a daily renewal of this trial. Accidents of another kind embittered it still further: often it would happen that the walking party returned drenched with rain; in which case, the young lady, with a laughing gaiety, and evidently unconscious of any liberty that she was taking, or any wound that she was inflicting, would run up to Mrs. Coleridge's wardrobe, array herself, without leave asked, in Mrs. Coleridge's dresses, and make herself merry with her own unceremoniousness and Mrs. Coleridge's gravity. In all this, she took no liberty that she would not most readily have granted in return; she confided too unthinkingly in what she regarded as the natural privileges of friendship; and as little thought that she had been receiving or exacting a favor, as, under an exchange of their relative positions, she would have claimed to confer one. But Mrs. Coleridge viewed her freedoms with a far different eye: she felt herself no longer the entire mistress of her own house; she held a divided empire; and it barbed the arrow to her womanly feelings that Coleridge treated any sallies of resentment which might sometimes escape her as narrow-mindedness; whilst, on the other hand, her own female servant, and others in the same rank of life, began to drop expressions which alternately implied pity for her as an injured woman, or contempt for her as a very tame one.

The reader will easily apprehend the situation, and the unfortunate results which it boded to the harmony of a young married couple, without further illustration. Whether Coleridge would not, under any circumstances, have become indifferent to a wife not eminently capable of enlightened sympathy with his own ruling pursuits, I do not undertake to pronounce. My own impression is that neither Coleridge nor Lord Byron could have failed, eventually, to quarrel with *any* wife, though a Pandora sent down from heaven to bless him. But, doubtless, this consummation must have been hastened by a situation which exposed Mrs. Coleridge to an invidious comparison with a more intellectual person; as, on the other hand, it was most unfortunate for Coleridge himself to be continually compared with one so ideally correct and regular in his habits as Mr. Southey. Thus was their domestic peace prematurely soured: embarrassments of a pecuniary nature would be likely to demand continual sacrifices; no depth of affection existing, these would create disgust or dissension; and at length each would believe that their union had originated in circumstances overruling their own deliberate choice.

The gloom, however, and the weight of dejection which sat upon Coleridge's countenance and deportment at this time could not be accounted for by a disappointment (if such it were) to which time must, long ago, have reconciled him. Mrs. Coleridge, if not turning to him the more amiable aspects of her character, was at any rate a respectable partner. And the season of youth was now passed. They had been married about ten years; had had four children, of whom three survived; and the interests of a father were now replacing those of a husband. Yet never had I beheld so profound an expression of cheerless despondency. And the restless activity of Coleridge's mind, in chasing abstract truths, and burying himself in the dark places of human speculation, seemed to me, in a great measure, an attempt to escape out of his own personal wretchedness. I was right. In this instance, at least, I had hit the mark; and Coleridge bore witness himself at an after period to the truth of my divination by some impressive verses. At dinner, when a very numerous party had assembled, he knew that he was expected to talk, and exerted himself to meet the expectation. But he was evidently struggling with gloomy thoughts that prompted him to silence and perhaps to solitude: he talked with effort, and passively resigned himself to the repeated misrepresentations of several amongst his hearers. The subject chiefly discussed was Arthur Young, not for his rural economy, but for his politics. It must be to this period of Coleridge's life that Wordsworth refers in those exquisite "Lines written in my pocket copy of the *Castle of Indolence.*" The passage which I mean comes after a description of Coleridge's countenance, and begins in some such terms as these:—

"A piteous sight it was to see this man,
  When he came back to us, a wither'd flow'r," &c.

Withered he was, indeed, and to all appearance blighted.

At night he entered into a spontaneous explanation of this unhappy overclouding of his life, on occasion of my saying accidentally that a toothache had obliged me to take a few drops of laudanum. At what time or on 5 what motive he had commenced the use of opium, he did not say; but the peculiar emphasis of horror with which he warned me against forming a habit of the same kind impressed upon my mind a feeling that he never hoped to liberate himself from the bondage. My belief is that 10 he never *did*. About ten o'clock at night I took leave of him; and, feeling that I could not easily go to sleep after the excitement of the day, and fresh from the sad spectacle of powers so majestic already besieged by decay, I determined to return to Bristol through the cool- 15 ness of the night. The roads, though, in fact, a section of the great highway between seaports so turbulent as Bristol and Plymouth, were as quiet as garden-walks. Once only I passed through the expiring fire of a village fair or wake: that interruption excepted, through 20 the whole stretch of forty miles from Bridgewater to the Hot-wells, I saw no living creature but a surly dog, who followed me for a mile along a park-wall, and a man, who was moving about in the half-way town of Cross. The turnpike-gates were all opened by a mechan- 25 ical contrivance from a bed-room window; I seemed to myself in solitary possession of the whole sleeping country. The summer night was divinely calm; no sound, except once or twice the cry of a child as I was passing the windows of cottages, ever broke upon 30 the utter silence; and all things conspired to throw back my thoughts upon that extraordinary man whom I had just quitted.

The fine saying of Addison is familiar to most readers —that Babylon in ruins is not so affecting a spectacle,

or so solemn, as a human mind overthrown by lunacy.
How much more awful, then, when a mind so regal as
that of Coleridge is overthrown, or threatened with over-
throw, not by a visitation of Providence, but by the
treachery of its own will, and by the conspiracy, as it
were, of himself against himself! Was it possible that
this ruin had been caused or hurried forward by the
dismal degradations of pecuniary difficulties? That was
worth inquiring. I will here mention briefly that I
did inquire two days after; and, in consequence of what
I heard, I contrived that a particular service should be
rendered to Mr. Coleridge, a week later, through the
hands of Mr. Cottle of Bristol, which might have the
effect of liberating his mind from anxiety for a year or
two, and thus rendering his great powers disposable to
their natural uses. That service was accepted by Coleridge. To save him any feelings of distress, all names
were concealed; but, in a letter written by him about
fifteen years after that time, I found that he had become
aware of all the circumstances, perhaps through some indiscretion of Mr. Cottle's. A more important question I
never ascertained, viz. whether this service had the effect
of seriously lightening his mind. For some succeeding
years, he did certainly appear to me released from that
load of despondency which oppressed him on my first
introduction. Grave, indeed, he continued to be, and
at times absorbed in gloom; nor did I ever see him in a
state of perfectly natural cheerfulness. But, as he strove
in vain for many years to wean himself from his captivity to opium, a healthy state of spirits could not be
much expected. Perhaps, indeed, where the liver and
other organs had, for so large a period in life, been
subject to a continual morbid stimulation, it might be
impossible for the system ever to recover a natural

action. Torpor, I suppose, must result from continued artificial excitement; and, perhaps, upon a scale of corresponding duration. Life, in such a case, may not offer a field of sufficient extent for unthreading the fatal
5 links that have been wound about the machinery of health, and have crippled its natural play.

Meantime—to resume the thread of my wandering narrative—on this serene summer night of 1807, as I moved slowly along, with my eyes continually settling
10 upon the northern constellations, which, like all the fixed stars, by their immeasurable and almost spiritual remoteness from human affairs, naturally throw the thoughts upon the perishableness of our earthly troubles, in contrast with their own utter peace and solemnity—
15 I reverted, at intervals, to all I had ever heard of Coleridge, and strove to weave it into some continuous sketch of his life. I hardly remember how much I then knew; I know but little now: that little I will here jot down upon paper.

MEETING WITH WORDSWORTH

20 IN 1807 it was, at the beginning of winter, that I first saw William Wordsworth. I have already mentioned that I had introduced myself to his notice by letter as early as the spring of 1803. To this hour it has continued, I believe, a mystery to Wordsworth, why it was
25 that I suffered an interval of four and a half years to slip away before availing myself of the standing invitation with which I had been honored to the poet's house. Very probably he accounted for this delay by supposing that the new-born liberty of an Oxford life, with its
30 multiplied enjoyments, acting upon a boy just emancipated from the restraints of a school, and, in one hour,

elevated into what we Oxonians so proudly and so exclusively denominate "a man,"[1] might have tempted me into pursuits alien from the pure intellectual passions which had so powerfully mastered my youthful heart some years before. Extinguished such a passion could not be; nor could he think, if remembering the fervor with which I had expressed it, the sort of "nympholepsy" which had seized upon me, and which, in some imperfect way, I had avowed with reference to the very lakes and mountains, amongst which the scenery of this most original poetry had chiefly grown up and moved. The very names of the ancient hills—Fairfield, Seat Sandal, Helvellyn, Blencathara, Glaramara; the names of the sequestered glens—such as Borrowdale, Martindale, Mardale, Wasdale, and Ennerdale; but, above all, the shy pastoral recesses, not garishly in the world's eye, like Windermere or Derwentwater, but lurking half unknown to the traveler of that day—Grasmere, for instance, the lovely abode of the poet himself, solitary, and yet sowed, as it were, with a thin diffusion of humble dwellings—here a scattering, and there a clustering, as in the starry heavens—sufficient to afford, at every turn and angle, human remembrances and memorials of time-honored affections, or of passions

---

[1] At the Universities at Oxford and Cambridge, where the town is viewed as a mere ministerial appendage to the numerous colleges—the civic Oxford, for instance, existing for the sake of the academic Oxford, and not *vice versa*—it has naturally happened that the students honor with the name of "*a man*" him only who wears a cap and gown. The word is not used with any reference to physical powers, or to age; but simply to the final object for which the places are supposed to have first arisen, and to maintain themselves. There is, however, a ludicrous effect produced in some instances by the use of this term in contradistinguishing parties. "Was he a man?" is a frequent question; and *as* frequent in the mouth of a stripling under nineteen, speaking, perhaps, of a huge, elderly tradesman—"Oh, no! not a man at all."

(as the *Churchyard amongst the Mountains* will
amply demonstrate) not wanting even in scenic and
tragical interest—these were so many local spells upon
me, equally poetic and elevating with the Miltonic names
5 of Valdarno and Vallombrosa.

Deep are the voices which seem to call, deep is the
lesson which would be taught even to the most thoughtless of men—

> "Could field, or grove, or any spot on earth,
> 10   Show to his eye an image of the pangs
>   Which it hath witness'd; render back an echo
>   Of the sad steps by which it hath been trod."[1]

Meantime, my delay was due to anything rather than to
waning interest. On the contrary, the real cause of my
15 delay was the too great profundity, and the increasing
profundity, of my interest in this regeneration of our
national poetry; and the increasing awe, in due proportion to the decaying thoughtlessness of boyhood,
which possessed me for the character of its author.
20 So far from neglecting Wordsworth, it is a fact that
twice I had undertaken a long journey expressly for the
purpose of paying my respects to Wordsworth; twice
I came so far as the little rustic inn (then the sole inn
of the neighborhood) at Church Coniston; and on
25 neither occasion could I summon confidence enough to
present myself before him. It was not that I had any
want of proper boldness for facing the most numerous
company of a mixed or ordinary character: reserved,
indeed, I was, perhaps even shy—from the character of
30 my mind, so profoundly meditative, and the character

---

[1] See the divine passage (in the Sixth Book of *The Excursion*)
beginning—

> "Ah, what a lesson to a thoughtless man," etc.

of my life, so profoundly sequestered—but still, from counteracting causes, I was not deficient in a reasonable self-confidence toward the world generally. But the very image of Wordsworth, as I prefigured it to my own planet-struck eye, crushed my faculties as before Elijah or St. Paul. Twice, as I have said, did I advance as far as the lake of Coniston; which is about eight miles from the church of Grasmere, and once I absolutely went forward from Coniston to the very gorge of Hammerscar, from which the whole Vale of Grasmere suddenly breaks upon the view in a style of almost theatrical surprise, with its lovely valley stretching before the eye in the distance, the lake lying immediately below, with its solemn ark-like island of four and a half acres in size seemingly floating on its surface, and its exquisite outline on the opposite shore, revealing all its little bays[1] and wild sylvan margin, feathered to the edge with wild flowers and ferns. In one quarter, a little wood, stretching for about half a mile toward the outlet of the lake; more directly in opposition to the spectator, a few green fields; and beyond them, just two bowshots from the water, a little white cottage gleaming from the midst of trees, with a vast and seemingly never-ending series of ascents rising above it to the height of more than three thousand feet. That little cottage was Wordsworth's from the time of his marriage, and earlier; in fact, from the beginning of the century to the year 1808. Afterward, for many a year, it was mine. Catching one hasty glimpse of this loveliest of landscapes, I retreated like a guilty thing, for fear I

[1] All which inimitable graces of nature have, by the hands of mechanic art, by solid masonry, by whitewashing, etc., been exterminated, as a growth of weeds and nuisances, for thirty years.—*August* 17, 1853.

might be surprised by Wordsworth, and then returned faint-heartedly to Coniston, and so to Oxford, *re infectâ*. This was in 1806. And thus far, from mere excess of nervous distrust in my own powers for sustaining a conversation with Wordsworth, I had for nearly five years shrunk from a meeting for which, beyond all things under heaven, I longed. In early youth I labored under a peculiar embarrassment and penury of words, when I sought to convey my thoughts adequately upon interesting subjects: neither was it words only that I wanted; but I could not unravel, I could not even make perfectly conscious to myself, the subsidiary thoughts into which one leading thought often radiates; or, at least, I could not do this with anything like the rapidity requisite for conversation. I labored like a sibyl instinct with the burden of prophetic woe, as often as I found myself dealing with any topic in which the understanding combined with deep feelings to suggest mixed and tangled thoughts: and thus partly—partly also from my invincible habit of reverie—at that era of my life, I had a most distinguished talent *"pour le silence."* Wordsworth, from something of the same causes, suffered (by his own report to myself) at the same age from pretty much the same infirmity. And yet, in more advanced years—probably about twenty-eight or thirty—both of us acquired a remarkable fluency in the art of unfolding our thoughts colloquially. However, at that period my deficiencies were what I have described. And, after all, though I had no absolute cause for anticipating contempt, I was so far right in my fears, that since that time I have had occasion to perceive a worldly tone of sentiment in Wordsworth, not less than in Mrs. Hannah More and other literary people, by which they were led to set a higher value upon a limited respect from a person high in the world's esteem than upon the most lavish spirit of devotion from an obscure quarter. Now, in that point, *my* feelings are far otherwise.

Meantime, the world went on; events kept moving; and, amongst them, in the course of 1807, occurred the event of Coleridge's return to England from his official station in the Governor's family at Malta. At Bridge-water, as I have already recorded, in the summer of 1807, I was introduced to him. Several weeks after he came with his family to the Bristol Hot-wells, at which, by accident, I was then visiting. On calling upon him, I found that he had been engaged by the Royal Institution to lecture at their theater in Albemarle Street during the coming winter of 1807–8, and, consequently, was embarrassed about the mode of conveying his family to Keswick. Upon this, I offered my services to escort them in a post-chaise. This offer was cheerfully accepted; and at the latter end of October we set forward —Mrs. Coleridge, viz., with her two sons—Hartley, aged nine, Derwent, about seven—her beautiful little daughter,[1] about five, and, finally, myself. Going by the direct route through Gloucester, Bridgenorth, etc., on the third day we reached Liverpool, where I took up my quarters at a hotel, whilst Mrs. Coleridge paid a visit of a few days to a very interesting family, who had become friends of Southey during his visit to Portugal. These

[1] That most accomplished, and to Coleridge most pious daughter, whose recent death afflicted so very many who knew her only by her writings. She had married her cousin, Mr. Serjeant Coleridge, and in that way retained her illustrious maiden name as a wife. At seventeen, when last I saw her, she was the most perfect of all pensive, nun-like, intellectual beauties that I have seen in real breathing life. The upper parts of her face were verily divine. See, for an artist's opinion, the Life of that admirable man Collins, by his son.

were the Misses Koster, daughters of an English gold-merchant of celebrity, who had recently quitted Lisbon on the approach of the French army under Junot. Mr. Koster did me the honor to call at my quarters, and 5 invite me to his house; an invitation which I very readily accepted, and had thus an opportunity of becoming acquainted with a family the most accomplished I had ever known. At dinner there appeared only the family party—several daughters, and one son, a fine 10 young man of twenty, but who was *consciously* dying of asthma. Mr. Koster, the head of the family, was distinguished for his good sense and practical information; but, in Liverpool, even more so by his eccentric and obstinate denial of certain notorious events; in par-15 ticular, some two years later, he denied that any such battle as Talavera had ever been fought, and had a large wager depending upon the decision. His house was the resort of distinguished foreigners; and, on the first evening of my dining there, as well as afterward, 20 I there met that marvel of women, Madame Catalani. I had heard her repeatedly; but never before been near enough to see her smile and converse—even to be honored with a smile myself. She and Lady Hamilton were the most effectively brilliant women I ever saw. 25 However, on this occasion, the Misses Koster outshone even La Catalani; to her they talked in the most fluent Italian; to some foreign men, in Portuguese; to one in French; and to most of the party in English; and each, by turns, seemed to be their native tongue. Nor did 30 they shrink, even in the presence of the mighty enchant-ress, from exhibiting their musical skill.

Leaving Liverpool, after about a week's delay, we pursued our journey northward. We had slept on the first day at Lancaster. Consequently, at the rate

of motion which then prevailed throughout England
—which, however, was rarely equaled on that western
road, where all things were in arrear by comparison with
the eastern and southern roads of the kingdom—we
found ourselves, about three o'clock in the afternoon, at 5
Ambleside, fourteen miles to the northwest of Kendal,
and thirty-six from Lancaster. There, for the last time,
we stopped to change horses; and about four o'clock
we found ourselves on the summit of the White Moss,
a hill which rises between the second and third mile- 10
stones on the stage from Ambleside to Keswick, and
which then retarded the traveler's advance by a full
fifteen minutes, but is now evaded by a lower line of
road. In ascending this hill, from weariness of moving
so slowly, I, with the two Coleridges, had alighted; and, 15
as we all chose to refresh ourselves by running down
the hill into Grasmere, we had left the chaise behind
us, and had even lost the sound of the wheels at times,
when all at once we came, at an abrupt turn of the
road, in sight of a white cottage, with two yew-trees 20
breaking the glare of its white walls. A sudden shock
seized me on recognizing this cottage, of which, in the
previous year, I had gained a momentary glimpse from
Hammerscar, on the opposite side of the lake. I paused,
and felt my old panic returning upon me; but just then, 25
as if to take away all doubt upon the subject, I saw
Hartley Coleridge, who had gained upon me considerably, suddenly turn in at a garden gate; this motion to
the right at once confirmed me in my belief that here at
last we had reached our port; that this little cottage 30
was tenanted by that man whom, of all the men from the
beginning of time, I most fervently desired to see; that
in less than a minute I should meet Wordsworth face
to face. Coleridge was of opinion that, if a man were

really and *consciously* to see an apparition, in such circumstances death would be the inevitable result; and, if so, the wish which we hear so commonly expressed for such experience is as thoughtless as that of Semele in the Grecian mythology, so natural in a female, that her lover should visit her *en grand costume*—presumptuous ambition, that unexpectedly wrought its own ruinous chastisement! Judged by Coleridge's test, my situation could not have been so terrific as *his* who anticipates a ghost; for, certainly, I survived this meeting; but at that instant it seemed pretty much the same to my own feelings.

Never before or since can I reproach myself with having trembled at the approaching presence of any creature that is born of woman, excepting only, for once or twice in my life, woman herself. Now, however, I *did* tremble; and I forgot, what in no other circumstances I could have forgotten, to stop for the coming up of the chaise, that I might be ready to hand Mrs. Coleridge out. Had Charlemagne and all his peerage been behind me, or Cæsar and his equipage, or Death on his pale horse, I should have forgotten them at that moment of intense expectation, and of eyes fascinated to what lay before me, or what might in a moment appear. Through the little gate I pressed forward; ten steps beyond it lay the principal door of the house. To this, no longer clearly conscious of my own feelings, I passed on rapidly; I heard a step, a voice, and, like a flash of lightning, I saw the figure emerge of a tallish man, who held out his hand, and saluted me with most cordial expressions of welcome. The chaise, however, drawing up to the gate at that moment, he (and there needed no Roman nomenclator to tell me that this *he* was Wordsworth) felt himself summoned to advance and receive Mrs. Coleridge. I, therefore, stunned almost with the actual accomplishment of a catastrophe so long anticipated and so long postponed, mechanically went forward into the house. A little semi-vestibule between two doors prefaced the entrance into what might be considered the principal room of the cottage. It was an oblong square, not above eight and a half feet high, sixteen feet long, and twelve broad; very prettily wainscoted from the floor to the ceiling with dark polished oak, slightly embellished with carving. One window there was—a perfect and unpretending cottage window, with little diamond panes, embowered at almost every season of the year with roses, and in the summer and autumn with a profusion of jasmine and other fragrant shrubs. From the exuberant luxuriance of the vegetation around it, and from the dark hue of the wainscoting, this window, though tolerably large, did not furnish a very powerful light to one who entered from the open air. However, I saw sufficiently to be aware of two ladies just entering the room, through a doorway opening upon a little staircase. The foremost, a tallish young woman, with the most winning expression of benignity upon her features, advanced to me, presenting her hand with so frank an air that all embarrassment must have fled in a moment before the native goodness of her manner. This was Mrs. Wordsworth, cousin of the poet, and, for the last five years or more, his wife. She was now mother of two children, a son and a daughter; and she furnished a remarkable proof how possible it is for a woman neither handsome nor even comely according to the rigor of criticism— nay, generally pronounced very plain—to exercise all the practical fascination of beauty, through the mere compensatory charms of sweetness all but angelic, of

simplicity the most entire, womanly self-respect and
purity of heart speaking through all her looks, acts, and
movements. *Words*, I was going to have added; but
her words were few. In reality, she talked so little that
5 Mr. Slave-Trade Clarkson used to allege against her
that she could only say *"God bless you!"* Certainly,
her intellect was not of an active order; but, in a qui-
escent, reposing, meditative way, she appeared always
to have a genial enjoyment from her own thoughts;
10 and it would have been strange, indeed, if she, who
enjoyed such eminent advantages of training, from
the daily society of her husband and his sister, failed
to acquire some power of judging for herself, and putting
forth some functions of activity. But undoubtedly that
15 was not her element: to feel and to enjoy in a luxurious
repose of mind—there was her *forte* and her peculiar
privilege; and how much better this was adapted to her
husband's taste, how much more adapted to uphold the
comfort of his daily life, than a blue-stocking loquacity,
20 or even a legitimate talent for discussion, may be
inferred from his verses, beginning—

> "She was a phantom of delight,
> When first she gleam'd upon my sight."

Once for all,[1] these exquisite lines were dedicated to
25 Mrs. Wordsworth; were understood to describe her—to
have been prompted by the feminine graces of her character; hers they are, and will remain for ever. To these,
therefore, I may refer the reader for an idea of what was
most important in the partner and second self of the poet.

[1] *Once for all, I say*—on recollecting that Coleridge's verses to
Sara were made transferable to any Sara who reigned at the time.
At least three Saras appropriated them; all three long since in the
grave.

And I will add to this abstract of her *moral* portrait these few concluding traits of her appearance in a physical sense. Her figure was tolerably good. In complexion she was fair, and there was something peculiarly pleasing even in this accident of the skin, for it was accompanied by an animated expression of health, a blessing which, in fact, she possesses uninterruptedly. Her eyes, the reader may already know, were

> "Like stars of twilight fair;
> Like twilight, too, her dark brown hair;
> But all things else about her drawn
> From May-time and the cheerful dawn."

Yet strange it is to tell that, in these eyes of vesper gentleness, there was a considerable obliquity of vision; and much beyond that slight obliquity which is often supposed to be an attractive foible in the countenance: this *ought* to have been displeasing or repulsive; yet, in fact, it was not. Indeed all faults, had they been ten times more and greater, would have been neutralized by that supreme expression of her features to the unity of which every lineament in the fixed parts, and every undulation in the moving parts, of her countenance, concurred, viz., a sunny benignity—a radiant graciousness—such as in this world I never saw surpassed.

Immediately behind her moved a lady, shorter, slighter, and perhaps, in all other respects, as different from her in personal characteristics as could have been wished for the most effective contrast. "Her face was of Egyptian brown"; rarely, in a woman of English birth, had I seen a more determinate gipsy tan. Her eyes were not soft, as Mrs. Wordsworth's, nor were they fierce or bold; but they were wild and startling, and hurried in their motion. Her manner was warm and even ardent;

her sensibility seemed constitutionally deep; and some
subtle fire of impassioned intellect apparently burned
within her, which, being alternately pushed forward into
a conspicuous expression by the irrepressible instincts
5 of her temperament, and then immediately checked, in
obedience to the decorum of her sex and age, and her
maidenly condition, gave to her whole demeanor, and
to her conversation, an air of embarrassment, and even
of self-conflict, that was almost distressing to witness.
10 Even her very utterance and enunciation often suffered,
in point of clearness and steadiness, from the agitation
of her excessive organic sensibility. At times, the self-
counteraction and self-baffling of her feelings caused
her even to stammer, and so determinately to stammer
15 that a stranger who should have seen her and quitted
her in that state of feeling would have certainly set her
down for one plagued with that infirmity of speech as
distressingly as Charles Lamb himself. This was Miss
Wordsworth, the only sister of the poet—his "Doro-
20 thy"; who naturally owed so much to the lifelong intercourse with her great brother in his most solitary and
sequestered years; but, on the other hand, to whom he
has acknowledged obligations of the profoundest nature;
and, in particular, this mighty one, through which we
25 also, the admirers and the worshipers of this great
poet, are become equally her debtors—that, whereas the
intellect of Wordsworth was, by its original tendency,
too stern, too austere, too much enamored of an ascetic
harsh sublimity, she it was—the lady who paced by his
30 side continually through sylvan and mountain tracks, in
Highland glens, and in the dim recesses of German charcoal-burners—that first *couched* his eye to the sense of
beauty, humanized him by the gentler charities, and en-
grafted, with her delicate female touch, those graces

upon the ruder growths of his nature which have since clothed the forest of his genius with a foliage corresponding in loveliness and beauty to the strength of its boughs and the massiness of its trunks. The greatest deductions from Miss Wordsworth's attractions, and from the exceeding interest which surrounded her in right of her character, of her history, and of the relation which she fulfilled toward her brother, were the glancing quickness of her motions, and other circumstances in her deportment (such as her stooping attitude when walking), which gave an ungraceful, and even an unsexual character to her appearance when out-of-doors. She did not cultivate the graces which preside over the person and its carriage. But, on the other hand, she was a person of very remarkable endowments intellectually; and, in addition to the other great services which she rendered to her brother, this I may mention, as greater than all the rest, and it was one which equally operated to the benefit of every casual companion in a walk—viz., the exceeding sympathy, always ready and always profound, by which she made all that one could tell her, all that one could describe, all that one could quote from a foreign author, reverberate, as it were, *à plusieurs reprises*, to one's own feelings, by the manifest impression it made upon *hers*. The pulses of light are not more quick or more inevitable in their flow and undulation, than were the answering and echoing movements of her sympathizing attention. Her knowledge of literature was irregular, and thoroughly unsystematic. She was content to be ignorant of many things; but what she knew and had really mastered lay where it could not be disturbed—in the temple of her own most fervid heart.

Such were the two ladies who, with himself and two children, and at that time one servant, composed the

poet's household. They were both, I believe, about
twenty-eight years old; and, if the reader inquires about
the single point which I have left untouched in their
portraiture—viz., the style of their manners—I may say
5 that it was, in *some* points, naturally of a plain household simplicity, but every way pleasing, unaffected, and
(as respects Mrs. Wordsworth) even dignified. Few
persons had seen so little as this lady of the world. She
had seen nothing of high life, for she had seen little of
10 any. Consequently, she was unacquainted with the conventional modes of behavior, prescribed in particular
situations by high breeding. But, as these modes are
little more than the product of dispassionate good sense,
applied to the circumstances of the case, it is surprising
15 how few deficiencies are perceptible, even to the most
vigilant eye—or, at least, essential deficiencies—in the
general demeanor of any unaffected young woman,
acting habitually under a sense of sexual dignity and
natural courtesy. Miss Wordsworth had seen more of
20 life and even of good company; for she had lived, when
quite a girl, under the protection of Dr. Cookson, a near
relative, canon of Windsor, and a personal favorite of
the Royal Family, especially of George III. Consequently, she ought to have been the more polished of the
25 two; and yet, from greater natural aptitudes for refinement of manner in her sister-in-law, and partly, perhaps,
from her more quiet and subdued manner, Mrs. Wordsworth would have been pronounced very much the more
lady-like person.
30   From the interest which attaches to anybody so nearly
connected as these two ladies with a great poet, I have
allowed myself a larger latitude than else might have
been justifiable in describing them. I now go on with
my narrative:—

I was ushered up a little flight of stairs, fourteen in all, to a little drawing-room, or whatever the reader chooses to call it. Wordsworth himself has described the fireplace of this room as his

> "Half-kitchen and half-parlor fire."   5

It was not fully seven feet six inches high, and, in other respects, pretty nearly of the same dimensions as the rustic hall below. There was, however, in a small recess, a library of perhaps three hundred volumes, which seemed to consecrate the room as the poet's study and 10 composing room; and such occasionally it was. But far oftener he both studied, as I found, and composed on the high road. I had not been two minutes at the fireside, when in came Wordsworth, returning from his friendly attentions to the travelers below, who, it 15 seemed, had been over-persuaded by hospitable solicitations to stay for this night in Grasmere, and to make out the remaining thirteen miles of their road to Keswick on the following day. Wordsworth entered. And *"what-like"* to use a Westmoreland as well as a Scot- 20 tish expression—*"what-like"* was Wordsworth? A reviewer in *Tait's Magazine*, noticing some recent collection of literary portraits, gives it as his opinion that Charles Lamb's head was the finest among them. This remark may have been justified by the engraved 25 portraits; but, certainly, the critic would have canceled it, had he seen the original heads—at least, had he seen them in youth or in maturity; for Charles Lamb bore age with less disadvantage to the intellectual expression of his appearance than Wordsworth, in whom a sanguine 30 complexion had, of late years, usurped upon the original bronze-tint; and this change of hue, and change in the quality of skin, had been made fourfold more conspicuous, and more unfavorable in its general effect, by the harsh contrast of grizzled hair which had displaced the original brown. No change in personal appearance ever can have been so unfortunate; for, generally speaking, whatever other disadvantages old age may bring along with it, one effect, at least in male subjects, has a compensating tendency—that it removes any tone of vigor too harsh, and mitigates the expression of power too unsubdued. But, in Wordsworth, the effect of the change has been to substitute an air of animal vigor, or, at least, hardiness, as if derived from constant exposure to the wind and weather, for the fine somber complexion which he once wore, resembling that of a Venetian senator or a Spanish monk.

Here, however, in describing the personal appearance of Wordsworth, I go back, of course, to the point of time at which I am speaking. He was, upon the whole, not a well-made man. His legs were pointedly condemned by all female connoisseurs in legs; not that they were bad in any way which *would* force itself upon your notice—there was no absolute deformity about them; and undoubtedly they had been serviceable legs beyond the average standard of human requisition; for I calculate, upon good data, that with these identical legs Wordsworth must have traversed a distance of 175,000 to 180,000 English miles—a mode of exertion which, to him, stood in the stead of alcohol and all other stimulants whatsoever to the animal spirits; to which, indeed, he was indebted for a life of unclouded happiness, and we for much of what is most excellent in his writings. But, useful as they have proved themselves, the Wordsworthian legs were certainly not ornamental; and it was really a pity, as I agreed with a lady in thinking, that he had not another pair for evening dress parties—when

no boots lend their friendly aid to mask our imperfections from the eyes of female rigorists—those *elegantes
formarum spectatrices*. A sculptor would certainly have
disapproved of their contour. But the worst part of
Wordsworth's person was the bust; there was a narrow- 5
ness and a droop about the shoulders which became
striking, and had an effect of meanness, when brought
into close juxtaposition with a figure of a more statuesque
build. Once on a summer evening, walking in the Vale
of Langdale with Wordsworth, his sister, and Mr. J——, 10
a native Westmoreland clergyman, I remember that Miss
Wordsworth was positively mortified by the peculiar illustration which settled upon this defective conformation.
Mr. J——, a fine towering figure, six feet high, massy and
columnar in his proportions, happened to be walking, a 15
little in advance, with Wordsworth; Miss Wordsworth
and myself being in the rear; and from the nature of the
conversation which then prevailed in our front rank, something or other about money, devises, buying and selling,
we of the rear-guard thought it requisite to preserve 20
this arrangement for a space of three miles or more;
during which time, at intervals, Miss Wordsworth would
exclaim, in a tone of vexation, "Is it possible,—can that
be William? How very mean he looks!" And she did
not conceal a mortification that seemed really painful, 25
until I, for my part, could not forbear laughing outright
at the serious interest which she carried into this trifle.
She was, however, right, as regarded the mere visual
judgment. Wordsworth's figure, with all its defects,
was brought into powerful relief by one which had been 30
cast in a more square and massy mould; and in such a
case it impressed a spectator with a sense of absolute
meanness, more especially when viewed from behind and
not counteracted by his countenance; and yet Words-

worth was of a good height (five feet ten), and not a
slender man; on the contrary, by the side of Southey,
his limbs looked thick, almost in a disproportionate
degree. But the total effect of Wordsworth's person
5 was always worse in a state of motion. Meantime, his
face—that was one which would have made amends for
greater defects of figure. Many such, and finer, I have
seen amongst the portraits of Titian, and, in a later
period, amongst those of Vandyke, from the great era of
10 Charles I, as also from the court of Elizabeth and of
Charles II, but none which has more impressed me in
my own time.

Haydon, in his great picture of *Christ's Entry into
Jerusalem*, has introduced Wordsworth in the character
15 of a disciple attending his Divine Master, and Voltaire
in the character of a sneering Jewish elder. This fact
is well known; and, as the picture itself is tolerably
well known to the public eye, there are multitudes now
living who will have seen a very impressive likeness of
20 Wordsworth—some consciously, some not suspecting
it. There will, however, always be many who have *not*
seen any portrait at all of Wordsworth; and therefore I
will describe its general outline and effect. It was a face
of the long order, often falsely classed as oval: but a
25 greater mistake is made by many people in supposing
the long face which prevailed so remarkably in the Elizabethan and Carolinian periods to have become extinct
in our own. Miss Ferrier, in one of her novels (*Marriage* I think), makes a Highland girl protest that
30 "no Englishman *with his round face*" shall ever wean
her heart from her own country; but England is not
the land of round faces; and those have observed
little, indeed, who think so: France it is that grows the
round face, and in so large a majority of her provinces

that it has become one of the national characteristics.
And the remarkable impression which an Englishman
receives from the eternal recurrence of the orbicular
countenance proves of itself, without any *conscious*
testimony, how the fact stands; in the blind sense of a   5
monotony, not felt elsewhere, lies involved an argument
that cannot be gainsaid. Besides, even upon an *a
priori* argument, how is it possible that the long face
so prevalent in England, by all confession, in certain
splendid eras of our history, should have had time, in   10
some five or six generations, to grow extinct? Again,
the character of face varies essentially in different provinces. Wales has no connection in this respect with
Devonshire, nor Kent with Yorkshire, nor either with
Westmoreland. England, it is true, tends, beyond all   15
known examples, to a general amalgamation of differences, by means of its unrivaled freedom of intercourse. Yet, even in England, law and necessity have
opposed as yet such and so many obstacles to the free
diffusion of labor that every generation occupies, by   20
at least five-sixths of its numbers, the ground of its
ancestors.

The movable part of a population is chiefly the higher
part; and it is the lower classes that, in every nation,
compose the *fundus*, in which lies latent the national   25
face, as well as the national character. Each exists here
in racy purity and integrity, not disturbed in the one by
alien intermarriages, nor in the other by novelties of
opinion, or other casual effects, derived from education
and reading. Now, look into this *fundus*, and you will   30
find, in many districts, no such prevalence of the round
orbicular face as some people erroneously suppose; and
in Westmoreland, especially, the ancient long face of the
Elizabethan period, powerfully resembling in all its

lineaments the ancient Roman face, and often (though
not so uniformly) the face of northern Italy in modern
times. The face of Sir Walter Scott, as Irving, the
pulpit orator, once remarked to me, was the indigenous
face of the Border: the mouth, which was bad, and the
entire lower part of the face, are seen repeated in thousands of working-men; or, as Irving chose to illustrate
his position, "in thousands of Border horse-jockeys."
In like manner, Wordsworth's face was, if not absolutely
the indigenous face of the Lake district, at any rate a
variety of that face, a modification of that original type.
The head was well filled out; and there, to begin with,
was a great advantage over the head of Charles Lamb,
which was absolutely truncated in the posterior region—
sawn off, as it were, by no timid sawyer. The forehead
was not remarkably lofty—and, by the way, some artists,
in their ardor for realizing their phrenological precon-
ceptions, not suffering nature to surrender quietly and
by slow degrees her real alphabet of signs and hiero-
glyphic characters, but forcing her language prematurely
into conformity with their own crude speculations, have
given to Sir Walter Scott a pile of forehead which is
unpleasing and cataphysical, in fact, a caricature of anything that is ever seen in nature, and would (if real) be
esteemed a deformity; in one instance—that which
was introduced in some annual or other—the forehead
makes about two-thirds of the entire face. Wordsworth's forehead is also liable to caricature misrepresentations in these days of phrenology: but, whatever
it may appear to be in any man's fanciful portrait, the
real living forehead, as I have been in the habit of seeing
it for more than five-and-twenty years, is not remarkable for its height; but it *is*, perhaps, remarkable for its
breadth and expansive development. Neither are the

eyes of Wordsworth "large," as is erroneously stated
somewhere in *Peter's Letters;* on the contrary, they
are (I think) rather small; but *that* does not interfere
with their effect, which at times is fine, and suitable to
his intellectual character. At times, I say, for the depth
and subtlety of eyes, even their coloring (as to con-
densation or dilation), varies exceedingly with the state
of the stomach; and, if young ladies were aware of the
magical transformations which can be wrought in the
depth and sweetness of the eye by a few weeks' walking
exercise, I fancy we should see their habits in this point
altered greatly for the better. I have seen Wordsworth's
eyes oftentimes affected powerfully in this respect; his
eyes are not, under any circumstances, bright, lustrous,
or piercing; but, after a long day's toil in walking, I
have seen them assume an appearance the most solemn
and spiritual that it is possible for the human eye to
wear. The light which resides in them is at no time
a superficial light; but, under favorable accidents, it
is a light which seems to come from unfathomed depths:
in fact, it is more truly entitled to be held "the light
that never was on land or sea," a light radiating from
some far spiritual world, than any the most idealizing
that ever yet a painter's hand created. The nose, a
little arched, is large; which, by the way (according to
a natural phrenology, existing centuries ago amongst
some of the lowest amongst the human species), has
always been accounted an unequivocal expression of
animal appetites organically strong. And that expressed
the simple truth: Wordsworth's intellectual passions
were fervent and strong: but they rested upon a basis
of preternatural animal sensibility diffused through *all*
the animal passions (or appetites); and something of
that will be found to hold of all poets who have been

great by original force and power, not (as Virgil) by means of fine management and exquisite artifice of composition applied to their conceptions. The mouth, and the whole circumjacencies of the mouth, composed 5 the strongest feature in Wordsworth's face; there was nothing specially to be noticed that I know of in the mere outline of the lips; but the swell and protrusion of the parts above and around the mouth are both noticeable in themselves, and also because they remind me of a 10 very interesting fact which I discovered about three years after this my first visit to Wordsworth.

Being a great collector of everything relating to Milton, I had naturally possessed myself, whilst yet very young, of Richardson the painter's thick octavo volume 15 of notes on the *Paradise Lost*. It happened, however, that my copy, in consequence of that mania for portrait collecting which has stripped so many English classics of their engraved portraits, wanted the portrait of Milton. Subsequently I ascertained that it ought to 20 have had a very good likeness of the great poet; and I never rested until I procured a copy of the book which had not suffered in this respect by the fatal admiration of the amateur. The particular copy offered to me was one which had been priced unusually high, on account of 25 the unusually fine specimen which it contained of the engraved portrait. This, for a particular reason, I was exceedingly anxious to see; and the reason was—that, according to an anecdote reported by Richardson himself, this portrait, of all that were shown to her, was the 30 only one acknowledged by Milton's last surviving daughter to be a strong likeness of her father. And her involuntary gestures concurred with her deliberate words:—for, on seeing all the rest, she was silent and inanimate; but the very instant she beheld that crayon drawing from which is derived the engraved head in Richardson's book, she burst out into a rapture of passionate recognition; exclaiming—"That is my father! that is my dear father!" Naturally, therefore, after such a testimony, so much stronger than any other person in the world could offer to the authentic value of this portrait, I was eager to see it.

Judge of my astonishment when, in this portrait of Milton, I saw a likeness nearly perfect of Wordsworth, better by much than any which I have since seen of those expressly painted for himself. The likeness is tolerably preserved in that by Carruthers, in which one of the little Rydal waterfalls, etc., composes a background; yet this is much inferior, as a mere portrait of Wordsworth, to the Richardson head of Milton; and this, I believe, is the last which represents Wordsworth in the vigor of his power. The rest, which I have not seen, may be better as works of art (for anything I know to the contrary), but they must labor under the great disadvantage of presenting the features when "defeatured," in the degree and the way I have described, by the peculiar ravages of old age, as it affects this family; for it is noticed of the Wordsworths, by those who are familiar with their peculiarities, that in their very blood and constitutional differences lie hidden causes that are able, in some mysterious way,

> "Those shocks of passion to prepare
> That kill the bloom before its time,
> And blanch, without the owner's crime,
> The most resplendent hair."

Some people, it is notorious, live faster by much than others, the oil is burned out sooner in one constitution than another: and the cause of this may be various;

but in the Wordsworths one part of the cause is, no
doubt, the secret fire of a temperament too fervid; the
self-consuming energies of the brain, that gnaw at the
heart and life-strings for ever. In that account which
5 *The Excursion* presents to us of an imaginary Scots-
man who, to still the tumult of his heart, when visiting the cataracts of a mountainous region, obliges
himself to study the laws of light and color as they
affect the rainbow of the stormy waters, vainly attempt-
10 ing to mitigate the fever which consumed him by en-
tangling his mind in profound speculations; raising a
cross-fire of artillery from the subtilizing intellect, under
the vain conceit that in this way he could silence the
mighty battery of his impassioned heart: there we read
15 a picture of Wordsworth and his own youth. In Miss
Wordsworth every thoughtful observer might read the
same self-consuming style of thought. And the effect
upon each was so powerful for the promotion of a premature old age, and of a premature expression of old
20 age, that strangers invariably supposed them fifteen to
twenty years older than they were. And I remember
Wordsworth once laughingly reporting to me, on returning from a short journey in 1809, a little personal
anecdote, which sufficiently showed what was the spon-
25 taneous impression upon that subject of casual strangers,
whose feelings were not confused by previous knowledge
of the truth. He was traveling by a stagecoach, and
seated outside, amongst a good half-dozen of fellow-
passengers. One of these, an elderly man, who confessed
30 to having passed the grand climacterical year (9 multiplied into 7) of 63, though he did not say precisely by
how many years, said to Wordsworth, upon some anticipations which they had been mutually discussing of
changes likely to result from enclosures, etc., then going

on or projecting—"Ay, ay, another dozen of years will show us strange sights; but you and I can hardly expect to see them."—"How so?" said Wordsworth. "How so, my friend? How old do you take me to be?"—"Oh, I beg pardon," said the other; "I meant no offence— but what?" looking at Wordsworth more attentively— "you'll never see threescore, I'm of opinion"; meaning to say that Wordsworth *had* seen it already. And, to show that he was not singular in so thinking, he appealed to all the other passengers; and the motion passed (*nem. con.*) that Wordsworth was rather over than under sixty. Upon this he told them the literal truth—that he had not yet accomplished his thirty-ninth year. "God bless me!" said the climacterical man; "so then, after all, you'll have a chance to see your childer get up like, and get settled! Only to think of that!" And so closed the conversation, leaving to Wordsworth an undeniable record of his own prematurely expressed old age in this unaffected astonishment, amongst a whole party of plain men, that he could really belong to a generation of the forward-looking, who live by hope; and might reasonably expect to see a child of seven years old matured into a man. And yet, as Wordsworth lived into his 82nd year, it is plain that the premature expression of decay does not argue any real decay.

Returning to the question of portraits, I would observe that this Richardson engraving of Milton has the advantage of presenting, not only by far the best likeness of Wordsworth, but of Wordsworth in the prime of his powers—a point essential in the case of one so liable to premature decay. It may be supposed that I took an early opportunity of carrying the book down to Grasmere, and calling for the opinions of Wordsworth's family upon this most remarkable coincidence. Not

one member of that family but was as much impressed
as myself with the accuracy of the likeness. All the
peculiarities even were retained—a drooping appearance
of the eyelids, that remarkable swell which I have noticed
about the mouth, the way in which the hair lay upon the
forehead. In two points only there was a deviation
from the rigorous truth of Wordsworth's features—
the face was a little too short and too broad, and the
eyes were too large. There was also a wreath of laurel
about the head, which (as Wordsworth remarked) disturbed the natural expression of the whole picture; else,
and with these few allowances, he also admitted that
the resemblance was, *for that period of his life*, perfect,
or as nearly so as art could accomplish.

I have gone into so large and circumstantial a review
of my recollections on this point as would have been
trifling and tedious in excess, had these recollections
related to a less important man; but I have a certain
knowledge that the least of them will possess a lasting
and a growing interest in connection with William
Wordsworth. How peculiar, how different from the
interest which we grant to the ideas of a great philosopher, a great mathematician, or a great reformer, is
that burning interest which settles on the great poets
who have made themselves necessary to the human
heart; who have first brought into consciousness, and
have clothed in words, those grand catholic feelings that
belong to the grand catholic situations of life through
all its stages; who have clothed them in such words that
human wit despairs of bettering them! Mighty were
the powers, solemn and serene is the memory, of Archimedes; and Apollonius shines like "the starry Galileo"
in the firmament of human genius; yet how frosty is the
feeling associated with these names by comparison with

that which, upon every sunny lawn, by the side of every
ancient forest, even in the farthest depths of Canada,
many a young innocent girl, perhaps at this very moment
—looking now with fear to the dark recesses of the infinite forest, and now with love to the pages of the 5
infinite poet, until the fear is absorbed and forgotten in
the love—cherishes in her heart for the name and person
of Shakespeare!

The English language is traveling fast toward the
fulfilment of its destiny. Through the influence of the 10
dreadful Republic[1] that within the last thirty years has
run through all the stages of infancy into the first stage
of maturity, and through the English colonies—African,
Canadian, Indian, Australian—the English language
(and, therefore, the English literature) is running for- 15
ward toward its ultimate mission of eating up, like
Aaron's rod, all other languages. Even the German
and the Spanish will inevitably sink before it; perhaps
within 100 or 150 years. In the recesses of California,
in the vast solitudes of Australia, *The Churchyard amongst* 20
the Mountains, from Wordsworth's *Excursion*, and
many a scene of his shorter poems, will be read, even as

[1] Not many months ago, the blind hostility of the Irish newspaper editors in America forged a ludicrous estimate of the Irish
numerical preponderance in the United States, from which it was
inferred, as at least a possibility, that the Irish Celtic language
might come to dispute the preëminence with the English. Others
anticipated the same destiny for the German. But, in the meantime, the unresting career of the law-courts, of commerce, and of
the national senate, that cannot suspend themselves for an hour,
reduce the case to this dilemma: If the Irish and the Germans
in the United States adapt their general schemes of education to
the service of their public ambition, they must begin by training
themselves to the use of the language now prevailing on all the
available stages of ambition. On the other hand, by refusing to do
this, they lose in the very outset every point of advantage. In
other words, adopting the English, they renounce the contest—
not adopting it, they disqualify themselves for the contest.

now Shakespeare is read amongst the forests of Canada.
All which relates to the writer of these poems will then
bear a value of the same kind as that which attaches to
our personal memorials (unhappily so slender) of
5 Shakespeare.

Let me now attempt to trace, in a brief outline, the
chief incidents in the life of William Wordsworth, which
are interesting, not only in virtue of their illustrious
subject, but also as exhibiting a most remarkable (almost
10 a providential) arrangement of circumstances, all tending
to one result—that of insulating from worldly cares, and
carrying onward from childhood to the grave, in a state
of serene happiness, one who was unfitted for daily toil,
and, at all events, who could not, under such demands
15 upon his time and anxieties, have prosecuted those genial
labors in which all mankind have an interest.

LEVANA AND OUR LADIES OF SORROW

OFTENTIMES at Oxford I saw Levana in my dreams. I
knew her by her Roman symbols. Who is Levana?
Reader, that do not pretend to have leisure for very much
20 scholarship, you will not be angry with me for telling
you. Levana was the Roman goddess that performed
for the new-born infant the earliest office of ennobling
kindness—typical, by its mode, of that grandeur which
belongs to man everywhere, and of that benignity in
25 powers invisible which even in pagan worlds sometimes
descends to sustain it. At the very moment of birth,
just as the infant tasted for the first time the atmosphere
of our troubled planet, it was laid on the ground. *That*
might bear different interpretations. But immediately,
30 lest so grand a creature should grovel there for more
than one instant, either the paternal hand, as proxy for

the goddess Levana, or some near kinsman, as proxy for the father, raised it upright, bade it look erect as the king of all this world, and presented its forehead to the stars, saying, perhaps, in his heart, "Behold what is greater than yourselves!" This symbolic act represented the function of Levana. And that mysterious lady, who never revealed her face (except to me in dreams), but always acted by delegation, had her name from the Latin verb (as still it is the Italian verb) *levare*, "to raise aloft."

This is the explanation of Levana. And hence it has arisen that some people have understood by Levana the tutelary power that controls the education of the nursery. She, that would not suffer at his birth even a prefigurative or mimic degradation for her awful ward, far less could be supposed to suffer the real degradation attaching to the non-development of his powers. She therefore watches over human education. Now, the word *edŭco*, with the penultimate short, was derived (by a process often exemplified in the crystallization of languages) from the word *edūco*, with the penultimate long. Whatsoever *educes*, or develops, *educates*. By the education of Levana, therefore, is meant, not the poor machinery that moves by spelling-books and grammars, but by that mighty system of central forces hidden in the deep bosom of human life, which by passion, by strife, by temptation, by the energies of resistance, works forever upon children, resting not day or night, any more than the mighty wheel of day and night themselves, whose moments, like restless spokes, are glimmering forever as they revolve.

If, then, *these* are the ministries by which Levana works, how profoundly must she reverence the agencies of grief! But you, reader, think that children generally are not liable to grief such as mine. There are two senses in the word "generally"—the sense of Euclid,

where it means "universally" (or in the whole extent
of the *genus*), and a foolish sense of this world, where it
means "usually."   Now, I am far from saying that children universally are capable of grief like mine.   But there
5 are more than you ever heard of who die of grief in this
island of ours.   I will tell you a common case.   The
rules of Eton require that a boy on the "foundation"
should be there twelve years: he is superannuated at
eighteen, consequently he must come at six.   Children
10 torn away from mothers and sisters at that age not un-
frequently die.   I speak of what I know.   The complaint is not entered by the registrar as grief; but *that*
it is.   Grief of that sort, and at that age, has killed more
than ever have been counted amongst its martyrs.

15   Therefore it is that Levana often communes with the
powers that shake man's heart; therefore it is that she
dotes upon grief.   "These ladies," said I softly to myself,
on seeing the ministers with whom Levana was conversing, "these are the Sorrows; and they are three in number:
20 as the Graces are three, who dress man's life with beauty;
the *Parcœ* are three, who weave the dark arras of man's
life in their mysterious loom, always with colors sad in
part, sometimes angry with tragic crimson and black;
the Furies are three, who visit with retributions, called
25 from the other side of the grave, offences that walk
upon this; and once even the Muses were but three, who
fit the harp, the trumpet, or the lute to the great burdens
of man's impassioned creations.   These are the Sorrows,
all three of whom I know."   The last words I say *now;*
30 but in Oxford I said, "one of whom I know, and the
others too surely I *shall* know."   For already, in my
fervent youth, I saw (dimly relieved upon the dark background of my dreams) the imperfect lineaments of the
awful Sisters.

These Sisters—by what name shall we call them? If I say simply "The Sorrows," there will be a chance of mistaking the term: it might be understood of individual sorrow, separate cases of sorrow, whereas I want a term expressing the mighty abstractions that incarnate themselves in all individual sufferings of man's heart; and I wish to have these abstractions presented as impersonations, that is, as clothed with human attributes of life, and with functions pointing to flesh. Let us call them, therefore, *Our Ladies of Sorrow.*

I know them thoroughly, and have walked in all their kingdoms. Three sisters they are, of one mysterious household; and their paths are wide apart; but of their dominion there is no end. Them I saw often conversing with Levana, and sometimes about myself. Do they talk, then? Oh, no! Mighty phantoms like these disdain the infirmities of language. They may utter voices through the organs of man when they dwell in human hearts, but amongst themselves is no voice nor sound; eternal silence reigns in their kingdoms. They spoke not as they talked with Levana; they whispered not; they sang not; though oftentimes methought they might have sung: for I upon earth had heard their mysteries oftentimes deciphered by harp and timbrel, by dulcimer and organ. Like God, whose servants they are, they utter their pleasure, not by sounds that perish or by words that go astray, but by signs in heaven, by changes on earth, by pulses in secret rivers, heraldries painted on darkness, and hieroglyphics written on the tablets of the brain. *They* wheeled in mazes; *I* spelled the steps. *They* telegraphed from afar; *I* read the signals. *They* conspired together; and on the mirrors of darkness *my* eye traced the plots. *Theirs* were the symbols; *mine* are the words.

What is it the Sisters are? What is it that they do?
Let me describe their form and their presence; if form
it were that still fluctuated in its outline, or presence it
were that forever advanced to the front or forever receded
5 amongst shades.

The eldest of the three is named *Mater Lachrymarum*,
Our Lady of Tears. She it is that night and day raves
and moans, calling for vanished faces. She stood in
Rama, where a voice was heard of lamentation—Rachel
10 weeping for her children, and refusing to be comforted.
She it was that stood in Bethlehem on the night when
Herod's sword swept its nurseries of Innocents, and the
little feet were stiffened forever, which, heard at times
as they trotted along floors overhead, woke pulses of
15 love in household hearts that were not unmarked in
heaven. Her eyes are sweet and subtle, wild and sleepy,
by turns; oftentimes rising to the clouds, oftentimes
challenging the heavens. She wears a diadem round her
head. And I knew by childish memories that she
20 could go abroad upon the winds, when she heard the
sobbing of litanies or the thundering of organs, and
when she beheld the mustering of summer clouds. This
Sister, the elder, it is that carries keys more than papal
at her girdle, which open every cottage and every palace.
25 She, to my knowledge, sat all last summer by the bedside
of the blind beggar, him that so often and so gladly I
talked with, whose pious daughter, eight years old, with
the sunny countenance, resisted the temptations of play
and village mirth, to travel all day long on dusty roads
30 with her afflicted father. For this did God send her a
great reward. In the springtime of the year, and
whilst yet her own spring was budding, he recalled her to
himself. But her blind father mourns forever over her;
still he dreams at midnight that the little guiding hand

is locked within his own; and still he wakens to a darkness
that is *now* within a second and a deeper darkness.   This
Mater Lachrymarum also has been sitting all this winter
of 1844–5 within the bedchamber of the Czar, bringing
before his eyes a daughter (not less pious) that vanished 5
to God not less suddenly, and left behind her a darkness
not less profound.   By the power of the keys it is that
Our Lady of Tears glides, a ghostly intruder, into the
chambers of sleepless men, sleepless women, sleepless
children, from Ganges to the Nile, from Nile to Mississippi. 10
And her, because she is the first-born of her house and
has the widest empire, let us honor with the title of
"Madonna."

The second Sister is called *Mater Suspiriorum*, Our
Lady of Sighs.   She never scales the clouds, nor walks 15
abroad upon the winds.   She wears no diadem.   And
her eyes, if they were even seen, would be neither sweet
nor subtle; no man could read their story; they would
be found filled with perishing dreams and with wrecks of
forgotten delirium.   But she raises not her eyes; her 20
head, on which sits a dilapidated turban, droops forever,
forever fastens on the dust.   She weeps not.   She groans
not.   But she sighs inaudibly at intervals.   Her sister
Madonna is oftentimes stormy and frantic, raging in
the highest against heaven, and demanding back her 25
darlings.   But Our Lady of Sighs never clamors, never
defies, dreams not of rebellious aspirations.   She is
humble to abjectness.   Hers is the meekness that
belongs to the hopeless.   Murmur she may, but it is
in her sleep.   Whisper she may, but it is to herself in the 30
twilight.   Mutter she does at times, but it is in solitary
places that are desolate as she is desolate, in ruined cities,
and when the sun has gone down to his rest.   This
Sister is the visitor of the Pariah, of the Jew, of the bonds-

man to the oar in the Mediterranean galleys; of the English criminal in Norfolk Island, blotted out from the books of remembrance in sweet far-off England; of the baffled penitent reverting his eyes forever upon a
5 solitary grave, which to him seems the altar overthrown of some past and bloody sacrifice, on which altar no oblation can now be availing, whether toward pardon that he might implore, or toward reparation that he might attempt. Every slave that at noonday looks
10 up to the tropical sun with timid reproach, as he points with one hand to the earth, our general mother, but for *him* a step-mother, as he points with the other hand to the Bible, our general teacher, but against *him* sealed and sequestered; every woman sitting in darkness,
15 without love to shelter her head, or hope to illumine her solitude, because the heaven-born instincts kindling in her nature germs of holy affections, which God implanted in her womanly bosom, having been stifled by social necessities, now burn sullenly to waste, like sepulchral
20 lamps amongst the ancients; every nun defrauded of her unreturning May-time by wicked kinsman, whom God will judge; every captive in every dungeon; all that are betrayed, and all that are rejected; outcasts by tradition-ary law, and children of hereditary disgrace—all these
25 walk with Our Lady of Sighs. She also carries a key; but she needs it little. For her kingdom is chiefly amongst the tents of Shem, and the houseless vagrant of every clime. Yet in the very highest ranks of man she finds chapels of her own; and even in glorious England
30 there are some that, to the world, carry their heads as proudly as the reindeer, yet who secretly have received her mark upon their foreheads.

But the third Sister, who is also the youngest—! Hush! whisper whilst we talk of *her!* Her kingdom is

not large, or else no flesh should live; but within that
kingdom all power is hers. Her head, turreted like that
of Cybele, rises almost beyond the reach of sight. She
droops not; and her eyes, rising so high, *might* be hidden
by distance. But, being what they are, they cannot be 5
hidden; through the treble veil of crape which she wears,
the fierce light of a blazing misery, that rests not for
matins or for vespers, for noon of day or noon of night,
for ebbing or for flowing tide, may be read from the very
ground. She is the defier of God. She also is the mother 10
of lunacies, and the suggestress of suicides. Deep lie
the roots of her power, but narrow is the nation that she
rules. For she can approach only those in whom a profound nature has been upheaved by central convulsions;
in whom the heart trembles and the brain rocks under 15
conspiracies of tempest from without and tempest from
within. Madonna moves with uncertain steps, fast or
slow, but still with tragic grace. Our Lady of Sighs
creeps timidly and stealthily. But this youngest Sister
moves with incalculable motions, bounding, and with 20
tiger's leaps. She carries no key; for, though coming
rarely amongst men, she storms all doors at which she is
permitted to enter at all. And *her* name is *Mater
Tenebrarum*, Our Lady of Darkness.

These were the *Semnai Theai*, or Sublime Goddesses, 25
these were the *Eumenides*, or Gracious Ladies (so called
by antiquity in shuddering propitiation), of my Oxford
dreams. Madonna spoke. She spoke by her mysterious
hand. Touching my head, she beckoned to Our Lady
of Sighs; and what she spoke, translated out of the signs 30
which (except in dreams) no man reads, was this:—

"Lo! here is he whom in childhood I dedicated to my
altars. This is he that once I made my darling. Him I
led astray, him I beguiled, and from heaven I stole away

his young heart to mine. Through me did he become idolatrous; and through me it was, by languishing desires, that he worshipped the worm and prayed to the wormy grave. Holy was the grave to him; lovely was its dark-
5 ness; saintly its corruption. Him, this young idolator, I have seasoned for thee, dear gentle Sister of Sighs! Do thou take him now to *thy* heart, and season him for our dreadful Sister. And thou"—turning to the *Mater Tenebrarum*, she said—"wicked Sister, that
10 temptest and hatest, do thou take him from *her*. See that thy scepter lie heavy on his head. Suffer not woman and her tenderness to sit near him in his darkness. Banish the frailties of hope; wither the relenting of love; scorch the fountains of tears; curse him as only thou
15 canst curse. So shall he be accomplished in the furnace; so shall he see the things that ought not to be seen, sights that are abominable, and secrets that are unutter- able. So shall he read elder truths, sad truth, grand truths, fearful truths. So shall he rise again *before* he
20 dies. And so shall our commission be accomplished which from God we had—to plague his heart until we had unfolded the capacities of his spirit."

WILLIAM MAKEPEACE THACKERAY

NIL NISI BONUM

ALMOST the last words which Sir Walter spoke to Lockhart, his biographer, were, "Be a good man, my dear!" and with the last flicker of breath on his dying lips, he sighed a farewell to his family, and passed away blessing them. 5

Two men, famous, admired, beloved, have just left us, the Goldsmith and the Gibbon of our time. Ere a few weeks are over, many a critic's pen will be at work, reviewing their lives, and passing judgment on their works. This is no review, or history, or criticism: only 10 a word in testimony of respect and regard from a man of letters, who owes to his own professional labor the honor of becoming acquainted with these two eminent literary men. One was the first ambassador whom the New World of Letters sent to the Old. He was born almost 15 with the republic; the *pater patriæ* had laid his hand on the child's head. He bore Washington's name: he came amongst us bringing the kindest sympathy, the most artless, smiling goodwill. His new country (which some people here might be disposed to regard rather super- 20 ciliously) could send us, as he showed in his own person, a gentleman, who, though himself born in no very high sphere, was most finished, polished, easy, witty, quiet; and, socially, the equal of the most refined Europeans. If Irving's welcome in England was a kind one, was it 25 not also gratefully remembered? If he ate our salt, did he not pay us with a thankful heart? Who can calculate the amount of friendliness and good feeling for our country which this writer's generous and untiring regard for us disseminated in his own? His books are read by millions of his countrymen, whom he has taught to love England, and why to love her? It would have been easy to speak otherwise than he did: to inflame national rancors, which, at the time when he first became known as a public writer, war had just renewed: to cry down the old civilization at the expense of the new: to point out our faults, arrogance, shortcomings, and give the republic to infer how much she was the parent state's superior. There are writers enough in the United States, honest and otherwise, who preach that kind of doctrine. But the good Irving, the peaceful, the friendly, had no place for bitterness in his heart, and no scheme but kindness. Received in England with extraordinary tenderness and friendship (Scott, Southey, Byron, a hundred others have borne witness to their liking for him), he was a messenger of goodwill and peace between his country and ours. "See, friends!" he seems to say, "these English are not so wicked, rapacious, callous, proud, as you have been taught to believe them. I went amongst them a humble man; won my way by my pen; and, when known, found every hand held out to me with kindliness and welcome. Scott is a great man, you acknowledge. Did not Scott's King of England give a gold medal to him, and another to me, your countryman, and a stranger?"

Tradition in the United States still fondly retains the history of the feasts and rejoicings which awaited Irving on his return to his native country from Europe. He had a national welcome; he stammered in his speeches, hid himself in confusion, and the people loved him all the better. He had worthily represented America in

Europe. In that young community a man who brings home with him abundant European testimonials is still treated with respect (I have found American writers, of wide-world reputation, strangely solicitous about the opinions of quite obscure British critics, and elated or depressed by their judgments); and Irving went home medaled by the King, diplomatized by the University, crowned and honored and admired. He had not in any way intrigued for his honors, he had fairly won them; and, in Irving's instance, as in others, the old country was glad and eager to pay them.

In America the love and regard for Irving was a national sentiment. Party wars are perpetually raging there, and are carried on by the press with a rancor and fierceness against individuals which exceed British, almost Irish, virulence. It seemed to me, during a year's travel in the country, as if no one ever aimed a blow at Irving. All men held their hand from that harmless, friendly peacemaker. I had the good fortune to see him at New York, Philadelphia, Baltimore, and Washington,[1] and remarked how in every place he was honored and welcome. Every large city has its "Irving House." The country takes pride in the fame of its men of letters. The gate of his own charming little domain on the beautiful Hudson River was for ever swinging before visitors who came to him. He shut out no one.[2] I had seen many pictures of his house, and

[1] At Washington, Mr. Irving came to a lecture given by the writer, which Mr. Filmore and General Pierce, the President and President Elect, were also kind enough to attend together. "Two Kings of Brentford smelling at one rose," says Irving, looking up with his good-humored smile.

[2] Mr. Irving described to me, with that humor and good humor which he always kept, how, amongst other visitors, a member of the British press who had carried his distinguished pen to America (where he employed it in vilifying his own country) came to Sunny-

read descriptions of it, in both of which it was treated with a not unusual American exaggeration. It was but a pretty little cabin of a place; the gentleman of the press who took notes of the place, whilst his kind old host was 5 sleeping, might have visited the whole house in a couple of minutes.

And how came it that this house was so small, when Mr. Irving's books were sold by hundreds of thousands, nay, millions, when his profits were known to be large, 10 and the habits of life of the good old bachelor were notoriously modest and simple? He had loved once in his life. The lady he loved died; and he, whom all the world loved, never sought to replace her. I can't say how much the thought of that fidelity has touched me. 15 Does not the very cheerfulness of his after-life add to the pathos of that untold story? To grieve always was not in his nature; or, when he had his sorrow, to bring all the world in, to condole with him and bemoan it. Deep and quiet he lays the love of his heart, and buries it; and 20 grass and flowers grow over the scarred ground in due time.

Irving had such a small house and such narrow rooms, because there was a great number of people to occupy them. He could only afford to keep one old horse 25 (which, lazy and aged as it was, managed once or twice to run away with that careless old horseman). He could only afford to give plain sherry to that amiable British paragraph-monger from New York, who saw the patriarch asleep over his modest, blameless cup, and fetched the

side, introduced himself to Irving, partook of his wine and lunch-eon, and in two days described Mr. Irving, his house, his nieces, his meal, and his manner of dozing afterward, in a New York paper. On another occasion, Irving said, laughing, "Two persons came to me, and one held me in conversation whilst the other miscreant took my portrait!"

public into his private chamber to look at him. Irving could only live very modestly, because the wifeless, childless man had a number of children to whom he was as a father. He had as many as nine nieces, I am told —I saw two of these ladies at his house—with all of whom the dear old man had shared the product of his labor and genius.

"Be a good man, my dear." One can't but think of these last words of the veteran Chief of Letters, who had tasted and tested the value of wordly success, admiration, prosperity. Was Irving not good, and, of his works, was not his life the best part? In his family, gentle, generous, good-humored, affectionate, self-denying: in society, a delightful example of complete gentlemanhood; quite unspoiled by prosperity; never obsequious to the great (or, worse still, to the base and mean, as some public men are forced to be in his and other countries); eager to acknowledge every contemporary's merit; always kind and affable to the young members of his calling: in his professional bargains and mercantile dealings delicately honest and grateful; one of the most charming masters of our lighter language; the constant friend to us and our nation; to men of letters doubly dear, not for his wit and genius merely, but as an exemplar of goodness, probity, and pure life:—I don't know what sort of testimonial will be raised to him in his own country, where generous and enthusiastic acknowledgment of American merit is never wanting: but Irving was in our service as well as theirs; and as they have placed a stone at Greenwich yonder in memory of that gallant young Bellot, who shared the perils and fate of some of our Arctic seamen, I would like to hear of some memorial raised by English writers and friends of letters in affectionate remembrance of the dear and good Washington Irving.

As for the other writer, whose departure many friends, some few most dearly-loved relatives, and multitudes of admiring readers deplore, our republic has already decreed his statue, and he must have known that he had 5 earned this posthumous honor. He is not a poet and man of letters merely, but citizen, statesmen, a great British worthy. Almost from the first moment when he appears, amongst boys, amongst college students, amongst men, he is marked, and takes rank as a great 10 Englishman. All sorts of successes are easy to him: as a lad he goes down into the arena with others, and wins all the prizes to which he has a mind. A place in the senate is straightway offered to the young man. He takes his seat there; he speaks, when so minded, without 15 party anger or intrigue, but not without party faith and a sort of heroic enthusiasm for his cause. Still he is poet and philosopher even more than orator. That he may have leisure and means to pursue his darling studies, he absents himself for a while, and accepts a 20 richly remunerative post in the East. As learned a man may live in a cottage or a college common-room; but it always seemed to me that ample means and recognized rank were Macaulay's as of right. Years ago there was a wretched outcry raised because Mr. Macaulay dated a 25 letter from Windsor Castle, where he was staying. Immortal gods! Was this man not a fit guest for any palace in the world? or a fit companion for any man or woman in it? I dare say, after Austerlitz, the old K. K. court officials and footmen sneered at Napoleon for 30 dating from Schönbrunn. But that miserable "Windsor Castle" outcry is an echo out of fast-retreating old-world remembrances. The place of such a natural chief was amongst the first of the land; and that country is best, according to our British notion at least, where the man of eminence has the best chance of investing his genius and intellect.

If a company of giants were got together, very likely one or two of the mere six-feet-six people might be angry at the incontestable superiority of the very tallest of the party: and so I have heard some London wits, rather peevish at Macaulay's superiority, complain that he occupied too much of the talk, and so forth. Now that wonderful tongue is to speak no more, will not many a man grieve that he no longer has the chance to listen? To remember the talk is to wonder: to think not only of the treasures he had in his memory, but of the trifles he had stored there, and could produce with equal readiness. Almost on the last day I had the fortune to see him, a conversation happened suddenly to spring up about senior wranglers, and what they had done in after-life. To the almost terror of the persons present, Macaulay began with the senior wrangler of 1801-2-3-4, and so on, giving the name of each, and relating his subsequent career and rise. Every man who has known him has his story regarding that astonishing memory. It may be that he was not ill pleased that you should recognize it; but to those prodigious intellectual feats, which were so easy to him, who would grudge his tribute of homage? His talk was, in a word, admirable, and we admired it.

Of the notices which have appeared regarding Lord Macaulay, up to the day when the present lines are written (the 9th of January), the reader should not deny himself the pleasure of looking especially at two. It is a good sign of the times when such articles as these (I mean the articles in the *Times* and *Saturday Review*) appear in our public prints about our public men. They educate us, as it were, to admire rightly. An uninstructed person in a museum or at a concert may pass by without recognizing a picture or a passage of music, which the connoisseur by his side may show him is a masterpiece of harmony, or a wonder of artistic skill. After reading these papers you like and respect more the person 5 you have admired so much already. And so with regard to Macaulay's style there may be faults of course— what critic can't point them out? But for the nonce we are not talking about faults: we want to say *nil nisi bonum*. Well—take at hazard any three pages of the 10 *Essays* or *History;*—and, glimmering below the stream of the narrative, as it were, you, an average reader, see one, two, three, a half-score of allusions to other historic facts, characters, literature, poetry, with which you are acquainted. Why is this epithet used? Whence is 15 that simile drawn? How does he manage, in two or three words to paint an individual, or to indicate a landscape? Your neighbor, who has *his* reading, and his little stock of literature stowed away in his mind, shall detect more points, allusions, happy touches, indicating 20 not only the prodigious memory and vast learning of this master, but the wonderful industry, the honest, humble previous toil of this great scholar. He reads twenty books to write a sentence: he travels a hundred miles to make a line of description.

25   Many Londoners—not all—have seen the British Museum Library. I speak *à coeur ouvert*, and pray the kindly reader to bear with me. I have seen all sorts of domes of Peters and Pauls, Sophia, Pantheon,—what not?—and have been struck by none of them so much as 30 by that catholic dome in Bloomsbury, under which our million volumes are housed. What peace, what love, what truth, what beauty, what happiness for all, what generous kindness for you and me, are here spread out! It seems to me one cannot sit down in that place without

a heart full of grateful reverence. I own to have said my grace at the table, and to have thanked heaven for this my English birthright, freely to partake of these bountiful books, and to speak the truth I find there. Under the dome which held Macaulay's brain, and from which his solemn eyes looked out on the world but a fortnight since, what a vast, brilliant, and wonderful store of learning was ranged! what strange lore would he not fetch for you at your bidding! A volume of law, or history, a book of poetry familiar or forgotten (except by himself who forgot nothing), a novel ever so old, and he had it at hand. I spoke to him once about *Clarissa*. "Not read *Clarissa!*" he cried out. "If you have once thoroughly entered on *Clarissa* and are infected by it, you can't leave it. When I was in India I passed one hot season at the hills, and there were the Governor-General, and the Secretary of Government, and the Commander-in-Chief, and their wives. I had *Clarissa* with me: and, as soon as they began to read, the whole station was in a passion of excitement about Miss Harlowe and her misfortunes, and her scoundrelly Lovelace! The Governor's wife seized the book, and the Secretary waited for it, and the Chief Justice could not read it for tears!" He acted the whole scene: he paced up and down the Athenæum library: I daresay he could have spoken pages of the book—of that book, and of what countless piles of others!

In this little paper let us keep to the text of *nil nisi bonum*. One paper I have read regarding Lord Macaulay says "he had no heart." Why, a man's books may not always speak the truth, but they speak his mind in spite of himself; and it seems to me this man's heart is beating through every page he penned. He is always in a storm of revolt and indignation against wrong, craft,

tyranny.   How he cheers heroic resistance; how he backs
and applauds freedom struggling for its own; how he
hates scoundrels, ever so victorious and successful; how
he recognizes genius, though selfish villains possess it!
5 The critic who says Macaulay had no heart might say
that Johnson had none; and two men more generous,
and more loving, and more hating, and more partial,
and more noble, do not live in our history.   Those
who knew Lord Macaulay knew how admirably tender
10 and generous,[1] and affectionate he was.   It was not his
business to bring his family before the theater footlights,
and call for bouquets from the gallery as he wept over
them.

If any young man of letters reads this little sermon—
15 and to him, indeed, it is addressed—I would say to him,
"Bear Scott's words in your mind, and 'be good, my
dear.'"   Here are two literary men gone to their account,
and, *laus Deo*, as far as we know, it is fair, and open, and
clean.   Here is no need of apologies for shortcomings, or
20 explanations of vices which would have been virtues but
for unavoidable etc.   Here are two examples of men
most differently gifted: each pursuing his calling; each
speaking his truth as God bade him; each honest in his
life; just and irreproachable in his dealings; dear to his
25 friends; honored by his country; beloved at his fireside.
It has been the fortunate lot of both to give incalculable
happiness and delight to the world, which thanks them
in return with an immense kindliness, respect, affection.
It may not be our chance, brother scribe, to be endowed
30 with such merit, or rewarded with such fame.   But
the rewards of these men are rewards paid to *our service*.

[1] Since the above was written, I have been informed that it has
been found, on examining Lord Macaulay's papers, that he was in
the habit of giving away *more than a fourth part* of his annual
income.

We may not win the bâton or epaulettes; but God give us strength to guard the honor of the flag!

DE FINIBUS

WHEN Swift was in love with Stella, and dispatching her a letter from London thrice a month by the Irish packet, you may remember how he would begin letter No. XXIII., we will say, on the very day when XXII. had been sent away, stealing out of the coffee-house or the assembly so as to be able to prattle with his dear; "never letting go her kind hand, as it were," as some commentator or other has said in speaking of the Dean and his amour. When Mr. Johnson, walking to Dodsley's, and touching the posts in Pall Mall as he walked, forgot to pat the head of one of them, he went back and imposed his hands on it—impelled I know not by what superstition. I have this I hope not dangerous mania too. As soon as a piece of work is out of hand, and before going to sleep, I like to begin another: it may be to write only half-a-dozen lines: but that is something toward Number the Next. The printer's boy has not yet reached Green Arbour Court with the copy. Those people who were alive half an hour since, Pendennis, Clive Newcome, and (what do you call him? what was the name of the last hero? I remember now!) Philip Firmin, have hardly drunk their glass of wine, and the mammas have only this minute got the children's cloaks on, and have been bowed out of my premises—and here I come back to the study again: *tamen usque recurro.* How lonely it looks now all these people are gone! My dear good friends, some folks are utterly tired of you, and say, "What a poverty of friends the man has! He is always asking us to meet those Pendennises, Newcomes, and so forth. Why does he not introduce us to some new characters? Why is he not thrilling like Twostars, learned and profound like Threestars, exquisitely humorous and human like Fourstars? Why, finally, is he not somebody else?" My good people, it is not 5 only impossible to please you all, but it is absurd to try. The dish which one man devours, another dislikes. Is the dinner of to-day not to your taste? Let us hope to-morrow's entertainment will be more agreeable. * *

I resume my original subject. What an odd, pleasant, 10 humorous, melancholy feeling it is to sit in the study, alone and quiet, now all these people are gone who have been boarding and lodging with me for twenty months! They have interrupted my rest: they have plagued me at all sorts of minutes: they have thrust themselves upon 15 me when I was ill, or wished to be idle, and I have growled out a "Be hanged to you, can't you leave me alone now?" Once or twice they have prevented my going out to dinner. Many and many a time they have prevented my coming home, because I knew they were there waiting in the 20 study, and a plague take them! and I have left home and family, and gone to dine at the Club, and told nobody where I went. They have bored me, those people. They have plagued me at all sorts of uncomfortable hours. They have made such a disturbance in my mind and 25 house, that sometimes I have hardly known what was going on in my family, and scarcely have heard what my neighbor said to me. They are gone at last; and you would expect me to be at ease? Far from it. I should almost be glad if Woolcomb would walk in and talk to 30 me; or Twysden reappear, take his place in that chair opposite me, and begin one of his tremendous stories.

Madmen, you know, see visions, hold conversations with, even draw the likeness of, people invisible to you and me. Is this making of people out of fancy madness?

and are novel-writers at all entitled to strait-waistcoats?
I often forget people's names in life; and in my own stories contritely own that I make dreadful blunders regarding them; but I declare, my dear sir, with respect to the
personages introduced into your humble servant's fables, 5
I know the people utterly—I know the sound of their
voices. A gentleman came in to see me the other day,
who was so like the picture of Philip Firmin in Mr.
Walker's charming drawings in the *Cornhill Magazine*,
that he was quite a curiosity to me. The same eyes, 10
beard, shoulders, just as you have seen them from month
to month. Well, he is not like the Philip Firmin in my
mind. Asleep, asleep in the grave, lies the bold, the
generous, the reckless, the tender-hearted creature whom
I have made to pass through those adventures which have 15
just been brought to an end. It is years since I heard
the laughter ringing, or saw the bright blue eyes. When
I knew him both were young. I become young as I
think of him. And this morning he was alive again in
this room, ready to laugh, to fight, to weep. As I write, 20
do you know, it is the grey of evening; the house is quiet;
everybody is out; the room is getting a little dark, and
I look rather wistfully up from the paper with perhaps
ever so little fancy that HE MAY COME IN.———
No? No movement. No grey shade, growing more 25
palpable, out of which at last look the well-known eyes.
No, the printer came and took him away with the last
page of the proofs. And with the printer's boy did the
whole cortège of ghosts flit away, invisible? Ha! stay!
what is this? Angels and ministers of grace! The door 30
opens, and a dark form—enters, bearing a black—a
black suit of clothes. It is John. He says it is time to
dress for dinner.

*　　　*　　　*　　　*　　　*　　　*

Every man who has had his German tutor, and has been coached through the famous *Faust* of Goethe (thou wert my instructor, good old Weissenborn, and these eyes beheld the great master himself in dear little Weimar
5 town!) has read those charming verses which are prefixed to the drama, in which the poet reverts to the time when his work was first composed, and recalls the friends now departed, who once listened to his song. The dear shadows rise up around him, he says; he lives in the past
10 again. It is to-day which appears vague and visionary. We humbler writers cannot create Fausts, or raise up monumental works that shall endure for all ages; but our books are diaries, in which our own feelings must of necessity be set down. As we look to the page written
15 last month, or ten years ago, we remember the day and its events: the child ill, mayhap, in the adjoining room, and the doubts and fears which racked the brain as it still pursued its work; the dear old friend who read the commencement of the tale, and whose gentle hand shall
20 be laid in ours no more. I own for my part that, in reading pages which this hand penned formerly, I often lose sight of the text under my eyes. It is not the words I see; but that past day; that bygone page of life's history; that tragedy, comedy it may be, which our little home
25 company was enacting; that merry-making which we shared; that funeral which we followed; that bitter, bitter grief which we buried.

And, such being the state of my mind, I pray gentle readers to deal kindly with their humble servant's mani-
30 fold shortcomings, blunders, and slips of memory. As sure as I read a page of my own composition, I find a fault or two, half-a-dozen. Jones is called Brown. Brown, who is dead, is brought to life. Aghast, and months after the number was printed, I saw that I had

called Philip Firmin, Clive Newcome. Now Clive Newcome is the hero of another story by the reader's most
obedient writer. The two men are as different, in my
mind's eye, as—as Lord Palmerston and Mr. Disraeli
let us say. But there is that blunder at page 990, line 5
76, volume 84 of the *Cornhill Magazine*, and it is past
mending; and I wish in my life I had made no worse
blunders or errors than that which is hereby acknowledged.

Another Finis written. Another mile-stone passed
on this journey from birth to the next world! Sure it is 10
a subject for solemn cogitation. Shall we continue this
story-telling business and be voluble to the end of our
age? Will it not be presently time, O prattler, to hold
your tongue, and let younger people speak? I have a
friend, a painter, who, like other persons who shall be 15
nameless, is growing old. He has never painted with
such laborious finish as his works now show. This
master is still the most humble and diligent of scholars.
Of Art, his mistress, he is always an eager, reverent pupil.
In his calling, in yours, in mine, industry and humility 20
will help and comfort us. A word with you. In a
pretty large experience, I have not found the men who
write books superior in wit or learning to those who don't
write at all. In regard of mere information, non-writers
must often be superior to writers. You don't expect a 25
lawyer in full practice to be conversant with all kinds of
literature; he is too busy with his law; and so a writer is
commonly too busy with his own books to be able to bestow attention on the works of other people. After a
day's work (in which I have been depicting, let us say, 30
the agonies of Louisa on parting with the Captain, or the
atrocious behavior of the wicked Marquis to Lady Emily)
I march to the Club, proposing to improve my mind and
keep myself "posted up," as the Americans phrase it, with

the literature of the day. And what happens? Given,
a walk after luncheon, a pleasing book, and a most comfortable arm-chair by the fire, and you know the rest. A
doze ensues. Pleasing book drops suddenly, is picked
5 up once with an air of some confusion, is laid presently
softly in lap: head falls on comfortable arm-chair cushion:
eyes close: soft nasal music is heard. Am I telling Club
secrets? Of afternoons, after lunch, I say, scores of sensible fogies have a doze. Perhaps I have fallen asleep
10 over that very book to which "Finis" has just been
written. "And if the writer sleeps, what happens to
the readers?" says Jones, coming down upon me with
his lightning wit. What? You *did* sleep over it? And
a very good thing too. These eyes have more than
15 once seen a friend dozing over pages which this hand
has written. There is a vignette somewhere in one of
my books of a friend so caught napping with *Pendennis*,
or the *Newcomes*, in his lap; and if a writer can give you a
sweet, soothing, harmless sleep, has he not done you a
20 kindness? So is the author who excites and interests
you worthy of your thanks and benedictions. I am
troubled with fever and ague, that seizes me at odd intervals and prostrates me for a day. There is cold fit,
for which, I am thankful to say, hot brandy-and-water is
25 prescribed, and this induces hot fit, and so on. In one
or two of these fits I have read novels with the most fearful contentment of mind. Once, on the Mississippi, it was
my dearly beloved *Jacob Faithful:* once at Frankfort O.
M., the delightful *Vingt Ans Après* of Monsieur Dumas:
30 once at Tunbridge Wells, the thrilling *Woman in White:*
and these books gave me amusement from morning till
sunset. I remember those ague fits with a great deal of
pleasure and gratitude. Think of a whole day in bed,
and a good novel for a companion! No cares: no remorse

about idleness: no visitors: and the Woman in White or the Chevalier d'Artagnan to tell me stories from dawn to night! "Please, ma'am, my master's compliments, and can he have the third volume?" (This message was sent to an astonished friend and neighbor, who lent me, volume by volume, the *W. in W.*) How do you like your novels? I like mine strong, "hot with," and no mistake: no love-making: no observations about society: little dialogue, except where the characters are bullying each other: plenty of fighting: and a villain in the cupboard, who is to suffer tortures just before Finis. I don't like your melancholy Finis. I never read the history of a consumptive heroine twice. If I might give a short hint to an impartial writer (as the *Examiner* used to say in old days), it would be to act, *not* à la mode le pays de Pole (I think that was the phraseology), but *always* to give quarter. In the story of Philip, just come to an end, I have the permission of the author to state that he was going to drown the two villains of the piece—a certain Doctor F—— and a certain Mr. T. H—— on board the *President,* or some other tragic ship—but you see I relented. I pictured to myself Firmin's ghastly face amid the crowd of shuddering people on that reeling deck in the lonely ocean, and thought, "Thou ghastly lying wretch, thou shalt not be drowned: thou shalt have a fever only; a knowledge of thy danger; and a chance—ever so small a chance—of repentance." I wonder whether he *did* repent when he found himself in the yellow-fever, in Virginia? The probability is, he fancied that his son had injured him very much, and forgave him on his death-bed. Do you imagine there is a great deal of genuine right-down remorse in the world? Don't people rather find excuses which make their minds easy; endeavor to prove to themselves that they have been lamentably

belied and misunderstood; and try and forgive the per-
secutors who *will* present that bill when it is due; and not
bear malice against the cruel ruffian who takes them to
the police-office for stealing the spoons?   Years ago I had
a quarrel with a certain well-known person (I believed
a statement regarding him which his friends imparted to
me, and which turned out to be quite incorrect).   To his
dying day that quarrel was never quite made up.   I said
to his brother, "Why is your brother's soul still dark
against me?   It is I who ought to be angry and unfor-
giving: for I was in the wrong."   In the region which they
now inhabit (for Finis has been set to the volumes of the
lives of both here below), if they take any cognizance of
our squabbles, and tittle-tattles, and gossips on earth
here, I hope they admit that my little error was not of a
nature unpardonable.   If you have never committed a
worse, my good sir, surely the score against you will not
be heavy.   Ha, *dilectissimi fratres!*   It is in regard of sins
not found out that we may say or sing (in an undertone,
in a most penitent and lugubrious minor key), *Miserere
nobis miseris peccatoribus.*

Among the sins of commission which novel-writers not
seldom perpetrate, is the sin of grandiloquence, or tall-
talking, against which, for my part, I will offer up a special *libera me*.   This is the sin of schoolmasters, govern-
esses, critics, sermoners, and instructors of young or old
people.   Nay (for I am making a clean breast, and
liberating my soul), perhaps of all the novel-spinners now
extant, the present speaker is the most addicted to
preaching.   Does he not stop perpetually in his story and
begin to preach to you?   When he ought to be engaged
with business, is he not forever taking the Muse by the
sleeve, and plaguing her with some of his cynical sermons?
I cry *peccavi* loudly and heartily.   I tell you I would like

to be able to write a story which should show no egotism whatever—in which there should be no reflections, no cynicism, no vulgarity (and so forth), but an incident in every other page, a villain, a battle, a mystery in every chapter. I should like to be able to feed a reader so spi- cily as to leave him hungering and thirsting for more at the end of every monthly meal.

Alexandre Dumas describes himself, when inventing the plan of a work, as lying silent on his back for two whole days on the deck of a yacht in a Mediterranean port. At the end of the two days he arose and called for dinner. In those two days he had built his plot. He had moulded a mighty clay, to be cast presently in per- ennial brass. The chapters, the characters, the incidents, the combinations were all arranged in the artist's brain ere he set a pen to paper. My Pegasus won't fly, so as to let me survey the field below me. He has no wings, he is blind of one eye certainly, he is restive, stubborn, slow; crops a hedge when he ought to be galloping, or gallops when he ought to be quiet. He never will show off when I want him. Sometimes he goes at a pace which surprises me. Sometimes, when I most wish him to make the running, the brute turns restive, and I am obliged to let him take his own time. I wonder do other novel- writers experience this fatalism? They *must* go a cer- tain way, in spite of themselves. I have been surprised at the observations made by some of my characters. It seems as if an occult Power was moving the pen. The personage does or says something, and I ask, how the dickens did he come to think of that? Every man has remarked in dreams, the vast dramatic power which is sometimes evinced; I won't say the surprising power, for nothing does surprise you in dreams. But those strange characters you meet make instant observations of which you never can have thought previously. In like manner, the imagination foretells things. We spake anon of the inflated style of some writers. What also if there is an *afflated* style—when a writer is like a Pythoness on her 5 oracle tripod, and mighty words, words which he cannot help, come blowing, and bellowing, and whistling, and moaning through the speaking pipes of his bodily organ? I have told you it was a very queer shock to me the other day when, with a letter of introduction in his hand, the 10 artist's (not my) Philip Firmin walked into this room, and sat down in the chair opposite. In the novel of *Pendennis*, written ten years ago, there is an account of a certain Costigan, whom I had invented (as I suppose authors invent their personages out of scraps, heel-taps, odds 15 and ends of characters). I was smoking in a tavern parlor one night—and this Costigan came into the room alive—the very man:—the most remarkable resemblance of the printed sketches of the man, of the rude drawings in which I had depicted him. He had 20 the same little coat, the same battered hat, cocked on one eye, the same twinkle in that eye. "Sir," said I, knowing him to be an old friend whom I had met in unknown regions, "Sir," I said, "may I offer you a glass of brandy-and-water?" "*Bedad, ye may,*" says 25 he, "*and I'll sing ye a song tu.*" Of course he spoke with an Irish brogue. Of course he had been in the army. In ten minutes he pulled out an Army Agent's account, whereon his name was written. A few months after we read of him in a police court. How had I come to know 30 him, to divine him? Nothing shall convince me that I have not seen that man in the world of spirits. In the world of spirits and water I know I did: but that is a mere quibble of words. I was not surprised when he spoke in an Irish brogue. I had had cognizance of him before somehow. Who has not felt that little shock which arises when a person, a place, some words in a book (there is always a collocation) present themselves to you, and you know that you have before met the same person, words, scene, and so forth?

They used to call the good Sir Walter the "Wizard of the North." What if some writer should appear who can write so *enchantingly* that he shall be able to call into actual life the people whom he invents? What if Mignon, and Margaret, and Goetz von Berlichingen are alive now (though I don't say they are visible), and Dugald Dalgetty and Ivanhoe were to step in at that open window by the little garden yonder? Suppose Uncas and our noble old Leather Stocking were to glide silent in? Suppose Athos, Porthos, and Aramis should enter with a noiseless swagger, curling their moustaches? And dearest Amelia Booth, on Uncle Toby's arm; and Tittlebat Titmouse, with his hair dyed green; and all the Crummles company of comedians, with the Gil Blas troop; and Sir Roger de Coverley; and the greatest of all crazy gentlemen, the Knight of La Mancha, with his blessed squire? I say to you, I look rather wistfully toward the window, musing upon these people. Were any of them to enter, I think I should not be very much frightened. Dear old friends, what pleasant hours I have had with them! We do not see each other very often, but when we do, we are ever happy to meet. I had a capital half hour with Jacob Faithful last night; when the last sheet was corrected, when "Finis" had been written, and the printer's boy, with the copy, was safe in Green Arbor Court.

So you are gone, little printer's boy, with the last scratches and corrections on the proof, and a fine flourish by way of Finis at the story's end. The last corrections? I say those last corrections seem never to be finished. A plague upon the weeds! Every day, when I walk in my own little literary garden-plot, I spy some, and should like to have a spud, and root them out. Those idle words, neighbor, are past remedy. That turning back to the 5 old pages produces anything but elation of mind. Would you not pay a pretty fine to be able to cancel some of them? Oh, the sad old pages, the dull old pages! Oh, the cares, the *ennui*, the squabbles, the repetitions, the old conversations over and over again! But now and 10 again a kind thought is recalled, and now and again a dear memory. Yet a few chapters more, and then the last: after which, behold Finis itself come to an end, and the Infinite begun.

RALPH WALDO EMERSON

MANNERS

"How near to good is what is fair!
    Which we no sooner see,
But with the lines and outward air
    Our senses taken be.

 Again yourselves compose,   5
And now put all the aptness on
    Of Figure, that Proportion
        Or Color can disclose;
That if those silent arts were lost,
Design and Picture, they might boast 10
        From you a newer ground,
Instructed by the heightening sense
    Of dignity and reverence
        In their true motions found."

        BEN JONSON. 15

HALF the world, it is said, knows not how the other
half lives. Our Exploring Expedition saw the Feejee
islanders getting their dinner off human bones; and
they are said to eat their own wives and children.
The husbandry of the modern inhabitants of Gournou 20
(west of old Thebes) is philosophical to a fault. To set
up their housekeeping, nothing is requisite but two or
three earthen pots, a stone to grind meal, and a mat
which is the bed. The house, namely, a tomb, is ready
without rent or taxes. No rain can pass through the 25
roof, and there is no door, for there is no want of one, as
there is nothing to lose. If the house do not please

215

them, they walk out and enter another, as there are several hundreds at their command. "It is somewhat singular," adds Belzoni, to whom we owe this account, "to talk of happiness among people who live in sep-
5 ulchers, among the corpses and rags of an ancient nation which they know nothing of." In the deserts of Borgoo, the rock-Tibboos still dwell in caves, like cliff swallows, and the language of these negroes is compared by their neighbors to the shrieking of bats, and to the whistling
10 of birds. Again, the Bornoos have no proper names; individuals are called after their height, thickness, or other accidental quality, and have nicknames merely. But the salt, the dates, the ivory, and the gold, for which these horrible regions are visited, find their way into
15 countries, where the purchaser and consumer can hardly be ranked in one race with these cannibals and man-stealers: countries where man serves himself with metals, wood, stone, glass, gum, cotton, silk, and wool; honors himself with architecture; writes laws, and contrives to
20 execute his will through the hands of many nations; and especially establishes a select society, running through all the countries of intelligent men, a self-constituted aris-tocracy, or fraternity of the best, which, without written law, or exact usage of any kind, perpetuates itself, colo-
25 nizes every new-planted island, and adopts and makes its own, whatever personal beauty or extraordinary native endowment anywhere appears.

What fact more conspicuous in modern history than the creation of the gentleman? Chivalry is that, and
30 loyalty is that, and, in English literature, half the drama, and all the novels, from Sir Philip Sidney to Sir Walter Scott, paint this figure. The word *gentleman*, which, like the word *Christian*, must hereafter characterize the present and the few preceding centuries, by the impor-

tance attached to it, is a homage to personal and incommunicable properties. Frivolous and fantastic additions have got associated with the name, but the steady interest of mankind in it must be attributed to the valuable properties which it designated. An element which unites all the most forcible persons of every country, makes them intelligible and agreeable to each other, and is somewhat so precise that it is at once felt if an individual lack the masonic sign, cannot be any casual product, but must be an average result of the character and faculties universally found in men. It seems a certain permanent average; as the atmosphere is a permanent composition, whilst so many gases are combined only to be decompounded. *Comme il faut*, is the Frenchman's description of good society, *as we must be*. It is a spontaneous fruit of talents and feelings of precisely that class who have most vigor, who take the lead in the world of this hour, and, though far from pure, far from constituting the gladdest and highest tone of human feeling, is as good as the whole society permits it to be. It is made of the spirit, more than of the talent of men, and is a compound result, into which every great force enters as an ingredient, namely, virtue, wit, beauty, wealth, and power.

There is something equivocal in all the words in use to express the excellence of manners and social cultivation, because the quantities are fluxional, and the last effect is assumed by the senses as the cause. The word *gentleman* has not any correlative abstract to express the quality. *Gentility* is mean, and *gentilesse* is obsolete. But we must keep alive in the vernacular the distinction between *fashion*, a word of narrow and often sinister meaning, and the heroic character which the gentleman imports. The usual words, however, must be respected: they will be found to contain the root of the matter.

The point of distinction in all this class of names, as
courtesy, chivalry, fashion, and the like, is, that the flower
and the fruit, not the grain of the tree, are contemplated.
It is beauty which is the aim this time, and not worth.
5 The result is now in question, although our words intimate well enough the popular feeling, that the appearance supposes a substance. The gentleman is a man of
truth, lord of his own actions, and expressing that lordship in his behavior, not in any manner dependent and
10 servile, either on persons, or opinions, or possessions.
Beyond this fact of truth and real force, the word denotes
good-nature or benevolence: manhood first, and then
gentleness. The popular notion certainly adds a condition of ease and fortune. But that is a natural result
15 of personal force and love, that they should possess and
dispense the goods of the world. In times of violence,
every eminent person must fall in with many opportunities to approve his stoutness and worth; therefore, every
man's name that emerged at all from the mass in the
20 feudal ages, rattles in our ear like a flourish of trumpets.
But personal force never goes out of fashion. That is
still paramount to-day, and, in the moving crowd of good
society, the men of valor and reality are known, and
rise to their natural place. The competition is trans-
25 ferred from war to politics and trade, but the personal
force appears readily enough in these new arenas.

Power first, or no leading class. In politics and in
trade, bruisers and pirates are of better promise than
talkers and clerks. God knows that all sorts of gentle-
30 men knock at the door; but whenever used in strictness
and with any emphasis, the name will be found to point
at original energy. It describes a man standing in his
own right, and working after untaught methods. In a
good lord, there must first be a good animal, at least to

the extent of yielding the incomparable advantage of animal spirits. The ruling class must have more, but they must have these, giving in every company the sense of power, which makes things easy to be done which daunt the wise. The society of the energetic class, in their friendly and festive meetings, is full of courage, and of attempts, which intimidate the pale scholar. The courage which girls exhibit is like the battle of Lundy's Lane, or a sea-fight. The intellect relies on memory to make some supplies to face these extemporaneous squadrons. But memory is a base mendicant with basket and badge, in the presence of these sudden masters. The rulers of society must be up to the work of the world, and equal to their versatile office: men of the right Cæsarian pattern, who have great range of affinity. I am far from believing the timid maxim of Lord Falkland ("that for ceremony there must go two to it; since a bold fellow will go through the cunningest forms"), and am of opinion that the gentleman is the bold fellow whose forms are not to be broken through; and only that plenteous nature is rightful master, which is the complement of whatever person it converses with. My gentleman gives the law where he is; he will out-pray saints in chapel, out-general veterans in the field, and outshine all courtesy in the hall. He is good company for pirates, and good with academicians; so that it is useless to fortify yourself against him; he has the private entrance to all minds, and I could as easily exclude myself as him. The famous gentlemen of Asia and Europe have been of the strong type: Saladin, Sapor, the Cid, Julius Cæsar, Scipio, Alexander, Pericles, and the lordliest personages. They sat very carelessly in their chairs, and were too excellent themselves, to value any condition at a high rate.

A plentiful fortune is reckoned necessary, in the popular judgment, to the completion of this man of the world: and it is a material deputy which walks through the dance which the first has led. Money is not essen-
5 tial, but this wide affinity is, which transcends the habits of clique and caste, and makes itself felt by men of all classes. If the aristocrat is only valid in fashionable circles, and not with truckmen, he will never be a leader in fashion; and if the man of the people cannot speak
10 on equal terms with the gentleman, so that the gentleman shall perceive that he is already really of his own order, he is not to be feared. Diogenes, Socrates, and Epaminondas, are gentlemen of the best blood, who have chosen the condition of poverty, when that of
15 wealth was equally open to them. I use these old names, but the men I speak of are my contemporaries. Fortune will not supply to every generation one of these well-appointed knights, but every collection of men furnishes some example of the class: and the politics of this
20 country, and the trade of every town, are controlled by these hardy and irresponsible doers, who have invention to take the lead, and a broad sympathy which puts them in fellowship with crowds, and makes their action popular.
25 The manners of this class are observed and caught with devotion by men of taste. The association of these masters with each other, and with men intelligent of their merits, is mutually agreeable and stimulating. The good forms, the happiest expressions of each, are re-
30 peated and adopted. By swift consent, everything superfluous is dropped, everything graceful is renewed. Fine manners show themselves formidable to the uncultivated man. They are a subtler science of defence to parry and intimidate; but once matched by the skill of

the other party, they drop the point of the sword—
points and fences disappear, and the youth finds himself
in a more transparent atmosphere, wherein life is a less
troublesome game, and not a misunderstanding arises
between the players. Manners aim to facilitate life, to
get rid of impediments, and bring the man pure to energize. They aid our dealings and conversation, as a
railway aids traveling, by getting rid of all avoidable
obstructions of the road, and leaving nothing to be conquered but pure space. These forms very soon become
fixed, and a fine sense of propriety is cultivated with the
more heed, that it becomes a badge of social and civil
distinctions. Thus grows up Fashion, an equivocal
semblance, the most puissant, the most fantastic and
frivolous, the most feared and followed, and which
morals and violence assault in vain.

There exists a strict relation between the class of
power, and the exclusive and polished circles. The last
are always filled or filling from the first. The strong
men usually give some allowance even to the petulances
of fashion, for that affinity they find in it. Napoleon,
child of the revolution, destroyer of the old noblesse,
never ceased to court the Faubourg St. Germain: doubtless with the feeling, that fashion is a homage to men of
his stamp. Fashion, though in a strange way, represents all manly virtue. It is virtue gone to seed: it is
a kind of posthumous honor. It does not often caress
the great, but the children of the great: it is a hall of the
Past. It usually sets its face against the great of this
hour. Great men are not commonly in its halls: they
are absent in the field: they are working, not triumph-
ing. Fashion is made up of their children; of those,
who through the value and virtue of somebody, have
acquired luster to their name, marks of distinction, means

of cultivation and generosity, and, in their physical organization, a certain health and excellence which secures to them, if not the highest power to work, yet high power to enjoy. The class of power, the working
5 heroes, the Cortez, the Nelson, the Napoleon, see that this is the festivity and permanent celebration of such as they; that fashion is funded talent; is Mexico, Marengo and Trafalgar, beaten out thin; that the brilliant names of fashion run back to just such busy names as their
10 own, fifty or sixty years ago. They are the sowers, their sons shall be the reapers, and *their* sons, in the ordinary course of things, must yield the possession of the harvest to new competitors with keener eyes and stronger frames. The city is recruited from the country. In
15 the year 1805, it is said, every legitimate monarch in Europe was imbecile. The city would have died out, rotted, and exploded long ago, but that it was reinforced from the fields. It is only country which came to town day before yesterday, that is city and court to-day.
20 Aristocracy and fashion are certain inevitable results. These mutual selections are indestructible. If they provoke anger in the least favored class, and the excluded majority revenge themselves on the excluding minority, by the strong hand, and kill them, at once a new class
25 finds itself at the top, as certainly as cream rises in a bowl of milk: and if the people should destroy class after class, until two men only were left, one of these would be the leader, and would be involuntarily served and copied by the other. You may keep this minority out
30 of sight and out of mind, but it is tenacious of life, and is one of the estates of the realm. I am the more struck with this tenacity, when I seek its work. It respects the administration of such unimportant matters, that we should not look for any durability in its rule. We

sometimes meet men under some strong moral influence,
as, a patriotic, a literary, a religious movement, and feel
that the moral sentiment rules man and nature. We
think all other distinctions and ties will be slight and
fugitive, this of caste or fashion, for example; yet come 5
from year to year, and see how permanent that is, in
this Boston or New York life of man, where, too, it has
not the least countenance from the law of the land.
Not in Egypt or in India, a firmer or more impassable
line. Here are associations whose ties go over, and under 10
and through it, a meeting of merchants, a military
corps, a college-class, a fire-club, a professional association, a political, a religious convention;—the persons
seem to draw inseparably near; yet, that assembly once
dispersed, its members will not in the year meet again. 15
Each returns to his degree in the scale of good society,
porcelain remains porcelain, and earthen earthen. The
objects of fashion may be frivolous, or fashion may be
objectless, but the nature of this union and selection
can be neither frivolous nor accidental. Each man's 20
rank in that perfect graduation depends on some symmetry in his structure, or some agreement in his structure to the symmetry of society. Its doors unbar in-
stantaneously to a natural claim of their own kind. A
natural gentleman finds his way in, and will keep the 25
oldest patrician out, who has lost his intrinsic rank.
Fashion understands itself; good breeding of every
country and personal superiority readily fraternize with
that of every other. The chiefs of savage tribes have
distinguished themselves in London and Paris, by the 30
purity of their tournure.

To say what good of fashion we can—it rests on
reality, and hates nothing so much as pretenders;—to
exclude and mystify pretenders, and send them into

everlasting "Coventry," is its delight. We contemn, in
turn, every other gift of men of the world; but the habit
even in little and the least matters, of not appealing
to any but our own sense of propriety, constitutes the
5 foundation of all chivalry. There is almost no kind of
self-reliance, so it be sane and proportioned, which fashion
does not occasionally adopt, and give it the freedom of
its saloons. A sainted soul is always elegant, and, if it
will, passes unchallenged into the most guarded ring.
10 But so will Jock the teamster pass, in some crisis that
brings him thither, and find favor, as long as his head is
not giddy with the new circumstance, and the iron shoes
do not wish to dance in waltzes and cotillions. For there
is nothing settled in manners, but the laws of behavior
15 yield to the energy of the individual. The maiden at
her first ball, the countryman at a city dinner, believes
that there is a ritual according to which every act and
compliment must be performed, or the failing party must
be cast out of this presence. Later, they learn that good
20 sense and character make their own forms every moment,
and speak or abstain, take wine or refuse it, stay or go,
sit in a chair or sprawl with children on the floor, or
stand on their head, or what else soever, in a new and
aboriginal way: and that strong will is always in fashion,
25 let who will be unfashionable. All that fashion demands
is composure, and self-content. A circle of men perfectly
well-bred, would be a company of sensible persons, in
which every man's native manners and character appeared. If the fashionist have not this quality, he is
30 nothing. We are such lovers of self-reliance, that we
excuse in a man many sins, if he will show us a complete
satisfaction in his position, which asks no leave to be, of
mine, or any man's good opinion. But any deference to
some eminent man or woman of the world, forfeits all

privilege of nobility. He is an underling: I have nothing to do with him; I will speak with his master. A man should not go where he cannot carry his whole sphere or society with him—not bodily, the whole circle of his friends, but atmospherically. He should preserve in a new company the same attitude of mind and reality of relation, which his daily associates draw him to, else he is shorn of his best beams, and will be an orphan in the merriest club. "If you could see Vich Ian Vohr with his tail on!——" But Vich Ian Vohr must always carry his belongings in some fashion, if not added as honor, then severed as disgrace.

There will always be in society certain persons who are Mercuries of its approbation, and whose glance will at any time determine for the curious their standing in the world. These are the chamberlains of the lesser gods. Accept their coldness as an omen of grace with the loftier deities, and allow them all their privilege. They are clear in their office, nor could they be thus formidable, without their own merits. But do not measure the importance of this class by their pretension, or imagine that a fop can be the dispenser of honor and shame. They pass also at their just rate; for how can they otherwise, in circles which exist as a sort of herald's office for the sifting of character?

As the first thing man requires of man, is reality, so, that appears in all the forms of society. We pointedly, and by name, introduce the parties to each other. Know you before all heaven and earth, that this is Andrew, and this is Gregory;—they look each other in the eye; they grasp each other's hand, to identify and signalize each other. It is a great satisfaction. A gentleman never dodges: his eyes look straight forward, and he assures the other party, first of all, that he has been met. For

what is it that we seek, in so many visits and hospitalities?
Is it your draperies, pictures, and decorations? Or do
we not insatiably ask, Was a man in the house? I may
easily go into a great household where there is much sub-
5 stance, excellent provision for comfort, luxury, and taste,
and yet not encounter there any Amphitryon, who shall
subordinate these appendages. I may go into a cottage,
and find a farmer who feels that he is the man I have
come to see, and fronts me accordingly. It was therefore
10 a very natural point of feudal etiquette, that a gentleman
who received a visit, though it were of his sovereign,
should not leave his roof, but should wait his arrival at
the door of his house. No house, though it were the
Tuileries, or the Escurial, is good for any thing without a
15 master. And yet we are not often gratified by this hospi-
tality. Every body we know surrounds himself with a
fine house, fine books, conservatory, gardens, equipage,
and all manner of toys, as screens to interpose between
himself and his guest. Does it not seem as if man was
20 of a very sly, elusive nature, and dreaded nothing so
much as a full rencontre front to front with his fellow?
It were unmerciful, I know, quite to abolish the use of
these screens, which are of eminent convenience, whether
the guest is too great, or too little. We call together
25 many friends who keep each other in play, or, by luxuries
and ornaments we amuse the young people, and guard our
retirement. Or if, perchance, a searching realist comes
to our gate, before whose eye we have no care to stand,
then again we run to our curtain, and hide as Adam at
30 the voice of the Lord God in the garden. Cardinal Cap-
rara, the Pope's legate at Paris, defended himself from
the glances of Napoleon, by an immense pair of green
spectacles. Napoleon remarked them, and speedily
managed to rally them off; and yet Napoleon, in his turn,

was not great enough with eight hundred thousand troops
at his back, to face a pair of freeborn eyes, but fenced
himself with etiquette, and within triple barriers of
reserve; and, as all the world knows from Madame de
Stael, was wont, when he found himself observed, to 5
discharge his face of all expression. But emperors and
rich men are by no means the most skilful masters of good
manners. No rent-roll nor army-list can dignify skulking
and dissimulation: and the first point of courtesy must
always be truth, as really all the forms of good-breeding 10
point that way.

I have just been reading, in Mr. Hazlitt's translation,
Montaigne's account of his journey into Italy, and am
struck with nothing more agreeably than the self-respect-
ing fashions of the time. His arrival in each place, the 15
arrival of a gentleman of France, is an event of some con- ·
sequence. Wherever he goes, he pays a visit to whatever
prince or gentleman of note resides upon his road, as a
duty to himself and to civilization. When he leaves
any house in which he has lodged for a few weeks, he 20
causes his arms to be painted and hung up as a perpetual
sign to the house, as was the custom of the gentlemen.

The complement of this graceful self-respect, and that
of all the points of good breeding I most require and
insist upon, is deference. I like that every chair should 25
be a throne, and hold a king. I prefer a tendency to
stateliness, to an excess of fellowship. Let the incommunicable objects of nature and the metaphysical isola-
tion of man teach us independence. Let us not be too
much acquainted. I would have a man enter his house 30
through a hall filled with heroic and sacred sculptures,
that he might not want the hint of tranquility and self-
poise. We should meet each morning, as from foreign
countries, and spending the day together, should depart

at night, as into foreign countries. In all things I would
have the island of a man inviolate. Let us sit apart as
the gods, talking from peak to peak all round Olympus.
No degree of affection need invade this religion. This is
5 myrrh and rosemary to keep the other sweet. Lovers
should guard their strangeness. If they forgive too
much, all slides into confusion and meanness. It is easy
to push this deference to a Chinese etiquette; but coolness and absence of heat and haste indicate fine qualities.
10 A gentleman makes no noise: a lady is serene. Pro-
portionate is our disgust at those invaders who fill a
studious house with blast or running, to secure some
paltry convenience. Not less I dislike a low sympathy
of each with his neighbor's needs. Must we have
15 good understanding with one another's palates? as
foolish people who have lived long together, know
when each wants salt or sugar. I pray my companion,
if he wishes for bread, to ask me for bread, and if he
wishes for sassafras or arsenic, to ask me for them,
20 and not to hold out his plate, as if I knew already. Every
natural function can be dignified by deliberation and
privacy. Let us leave hurry to slaves. The compliments and ceremonies of our breeding should signify,
however remotely, the recollection of the grandeur of
25 our destiny.

The flower of courtesy does not very well bide handling, but if we dare to open another leaf, and explore
what parts go to its conformation, we shall find also an
intellectual quality. To the leaders of men, the brain as
30 well as the flesh and the heart must furnish a proportion.
Defect in manners is usually the defect of fine perceptions.
Men are too coarsely made for the delicacy of beautiful
carriage and customs. It is not quite sufficient to good
breeding, a union of kindness and independence. We

imperatively require a perception of, and a homage to
beauty in our companions. Other virtues are in request
in the field and work-yard, but a certain degree of taste is
not to be spared in those we sit with. I could better eat
with one who did not respect the truth or the laws, than 5
with a sloven and unpresentable person. Moral qualities
rule the world, but at short distances, the senses are des-
potic. The same discrimination of fit and fair runs
out, if with less rigor, into all parts of life. The average
spirit of the energetic class is good sense, acting under 10
certain limitations and to certain ends. It entertains
every natural gift. Social in its nature, it respects every
thing which tends to unite men. It delights in measure.
The love of beauty is mainly the love of measure or proportion. The person who screams, or uses the super- 15
lative degree, or converses with heat, puts whole draw-
ing-rooms to flight. If you wish to be loved, love measure. You must have genius, or a prodigious usefulness,
if you will hide the want of measure. This perception
comes in to polish and perfect the parts of the social 20
instrument. Society will pardon much to genius and
special gifts, but, being in its nature a convention, it
loves what is conventional, or what belongs to coming
together. That makes the good and bad of manners,
namely, what helps or hinders the fellowship. For 25
fashion is not good sense absolute, but relative; not good
sense private, but good sense entertaining company.
It hates corners and sharp points of character, hates
quarrelsome, egotistical, solitary, and gloomy people;
hates whatever can interfere with total blending of par- 30
ties; whilst it values all peculiarities as in the highest
degree refreshing, which can consist with good fellowship.
And besides the general infusion of wit to heighten
civility, the direct splendor of intellectual power is ever

welcome in fine society as the costliest addition to its
rule and its credit.

The dry light must shine in to adorn our festival,
but it must be tempered and shaded, or that will also
5 offend. Accuracy is essential to beauty, and quick perceptions to politeness, but not too quick perceptions.
One may be too punctual and too precise. He must
leave the omniscience of business at the door, when he
comes into the palace of beauty. Society loves creole
10 natures, and sleepy, languishing manners, so that they
cover sense, grace, and good-will; the air of drowsy
strength, which disarms criticism; perhaps, because such
a person seems to reserve himself for the best of the
game, and not spend himself on surfaces; an ignoring
15 eye, which does not see the annoyances, shifts, and inconveniences that cloud the brow and smother the voice
of the sensitive.

Therefore, besides personal force and so much perception as constitutes unerring taste, society demands, in
20 its patrician class, another element already intimated,
which it significantly terms good-nature, expressing all
degrees of generosity from the lowest willingness and
faculty to oblige, up to the heights of magnanimity and
love. Insight we must have, or we shall run against one
25 another, and miss the way to our food; but intellect is
selfish and barren. The secret of success in society, is
a certain heartiness and sympathy. A man who is not
happy in the company, cannot find any word in his
memory that will fit the occasion. All his information
30 is a little impertinent. A man who is happy there, finds
in every turn of the conversation equally lucky occasions
for the introduction of that which he has to say. The
favorites of society, and what it calls *whole souls*, are
able men, and of more spirit than wit, who have no

uncomfortable egotism, who but exactly fill the hour and the company, contented and contenting, at a marriage or a funeral, a ball or a jury, a water-party or a shooting march. England, which is rich in gentlemen, furnished, in the beginning of the present century, a good model of that genius which the world loves, in Mr. Fox, who added to his great abilities the most social disposition, and real love of men. Parliamentary history has few better passages than the debate, in which Burke and Fox separated in the House of Commons; when Fox urged on his old friend the claims of old friendship with such tenderness that the house was moved to tears. Another anecdote is so close to my matter, that I must hazard the story. A tradesman who had long dunned him for a note of three hundred guineas, found him one day counting gold, and demanded payment: "No," said Fox, "I owe this money to Sheridan; it is a debt of honor: if an accident should happen to me, he has nothing to show." "Then," said the creditor, "I change my debt into a debt of honor," and tore the note in pieces. Fox thanked the man for his confidence, and paid him, saying, "his debt was of older standing, and Sheridan must wait." Lover of liberty, friend of the Hindoo, friend of the African slave, he possessed a great personal popularity; and Napoleon said to him on the occasion of his visit to Paris, in 1805, "Mr. Fox will always hold the first place in an assembly of the Tuileries."

We may easily seem ridiculous in our eulogy of courtesy, whenever we insist on benevolence as its foundation. The painted phantasm Fashion rises to cast a species of derision on what we say. But I will neither be driven from some allowance to Fashion, as a symbolic institution, nor from the belief that love is the basis of courtesy. We must obtain *that*, if we can;

but by all means we must affirm *this*. Life owes much of its spirit to these sharp contrasts. Fashion which affects to be honor, is often, in all men's experience, only a ball-room code. Yet, so long as it is the highest 5 circle in the imagination of the best heads on the planet, there is something necessary and excellent in it; for it is not to be supposed that men have agreed to be the dupes of any thing preposterous; and the respect which these mysteries inspire in the most rude and sylvan characters, 10 and the curiosity with which details of high life are read, betray the universality of the love of cultivated manners. I know that a comic disparity would be felt, if we should enter the acknowleged "first circles," and apply these terrific standards of justice, beauty, and benefit, to the 15 individuals actually found there. Monarchs and heroes, sages and lovers, these gallants are not. Fashion has many classes and many rules of probation and admission; and not the best alone. There is not only the right of conquest, which genius pretends—the individual demon- 20 strating his natural aristocracy best of the best;—but less claims will pass for the time; for Fashion loves lions, and points, like Circe, to her horned company. This gentleman is this afternoon arrived from Denmark; and that is my Lord Ride, who came yesterday from 25 Bagdat; here is Captain Friese, from Cape Turnagain; and Captain Symmes, from the interior of the earth; and Monsieur Jovaire, who came down this morning in a balloon; Mr. Hobnail, the reformer; and Reverend Jul Bat, who has converted the whole torrid zone in his 30 Sunday-school; and Signor Torre del Greco, who ex- tinguished Vesuvius, by pouring into it the Bay of Naples; Spahi, the Persian ambassador; and Tul Wil Shan, the exiled nabob of Nepaul, whose saddle is the new moon.— But these are monsters of one day, and to-morrow will be dismissed to their holes and dens; for, in these rooms, every chair is waited for. The artist, the scholar, and, in general, the clerisy, wins its way up into these places, and gets represented here, somewhat on this footing of conquest. Another mode is to pass through all the degrees, spending a year and a day in St. Michael's Square, being steeped in Cologne water, and perfumed, and dined, and introduced, and properly grounded in all the biography, and politics, and anecdotes of the boudoirs.

Yet these fineries may have grace and wit. Let there be grotesque sculpture about the gates and offices of temples. Let the creed and commandments even have the saucy homage of parody. The forms of politeness universally express benevolence in superlative degrees. What if they are in the mouths of selfish men, and used as means of selfishness? What if the false gentleman almost bows the true out of the world? What if the false gentleman contrives so to address his companion, as civilly to exclude all others from his discourse, and also to make them feel excluded? Real service will not lose its nobleness. All generosity is not merely French and sentimental; nor is it to be concealed, that living blood and a passion of kindness does at last distinguish God's gentleman from Fashion's. The epitaph of Sir Jenkin Grout is not wholly unintelligible to the present age. "Here lies Sir Jenkin Grout, who loved his friend, and persuaded his enemy: what his mouth ate, his hand paid for: what his servants robbed, he restored: if a woman gave him pleasure, he supported her in pain: he never forgot his children: and whoso touched his finger, drew after it his whole body." Even the line of heroes is not utterly extinct. There is still ever some admirable person in plain clothes, standing on the wharf, who jumps in to rescue a drowning man; there is still some absurd inventor of charities; some guide and comforter of runaway slaves; some friend of Poland; some Philhellene; some fanatic who plants shade-trees for the second and third generation, and orchards when he is grown old; some well-concealed piety; some just man happy in an ill-fame; some youth ashamed of the favors of fortune, and impatiently casting them on other shoulders. And these are the centers of society, on which it returns for fresh impulses. These are the creators of Fashion, which is an attempt to organize beauty of behavior. The beautiful and the generous are, in the theory, the doctors and apostles of this church: Scipio, and the Cid, and Sir Philip Sidney, and Washington, and every pure and valiant heart, who worshipped Beauty by word and by deed. The persons who constitute the natural aristocracy, are not found in the actual aristocracy, or, only on its edge; as the chemical energy of the spectrum is found to be greatest, just outside of the spectrum. Yet that is the infirmity of the seneschals, who do not know their sovereign when he appears. The theory of society supposes the existence and sovereignty of these. It divines afar off their coming. It says with the elder gods—

"As Heaven and Earth are fairer far
   Than Chaos and blank Darkness, though once chiefs;
And as we show beyond that Heaven and Earth,
   In form and shape compact and beautiful;
So, on our heels a fresh perfection treads;
A power, more strong in beauty, born of us,
   And fated to excel us, as we pass
   In glory that old Darkness:
——— for, 'tis the eternal law,
That first in beauty shall be first in might."

Therefore, within the ethnical circle of good society, there is a narrower and higher circle, concentration of its light, and flower of courtesy, to which there is always a tacit appeal of pride and reference, as to its inner and imperial court, the parliament of love and chivalry. And this is constituted of those persons in whom heroic dispositions are native, with the love of beauty, the delight in society, and the power to embellish the passing day. If the individuals who compose the purest circles of aristocracy in Europe, the guarded blood of centuries, should pass in review, in such a manner as that we could, at leisure, and critically, inspect their behavior, we might find no gentleman, and no lady; for, although excellent specimens of courtesy and high-breeding would gratify us in the assemblage, in the particulars we should detect offence; because elegance comes of no breeding, but of birth. There must be romance of character, or the most fastidious exclusion of impertinencies will not avail. It must be genius which takes that direction: it must be not courteous, but courtesy. High behavior is as rare in fiction, as it is in fact. Scott is praised for the fidelity with which he painted the demeanor and conversation of the superior classes. Certainly, kings and queens, nobles and great ladies, had some right to complain of the absurdity that had been put in their mouths, before the days of Waverley: but neither does Scott's dialogue bear criticism. His lords brave each other in smart epigrammatic speeches, but the dialogue is in costume, and does not please on the second reading: it is not warm with life. In Shakespeare alone, the speakers do not strut and bridle, the dialogue is easily great, and he is the best-bred man in all England, in all Christendom. Once or twice, in real life, we are permitted to enjoy the charm of noble manners, in the

presence of a man or woman who have no bar in their
nature, but whose character emanates freely in their word
and gesture. A beautiful form is better than a beautiful
face; a beautiful behavior is better than a beautiful
5 form: it gives a higher pleasure than statues or pictures;
it is the finest of the fine arts. A man is but a little thing
in the midst of the objects of nature, yet, by the moral
quality radiating from his countenance, he may abolish
all considerations of magnitude, and in his manners
10 equal the majesty of the world. I have seen an individual, whose manners, though wholly within the
conventions of elegant society, were never learned there,
but were original and commanding, and held out protection and prosperity; one who did not need the aid of
15 a court-suit, but carried the holiday in his eye; who
exhilarated the fancy by flinging wide the doors of new
modes of existence; who shook off the captivity of
etiquette, with happy, spirited bearing, good-natured and
free as Robin Hood; yet with the port of an emperor—
20 if need be, calm, serious, and fit to stand the gaze of
millions.

The open air and the fields, the streets and public
chambers, are the places where man executes his will;
let him yield or divide the scepter at the door of the
25 house. Woman, with her instinct of behavior, instantly
detects in man a love of trifles, any coldness or imbecility,
or, in short, any want of that large, flowing, and magnanimous deportment, which is indispensable as an exterior
in the hall. Our American institutions have been friendly
30 to her, and, at this moment, I esteem it a chief felicity of
this country, that it excels in women. A certain awkward
consciousness of inferiority in the men, may give rise to
the new chivalry in behalf of Women's Rights. Certainly
let her be as much better placed in the laws and in social

forms, as the most zealous reformer can ask, but I con-
fide so entirely in her inspiring and musical nature, that
I believe only herself can show us how she shall be served.
The wonderful generosity of her sentiments raises her at
times into heroical and godlike regions, and verifies the 5
pictures of Minerva, Juno, or Polymnia; and, by the
firmness with which she treads her upward path, she con-
vinces the coarsest calculators that another road exists,
than that which their feet know. But besides those who
make good in our imagination the place of muses and of 10
Delphic Sybils, are there not women who fill our vase
with wine and roses to the brim, so that the wine runs
over and fills the house with perfume; who inspire us
with courtesy; who unloose out tongues, and we speak;
who anoint our eyes, and we see? We say things we 15
never thought to have said; for once, our walls of habitual
reserve vanished, and left us at large; we were children
playing with children in a wide field of flowers. Steep
us, we cried, in these influences for days, for weeks, and
we shall be sunny poets, and will write out in many- 20
colored words the romance that you are. Was it Hafiz
or Firdousi that said of his Persian, Lilla, she was an
elemental force, and astonished me by her amount of
life, when I saw her day after day radiating, every instant,
redundant joy and grace on all around her? She was a 25
solvent powerful to reconcile all heterogeneous persons
into one society. Like air or water, an element of such
a great range of affinities, that it combines readily with a
thousand substances. Where she is present, all others
will be more than they are wont. She was a unit and 30
whole, so that whatsoever she did, became her. She had
too much sympathy and desire to please, than that you
could say, her manners were marked with dignity, yet no
princess could surpass her clear and direct demeanor

on each occasion. She did not study the Persian grammar, nor the books of the seven poets, but all the poems of the seven seemed to be written upon her. For, though the bias of her nature was not to thought, but to sympathy, yet was she so perfect in her own nature, as to meet intellectual persons by the fulness of her heart, warming them by her sentiments; believing, as she did, that by dealing nobly with all, all would show themselves noble.

I know that this Byzantine pile of Chivalry or Fashion, which seems so fair and picturesque to those who look at the contemporary facts for science or for entertainment, is not equally pleasant to all spectators. The constitution of our society makes it a giant's castle to the ambitious youth who have not found their names enrolled in its Golden Book, and whom it has excluded from its coveted honors and privileges. They have yet to learn that its seeming grandeur is shadowy and relative: it is great by their allowance: its proudest gates will fly open at the approach of their courage and virtue. For the present distress, however, of those who are predisposed to suffer from the tyrannies of this caprice, there are easy remedies. To remove your residence a couple of miles, or at most four, will commonly relieve the most extreme susceptibility. For, the advantages which fashion values, are plants, which thrive in very confined localities, in a few streets, namely. Out of this precinct, they go for nothing; are of no use in the farm, in the forest, in the market, in war, in the nuptial society, in the literary or scientific circle, at sea, in friendship, in the heaven of thought or virtue.

But we have lingered long enough in these painted courts. The worth of the thing signified must vindicate our taste for the emblem. Every thing that is called fashion and courtesy humbles itself before the cause and

fountain of honor, creator of titles and dignities, namely,
the great heart of love.   This is the royal blood, this the
fire, which, in all countries and contingencies, will work
after its kind, and conquer and expand all that approaches it.   This gives new meaning to every fact. 5
This impoverishes the rich, suffering no grandeur but
its own.   What *is* rich?   Are you rich enough to help
anybody? to succor the unfashionable and the eccentric?
rich enough to make the Canadian in his wagon, the
itinerant with his consul's paper which commends him 10
"to the charitable," the swarthy Italian with his few
broken words of English, the lame pauper hunted by
overseers from town to town, even the poor insane be-
sotted wreck of man or woman, feel the noble exception
of your presence and your house, from the general bleak- 15
ness and stoniness; to make such feel that they were
greeted with a voice which made them both remember
and hope?   What is vulgar, but to refuse the claim on
acute and conclusive reasons?   What is gentle, but to
allow it, and give their heart and yours one holiday from 20
the national caution?   Without the rich heart, wealth
is an ugly beggar.   The king of Schiraz could not afford
to be so bountiful as the poor Osman who dwelt at his
gate.   Osman had a humanity so broad and deep, that
although his speech was so bold and free with the Koran, 25
as to disgust all the dervishes, yet was there never a poor
outcast, eccentric, or insane man, some fool who had cut
off his beard, or who had been mutilated under a vow, or
had a pet madness in his brain, but fled at once to him,
—that great heart lay there so sunny and hospitable in 30
the center of the country—that it seemed as if the instinct of all sufferers drew them to his side.   And the
madness which he harbored, he did not share.   Is not
this to be rich? this only to be rightly rich?

But I shall hear without pain, that I play the courtier very ill, and talk of that which I do not well understand. It is easy to see, that what is called by distinction society and fashion, has good laws as well as bad, has much that
5 is necessary, and much that is absurd. Too good for banning, and too bad for blessing, it reminds us of a tradition of the pagan mythology, in any attempt to settle its character. "I overheard Jove, one day," said Silenus, "talking of destroying the earth; he said it had
10 failed; they were all rogues and vixens, who went from bad to worse, as fast as the days succeeded each other. Minerva said, she hoped not; they were only ridiculous little creatures, with this odd circumstance, that they had a blur, or indeterminate aspect, seen far or seen near: if
15 you called them bad, they would appear so; if you called them good, they would appear so; and there was no one person or action among them which would not puzzle her owl, much more all Olympus, to know whether it was fundamentally bad or good."

JAMES RUSSELL LOWELL

ON A CERTAIN CONDESCENSION IN FOREIGNERS[1]

WALKING one day toward the Village, as we used to call it in the good old days when almost every dweller in the town had been born in it, I was enjoying that delicious sense of disenthralment from the actual which the deepening twilight brings with it, giving as it does a 5 sort of obscure novelty to things familiar. The coolness, the hush, broken only by the distant bleat of some belated goat, querulous to be disburthened of her milky load, the few faint stars, more guessed as yet than seen, the sense that the coming dark would so soon fold me in the 10 secure privacy of its disguise—all things combined in a result as near absolute peace as can be hoped for by a man who knows that there is a writ out against him in the hands of the printer's devil. For the moment, I was enjoying the blessed privilege of thinking without 15 being called on to stand and deliver what I thought to the small public who are good enough to take any interest therein. I love old ways, and the path I was walking felt kindly to the feet it had known for almost fifty years. How many fleeting impressions it had 20 shared with me! How many times I had lingered to study the shadows of the leaves mezzotinted upon the turf that edged it by the moon, of the bare boughs etched

[1] This essay is included by special arrangement with the Houghton Mifflin Company, the authorized publishers of Lowell's works.

with a touch beyond Rembrandt by the same unconscious
artist on the smooth page of snow! If I turned round,
through dusky tree-gaps came the first twinkle of evening lamps in the dear old homestead. On Corey's hill I
5 could see these tiny pharoses of love and home and sweet
domestic thoughts flash out one by one across the black-
ening salt-meadow between. How much has not kero-
sene added to the cheerfulness of our evening landscape!
A pair of night-herons flapped heavily over me toward the
10 hidden river. The war was ended. I might walk townward without that aching dread of bulletins that had
darkened the July sunshine and twice made the scarlet
leaves of October seem stained with blood. I remembered with a pang, half-proud, half-painful, how, so many
15 years ago I had walked over the same path and felt
round my finger the soft pressure of a little hand that
was one day to harden with faithful grip of saber. On
how many paths, leading to how many homes where
proud Memory does all she can to fill up the fireside gaps
20 with shining shapes, must not men be walking in just
such pensive mood as I? Ah, young heroes, safe in
immortal youth as those of Homer, you at least carried
your ideal hence untarnished! It is locked for you
beyond moth or rust in the treasure-chamber of Death.

25 Is not a country, I thought, that has had such as they
in it, that could give such as they a brave joy in dying
for it, worth something, then? And as I felt more and
more the soothing magic of evening's cool palm upon my
temples, as my fancy came home from its reverie, and my
30 senses, with reawakened curiosity, ran to the front windows again from the viewless closet of abstraction, and
felt a strange charm in finding the old tree and shabby
fence still there under the travesty of falling night, nay,
were conscious of an unsuspected newness in familiar

stars and the fading outlines of hills my earliest horizon,
I was conscious of an immortal soul, and could not but
rejoice in the unwaning goodliness of the world into which
I had been born without any merit of my own. I thought
of dear Henry Vaughan's rainbow, "Still young and
fine!" I remembered people who had to go over to the
Alps to learn what the divine silence of snow was, who
must run to Italy before they were conscious of the miracle wrought every day under their very noses by the
sunset, who must call upon the Berkshire hills to teach
them what a painter autumn was, while close at hand
the Fresh Pond meadows made all oriels cheap with hues
that showed as if a sunset-cloud had been wrecked
among their maples. One might be worse off than even
in America, I thought. There are some things so elastic
that even the heavy roller of democracy cannot flatten
them altogether down. The mind can weave itself
warmly in the cocoon of its own thoughts and dwell a
hermit anywhere. A country without traditions, without ennobling associations, a scramble of *parvenus*, with
a horrible consciousness of shoddy running through
politics, manners, art, literature, nay, religion itself? I
confess, it did not seem so to me there in that illimitable
quiet, that serene self-possession of nature, where Collins
might have brooded his "Ode to Evening," or where those
verses on Solitude in Dodsley's Collection, that Hawthorne liked so much, might have been composed.
Traditions? Granting that we had none, all that is
worth having in them is the common property of the soul
—an estate in gavelkind for all the sons of Adam—and,
moreover, if a man cannot stand on his two feet (the
prime quality of whoever has left any tradition behind
him), were it not better for him to be honest about it at
once, and go down on all fours? And for associations, in

one have not the wit to make them for himself out of his native earth, no ready-made ones of other men will avail him much. Lexington is none the worse to me for not being in Greece, nor Gettysburg that its name is not
5 Marathon. "Blessed old fields," I was just exclaiming to myself, like one of Mrs. Radcliffe's heroes, "dear acres, innocently secure from history, which these eyes first beheld, may you be also those to which they shall at last slowly darken!" when I was interrupted by a voice
10 which asked me in German whether I was the Herr Professor, Doctor, So-and-so? The "Doctor" was by brevet or vaticination, to make the grade easier to my pocket.

One feels so intimately assured that he is made up, in part, of shreds and leavings of the past, in part of
15 the interpolations of other people, that an honest man would be slow in saying *yes* to such a question. But "my name is So-and-so" is a safe answer, and I gave it. While I had been romancing with myself, the street-lamps had been lighted, and it was under one of these
20 detectives that have robbed the Old Road of its privilege of sanctuary after nightfall that I was ambushed by my foe. The inexorable villain had taken my description, it appears, that I might have the less chance to escape him. Dr. Holmes tells us that we change our substance, not
25 every seven years, as was once believed, but with every breath we draw. Why had I not the wit to avail myself of the subterfuge, and, like Peter, to renounce my identity, especially, as in certain moods of mind, I have often more than doubted of it myself? When a man is, as it
30 were, his own front-door, and is thus knocked at, why may he not assume the right of that sacred wood to make every house a castle, by denying himself to all visitations? I was truly not at home when the question was put to me, but had to recall myself from all out-of-doors, and to

piece my self-consciousness hastily together as well as I could before I answered it.

I knew perfectly well what was coming. It is seldom that debtors or good Samaritans waylay people under gas-lamps in order to force money upon them, so far as I have seen or heard. I was also aware, from considerable experience, that every foreigner is persuaded that, by doing this country the favor of coming to it, he has laid every native thereof under an obligation, pecuniary or other, as the case may be, whose discharge he is entitled to on demand duly made in person or by letter. Too much learning (of this kind) had made me mad in the provincial sense of the word. I had begun life with the theory of giving something to every beggar that came along, though sure of never finding a native-born countryman among them. In a small way, I was resolved to emulate Hatem Tai's tent, with its three hundred and sixty-five entrances, one for every day in the year— I know not whether he was astronomer enough to add another for leap-years. The beggars were a kind of German-silver aristocracy; not real plate, to be sure, but better than nothing. Where everybody was overworked, they supplied the comfortable equipoise of absolute leisure, so æsthetically needful. Besides, I was but too conscious of a vagrant fiber in myself, which too often thrilled me in my solitary walks with the temptation to wander on into infinite space, and by a single spasm of resolution to emancipate myself from the drudgery of prosaic serfdom to respectability and the regular course of things. This prompting has been at times my familiar demon, and I could not but feel a kind of respectful sympathy for men who had dared what I had only sketched out to myself as a splendid possibility. For seven years I helped maintain one heroic man on an

imaginary journey to Portland—as fine an example as
I have ever known of hopeless loyalty to an ideal. I
assisted another so long in a fruitless attempt to reach
Mecklenburg-Schwerin, that at last we grinned in each
5 other's faces when we met, like a couple of augurs.
He was possessed by this harmless mania as some are by
the North Pole, and I shall never forget his look of regret-
ful compassion (as for one who was sacrificing his higher
life to the fleshpots of Egypt) when I at last advised him
10 somewhat strenuously to go to the D——, whither the
road was so much traveled that he could not miss it.
General Banks, in his noble zeal for the honor of his country, would confer on the Secretary of State the power
of imprisoning, in case of war, all these seekers of the
15 unattainable, thus by a stroke of the pen annihilating
the single poetic element in our humdrum life. Alas!
not everybody has the genius to be a Bobbin-Boy, or
doubtless all these also would have chosen that more
prosperous line of life! But moralists, sociologists,
20 political economists, and taxes have slowly convinced me
that my beggarly sympathies were a sin against society.
Especially was the Buckle doctrine of averages (so
flattering to our free-will) persuasive with me; for as
there must be in every year a certain number who would
25 bestow an alms on these abridged editions of the Wandering Jew, the withdrawal of my quota could make no
possible difference, since some destined proxy must always
step forward to fill my gap. Just so many misdirected
letters every year and no more! Would it were as
30 easy to reckon up the number of men on whose backs
fate has written the wrong address, so that they arrive
by mistake in Congress and other places where they
do not belong! May not these wanderers of whom I
speak have been sent into the world without any proper

address at all? Where is our Dead-Letter Office for such?
And if wiser social arrangements should furnish us
with something of the sort, fancy (horrible thought!)
how many a workingman's friend (a kind of industry
in which the labor is light and the wages heavy) would 5
be sent thither because not called for in the office where
he at present lies!

But I am leaving my new acquaintance too long under
the lamp-post. The same Gano which had betrayed me
to him revealed to me a well-set young man of about 10
half my own age, as well dressed, so far as I could see,
as I was, and with every natural qualification for getting
his own livelihood as good, if not better, than my own.
He had been reduced to the painful necessity of calling
upon me by a series of crosses beginning with the Baden 15
Revolution (for which, I own, he seemed rather young
—but perhaps he referred to a kind of revolution practised every season at Baden-Baden), continued by repeated failures in business, for amounts which must
convince me of his entire respectability, and ending with 20
our Civil War. During the latter, he had served with
distinction as a soldier, taking a main part in every important battle, with a rapid list of which he favored me,
and no doubt would have admitted that, impartial as
Johnathan Wild's great ancestor, he had been on both 25
sides, had I baited him with a few hints of conservative
opinions on a subject so distressing to a gentleman wishing to profit by one's sympathy and unhappily doubtful
as to which way it might lean. For all these reasons,
and, as he seemed to imply, for his merit in consenting 30
to be born in Germany, he considered himself my natural
creditor to the extent of five dollars, which he would
handsomely consent to accept in greenbacks, though he
preferred specie. The offer was certainly a generous

one, and the claim presented with an assurance that
carried conviction. But, unhappily, I had been led to
remark a curious natural phenomenon. If I was ever
weak enough to give anything to a petitioner of what-
5 ever nationality, it always rained decayed compatriots
of his for a month after. *Post hoc ergo propter hoc* may
not be always safe logic, but here I seemed to perceive a
natural connection of cause and effect. Now, a few days
before I had been so tickled with a paper (professedly
10 written by a benevolent American clergyman) certifying
that the bearer, a hard-working German, had long
"sofered with rheumatic paints in his limps," that, after
copying the passage into my note-book, I thought it but
fair to pay a trifling *honorarium* to the author. I had
15 pulled the string of the shower-bath! It had been running shipwrecked sailors for some time, but forthwith it
began to pour Teutons, redolent of *lager-bier*. I could
not help associating the apparition of my new friend
with this series of otherwise unaccountable phenomena.
20 I accordingly made up my mind to deny the debt, and
modestly did so, pleading a native bias toward impecu-
niosity to the full as strong as his own. He took a high
tone with me at once, such as an honest man would
naturally take with a confessed repudiator. He even
25 brought down his proud stomach so far as to join himself to me for the rest of my townward walk, that he
might give me his views of the American people, and
thus inclusively of myself.

I know not whether it is because I am pigeon-livered
30 and lack gall, or whether it is from an overmastering
sense of drollery, but I am apt to submit to such bast-
ings with a patience which afterward surprises me,
being not without my share of warmth in the blood.
Perhaps it is because I so often meet with young per-

sons who know vastly more than I do, and especially with so many foreigners whose knowledge of this country is superior to my own. However it may be, I listened for some time with tolerable composure as my self-appointed lecturer gave me in detail his opinions of my country and its people. America, he informed me, was without arts, science, literature, culture, or any native hope of supplying them. We were a people wholly given to money-getting, and who, having got it, knew no other use for it than to hold it fast. I am fain to confess that I felt a sensible itching of the biceps, and that my fingers closed with such a grip as he had just informed me was one of the effects of our unhappy climate. But happening just then to be where I could avoid temptation by dodging down a by-street, I hastily left him to finish his diatribe to the lamp-post, which could stand it better than I. That young man will never know how near he came to being assaulted by a respectable gentleman of middle age, at the corner of Church Street. I have never felt quite satisfied that I did all my duty by him in not knocking him down. But perhaps he might have knocked *me* down, and then?

The capacity of indignation makes an essential part of the outfit of every honest man, but I am inclined to doubt whether he is a wise one who allows himself to act upon its first hints. It should be rather, I suspect, a *latent* heat in the blood, which makes itself felt in character, a steady reserve for the brain, warming the ovum of thought to life, rather than cooking it by a too hasty enthusiasm in reaching the boiling-point. As my pulse gradually fell back to its normal beat, I reflected that I had been uncomfortably near making a fool of myself—a handy salve of euphuism for our vanity, though it does not always make a just allowance to Nature for her

share in the business. What possible claim had my
Teutonic friend to rob me of my composure? I am not,
I think, specially thin-skinned as to other people's opinions of myself, having, as I conceive, later and fuller
5 intelligence on that point than anybody else can give
me. Life is continually weighing us in very sensitive
scales, and telling every one of us precisely what his
real weight is to the last grain of dust. Whoever at
fifty does not rate himself quite as low as most of his
10 acquaintance would be likely to put him, must be either
a fool or a great man, and I humbly disclaim being either.
But if I was not smarting in person from any scattering
shot of my late companion's commination, why should
I grow hot at any implication of my country therein?
15 Surely *her* shoulders are broad enough, if yours or mine
are not, to bear up under a considerable avalanche of
this kind. It is the bit of truth in every slander, the
hint of likeness in every caricature, that makes us smart.
"Art thou *there*, old Truepenny?" How did your blade
20 know its way so well to that one loose rivet in our armor?
I wondered whether Americans were over-sensitive in
this respect, whether they were more touchy than other
folks. On the whole, I thought we were not. Plu-
tarch, who at least had studied philosophy, if he had not
25 mastered it, could not stomach something Herodotus
had said of Bœotia, and devoted an essay to showing
up the delightful old traveler's malice and ill-breeding.
French editors leave out of Montaigne's *Travels* some
remarks of his about France, for reasons best known
30 to themselves. Pachydermatous Deutschland, covered
with trophies from every field of letters, still winces
under that question which Père Bouhours put two centuries ago, *Si un Allemand peut être bel-esprit?* John
Bull grew apoplectic with angry amazement at the auda-

cious persiflage of Pückler-Muskau. To be sure, he was
a prince—but that was not all of it, for a chance phrase
of gentle Hawthorne sent a spasm through all the journals of England. Then this tenderness is not peculiar
to *us?* Console yourself, dear man and brother, what- 5
ever you may be sure of, be sure at least of this, that
you are dreadfully like other people. Human nature
has a much greater genius for sameness than for originality, or the world would be at a sad pass shortly. The
surprising thing is that men have such a taste for this 10
somewhat musty flavor, that an Englishman, for example, should feel himself defrauded, nay, even outraged,
when he comes over here and finds a people speaking
what he admits to be something like English, and yet
so very different from (or, as he would say, to) those 15
he left at home. Nothing, I am sure, equals *my* thank-
fulness when I meet an Englishman who is *not* like
every other, or, I may add, an American of the same
odd turn.

Certainly it is no shame to a man that he should be 20
as nice about his country as about his sweetheart, and
who ever heard even the friendliest appreciation of that
unexpressive she that did not seem to fall infinitely
short? Yet it would hardly be wise to hold every one
an enemy who could not see her with our own enchanted 25
eyes. It seems to be the common opinion of foreigners
that Americans are *too* tender upon this point. Perhaps we are; and if so, there must be a reason for it.
Have we had fair play? Could the eyes of what is
called Good Society (though it is so seldom true either to 30
the adjective or noun) look upon a nation of democrats
with any chance of receiving an undistorted image?
Were not those, moreover, who found in the old order
of things an earthly paradise, paying them quarterly

dividends for the wisdom of their ancestors, with the punctuality of the seasons, unconsciously bribed to misunderstand if not to misrepresent us? Whether at war or at peace, there we were, a standing menace to all 5 earthly paradises of that kind, fatal underminers of the very credit on which the dividends were based, all the more hateful and terrible that our destructive agency was so insidious, working invisible in the elements, as it seemed, active while they slept, and coming upon them 10 in the darkness like an armed man. *Could* Laius have the proper feelings of a father toward Œdipus, announced as his destined destroyer by infallible oracles, and felt to be such by every conscious fiber of his soul? For more than a century the Dutch were the laughing-stock of 15 polite Europe. They were butter-firkins, swillers of beer and schnaps, and their *vrouws* from whom Holbein painted the all-but loveliest of Madonnas, Rembrandt the graceful girl who sits immortal on his knee in Dresden, and Rubens his abounding goddesses, were the syno- 20 nyms of clumsy vulgarity. Even so late as Irving the ships of the greatest navigators in the world were represented as sailing equally well stern-foremost. That the aristocratic Venetians should have

"Riveted with gigantic piles
25　　　Thorough the center their new-catchèd miles,"

was heroic. But the far more marvelous achievement of the Dutch in the same kind was ludicrous even to republican Marvell. Meanwhile, during that very century 30 of scorn, they were the best artists, sailors, merchants, bankers, printers, scholars, jurisconsults, and statesmen in Europe, and the genius of Motley has revealed them to us, earning a right to themselves by the most heroic struggle in human annals. But, alas! they were not

merely simple burghers who had fairly made themselves
High Mightinesses, and could treat on equal terms with
anointed kings, but their commonwealth carried in its
bosom the germs of democracy. They even unmuzzled,
at least after dark, that dreadful mastiff, the Press, whose   5
scent is, or ought to be, so keen for wolves in sheep's
clothing and for certain other animals in lions' skins.
They made fun of Sacred Majesty, and, what was worse,
managed uncommonly well without it. In an age when
periwigs made so large a part of the natural dignity of 10
man, people with such a turn of mind were dangerous.
How could they seem other than vulgar and hateful?

In the natural course of things we succeeded to this un-
enviable position of general butt. The Dutch had thriven
under it pretty well, and there was hope that we could 15
at least contrive to worry along. And we certainly did
in a very redoubtable fashion. Perhaps we deserved
some of the sarcasm more than our Dutch predecessors
in office. We had nothing to boast of in arts or letters,
and were given to bragging overmuch of our merely ma- 20
terial prosperity, due quite as much to the virtue of our
continent as to our own. There was some truth in Carlyle's sneer, after all. Till we had succeeded in some
higher way than this, we had only the success of physical
growth. Our greatness, like that of enormous Russia, 25
was greatness on the map—barbarian mass only; but
had we gone down, like that other Atlantis, in some vast
cataclysm, we should have covered but a pin's point on
the chart of memory, compared with those ideal spaces
occupied by tiny Attica and cramped England. At the 30
same time, our critics somewhat too easily forgot that
material must make ready the foundation for ideal tri-
umphs, that the arts have no chance in poor countries.
But it must be allowed that democracy stood for a great

deal in our shortcoming. The *Edinburgh Review* never would have thought of asking, "Who reads a Russian book?" and England was satisfied with iron from Sweden without being impertinently inquisitive after her painters
5 and statuaries. Was it that they expected too much from the mere miracle of Freedom? Is it not the highest art of a republic to make men of flesh and blood, and not the marble ideals of such? It may be fairly doubted whether we have produced this higher type of man yet.
10 Perhaps it is the collective, not the individual, humanity that is to have a chance of nobler development among us. We shall see. We have a vast amount of imported ignorance, and, still worse, of native ready-made knowledge, to digest before even the preliminaries of such a
15 consummation can be arranged. We have got to learn that statesmanship is the most complicated of all arts, and to come back to the apprenticeship-system too hastily abandoned. At present, we trust a man with making constitutions on less proof of competence than we
20 should demand before we gave him our shoe to patch. We have nearly reached the limit of the reaction from the old notion, which paid too much regard to birth and station as qualifications for office, and have touched the extreme point in the opposite direction, putting the highest of
25 human functions up at auction to be bid for by any creature capable of going upright on two legs. In some places, we have arrived at a point at which civil society is no longer possible, and already another reaction has begun, not backward to the old system, but toward' fitness
30 either from natural aptitude or special training. But will it always be safe to let evils work their own cure by becoming unendurable? Every one of them leaves its taint in the constitution of the body-politic, each in itself, perhaps, trifling, yet all together powerful for evil.

But whatever we might do or leave undone, we were not genteel, and it was uncomfortable to be continually reminded that, though we should boast that we were the Great West till we were black in the face, it did not bring us an inch nearer to the world's West-End. That sacred enclosure of respectability was tabooed to us. The Holy Alliance did not inscribe us on its visiting-list. The Old World of wigs and orders and liveries would shop with us, but we must ring at the area-bell, and not venture to awaken the more august clamors of the knocker. Our manners, it must be granted, had none of those graces that stamp the caste of Vere de Vere, in whatever museum of British antiquities they may be hidden. In short, we were vulgar.

This was one of those horribly vague accusations, the victim of which has no defense. An umbrella is of no avail against a Scotch mist. It envelops you, it penetrates at every pore, it wets you through without seeming to wet you at all. Vulgarity is an eighth deadly sin, added to the list in these latter days, and worse than all the others put together, since it perils your salvation in *this* world—far the more important of the two in the minds of most men. It profits nothing to draw nice distinctions between essential and conventional, for the convention in this case *is* the essence, and you may break every command of the decalogue with perfect good-breeding, nay, if you are adroit, without losing caste. We, indeed, had it not to lose, for we had never gained it. "*How* am I vulgar?" asks the culprit, shudderingly. "Because thou art not like unto Us," answers Lucifer, Son of the Morning, and there is no more to be said. The god of this world may be a fallen angel, but he has us *there!* We were as clean—so far as my observation goes, I think we were cleaner, morally and physically,

than the English, and therefore, of course, than every-body else. But we did not pronounce the diphthong *ou* as they did, and we said *eether* and not *eyther*, following therein the fashion of our ancestors, who unhappily could
5 bring over no English better than Shakespeare's; and we did not stammer as they had learned to do from the courtiers, who in this way flattered the Hanoverian king, a foreigner among the people he had come to reign over. Worse than all, we might have the noblest ideas and the
10 finest sentiments in the world, but we vented them through that organ by which men are led rather than leaders, though some physiologists would persuade us that Nature furnishes her captains with a fine handle to their faces that Opportunity may get a good purchase on
15 them for dragging them to the front.

This state of things was so painful that excellent people were not wanting who gave their whole genius to reproducing here the original Bull, whether by gaiters, the cut of their whiskers, by a factitious brutality in
20 their tone, or by an accent that was forever tripping and falling flat over the tangled roots of our common tongue. Martyrs to a false ideal, it never occurred to them that nothing is more hateful to gods and men than a second-rate Englishman, and for the very reason that this planet
25 never produced a more splendid creature than the first-rate one, witness Shakespeare and the Indian Mutiny. Witness that truly sublime self-abnegation of those prisoners lately among the bandits of Greece, where average men gave an example of quiet fortitude for which all
30 the stoicism of antiquity can show no match. If we could contrive to be not too unobtrusively our simple selves, we should be the most delightful of human beings, and the most original; whereas, when the plating of Anglicism rubs off, as it always will in points that

come to much wear, we are liable to very unpleasing conjectures about the quality of the metal underneath. Perhaps one reason why the average Briton spreads himself here with such an easy air of superiority may be owing to the fact that he meets with so many bad imitations 5 as to conclude himself the only real thing in a wilderness of shams. He fancies himself moving through an endless Bloomsbury, where his mere apparition confers honor as an avatar of the court-end of the universe. Not a Bull of them all but is persuaded he bears Europa 10 upon his back. This is the sort of fellow whose patronage is so divertingly insufferable. Thank Heaven he is not the only specimen of cater-cousinship from the dear old Mother Island that is shown to us! Among genuine things, I know nothing more genuine than the better 15 men whose limbs were made in England. So manly-tender, so brave, so true, so warranted to wear, they make us proud to feel that blood is thicker than water.

But it is not merely the Englishman; every European 20 candidly admits in himself some right of primogeniture in respect to us, and pats this shaggy continent on the back with a lively sense of generous unbending. The German who plays the bass-viol has a well-founded contempt, which he is not always nice in concealing, for a 25 country so few of whose children ever take that noble instrument between their knees. His cousin, the Ph. D. from Göttingen, cannot help despising a people who do not grow loud and red over Aryans and Turanians, and are indifferent about their descent from either. The 30 Frenchman feels an easy mastery in speaking his mother tongue, and attributes it to some native superiority of parts that lifts him high above us barbarians of the West. The Italian *prima donna* sweeps a courtesy of

careless pity to the over-facile pit which unsexes her
with the *bravo!* innocently meant to show a familiarity
with foreign usage. But all without exception make no
secret of regarding us as the goose bound to deliver
5 them a golden egg in return for *their* cackle. Such
men as Agassiz, Guyot, and Goldwin Smith come with
gifts in their hands; but since it is commonly European
failures who bring hither their remarkable gifts and
acquirements, this view of the case is sometimes just
10 the least bit in the world provoking. To think what
a delicious seclusion of contempt we enjoyed till California and our own ostentatious *parvenus*, flinging gold
away in Europe that might have endowed libraries at
home, gave us the ill repute of riches! What a shabby
15 downfall from the Arcadia which the French officers of
our Revolutionary War fancied they saw here through
Rousseau-tinted spectacles! Something of Arcadia there
really was, something of the Old Age; and that divine
provincialism were cheaply repurchased could we have
20 it back again in exchange for the tawdry upholstery
that has taken its place.

For some reason or other, the European has rarely
been able to see America except in caricature. Would
the first Review of the world have printed the *niaiseries*
25 of Mr. Maurice Sand as a picture of society in any civilized country? Mr. Sand, to be sure, has inherited
nothing of his famous mother's literary outfit, except
the pseudonyme. But since the conductors of the
Revue could not have published his story because it was
30 clever, they must have thought it valuable for its truth.
As true as the last-century Englishman's picture of Jean
Crapaud! We do not ask to be sprinkled with rose-
water, but may perhaps fairly protest against being
drenched with the rinsings of an unclean imagination.

The next time the *Revue* allows such ill-bred persons to throw their slops out of its first-floor windows, let it honestly preface the discharge with a *gare de l'eau!* that we may run from under in season. And Mr. Duvergier d'Hauranne, who knows how to be entertaining! I know *le Français est plutôt indiscret que confiant*, and the pen slides too easily when indiscretions will fetch so much a page; but should we not have been *tant-soit-peu* more cautious had we been writing about people on the other side of the Channel? But then it is a fact in the natural history of the American long familiar to Europeans, that he abhors privacy, knows not the meaning of reserve, lives in hotels because of their greater publicity, and is never so pleased as when his domestic affairs (if he may be said to have any) are paraded in the newspapers. Barnum, it is well known, represents perfectly the average national sentiment in this respect. However it be, we are not treated like other people, or perhaps I should say like people who are ever likely to be met with in society.

Is it in the climate? Either I have a false notion of European manners, or else the atmosphere affects them strangely when exported hither. Perhaps they suffer from the sea-voyage like some of the more delicate wines. During our Civil War an English gentleman of the highest description was kind enough to call upon me, mainly, as it seemed, to inform me how entirely he sympathized with the Confederates, and how sure he felt that we could never subdue them—"they were the *gentlemen* of the country, you know." Another, the first greetings hardly over, asked me how I accounted for the universal meagerness of my countrymen. To a thinner man than I, or from a stouter man than he, the question *might* have been offensive. The Marquis of

Hartington[1] wore a secession badge at a public ball in New York. In a civilized country he might have been roughly handled; but here, where the *biensèances* are not so well understood, of course nobody minded it. A French traveler told me he had been a good deal in the British colonies, and had been astonished to see how soon the people became Americanized. He added, with delightful *bonhomie*, and as if he were sure it would charm me, that "they even began to talk through their noses, just like you!" I was naturally ravished with this testimony to the assimilating power of democracy, and could only reply that I hoped they would never adopt our democratic patent-method of seeming to settle one's honest debts, for they would find it paying through the nose in the long run. I am a man of the New World, and do not know precisely the present fashion of May-Fair, but I have a kind of feeling that if an American (*mutato nomine, de te* is always frightfully possible) were to do this kind of thing under a European roof, it would induce some disagreeable reflections as to the ethical results of democracy. I read the other day in print the remark of a British tourist who had eaten large quantities of our salt, such as it is (I grant it has not the European savor), that the Americans were hospitable, no doubt, but that it was partly because they longed for foreign visitors to relieve the tedium of their dead-level existence, and partly from ostentation. What shall we do? Shall we close our doors? Not I, for one,

---

[1] One of Mr. Lincoln's neatest strokes of humor was his treatment of this gentleman when a laudable curiosity induced him to be presented to the President of the Broken Bubble. Mr. Lincoln persisted in calling him Mr. Partington. Surely the refinement of good-breeding could go no further. Giving the young man his real name (already notorious in the newspapers) would have made his visit an insult. Had Henri IV. done this, it would have been famous.

if I should so have forfeited the friendship of L. S., most lovable of men. He somehow seems to find us human, at least, and so did Clough, whose poetry will one of these days, perhaps, be found to have been the best utterance in verse of this generation. And T. H. the mere grasp of whose manly hand carries with it the pledge of frankness and friendship, of an abiding simplicity of nature as affecting as it is rare!

The fine old Tory aversion of former times was not hard to bear. There was something even refreshing in it, as in a northeaster to a hardy temperament. When a British parson, traveling in Newfoundland while the slash of our separation was still raw, after prophesying a glorious future for an island that continued to dry its fish under the ægis of Saint George, glances disdainfully over his spectacles in parting at the U. S. A., and forebodes for them a "speedy relapse into barbarism," now that they have madly cut themselves off from the humanizing influences of Britain, I smile with barbarian self-conceit. But this kind of thing became by degrees an unpleasant anachronism. For meanwhile the young giant was growing, was beginning indeed to feel tight in his clothes, was obliged to let in a gore here and there in Texas, in California, in New Mexico, in Alaska, and had the scissors and needle and thread ready for Canada when the time came. His shadow loomed like a Brocken-specter over against Europe—the shadow of what they were coming to, that was the unpleasant part of it. Even in such misty image as they had of him, it was painfully evident that his clothes were not of any cut hitherto fashionable, nor conceivable by a Bond Street tailor—and this in an age, too, when everything depends upon clothes, when, if we do not keep up appearances, the seeming-solid frame of this universe, nay,

your very God, would slump into himself, like a mockery
king of snow, being nothing, after all, but a prevailing
mode. From this moment the young giant assumed the
respectable aspect of a phenomenon, to be got rid of if
5 possible, but at any rate as legitimate a subject of human
study as the glacial period or the silurian what-d'ye-call-
ems. If the man of the primeval drift-heaps is so ab-
sorbingly interesting, why not the man of the drift that
is just beginning, of the drift into whose irresistible cur-
10 rent we are just being sucked whether we will or no? If
I were in their place, I confess I should not be frightened. Man has survived so much, and contrived to be
comfortable on this planet after surviving so much! I
am something of a protestant in matters of government
15 also, and am willing to get rid of vestments and ceremonies and to come down to bare benches, if only faith
in God take the place of a general agreement to profess
confidence in ritual and sham. Every mortal man of us
holds stock in the only public debt that is absolutely
20 sure of payment, and that is the debt of the Maker of
this Universe to the Universe he has made. I have no
notion of selling out my stock in a panic.

It was something to have advanced even to the dignity
of a phenomenon, and yet I do not know that the rela-
25 tion of the individual American to the individual European was bettered by it; and that, after all, must adjust
itself comfortably before there can be a right understanding between the two. We had been a desert, we
became a museum. People came hither for scientific
30 and not social ends. The very cockney could not complete his education without taking a vacant stare at us
in passing. But the sociologists (I think they call themselves so) were the hardest to bear. There was no escape. I have even known a professor of this fearful

science to come disguised in petticoats. We were cross-examined as a chemist cross-examines a new substance. Human? yes, all the elements are present, though abnormally combined. Civilized? Hm! that needs a stricter assay. No entomologist could take a more friendly interest in a strange bug. After a few such experiences, I, for one, have felt as if I were merely one of those horrid things preserved in spirits (and very bad spirits too) in a cabinet. I was not the fellow-being of these explorers: I was a curiosity; I was a *specimen*. Hath not an American organs, dimensions, senses, affections, passions even as a European hath? If you prick us, do we not bleed? If you tickle us, do we not laugh? I will not keep on with Shylock to his next question but one.

Till after our Civil War it never seemed to enter the head of any foreigner, especially of any Englishman, that an American had what could be called a country, except as a place to eat, sleep, and trade in. Then it seemed to strike them suddenly. "By Jove, you know, fellahs don't fight like that for a shop-till!" No, I rather think not. To Americans America is something more than a promise and an expectation. It has a past and traditions of its own. A descent from men who sacrificed everything and came hither, not to better their fortunes, but to plant their idea in virgin soil, should be a good pedigree. There was never colony save this that went forth, not to seek gold, but God. Is it not as well to have sprung from such as these as from some burly beggar who came over with Wilhelmus Conquestor, unless, indeed, a line grow better as it runs farther away from stalwart ancestors? And for history, it is dry enough, no doubt, in the books, but, for all that, is of a kind that tells in the blood. I have admitted that Carlyle's sneer had a show of truth in it. But what does he himself, like a true Scot, admire in the Hohenzollerns? First of all, that they were *canny*, a thrifty, forehanded race. Next, that they made a good fight from generation to generation with the chaos around them. That is precisely the battle which the English race on this continent has been carrying doughtily on for two centuries and a half. Doughtily and silently, for you cannot hear in Europe "that crash, the death-song of the perfect tree," that has been going on here from sturdy father to sturdy son, and making this continent habitable for the weaker Old World breed that has swarmed to it during the last half-century. If ever men did a good stroke of work on this planet, it was the forefathers of those whom you are wondering whether it would not be prudent to acknowledge as far-off cousins. Alas, man of genius, to whom we owe so much, could you see nothing more than the burning of a foul chimney in that clash of Michael and Satan which flamed up under your very eyes?

Before our war we were to Europe but a huge mob of adventurers and shop-keepers. Leigh Hunt expressed it well enough when he said that he could never think of America without seeing a gigantic counter stretched all along the seaboard. Feudalism had by degrees made commerce, the great civilizer, contemptible. But a tradesman with sword on thigh and very prompt of stroke was not only redoubtable, he had become respectable also. Few people, I suspect, alluded twice to a needle in Sir John Hawkwood's presence, after that doughty fighter had exchanged it for a more dangerous tool of the same metal. Democracy had been hitherto only a ludicrous effort to reverse the laws of nature by thrusting Cleon into the place of Pericles. But a democ-

racy that could fight for an abstraction, whose members
held life and goods cheap compared with that larger life
which we call country, was not merely unheard-of, but
portentous. It was the nightmare of the Old World
taking upon itself flesh and blood, turning out to be
substance and not dream. Since the Norman crusader
clanged down upon the throne of the *porphyro-geniti*,
carefully-draped appearances had never received such a
shock, had never been so rudely called on to produce
their titles to the empire of the world. Authority has
had its periods not unlike those of geology, and at last
comes Man claiming kingship in right of his mere manhood. The world of the Saurians might be in some
respects more picturesque, but the march of events is
inexorable, and it is bygone.

The young giant had certainly got out of long-clothes.
He had become the *enfant terrible* of the human household. It was not and will not be easy for the world
(especially for our British cousins) to look upon us as
grown up. The youngest of nations, its people must also
be young and to be treated accordingly, was the syllogism—as if libraries did not make all nations equally
old in all those respects, at least, where age is an advantage and not a defect. Youth, no doubt, has its good
qualities, as people feel who are losing it, but boyishness
is another thing. We had been somewhat boyish as a
nation, a little loud, a little pushing, a little braggart.
But might it not partly have been because we felt that
we had certain claims to respect that were not admitted?
The war which established our position as a vigorous
nationality has also sobered us. A nation, like a man
cannot look death in the eye for four years, without some
strange reflections, without arriving at some clearer consciousness of the stuff it is made of, without some great

moral change. Such a change, or the beginning of it, no observant person can fail to see here. Our thought and our politics, our bearing as a people, are assuming a manlier tone. We have been compelled to see what was
5 weak in democracy as well as what was strong. We have begun obscurely to recognize that things do not go of themselves, and that popular government is not in itself a panacea, is no better than any other form except as the virtue and wisdom of the people make it so, and
10 that when men undertake to do their own kingship, they enter upon the dangers and responsibilities as well as the privileges of the function. Above all, it looks as if we were on the way to be persuaded that no government can be carried on by declamation. It is noticeable also
15 that facility of communication has made the best English and French thought far more directly operative here than ever before. Without being Europeanized, our discussion of important questions in statesmanship, political economy, in æsthetics, is taking a broader scope
20 and a higher tone. It had certainly been provincial, one might almost say local, to a very unpleasant extent. Perhaps our experience in soldiership has taught us to value training more than we have been popularly wont. We may possibly come to the conclusion, one of these
25 days, that self-made men may not be always equally skilful in the manufacture of wisdom, may not be divinely commissioned to fabricate the higher qualities of opinion on all possible topics of human interest.

So long as we continue to be the most common-
30 schooled and the least cultivated people in the world, I suppose we must consent to endure this condescending manner of foreigners toward us. The more friendly they mean to be the more ludicrously prominent it becomes. They can never appreciate the immense amount

of silent work that has been done here, making this continent slowly fit for the abode of man, and which will demonstrate itself, let us hope, in the character of the people. Outsiders can only be expected to judge a nation by the amount it has contributed to the civilization of the world; the amount, that is, that can be seen and handled. A great place in history can only be achieved by competitive examinations, nay, by a long course of them. How much new thought have we contributed to the common stock? Till that question can be triumphantly answered, or needs no answer, we must continue to be simply interesting as an experiment, to be studied as a problem, and not respected as an attained result or an accomplished solution. Perhaps, as I have hinted, their patronizing manner toward us is the fair result of their failing to see here anything more than a poor imitation, a plaster-cast of Europe. And are they not partly right? If the tone of the uncultivated American has too often the arrogance of the barbarian, is not that of the cultivated as often vulgarly apologetic? In the America they meet with is there the simplicity, the manliness, the absence of sham, the sincere human nature, the sensitiveness to duty and implied obligation, that in any way distinguishes us from what our orators call "the effete civilization of the Old World"? Is there a politician among us daring enough (except a Dana here and there) to risk his future on the chance of our keeping our word with the exactness of superstitious communities like England? Is it certain that we shall be ashamed of a bankruptcy of honor, if we can only keep the letter of our bond? I hope we shall be able to answer all these questions with a frank *yes*. At any rate, we would advise our visitors that we are not merely curious creatures, but belong to the family

of man, and that, as individuals, we are not to be always subjected to the competitive examination above mentioned, even if we acknowledged their competence as an examining board.   Above all, we beg them to re-
5 member that America is not to us, as to them, a mere object of external interest to be discussed and analyzed, but *in* us, part of our very marrow.   Let them not suppose that we conceive of ourselves as exiles from the graces and amenities of an older date than we, though
10 very much at home in a state of things not yet all it might be or should be, but which we mean to make so, and which we find both wholesome and pleasant for men (though perhaps not for *dilettanti*) to live in.   "The full tide of human existence" may be felt here as keenly as
15 Johnson felt it at Charing Cross, and in a larger sense. I know one person who is singular enough to think Cambridge the very best spot on the habitable globe. "Doubtless God *could* have made a better, but doubtless he never did."

20   It will take England a great while to get over her airs of patronage toward us, or even passably to conceal them. She cannot help confounding the people with the country, and regarding us as lusty juveniles.   She has a conviction that whatever good there is in us is wholly
25 English, when the truth is that we are worth nothing except so far as we have disinfected ourselves of Anglicism. She is especially condescending just now, and lavishes sugar-plums on us as if we had not outgrown them.   I am no believer in sudden conversions, especially in sud-
30 den conversions to a favorable opinion of people who have just proved you to be mistaken in judgment and therefore unwise in policy.   I never blamed her for not wishing well to democracy—how should she?—but Alabamas are not wishes.   Let her not be too hasty in be-

lieving Mr. Reverdy Johnson's pleasant words. Though there is no thoughtful man in America who would not consider a war with England the greatest of calamities, yet the feeling toward her here is very far from cordial, whatever our Minister may say in the effusion that comes after ample dining. Mr. Adams, with his famous " My Lord, this means war," perfectly represented his country. Justly or not, we have a feeling that we have been wronged, not merely insulted. The only sure way of bringing about a healthy relation between the two countries is for Englishmen to clear their minds of the notion that we are always to be treated as a kind of inferior and deported Englishman whose nature they perfectly understand, and whose back they accordingly stroke the wrong way of the fur with amazing perseverance. Let them learn to treat us naturally on our merits as human beings, as they would a German or a Frenchman, and not as if we were a kind of counterfeit Briton whose crime appeared in every shade of difference, and before long there would come that right feeling which we naturally call a good understanding. The common blood, and still more the common language, are fatal instruments of misapprehension. Let them give up *trying* to understand us, still more thinking that they do, and acting in various absurd ways as the necessary consequence, for they will never arrive at that devout-to-be-wished consummation, till they learn to look at us as we are and not as they suppose us to be. Dear old long-estranged mother-in-law, it is a great many years since we parted. Since 1660, when you married again, you have been a stepmother to us. Put on your spectacles, dear madam. Yes, we *have* grown, and changed likewise. You would not let us darken your doors, if you could help it. We know that perfectly well. But pray, when we look to be treated as men, don't shake that rattle in our faces, nor talk baby to us any longer.

> "Do, child, go to it grandam, child;
> Give grandam kingdom, and it grandam will
> 5   Give it a plum, a cherry, and a fig!"

ROBERT LOUIS STEVENSON

·EL DORADO

It seems as if a great deal were attainable in a world where there are so many marriages and decisive battles, and where we all, at certain hours of the day, and with great gusto and despatch, stow a portion of victuals finally and irretrievably into the bag which contains us. And it would seem also, on a hasty view, that the attainment of as much as possible was the one goal of man's contentious life. And yet, as regards the spirit, this is but a semblance. We live in an ascending scale when we live happily, one thing leading to another in an endless series. There is always a new horizon for onward-looking men, and although we dwell on a small planet, immersed in petty business and not enduring beyond a brief period of years, we are so constituted that our hopes are inaccessible, like stars, and the term of hoping is prolonged until the term of life. To be truly happy is a question of how we begin and not of how we end, of what we want and not of what we have. An aspiration is a joy for ever, a possession as solid as a landed estate, a fortune which we can never exhaust and which gives us year by year a revenue of pleasurable activity. To have many of these is to be spiritually rich. Life is only a very dull and ill-directed theater unless we have some interests in the piece; and to those who have neither art nor science, the world is a mere arrangement of colors, or a rough footway where they may very well

break their shins. It is in virtue of his own desires and curiosities that any man continues to exist with even patience, that he is charmed by the look of things and people, and that he wakens every morning with a renewed
5 appetite for work and pleasure. Desire and curiosity are the two eyes through which he sees the world in the most enchanted colors: it is they that make women beautiful or fossils interesting: and the man may squander his estate and come to beggary, but if he keeps these two
10 amulets he is still rich in the possibilities of pleasure. Suppose he could take one meal so compact and comprehensive that he should never hunger any more; suppose him, at a glance, to take in all the features of the world and allay the desire for knowledge; suppose him to do the
15 like in any province of experience—would not that man be in a poor way for amusement ever after?

One who goes touring on foot with a single volume in his knapsack reads with circumspection, pausing often to reflect, and often laying the book down to contemplate the
20 landscape or the prints in the inn parlor; for he fears to come to an end of his entertainment, and be left companionless on the last stages of his journey. A young fellow recently finished the works of Thomas Carlyle, winding up, if we remember aright, with the ten note-books upon
25 Frederick the Great. "What!" cried the young fellow, in consternation, "is there no more Carlyle? Am I left to the daily papers?" A more celebrated instance is that of Alexander, who wept bitterly because he had no more worlds to subdue. And when Gibbon had finished
30 the *Decline and Fall*, he had only a few moments of joy; and it was with a "sober melancholy" that he parted from his labors.

Happily we all shoot at the moon with ineffectual arrows; our hopes are set on inaccessible El Dorado;

we come to an end of nothing here below. Interests are only plucked up to sow themselves again, like mustard. You would think, when the child was born, there would be an end to trouble; and yet it is only the beginning of fresh anxieties; and when you have seen it through its teething and its education, and at last its marriage, alas! it is only to have new fears, new quivering sensibilities, with every day; and the health of your children's children grows as touching a concern as that of your own. Again, when you have married your wife, you would think you were got upon a hilltop, and might begin to go downward by an easy slope. But you have only ended courting to begin marriage. Falling in love and winning love are often difficult tasks to overbearing and rebellious spirits; but to keep in love is also a business of some importance, to which both man and wife must bring kindness and good-will. The true love story commences at the altar, when there lies before the married pair a most beautiful contest of wisdom and generosity, and a life-long struggle toward an unattainable ideal. Unattainable? Ay, surely unattainable, from the very fact that they are two instead of one.

"Of making books there is no end," complained the Preacher; and did not perceive how highly he was praising letters as an occupation. There is no end, indeed, to making books or experiments, or to travel, or to gathering wealth. Problem gives rise to problem. We may study for ever, and we are never as learned as we would. We have never made a statue worthy of our dreams. And when we have discovered a continent, or crossed a chain of mountains, it is only to find another ocean or another plain upon the further side. In the infinite universe there is room for our swiftest diligence and to spare. It is not like the works of Carlyle, which can be read to an end. Even in a corner of it, in a private park, or in the neighborhood of a single hamlet, the weather and the seasons keep so deftly changing that although we walk there for a lifetime there will be always something 5 new to startle and delight us.

There is only one wish realizable on the earth; only one thing that can be perfectly attained: Death. And from a variety of circumstances we have no one to tell us whether it be worth attaining.

10 A strange picture we make on our way to our chimæras, ceaselessly marching, grudging ourselves the time for rest; indefatigable, adventurous pioneers. It is true that we shall never reach the goal; it is even more than probable that there is no such place; and if we lived for centuries 15 and were endowed with the powers of a god, we should find ourselves not much nearer what we wanted at the end. O toiling hands of mortals! O unwearied feet, traveling ye know not whither! Soon, soon, it seems to you, you must come forth on some conspicuous hilltop, 20 and but a little way further, against the setting sun, descry the spires of El Dorado. Little do ye know your own blessedness; for to travel hopefully is a better thing than to arrive, and the true success is to labor.

WALKING TOURS

It must not be imagined that a walking tour, as some 25 would have us fancy, is merely a better or worse way of seeing the country. There are many ways of seeing landscape quite as good; and none more vivid, in spite of canting dilettantes, than from a railway train. But landscape on a walking tour is quite accessory. He who is indeed 30 of the brotherhood does not voyage in quest of the picturesque, but of certain jolly humors—of the hope and spirit with which the march begins at morning, and the peace and spiritual repletion of the evening's rest. He cannot tell whether he puts his knapsack on, or takes it off, with more delight. The excitement of the departure puts him in key for that of the arrival. Whatever he does is 5 not only a reward in itself, but will be further rewarded in the sequel; and so pleasure leads on to pleasure in an endless chain. It is this that so few can understand; they will either be always lounging or always at five miles an hour; they do not play off the one against the other, 10 prepare all day for the evening, and all evening for the next day. And, above all, it is here that your overwalker fails of comprehension. His heart rises against those who drink their curaçoa in liqueur glasses, when he himself can swill it in a brown john. He will not believe that the 15 flavor is more delicate in the smaller dose. He will not believe that to walk this unconscionable distance is merely to stupefy and brutalize himself, and come to his inn, at night, with a sort of frost on his five wits, and a starless night of darkness in his spirit. Not for him the 20 mild luminous evening of the temperate walker! He has nothing left of man but a physical need for bedtime and a double nightcap; and even his pipe, if he be a smoker, will be savorless and disenchanted. It is the fate of such an one to take twice as much trouble as is needed to obtain 25 happiness, and miss the happiness in the end; he is the man of the proverb, in short, who goes further and fares worse.

Now, to be properly enjoyed, a walking tour should be gone upon alone. If you go in a company, or even in pairs, 30 it is no longer a walking tour in anything but name; it is something else and more in the nature of a picnic. A walking tour should be gone upon alone, because freedom is of the essence; because you should be able to stop and

go on, and follow this way or that, as the freak takes you; and because you must have your own pace, and neither trot alongside a champion walker, nor mince in time with a girl. And then you must be open to all impressions and
5 let your thoughts take color from what you see. You should be as a pipe for any wind to play upon. "I cannot see the wit," says Hazlitt, "of walking and talking at the same time. When I am in the country I wish to vegetate like the country"—which is the gist of all that can
10 be said upon the matter. There should be no cackle of voices at your elbow, to jar on the meditative silence of the morning. And so long as a man is reasoning he cannot surrender himself to that fine intoxication that comes of much motion in the open air, that begins in a sort of
15 dazzle and sluggishness of the brain, and ends in a peace that passes comprehension.

During the first day or so of any tour there are moments of bitterness, when the traveler feels more than coldly toward his knapsack, when he is half in a mind to throw
20 it bodily over the hedge and, like Christian on a similar occasion, "give three leaps and go on singing." And yet it soon acquires a property of easiness. It becomes magnetic; the spirit of the journey enters into it. And no sooner have you passed the straps over your shoulder than
25 the lees of sleep are cleared from you, you pull yourself together with a shake, and fall at once into your stride. And surely, of all possible moods, this, in which a man takes the road, is the best. Of course, if he *will* keep thinking of his anxieties, if he *will* open the merchant
30 Abudah's chest and walk arm-in-arm with the hag—why wherever he is, and whether he walk fast or slow, the chances are that he will not be happy. And so much the more shame to himself! There are perhaps thirty men setting forth at that same hour, and I would lay a

large wager there is not another dull face among the
thirty. It would be a fine thing to follow, in a coat of
darkness, one after another of these wayfarers, some
summer morning, for the first few miles upon the
road. This one, who walks fast, with a keen look in 5
his eyes, is all concentrated in his own mind; he is up
at his loom, weaving and weaving, to set the landscape
to words. This one peers about, as he goes, among the
grasses; he waits by the canal to watch the dragon-flies;
he leans on the gate of the pasture, and cannot look 10
enough upon the complacent kine. And here comes
another, talking, laughing, and gesticulating to himself.
His face changes from time to time, as indignation flashes
from his eyes or anger clouds his forehead. He is composing articles, delivering orations, and conducting the 15
most impassioned interviews, by the way. A little
farther on, and it is as like as not he will begin to
sing. And well for him, supposing him to be no great
master in that art, if he stumble across no stolid peasant
at a corner; for on such occasion, I scarcely know which is 20
the more troubled, or whether it is worse to suffer the confusion of your troubador, or the unfeigned alarm of your
clown. A sedentary population, accustomed, besides,
to the strange mechanical bearing of the common tramp,
can in no wise explain to itself the gaiety of these passers- 25
by. I knew one man who was arrested as a runaway
lunatic, because, although a full-grown person with a red
beard, he skipped as he went like a child. And you
would be astonished if I were to tell you all the grave
and learned heads who have confessed to me that, when 30
on walking tours, they sang—and sang very ill—and had
a pair of red ears when, as described above, the inau-
spicious peasant plumped into their arms from round a
corner. And here, lest you think I am exaggerating, is

Hazlitt's own confession, from his essay *On Going a Journey*, which is so good that there should be a tax levied on all who have not read it:

5 "Give me the clear blue sky over my head," says he, "and the green turf beneath my feet, a winding road before me, and a three hours' march to dinner—and then to thinking! It is hard if I cannot start some game on these lone heaths. I laugh, I run, I leap, I sing for joy."

Bravo! After that adventure of my friend with the
10 policeman, you would not have cared, would you, to publish that in the first person? But we have no bravery nowadays, and, even in books, must all pretend to be dull and foolish as our neighbors. It was not so with Hazlitt. And notice how learned he is (as, indeed, through-
15 out the essay) in the theory of walking tours. He is none of your athletic men in purple stockings, who walk their fifty miles a day: three hours' march is his ideal. And then he must have a winding road, the epicure!

Yet there is one thing I object to in these words of his,
20 one thing in the great master's practice that seems to me not wholly wise. I do not approve of that leaping and running. Both of these hurry the respiration; they both shake up the brain out of its glorious open-air confusion; and they both break the pace. Uneven walking is not so
25 agreeable to the body, and it distracts and irritates the mind. Whereas, when once you have fallen into an equable stride, it requires no conscious thought from you to keep it up, and yet it prevents you from thinking earnestly of anything else. Like knitting, like the work of a
30 copying clerk, it gradually neutralizes and sets to sleep the serious activity of the mind. We can think of this or that, lightly and laughingly, as a child thinks, or as we think in a morning doze; we can make puns or puzzle out acrostics, and trifle in a thousand ways with words and

rimes; but when it comes to honest work, when we come to gather ourselves together for an effort, we may sound the trumpet as loud and long as we please; the great barons of the mind will not rally to the standard, but sit, each one, at home, warming his hands over his own fire and brooding on his own private thought!

In the course of a day's walk, you see, there is much variance in the mood. From the exhilaration of the start, to the happy phlegm of the arrival, the change is certainly great. As the day goes on, the traveler moves from the one extreme toward the other. He becomes more and more incorporated with the material landscape, and the open-air drunkenness grows upon him with great strides, until he posts along the road, and sees everything about him, as in a cheerful dream. The first is certainly brighter, but the second stage is more peaceful. A man does not make so many articles toward the end, nor does he laugh aloud; but the purely animal pleasures, the sense of physical wellbeing, the delight of every inhalation, of every time the muscles tighten down the thigh, console him for the absence of the others, and bring him to his destination still content.

Nor must I forget to say a word on bivouacs. You come to a milestone on a hill, or some place where deep ways meet under trees; and off goes the knapsack, and down you sit to smoke a pipe in the shade. You sink into yourself, and the birds come round and look at you; and your smoke dissipates upon the afternoon under the blue dome of heaven; and the sun lies warm upon your feet, and the cool air visits your neck and turns aside your open shirt. If you are not happy, you must have an evil conscience. You may dally as long as you like by the roadside. It is almost as if the millennium were arrived, when we shall throw our clocks and watches over the

housetop, and remember time and seasons no more.
Not to keep hours for a lifetime is, I was going to
say, to live for ever. You have no idea, unless you
have tried it, how endlessly long is a summer's day,
5 that you measure out only by hunger, and bring to an
end only when you are drowsy. I know a village where
there are hardly any clocks, where no one knows more
of the days of the week than by a sort of instinct for
the fête on Sundays, and where only one person can
10 tell you the day of the month, and she is generally
wrong; and if people were aware how slow Time journeyed
in that village, and what armfuls of spare hours he gives,
over and above the bargain, to its wise inhabitants, I
believe there would be a stampede out of London, Liver-
15 pool, Paris, and a variety of large towns, where the clocks
lose their heads, and shake the hours out each one faster
than the other, as though they were all in a wager. And
all these foolish pilgrims would each bring his own misery
along with him, in a watch-pocket! It is to be noticed,
20 there were no clocks and watches in the much-vaunted
days before the flood. It follows, of course, there were no
appointments, and punctuality was not yet thought
upon. "Though ye take from a covetous man all his
treasure," says Milton "he has yet one jewel left; ye
25 cannot deprive him of his covetousness." And so I
would say of a modern man of business, you may do
what you will for him, put him in Eden, give him the
elixir of life—he has still a flaw at heart, he still has
his business habits. Now, there is no time when busi-
30 ness habits are more mitigated than on a walking tour.
And so during these halts, as I say, you will feel almost
free.

But it is at night, and after dinner, that the best hour
comes. There are no such pipes to be smoked as those

that follow a good day's march; the flavor of the tobacco
is a thing to be remembered, it is so dry and aromatic, so
full and so fine. If you wind up the evening with grog,
you will own there was never such grog; at every sip a
jocund tranquility spreads about your limbs, and sits
easily in your heart. If you read a book—and you will
never do so save by fits and starts—you find the language
strangely racy and harmonious; words take a new meaning; single sentences possess the ear for half an hour together; and the writer endears himself to you, at every
page, by the nicest coincidence of sentiment. It seems as
if it were a book you had written yourself in a dream. To
all we have read on such occasions we look with special
favor. "It was on the 10th of April, 1798," says Hazlitt,
with amorous precision, "that I sat down to a volume
of the new *Héloïse*, at the Inn at Llangollen, over a
bottle of sherry and a cold chicken." I should wish
to quote more, for though we are mighty fine fellows
nowadays, we cannot write like Hazlitt. And, talking of
that, a volume of Hazlitt's essays would be a capital
pocket-book on such a journey; so would a volume of
Heine's songs; and for *Tristram Shandy* I can pledge a
fair experience.

If the evening be fine and warm, there is nothing better
in life than to lounge before the inn door in the sunset,
or lean over the parapet of the bridge, to watch the weeds
and the quick fishes. It is then, if ever, that you taste
Joviality to the full significance of that audacious word.
Your muscles are so agreeably slack, you feel so clean and
so strong and so idle, that whether you move or sit still,
whatever you do is done with pride and a kingly sort of
pleasure. You fall in talk with any one, wise or foolish,
drunk or sober. And it seems as if a hot walk purged
you, more than of anything else, of all narrowness and

pride, and left curiosity to play its part freely, as in a child or a man of science. You lay aside all your own hobbies, to watch provincial humors develop themselves before you, now as a laughable farce, and now grave and 5 beautiful like an old tale.

Or perhaps you are left to your own company for the night, and surly weather imprisons you by the fire. You may remember how Burns, numbering past pleasures, dwells upon the hours when he has been "happy 10 thinking." It is a phrase that may well perplex a poor modern, girt about on every side by clocks and chimes, and haunted, even at night, by flaming dial-plates. For we are all so busy, and have so many far-off projects to realize, and castles in the fire to turn into solid habitable 15 mansions on a gravel soil, that we can find no time for pleasure trips into the Land of Thought and among the Hills of Vanity. Changed times, indeed, when we must sit all night, beside the fire, with folded hands; and a changed world for most of us, when we find we can pass 20 the hours without discontent, and be happy thinking. We are in such haste to be doing, to be writing, to be gathering gear, to make our voice audible a moment in the derisive silence of eternity, that we forget that one thing, of which these are but the parts—namely, to live. 25 We fall in love, we drink hard, we run to and fro upon the earth like frightened sheep. And now you are to ask yourself if, when all is done, you would not have been better to sit by the fire at home, and be happy thinking. To sit still and contemplate—to remember the faces of 30 women without desire, to be pleased by the great deeds of men without envy, to be everything and everywhere in sympathy, and yet content to remain where and what you are—is not this to know both wisdom and virtue, and to dwell with happiness? After all, it is not they who carry flags, but they who look upon it from a private chamber, who have the fun of the procession. And once you are at that, you are in the very humor of all social heresy. It is no time for shuffling, or for big, empty words. If you ask yourself what you mean by fame, riches, or 5 learning, the answer is far to seek; and you go back into that kingdom of light imaginations, which seem so vain in the eyes of Philistines perspiring after wealth, and so momentous to those who are stricken with the disproportions of the world, and, in the face of the gigantic stars, 10 cannot stop to split differences between two degrees of the infinitesimally small, such as a tobacco pipe or the Roman Empire, a million of money or a fiddlestick's end.

You lean from the window, your last pipe reeking whitely into the darkness, your body full of delicious 15 pains, your mind enthroned in the seventh circle of content; when suddenly the mood changes, the weathercock goes about, and you ask yourself one question more; whether, for the interval, you have been the wisest philosopher or the most egregious of donkeys? Human 20 experience is not yet able to reply; but at least you have had a fine moment, and looked down upon all the kingdoms of the earth. And whether it was wise or foolish, to-morrow's travel will carry you, body and mind, into some different parish of the infinite. 25

ÆS TRIPLEX

THE changes wrought by death are in themselves so sharp and final, and so terrible and melancholy in their consequences, that the thing stands alone in man's experience, and has no parallel upon earth. It outdoes all other accidents because it is the last of them. Some- 30 times it leaps suddenly upon its victims, like a Thug;

sometimes it lays a regular siege and creeps upon their citadel during a score of years. And when the business is done, there is sore havoc made in other people's lives, and a pin knocked out by which many subsidiary friend-
5 ships hung together. There are empty chairs, solitary walks, and single beds at night. Again, in taking away our friends, death does not take them away utterly, but leaves behind a mocking, tragical, and soon intolerable residue, which must be hurriedly concealed. Hence a
10 whole chapter of sights and customs striking to the mind, from the pyramids of Egypt to the gibbets and dule trees of mediæval Europe. The poorest persons have a bit of pageant going toward the tomb; memorial stones are set up over the least memorable; and, in order to preserve
15 some show of respect for what remains of our old loves and friendships, we must accompany it with much grimly ludicrous ceremonial, and the hired undertaker parades before the door. All this, and much more of the same sort, accompanied by the eloquence of poets, has gone a
20 great way to put humanity in error; nay, in many phil-osophies the error has been embodied and laid down with every circumstance of logic; although in real life the bus-tle and swiftness, in leaving people little time to think, have not left them time enough to go dangerously wrong
25 in practice.

As a matter of fact, although few things are spoken of with more fearful whisperings than this prospect of death, few have less influence on conduct under healthy circum-stances. We have all heard of cities in South America
30 built upon the side of fiery mountains, and how, even in this tremendous neighborhood, the inhabitants are not a jot more impressed by the solemnity of mortal conditions than if they were delving gardens in the greenest corner of England. There are serenades and suppers and much

gallantry among the myrtles overhead; and meanwhile the foundation shudders underfoot, the bowels of the mountain growl, and at any moment living ruin may leap sky-high into the moonlight, and tumble man and his merry-making in the dust. In the eyes of very young people, and very dull old ones, there is something indescribably reckless and desperate in such a picture. It seems not credible that respectable married people, with umbrellas, should find appetite for a bit of supper within quite a long distance of a fiery mountain; ordinary life begins to smell of high-handed debauch when it is carried on so close to a catastrophe; and even cheese and salad, it seems, could hardly be relished in such circumstances without something like a definace of the Creator. It should be a place for nobody but hermits dwelling in prayer and maceration, or mere born-devils drowning care in a perpetual carouse.

And yet, when one comes to think upon it calmly, the situation of these South American citizens forms only a very pale figure for the state of ordinary mankind. This world itself, traveling blindly and swiftly in overcrowded space, among a million other worlds traveling blindly and swiftly in contrary directions, may very well come by a knock that would set it into explosion like a penny squib. And what, pathologically looked at, is the human body with all its organs, but a mere bagful of petards? The least of these is as dangerous to the whole economy as the ship's powder-magazine to the ship; and with every breath we breathe, and every meal we eat, we are putting one or more of them in peril. If we clung as devotedly as some philosophers pretend we do to the abstract idea of life, or were half as frightened as they make out we are, for the subversive accident that ends it all, the trumpets might sound by the hour and no

one would follow them into battle—the blue-peter might
fly at the truck, but who would climb into a sea-going
ship? Think (if these philosophers were right) with what
a preparation of spirit we should affront the daily peril
5 of the dinner-table: a deadlier spot than any battle-field
in history, where the far greater proportion of our ancestors have miserably left their bones! What woman
would ever be lured into marriage, so much more dangerous than the wildest sea? And what would it be to grow
10 old? For, after a certain distance, every step we take in
life we find the ice growing thinner below our feet, and
all around us and behind us we see our contemporaries
going through. By the time a man gets well into the
seventies, his continued existence is a mere miracle; and
15 when he lays his old bones in bed for the night, there is an
overwhelming probability that he will never see the day.
Do the old men mind it, as a matter of fact? Why, no.
They were never merrier; they have their grog at night,
and tell the raciest stories; they hear of the death of
20 people about their own age, or even younger, not as if it
was a grisly warning, but with a simple childlike pleasure
at having outlived someone else; and when a draught
might puff them out like a guttering candle, or a bit of a
stumble shatter them like so much glass, their old hearts
25 keep sound and unaffrighted, and they go on, bubbling
with laughter, through years of man's age compared to
which the valley of Balaclava was as safe and peaceful
as a village cricket-green on Sunday. It may fairly be
questioned (if we look to the peril only) whether it was a
30 much more daring feat for Curtius to plunge into the gulf,
than for any old gentleman of ninety to doff his clothes
and clamber into bed.

Indeed, it is a memorable subject for consideration,
with what unconcern and gaiety mankind pricks on along

the Valley of the Shadow of Death. The whole way is
one wilderness of snares, and the end of it, for those who
fear the last pinch, is irrevocable ruin. And yet we go
spinning through it all, like a party for the Derby.
Perhaps the reader remembers one of the humorous
devices of the deified Caligula: how he encouraged a
vast concourse of holiday-makers on to his bridge over
Baiæ bay; and when they were in the height of their
enjoyment, turned loose the Prætorian guards among the
company, and had them tossed into the sea. This is no
bad miniature of the dealings of nature with the transi-
tory race of man. Only, what a checkered picnic
we have of it, even while it lasts! and into what great
waters, not to be crossed by any swimmer, God's pale
Prætorian throws us over in the end!

We live the time that a match flickers; we pop the
cork of a ginger-beer bottle, and the earthquake swallows
us on the instant. Is it not odd, is it not incongruous, is
it not, in the highest sense of human speech, incredible,
that we should think so highly of the ginger-beer, and
regard so little the devouring earthquake? The love of
Life and the fear of Death are two famous phrases that
grow harder to understand the more we think about them.
It is a well-known fact that an immense proportion of
boat accidents would never happen if people held the
sheet in their hands instead of making it fast; and yet,
unless it be some martinet of a professional mariner or
some landsman with shattered nerves, every one of God's
creatures makes it fast. A strange instance of man's
unconcern and brazen boldness in the face of death!

We confound ourselves with metaphysical phrases,
which we import into daily talk with noble inappro-
priateness. We have no idea of what death is, apart from
its circumstances and some of its consequences to others;

and although we have some experience of living, there is
not a man on earth who has flown so high into abstraction
as to have any practical guess at the meaning of the word
life. All literature, from Job and Omar Khayyam to
5 Thomas Carlyle or Walt Whitman, is but an attempt
to look upon the human state with such largeness of
view as shall enable us to rise from the consideration of
living to the Definition of Life. And our sages give us
about the best satisfaction in their power when they say
10 that it is a vapor, or a show, or made out of the same stuff
with dreams. Philosophy, in its more rigid sense, has
been at the same work for ages; and after a myriad bald
heads have wagged over the problem, and piles of words
have been heaped one upon another into dry and cloudy
15 volumes without end, philosophy has the honor of laying
before us, with modest pride, her contribution toward
the subject: that life is a Permanent Possibility of Sensation. Truly a fine result! A man may very well love
beef, or hunting, or a woman; but surely, surely, not a
20 Permanent Possibility of Sensation! He may be afraid
of a precipice, or a dentist, or a large enemy with a club,
or even an undertaker's man; but not certainly of
abstract death. We may trick with the word life in its
dozen senses until we are weary of tricking; we may argue
25 in terms of all the philosophies on earth, but one fact
remains true throughout—that we do not love life, in the
sense that we are greatly preoccupied about its conserva-
tion; that we do not, properly speaking, love life at all,
but living. Into the views of the least careful there will
30 enter some degree of providence; no man's eyes are fixed
entirely on the passing hour; but although we have some
anticipation of good health, good weather, wine, active
employment, love, and self-approval, the sum of these
anticipations does not amount to anything like a general

view of life's possibilities and issues; nor are those who
cherish them most vividly, at all the most scrupulous of
their personal safety. To be deeply interested in the
accidents of our existence, to enjoy keenly the mixed
texture of human experience, rather leads a man to dis- 5
regard precautions, and risk his neck against a straw.
For surely the love of living is stronger in an Alpine
climber roping over a peril, or a hunter riding merrily
at a stiff fence, than in a creature who lives upon a diet
and walks a measured distance in the interest of his 10
constitution.

There is a great deal of very vile nonsense talked upon
both sides of the matter: tearing divines reducing life to
the dimensions of a mere funeral procession, so short as to
be hardly decent; and melancholy unbelievers yearning 15
for the tomb as if it were a world too far away. Both
sides must feel a little ashamed of their performances
now and again when they draw in their chairs to dinner.
Indeed, a good meal and a bottle of wine is an answer to
most standard works upon the question. When a man's 20
heart warms to his viands, he forgets a great deal of
sophistry, and soars into a rosy zone of contemplation.
Death may be knocking at the door, like the Commander's statue; we have something else in hand, thank God,
and let him knock. Passing bells are ringing all the world 25
over. All the world over, and every hour, some one is
parting company with all his aches and ecstasies. For us
also the trap is laid. But we are so fond of life that we
have no leisure to entertain the terror of death. It is a
honeymoon with us all through, and none of the longest. 30
Small blame to us if we give our whole hearts to this
glowing bride of ours, to the appetites, to honor, to the
hungry curiosity of the mind, to the pleasure of the eyes
in nature, and the pride of our own nimble bodies.

We all of us appreciate the sensations; but as for caring about the Permanence of the Possibility, a man's head is generally very bald, and his senses very dull, before he comes to that. Whether we regard life as a lane leading to a dead wall—a mere bag's end, as the French say—or whether we think of it as a vestibule or gymnasium, where we wait our turn and prepare our faculties for some more noble destiny; whether we thunder in a pulpit, or pule in a little atheistic poetry-book, about its vanity and brevity; whether we look justly for years of health and vigor, or are about to mount into a Bath-chair as a step toward the hearse; in each and all of these views and situations there is but one conclusion possible: that a man should stop his ears against paralyzing terror, and run the race that is set before him with a single mind. No one surely could have recoiled with more heartache and terror from the thought of death than our respected lexicographer; and yet we know how little it affected his conduct, how wisely and boldly he walked, and in what a fresh and lively vein he spoke of life. Already an old man, he ventured on his Highland tour; and his heart, bound with triple brass, did not recoil before twenty-seven individual cups of tea. As courage and intelligence are the two qualities best worth a good man's cultivation, so it is the first part of intelligence to recognize our precarious estate in life, and the first part of courage to be not at all abashed before the fact. A frank and somewhat headlong carriage, not looking too anxiously before, not dallying in maudlin regret over the past, stamps the man who is well armored for this world.

And not only well armored for himself, but a good friend and a good citizen to boot. We do not go to cowards for tender dealing; there is nothing so cruel as panic; the man who has least fear for his own carcass, has most time to consider others. That eminent chemist who took his walks abroad in tin shoes, and subsisted wholly upon tepid milk, had all his work cut out for him in considerate dealings with his own digestion. So soon as prudence has begun to grow up in the brain, like a dismal fungus, it finds its first expression in a paralysis of generous acts. The victim begins to shrink spiritually; he develops a fancy for parlors with a regulated temperature, and takes his morality on the principle of tin shoes and tepid milk. The care of one important body or soul becomes so engrossing, that all the noises of the outer world begin to come thin and faint into the parlor with the regulated temperature; and the tin shoes go equably forward over blood and rain. To be overwise is to ossify; and the scruple-monger ends by standing stockstill. Now the man who has his heart on his sleeve, and a good whirling weathercock of a brain, who reckons his life as a thing to be dashingly used and cheerfully hazarded, makes a very different acquaintance of the world, keeps all his pulses going true and fast, and gathers impetus as he runs, until, if he be running toward anything better than wildfire, he may shoot up and become a constellation in the end. Lord look after his health, Lord have a care of his soul, says he; and he has at the key of the position, and swashes through incongruity and peril toward his aim. Death is on all sides of him with pointed batteries, as he is on all sides of all of us; unfortunate surprises gird him round; mimmouthed friends and relations hold up their hands in quite a little elegiacal synod about his path: and what cares he for all this? Being a true lover of living, a fellow with something pushing and spontaneous in his inside, he must, like any other soldier, in any other stirring, deadly warfare, push on at his best pace until

he touch the goal. "A peerage or Westminster Abbey!"
cried Nelson in his bright, boyish, heroic manner. These
are great incentives; not for any of these, but for the
plain satisfaction of living, of being about their business
5 in some sort or other, do the brave, serviceable men of
every nation tread down the nettle danger, and pass
flyingly over all the stumbling-blocks of prudence.
Think of the heroism of Johnson, think of that superb
indifference to mortal limitation that set him upon his
10 dictionary, and carried him through triumphantly until
the end! Who, if he were wisely considerate of things
at large, would ever embark upon any work much more
considerable than a halfpenny post card? Who would
project a serial novel, after Thackeray and Dickens had
15 each fallen in mid-course? Who would find heart enough
to begin to live, if he dallied with the consideration of
death?

  And, after all, what sorry and pitiful quibbling all this
is! To forego all the issues of living in a parlor with a
20 regulated temperature—as if that were not to die a hundred times over, and for ten years at a stretch! As if it
were not to die in one's own lifetime, and without even
the sad immunities of death! As if it were not to die,
and yet be the patient spectators of our own pitiable
25 change! The Permanent Possibility is preserved, but the
sensations carefully held at arm's length, as if one kept a
photographic plate in a dark chamber. It is better to lose
health like a spendthrift than to waste it like a miser. It
is better to live and be done with it, than to die daily in
30 the sickroom. By all means begin your folio; even if the
doctor does not give you a year, even if he hesitates about
a month, make one brave push and see what can be accomplished in a week. It is not only in finished undertakings
that we ought to honor useful labor. A spirit goes out of

the man who means execution, which outlives the most
untimely ending. All who have meant good work with
their whole hearts, have done good work, although they
may die before they have the time to sign it. Every
heart that has beat strong and cheerfully has left a hope- 5
ful impulse behind it in the world, and bettered the tradition of mankind. And even if death catch people, like
an open pitfall, and in mid-career, laying out vast projects, and planning monstrous foundations, flushed with
hope, and their mouths full of boastful language, they 10
should be at once tripped up and silenced: is there not
something brave and spirited in such a termination?
and does not life go down with a better grace, foaming in
full body over a precipice, than miserably straggling to
an end in sandy deltas? When the Greeks made their 15
fine saying that those whom the gods love die young, I
cannot help believing they had this sort of death also
in their eye. For surely, at whatever age it overtake the
man, this is to die young. Death has not been suffered
to take so much as an illusion from his heart. In the 20
hot-fit of life, a-tiptoe on the highest point of being, he
passes at a bound on to the other side. The noise of the
mallet and chisel is scarcely quenched, the trumpets are
hardly done blowing, when, trailing with him clouds of
glory, this happy-starred, full-blooded spirit shoots into 25
the spiritual land.

BIOGRAPHICAL SKETCHES AND NOTES

FRANCIS BACON

Francis Bacon was born in 1561, three years after the accession of Queen Elizabeth, and three years before the birth of Shakespeare. His father was Sir Nicholas Bacon, Keeper of the Seals to the queen; his uncle was the queen's famous prime minister, Cecil, Lord Burleigh.

Bacon himself, from his earliest years, was ambitious of political power and place; but his powerful kinsmen seem not to have favored this ambition, and he was unable to secure any considerable advancement so long as Elizabeth lived. But with the accession of James First, his fortunes began to look up. His assiduous court to that monarch and to his favorite the Duke of Buckingham was rewarded by substantial and rapid promotion. In 1607 he was made Solicitor General, in 1613 Attorney General, in 1617 Lord Chancellor. Next year the king conferred upon him the title of Baron Verulam, and a little later he was made Viscount of St. Albans.

His character, however, was not proof against some meaner temptations than those of power. In 1621 he was charged with taking bribes in his judicial office, and brought to trial before the House of Lords. He pleaded guilty, was sentenced to pay a heavy fine and to be imprisoned during the pleasure of the king. His imprisonment lasted but a few days, and he soon received a practical pardon from the king; but he never entered public life again. After his disgrace he retired to his estate at St. Albans, and spent the few remaining years of his life in those philosophical studies in which he had long been interested, and to which the noblest efforts of his career had been given. He died in 1626.

It must be admitted that the moral character of Bacon was not commensurate with his intellectual power. Later students of his life, it is true, have shown that he hardly deserves the last epithet of Pope's famous characterization—

"The wisest, brightest, meanest of mankind."

It is probable that the judicial misconduct which caused his downfall was no worse than that of other men in the corrupt times of James First; but it is impossible to deny that his motives throughout his career were alloyed with a certain mean selfishness that led him sometimes into sycophancy, sometimes into ingratitude if not treachery, and later resulted in those acts that drove him out of public life.

Most of the works on which Bacon's fame as a philosopher must rest were written in Latin, and belong to the later period of his life. Even his early scientific work, the *Advancement of Learning*, 1605, reappeared nearly twenty years later in a Latin translation, as *DeAugmentis Scientiarum*. The *Essays*, which give him his claim to a high place among English writers, were the product of his earlier years. The original edition, of only ten essays, was issued in 1597. By 1612 the number had grown to thirty-eight; and the final edition of 1625 contains fifty-eight. In each successive edition the essays were revised and expanded; some of those in the 1597 edition had grown by 1625 to almost twice their original length.

Bacon's *Essays* may be said to be the first specimens of this literary form in English literature. Both the name and the form, indeed, were doubtless suggested to Bacon by the *Essais* of Montaigne, which were popular before 1597 in two good English translations. Bacon's essays could not have that delightful personal charm so characteristic of those of Montaigne; but they are the record of an observation remarkably acute and a reflection remarkably profound. Bacon himself declared that of all his writings they had been "most current, for that, it seems, they come home to men's business and bosoms." They probably come nearer to men's business than to men's bosoms; for Bacon sees all things through the cold, dry light of the intellect. He has largeness and vigor of thought, and a gift of imaginative illustration; but he is singularly deficient in either warmth or elevation of feeling. Yet nowhere else in our literature can there be found so much of the wisdom of prudence packed in so small a compass. What another writer would spread over a page, Bacon crowds into a sentence. A style so condensed cannot be easy and flowing; the essay becomes a bundle of apothegms. But, although Bacon deemed Latin the only language fit for permanent record, his diction is not highly Latinized, and his structure, though so condensed, is seldom involved or perplexed. No writing is more pithy; none more stimulating to the intellect.

OF RICHES

1, 2. Impedimenta: those things which impede, hindrances.

1, 7. Conceit: imagination.

1, 8. Where much is, etc. See *Ecclesiastes*, v, 11. The text given by Bacon is that of the Latin or Vulgate, Version of the Bible.

1, 10. Fruition: enjoyment. The lines may be paraphrased: "A man cannot realize any enjoyment of great riches; he has the custody of them, or the power of charity and gift from them, or the reputation of possessing them."

1, 18. Saith Salomon. See *Proverbs*, xxiii, 11.

2, 4. In studio rei, etc. " In his desire to increase his fortune, it was evident that he sought not the gratification of avarice but the means of benevolence." The quotation is from an oration of Cicero in defence of a Roman knight accused of having lent moneys to a king of Egypt.

2, 6. Salomon. See *Proverbs*, xxviii, 20: "He that maketh haste to be rich shall not be innocent."

2, 8. The poets feign. The story is found in the *Dialogues* of Lucian.

2, 26. Audits: rent-rolls, accounts rendered.

2, 34. Expect: wait for.

3, 1. Overcome: take advantage of those business transactions which are beyond the means of most men.

3, 7. Wait upon: watch for.

3, 8. Broke by: profit by; make use of servants or other means to draw men into further business difficulties.

3, 10. Better chapmen: better buyers or lenders.

3, 11. Naught: bad, naughty.

Chopping: barter or exchange; chopping of bargains, means, therefore, buying something in large amounts in order to raise the price—what is now called "making a corner."

3, 15. Usury: interest on money loaned.

3, 17. In sudore vultus alieni: "in the sweat of another man's brow."

3, 18. Plow upon Sundays. In his essay upon Usury, Bacon cites, among other "witty invectives" against the taking of interest, that the "Usurer is the greatest Sabbath breaker, because his plow goeth on Sunday."

3, 19. Scrivener: literally a writer; one who draws contracts and other business papers.

3, 20. Value unsound men: rate highly financially unsound men.

3, 23. Sugar man in the Canaries. The cultivation of sugar-cane was introduced into the Canary islands in 1507, and sugar soon became one of the most important articles of British commerce.

3, 26. Resteth: relies.

3, 31. Monopolies. Monopolies giving the exclusive privilege of dealing in certain commodities were often granted by the crown during the reign of Elizabeth, and still more freely by her successor, James First; but the outcry against the system became so general that in 1624 Parliament abolished monopolies, save in a few specified cases. See Traill's *Social England*, Vol. IV, ch. 13.

4, 1. Service: i.e., public service.

Of the best rise: best way of rising.

4, 5. Testamenta, etc.: wills and orphans drawn into a net.

4, 9. Despise them: i.e., riches.

4, 10. None worse: i.e., none despise them less.

4, 15. State: estate, fortune.

4, 21. Advancements: givings, charities.

Of Studies

5, 8. Bounded in: checked.

5, 9. Crafty men: men of practical ability.

Admire: wonder at.

5, 21. Would be: should be.

Arguments: subjects.

5, 24. Conference: conversation, speaking.

5, 31. Abeunt studia in mores: "Studies pass into habits."

5, 32. Stond: obstacle.

5, 33. Wrought out: worked out, removed.

6, 7. The schoolmen: the philosophers of the middle ages who held and taught the philosophy of Aristotle, especially as applied to religion.

6, 8. Cymini sectores: splitters of cumin seeds; as we say, hair splitters; prone to over-subtle distinctions.

Beat over matters: turn over matters, investigate.

Of Atheism

6, 12. The Legend. The Legenda Aurea or Golden Legend, stories of saints and their miracles, by Jacobus de Voragine, a Dominican friar, who died in 1292.

6, 13. **The Talmud.** A body of Jewish traditions and customs, with Commentary; the Alcoran, or Koran, the Mohammedan Scriptures, alleged to have been divinely revealed to Mohammed.

6, 19. **Second causes:** immediate or efficient causes, as distinguished from the ultimate or First Cause.

6, 25. **Leucippus:** a Greek philosopher, about 500 B. C., founder of the atomic school of philosophy. His views were adopted by his pupil, Democritus, and more fully expounded, 250 years later, by Epicurus.

6, 27. **Four mutable elements.** Aristotle taught that all terrestrial things were composed of the four elements, fire, air, earth, and water; but that there was a fifth, immutable element, ether, of which the heavenly bodies were made.

6, 29. **Seeds unplaced.** The atomic philosophers held that the world may have been formed by the chance arrangement of atoms.

6, 31. **The fool hath said.** See *Psalm* xiv, 1.

7, 5. **For whom it maketh:** for whose advantage it is.

7, 22. **Non deos,** etc.: "It is not profane to deny the gods of the vulgar, but profane to attribute to the gods the opinions of the vulgar."

7, 25. **Deny the administration,** etc. He dared to deny the influence of the gods, but he could not deny their existence.

7, 27. **Of the West:** i.e., of America.

8, 1. **Diagoras,** banished from Athens about 420 B. C. for his attacks upon the popular religion; **Bion,** a student of philosophy in Athens about 260 B. C. who was a pronounced disbeliever in the gods; **Lucian,** a brilliant Greek satirist and freethinker of the second century, who in his *Dialogues of the Gods* ridiculed Greek religious conceptions.

8, 11. **St. Bernard:** Abbot of Clairvaux, died 1153. His Latin may be interpreted: "We cannot now say, as is the people so are the priests, for now the people are not so (bad) as the priests."

8, 25. **Melior natura:** a better, i.e., a higher, nature.

9, 2. **Cicero.** The quotation is from *De Haruspicum Responsis*, IX, 19. It may be translated: "We may admire ourselves, Conscript Fathers, if we will, yet we have not surpassed the Spaniards in numbers, the Gauls in physical strength, the Carthagenians in craft, the Greeks in arts, nor, finally, the Italians and Latins themselves in homely, native sense of race and country; but we do surpass other races and nations in that we are wise enough to perceive all things to be ruled and governed by the power of the immortal gods."

QUERIES AND SUGGESTIONS

I. Of Riches.

1. Explain more fully what Bacon means by calling Riches the "baggage of virtue."

2. Bacon says the "gains of bargains are of a doubtful nature." What does he mean by "the gains of bargains"? And why are they doubtful?

3. Do you think Bacon right in pronouncing usury—i.e., interest on money loaned—one of the worst means of gain?

4. Do you know of any modern examples of what Bacon says of Monopolies?

5. Was Bacon's own practice consistent at every point with the teaching of this essay?

II. Of Studies.

1. "Studies serve for delight, for ornament, and for ability." Explain this statement and mention certain books or studies that seem to you well fitted for each of these purposes.

2. Explain more fully Bacon's meaning in each of the members of the statement "To spend too much time in studies is sloth; to use them too much for ornament is affectation; to make judgment wholly by their rules is the humor of a scholar."

3. "Some books are to be tasted, others to be swallowed, and some few to be chewed and digested." Give an example of each kind.

4. Why should "poets" make men witty? A little further on Bacon says that "if a man's wit be wandering, let him study the mathematics." Are the two statements consistent?

III. Of Atheism.

1. What is the meaning of the word Atheism?

2. "A little philosophy inclineth man's mind to atheism, but depth in philosophy bringeth men's minds about to religion." Explain somewhat more fully Bacon's reasons for that statement.

3. What reasons does Bacon give for charging professing atheists with inconsistency?

4. What causes of atheism are enumerated by Bacon? Can you think of any that he has not mentioned?

ABRAHAM COWLEY

Abraham Cowley was born in London, in the year 1618. His parents, says his friend and biographer, Bishop Sprat, were "citizens of a virtuous life and sufficient estate"; which handsome phrase, Dr. Samuel Johnson thinks, is meant to disguise the fact that the father was a Puritan and a grocer. The father, we know, died before the birth of his son, and young Cowley's early education was directed by his mother. If we can trust his own account, he felt the call to poetry at a very tender age. It was when he was just beginning to read, that a copy of Spenser's Faery Queen which was wont to lie in his mother's parlor awoke his childish imagination; before he was twelve years of age he had read it over and over, and "was thus made irrevocably a poet." The following year he gave proof of his calling by issuing a thin volume of his own verses, which, as he said with pardonable indulgence in his later life, contained some things he was not ashamed of.

His plans for a poetic career were, however, destined to interruption. After passing through Westminister school, he went on to Cambridge. When that university, in the troublous times of the Civil War, passed under the control of the Puritans, Cowley indignantly quitted it for Oxford, then the seat of the royal government. For, even if, as Johnson asserts, his father was a Puritan, Cowley himself was always a sturdy royalist. At Oxford he formed the acquaintance of a number of prominent noblemen, and accepted a position as secretary in the household of Lord Henry Jermyn, one of the closest friends of King Charles. Cowley seems to have made himself so useful in the circle immediately about the king that when Queen Henrietta Maria was forced to flee to France, in 1644, he accompanied her, and for several years thereafter was entrusted with the charge of the cipher correspondence between Charles and his exiled queen. He remained abroad twelve years, occupied in various services for the royalist party, both before and after the execution of Charles. In 1656, he came over to England that he might, as his biographer puts it, "under pretence of privacy and retirement, take occasion of giving notice of the posture of affairs in this kingdom"—that is, in homelier language, serve as a kind of spy in the interest of the king over the water. But he found that service rather hazardous; and after escaping from arrest once, he concluded to return to France, where he remained until the Restoration. He always regretted this long interruption of his favorite studies; and in later life was inclined to think it had been fatal to his chosen ambition as a poet.

On his return to England for permanent residence, he failed to secure from Charles Second, whose family he had served so long, any substantial recognition of his service. Disappointed in his hopes, and vexed by the ingratitude of men in high place, he now persuaded himself that he wished only to retire from public life, and to find somewhere leisure and seclusion. At one time he professes to have had serious thoughts of emigrating to America. He chose, instead, to accept a much less distant retreat. He went into the country, first to Barn Elms, a village on the Thames, and then to Chertsey, where, through the influence of his old patron Lord Jermyn—now created first Earl of St. Albans—he was given the lease of a considerable estate. It is said, however, that he did not find his rustic seclusion as attractive as he had pictured it. Dr. Johnson, who never had any desire for seclusion, rather cruelly prints a letter in which the lonesome poet complains that the wretched weather has given him a severe cold, that he has fallen down and nearly broken a rib, that his tenants will not pay their rents but pester him by turning their cattle into his meadow every night, with such other annoyances as, God knows, have brought him near to suicide. His retirement, whether fortunate or not, he did not long survive. Having overheated himself by working with the laborers one day, he was seized with a "defluxion and stoppage in the throat," which speedily carried him off. He died in 1667. At his funeral in Westminster Abbey, King Charles declared in over-late recognition of his merit, "Mr. Cowley has not left behind him a better man in England"—a remark very characteristic of this ungrateful king, "Who never said a foolish thing, and never did a wise one."

So far as can be gathered from the testimony of those who knew him, Cowley seems to have been of a singularly refined and gentle temperament, a thoughtful, kindly, courteous man, with a slender vein of melancholy sentiment. The disappointments of his life had depressed but not embittered him; if he had not the gift of a more vigorous nature to make powerful friends, he seems to have made no enemies.

The poetry of Cowley, it does not fall within the purpose of this volume to discuss. He wrote a good deal of it; and for a time enjoyed a fame which it is now difficult to understand. Even Milton, in those years when he was himself writing the *Paradise Lost*, is said to have pronounced Spenser, Shakespeare and Cowley the three greatest English poets. But this eminence was very brief. There is no better example of the transiency of literary fashions. Even as early as 1737, Pope could ask

> "Who now reads Cowley? If he pleases yet,
> His moral pleases, not his pointed wit."

Certainly later generations have not learned to read him. *The Mistress*, a collection of love lyrics, seems to the reader of to-day to have neither love nor music. The *Davideis*, a tedious epic on the story of King David, he hoped to carry through twelve books, but finished only four—and no one has been found to wish it longer. The *Pindaric Odes*, his most ambitious effort, were much admired in their own day, as introducing into English poetry a new and lofty form; but most readers of to-day will pronounce them, in spite of fine lines, grandiose and stilted. There are passages here and there, and two or three entire short poems, that well deserve preservation; but it is to be feared that Cowley's extravagant statements, ingenious conceits, and chill rhetoric, produce in the modern reader only a mixed feeling of wonder and irritation.

But if Cowley is forgotten as a poet he well deserves to be remembered as an essayist. His prose is as good as his poetry is bad. Curiously enough, it is almost entirely free from the unnatural artifice and ingeniously bad taste that disfigure his verse. The group of short essays, of which two are given in this volume, were all written in the closing years of his life. They have in them the wisdom of ripened experience with the charm of a genial and kindly temperament. They are the reflections of a thoughtful, observant scholar, who knows both men and books; and they are written in a in a style pure, natural, and easy. Cowley was an excellent classical scholar, and Johnson pronounces his Latin verse superior to Milton's; but his English prose is singularly free from the heavy Latinisms that mark much of the writing of his age. No more lucid, attractive prose was written in England during the last forty years of the seventeenth century.

OF SOLITUDE

10, 1. Nunquam minus solus, quam cum solus: "Never less alone than when alone." The saying is generally attributed to Cicero, but Cowley gives it to Scipio.

10, 5. Scipio: Publius Cornelius Scipio, surnamed Africanus (B. C. 237–183), the most famous and popular of the generals of early Rome. After successful campaigns against the Carthaginians in Spain, he carried the war into Africa, and in the great battle of Zama defeated the Carthaginians, and so ended the long struggle between Rome and Carthage. In the year 185 B. C. he retired from public life and spent his last years on his country seat at Liternum, in Campania.

10, 15. Seneca: L. Annaeus Seneca, Roman philosopher and statesman (circa 5–65 A. D.). In one of his *Epistles*, No. 86, he describes at considerable length the villa of Scipio, dwelling especially upon the plainness of the great Scipio's bath as compared with the luxurious appointments of the Roman baths in his day, and then exclaims—"*Quantæ nunc aliqui rusticitatis damnant Scipionem . . . O hominem calamitosum! Nesciit vivere!*"

10, 22. Hannibal. The great Carthaginian general who, after several important victories over the Romans in Italy, was finally defeated by Scipio in Africa. Cowley thinks him unfortunate because he did not, like Scipio, retire into private life after the battle that closed his career, but gave his attention to civil reforms and remained in public life, until, in order to avoid surrender to the Romans, he ended his life by poison.

10, 26. Montaigne: Michel Eyquem, Seigneur de Montaigne (1533–1592), one of the wisest and most delightful of French writers, the real founder of the Essay as a literary form. The passage quoted is in the essay *On Solitude*, Book I, Essay 38: "*Respondons à l'ambition. Que c'est elle mesme qui nous donne goust de la solitude: car que fuit elle tant que la sociéte?*"

11, 18. Sic ego secretis possum, etc. Quoted from Tibullus, XIII, 9.

11, 31. Odi, et amo, etc. Quoted from Catullus, *De Amore Suo*, LXXXIII.

13, 8. O vita, stulto longa, sapienti brevis! This seems to be a modification of a line by Publius Syrus—

> "*O vita, misero longa, felici brevis.*"
> "O life, long to the unhappy, to the happy brief."

Publius (or Publilius) Syrus was a late Latin writer, about 50 B. C. Short sayings or proverbs by him, or attributed to him were popular through the middle ages.

13, 18. Methuselah in the nine hundred and sixty-ninth year of his life. Genesis v, 27.

14, 9. O qui me gelidis in vallibus Haemi, etc. The lines are from the Second *Georgic* of Virgil, 489–490. The pleasing stanzas that follow this essay, in sentiment and in imagery, are evidently suggested by the closing passage of this Georgic.

Of Myself

16, 25. These precedent discourses. This paper stood last in the collection of essays.

17, 16. in which they dispensed with me alone: i.e., which they dispensed with in my case only. "He was wont to relate that he had this defect in memory at that time, that his teachers could never bring it to retain the ordinary rules of grammar. However, he supplied that want by conversing with the books themselves from whence those rules had been drawn. That was no doubt a better way, though much more difficult, and he afterwards found this benefit by it, that having got the Greek and Roman languages, as he had done his own, not by precept but use, he practised them not as a scholar but as a native." Sprat's *Memoir*.

17, 21. An ode, which I made when I was but thirteen years old. This is the ode entitled "The Wish," beginning—

"Lest the misjudging world should chance to say."

The first eight stanzas, though somewhat "boyish" in manner, describe with a good deal of vigor the various types of character of which he is not envious, as the Puritan, the School Master, the Justice, the Courtier, the Lawyer, the Singing Man, the Court Beauty.

18, 18. The conclusion is taken out of Horace. The last five lines of Cowley's ode are a free rendering of Horace's Ode, Book III, 29, lines 41ff.

18, 31. Spenser's works: i.e., Edmund Spenser's *Faery Queen*.

19, 9. Went to the university: but was soon torn from thence. Cowley was entered at Cambridge; but when that university passed under Puritan influence, he left Cambridge for Oxford, 1643, Oxford then being the seat of the royalist party.

19, 14. The family of one of the best persons: Henry Jermyn, created first earl of St. Albans in 1660.

19, 15. The court of one of the best princesses. Henrietta Maria, queen of Charles First.

20, 2. In business of great and honorable trust. Cowley had charge of the correspondence in cipher between Charles and his absent queen.

20, 8. Well then; I now do plainly see: the opening line of one of the lyrics in Cowley's poem The Mistress, which he entitled "The Wish." It is, as he says, another version of the earlier poem bearing the same title.

20, 19. Thou neither great at court, nor in the war. These two stanzas are from one of Cowley's Pindaric Odes entitled "Destiny."

21, 12. Ben: i.e., Ben Jonson, dramatist contemporary with

Shakespeare. He was accounted in his own day the first poet and critic of the age.

21, 17. **Take thy ease.** See *Luke* xii, 19.

21, 22. **Non ego perfidum dixi sacramentum.** "I have not made a false promise."

21, 27. **Nec vos, dulcissima mundi.** I have not been able to locate this quotation.

QUERIES AND SUGGESTIONS

1. What would you infer from the two essays given in the text as to the temperament, habits, tastes, culture, of Cowley himself?

How far do you judge the desire for retirement and solitude expressed in both essays was native to him, and how far produced by the disappointments and vexations of his career?

2. Most of the poetry of Cowley, like that which he quotes in these essays, was in the form of odes; what is an ode?

3. Can you point out any manifest differences in diction and structure between the style of these essays and that of the essays of Bacon which precede them in this volume?

RICHARD STEELE AND JOSEPH ADDISON

Richard Steele and Joseph Addison will always be remembered together. There was but a little more than a year's difference in their ages; they were close friends from the days when they first met in the Charterhouse school; they were associated in the one form of literary endeavor on which their fame must chiefly rest.

Steele was born in Dublin, in 1672. One of his earliest recollections, as he says in a characteristic paper, was that of the death of his father and the grief of his widowed mother. The father left no fortune; but young Steele was sent up to the Charterhouse school in London, when he was twelve years old, on the recommendation of a distant relative, the Duke of Ormond. Two years later young Joseph Addison entered the same school. The fatherless lad from Dublin and the son of the cultured and scholarly dean Addison of Lichfield cathedral soon became fast friends. Addison was always much the better scholar, and after only a year's stay at the Charterhouse, he went up to Oxford, in 1687, and was entered at Queen's college. It was not until three years later that Steele followed him and was matriculated at Christ's Church. But the cloistered life of the university had little attraction for the active spirit of Steele; after some years' stay, he left Oxford without a degree and entered the army as an ensign in Lord Cutt's regiment of foot-guards. We know little of his life for the next six or seven years, save that he was for some time secretary to Lord Cutts, and by 1700 is spoken of as Captain Steele. His regiment was quartered in London, and Steele's military duties seem to have left him ample leisure to become acquainted with the wit and fashion of the town. His life in the Guards and as a young fellow about town was exposed to many temptations; his first book is proof that he felt himself not always proof against them. This curious little volume appeared in 1701, with the title *The Christian Hero, an Argument proving that no Principles but those of Religion are sufficient to make a great Man.* Steele wrote it, he said, as a kind of confession of faith, with the hope that by setting down his principles in black and white he might make his conduct better conform to them. From which we should infer, I think, not the irregularity of his life, but the activity of his conscience.

The *Christian Hero*, at all events, had one good result; it made Steele in love with the pen. He had found his vocation. He turned first to the stage, as affording the readiest opportunity to a young fellow of literary aspirations. In December of that same year, 1701, his first comedy, *The Funeral*, was produced at the Drury Lane theater, and by the aid of his fellow soldiers of the Guards, scored a success. It is a satire on the silly fashion of hired mourning, and in spite of its lugubrious title contains some excellent humor. A second comedy, *The Lying Lover*, the plot of which was suggested by Corneille's *Menteur*, appeared early in 1704, and a third—the best of the series—*The Tender Husband*, in 1705. It ought to be said that Steele did not in these plays belie the principles he had avowed in the *Christian Hero*. Their humor, in most refreshing contrast to that of other English comedies of the time, was clean and wholesome throughout.

In 1706 Steele decided to retire from the army and give himself to literature and politics. He had only the very small fortune left him at her death by the wife whom he had married the previous year; but he was emboldened by the success of his plays, and determined to live thereafter by his wits. The glimpses we get of him during the next half dozen years prove that the venture was not always very successful. Steele's prudence was never equal to his assurance; and he never was quite secure from the bailiffs. About a year after the death of his first wife, he began to pay court to a Miss Mary Scurlock, a young lady of wit, beauty, and some little fortune. The wooing was not long adoing, and they were married in September, 1707. The marriage was an almost ideally happy one; but Mrs. Steele, who was evidently much the better economist of the two, was to hear a good many explanations of her husband's business irregularities. The series of letters and notelets written to his "Prue," both before and after the marriage, full of all fond endearments and ingeneous excuses, form quite the most delightful set of domestic correspondence in our literary history.

All through those years Steele had kept up his early intimacy with Addison, and by 1709 had formed the acquaintance of Swift, Pope, Arbuthnot, and most of the lesser wits about town. It was in this year that he hit upon the scheme which was to make him famous, and to introduce a new and distinct form into English literature. He founded the *Tatler*. Two years before, in 1707, Daniel Defoe had started his *Review* which may be called the beginning of political journalism; it was left for Steele to found the first literary journal. The *Tatler* contained one short essay or sometimes two or three brief letters, usually with a tag of notices and advertisements. Who wrote the new paper no one knew at first; for Steele concealed his editorship under the pseudonym of Isaac Bickerstaff, a name that Swift had made the town-talk a year before by a clever pamphlet ridiculing the pretensions of a notorious quack and almanac maker. The *Tatler* was to be issued three times a week, on post days, and was at first sold for one penny. After the twenty-fifth number, a blank page was added for correspondence, and in this form the price was three halfpence. It excluded party politics and all graver questions of theology or religion. Steele's purpose, which became clearer to himself as he proceeded, was to furnish the town from day to day, with a picture of the more entertaining phases of manners and society and at the same time to correct its follies and vices by a kindly and genial satire. "The general purpose of this paper" he said in the dedication to the first volume, "is to expose the false arts of life, to pull off the disguises of cunning, vanity and affectation, and to recommend a general simplicity in our dress, our discourse, and our behavior." For such a task no one could have been better fitted. Nobody knew the town better; nobody loved it more. As the weeks go by, we find in the pages of the *Tatler* a constantly changing series of glimpses of London life—brief stories, sketches of humorous characters, satire on fashionable follies, short sermons on minor morals, all filled with Steele's delightful humor and told in his easy and familiar manner. For all which we have to thank Richard Steele. The plan of the *Tatler* was his own devising, and the early numbers seem to have been written almost exclusively by him. He did not consult Addison before starting the paper; and it was only after about five months that he received any very substantial aid from the pen of his old friend.

By this time Mr. Addison had attained considerable fame both in literature and in politics. His career at first, indeed, had not seemed one of very brilliant promise. He had entered the university two years before Steele; he remained there five years after Steele had left. He had been granted a fellowship in Magdalen college and seemed contented with that life of studious ease. In 1699, after twelve years residence in Oxford, he received from Lord Halifax a pension which enabled him to spend nearly three years on the continent in travel and study. In 1703, as his pension had lapsed, and the war with France made further residence abroad hazardous, he came back to London, and for a time lived quietly in humble lodgings in the Haymarket. But in 1704 Marlborough won the famous victory of Blenheim, and the Whig ministers at the suggestion of his patron Halifax, invited the scholarly Mr. Addison to celebrate that glorious event in verse. The poem of *The Campaign*, which Addison wrote in response to this august invitation, will be voted dull by most readers of to-day; but it won a surprising admiration then, and at once placed Mr. Addison in the public eye. He was rewarded by an appointment as Under Secretary of State; in 1707 was elected to parliament, and was never out of office again so long as he lived. Yet nothing Addison ever did in political life would have preserved his name. His fame will always rest upon the literary work he did in association with Richard Steele. As Steele's biographer, Mr. Aitken, truly says, "The world owes Addison to Steele." Thenceforward the best work of either man was done in coöperation with the other.

Steele brought the *Tatler* to an end in January, 1711. He had, however, no thought of abandoning that form of literary effort; on the first day of the following March appeared the first number of that more famous paper the *Spectator*. In plan and manner the *Spectator* was similar to its predecessor; but it was to be issued daily. It is customary to speak of "Addison's *Spectator*"; but, although Addison was associated with Steele in the conduct of the new paper from the first, it seems to have been Steele's venture. The contributions of the two men, also, were about equal in number. The *Spectator* continued under this joint management until 1713, when Steele, chafing under the agreement to keep the paper out of politics, withdrew and set up the *Guardian*, which was not so rigidly closed to party discussion. Addison continued the *Spectator* another year, when it was finally abandoned, in 1714. Steele later set up two or three periodicals, each of which ran for a few weeks or months; but neither he nor Addison ever succeeded in such an enterprise alone. Addison greatly increased his contemporary reputation by producing, in 1713, that now forgotten drama, *Cato*, and continued in public life, filling one office after another, till he rose to his highest dignity, in 1717, as Secretary of State. He died in 1719.

Steele survived his friend ten years. He could never learn the lesson of careful prudence, and was never quite free from financial troubles. The great grief of his life fell upon him when his wife died, in 1716; but he retained much of the genial and buoyant spirit of youth till the end. After 1720 he retired from public life and spent his last years in the pleasant old town of Hereford, or over the Welsh border in Carmarthen, where he died in 1729.

The periodical essay, as Steele and Addison wrote it, was a distinctly new form in our literature. Brief and entertaining, meant to be read at a sitting, it is ill-suited to the discussion of matters serious or profound. The reader of to-day will probably omit most of Addison's careful critical and philosophic papers. But no form could be better fitted for the depiction of the lighter and more humorous phases of daily life. The *Tatler* and *Spectator* mark that quickened interest in what we call society that was so characteristic of the early years of the eighteenth century. It is in their pages that we may best see the social life of the town in the time of Queen Anne, with its new feeling for the charm of manners, its rather shallow vein of sentiment, its immense admiration for wit, good sense and good breeding. These essays were written for the town, for the club and the drawing-room. They would be four days old before they could reach Edinburgh or Dublin; but they could be laid damp from the press on five hundred coffee-house tables and be read before nightfall by ten thousand people. In these circumstances literature inevitably became polished, urbane. The essayist must not be too much in earnest; he must not preach; he must not lose the air of good society, the dignified ease of good conversation. To read much in the *Tatler* and *Spectator* is to take a lesson in manners as well as in literature.

Now in this form of writing Steele and Addison have never been surpassed. Unlike in temperament and in style, each was the complement of the other. Steele was the more hearty, spontaneous; Addison the more thoughtful, observant. Steele's humor is the more exuberant; Addison's the more subtle, delicate. Steele was a warm-hearted impulsive man, who threw himself into the life he described with generous sympathy for all its humor and its pathos; Addison was a spectator of that life from the outside, and depicted it with a suave and quiet irony. Steele's literary style is often careless, almost slip-shod; but we forget these imperfections of his work in our love for the man. His short stories often have a warmth of natural feeling that Addison never could command. Addison, on the other hand, was master of a style that has ever since been justly admired for the union of accuracy with perfect ease and grace. The most careful, almost finical of writers, his writing yet shows no trace of labor or effort. His manner has never been better characterized than in the famous dictum of Johnson: "Whoever would attain an English style, familiar but not coarse, elegant but not ostentatious, must give his days and nights to the study of Addison."

Finally, in the writings of both these men, underneath all external charm of manner, is a broad and genial humanity, and an earnest moral purpose. They were good men, sincerely intent upon making the world about them a cleaner, brighter, more joyous place to live in. It is no exaggeration to say that the *Tatler* and *Spectator* rendered a better service to their age than all the sermons preached in the reign of Anne; for they brought morality into fashion.

RECOLLECTIONS OF CHILDHOOD.   STEELE: *Tatler, No.* 181

26, 15. **Manes:** Latin term for the spirits of the departed; hence sometimes used, as here, for the memory of the dead.

27, 31. **The death of my father.** Dobson, in his volume of *Selections from Steele*, quotes the beautiful passage in which Thackeray contrasts the simple pathos of Steele in this paragraph with the "lonely serenity" of Addison's mood in the closing passage of the essay on Westminster Abbey: "The third whose theme is death, too, and who will speak his moral as Heaven teaches him, leads you up to his father's coffin, and shows you his beautiful mother weeping, and himself an unconscious little boy wondering at her side. His own natural tears flow as he takes your hand, and confidingly asks for your sympathy; 'See how good and innocent and beautiful women are' he says, 'how tender little children. Let us love these and one another, brother—God knows we have need of love and pardon!'"—*English Humorists.*

29, 29. **The first object my eyes ever beheld with love.** Nothing is known with reference to this early attachment.

30, 10. **Garraway's coffee-house.** The coffee-house was one of the most interesting features of London life in the time of Queen Anne. It was the center of news, the resort of the men of business, the men of letters, the men of fashion. Says Misson, a traveler who visited London in 1719, "These coffee-houses are very numerous in London and extremely convenient. You have all manner of news there; you have a good fire which you may sit by as long as you please; you have a dish of coffee, you meet your friends for the transaction of business, and all for a penny, if you don't care to spend more." The coffee-house served as a kind of club. Steele gives a pleasant and gossiping account of a coffee-house morning, in *Spectator* No. 49. Although any coffee-house was open to everybody, naturally many of them came to be patronized especially by men of particular professions; the Grecian, by scholars, Child's by physicians, Jonathan's by stock-brokers. It will be remembered that Steele proposed to date all *Tatler* papers upon poetry from Will's coffee-house, which had been the favorite resort of Dryden in his later years. Buttons', near by, was Addison's headquarters. Garraway's, mentioned in the text, was patronized almost exclusively by merchants; Garraway, who opened it in the later years of the seventeenth century, is said to have been the first man who sold tea by retail in London.

For a good account of London coffee-houses, see Ashton's *Social Life in the Reign of Queen Anne*, where over 500 are named.

A Visit to a Friend.   Steele: *Tatler, No.* 95

31, 29. **Mrs. Mary.** Young unmarried women were commonly addressed as Mrs. or Mistress in Steele's time. The term Miss was reserved for girls under ten, or for older ones who misbehaved.

33, 30. **Her baby:** i.e., her doll. The word doll, with its present meaning did not come into general use until after 1750.

34, 18. **Full-bottomed periwigs.** Wigs were universally worn by gentlemen in the time of Queen Anne. The full-bottomed wig was one in which the hair fell in rolls or curls about the neck, instead of being tied in a cue, as in the "tie-wig." The periwig attained its greatest size at this time and sometimes seems to have been costly. An earlier number of the *Tatler*, 54, gives an account of a petty quarrel, where Phillis, angered by a sharp remark from her lover, snatches off his wig and throws it in the fire. "There," said he.

"thou art a brave termagant jade; do you know, hussy, that wig cost me forty guineas." For a full account of the wig, see Ashton's *Social Life in the Reign of Queen Anne*, Chap. XIII.

34, 19. Open-breasted. It was a fashion at this time to leave the waist-coat unbuttoned nearly down to the waist, in order to show the ruffled shirt underneath. The fashion was thought to have an irresistible effect upon the ladies. "A sincere heart has not made half so many conquests as an open waistcoat."—*Tatler*, 151.

35, 3. A point of war: a martial roll of the drum.

35, 15. Don Belianis of Greece, etc. These were popular chap-books or story-books, founded on older romances. Don Belianis was one of the continuations of the Spanish romance of Amadis of Gaul. Guy of Warwick was the hero of a romance originating in England in the twelfth century. The Seven Champions were national heroes, connected in a romance dating from the sixteenth century. The four probably most interesting to the English lad were St. George of England, St. Andrew of Scotland, St. Patrick of Ireland, and St. David of Wales. The other three were St. Denis of France, St. Anthony of Italy, and St. James of Spain.

35, 22. John Hickerthrift: a legendary strong man, whose adventures were recounted in several chap-books. A character like that of Jack the Giant killer.

35, 23. Bevis of Southampton: one of the heroes of the Arthurian romance. His story was put into a popular prose form about 1650.

MR. BICKERSTAFF'S THREE NEPHEWS. STEELE: *Tatler, No.* 30

36, 25. The lions, the tombs, Bedlam. Lions were kept on exhibition in the Tower of London. "To see the lions" thus early became a popular phrase. In 1703 there were "two lions, two lionesses, and a cub." The tombs were those in Westminster Abbey, then, as now, one of the sights of London. See Addison's famous paper, *Spectator*, No. 26, on p. 48 of this volume. Bedlam was the St. Bartholomew's hospital for the insane. It is a curious comment on the temper of the age that Bedlam should have been thought one of the sights of London, visited daily by crowds for entertainment, with only the restriction that, "No person can be admitted to come or stay as a spectator after sunsetting."

37, 12. Taws: marbles used as shooters.

37, 21. Provident conduct. Steele perhaps naturally expressed admiration for this virtue in which he was himself most deficient.

38, 13. A citizen: i.e., a resident of the city (of London), and therefore assumed to be in trade.

NED SOFTLY. ADDISON: *Tatler, No.* 163

40, 1. (Motto.) The motto is translated in the edition of 1764: "Suffenus has no more wit than a mere clown when he attempts to write verses; and yet he is never happier than when he is scribbling, so much does he admire himself and his compositions. And, indeed, this is the foible of every one of us; for there is no man living who is not a Suffenus in one thing or another." Catullus, *De Suffeno, XXII,* 14*ff.*

40, 16. A late paper of yours: No. 155 of the *Tatler,* in which Mr. Bickerstaff describes a troublesome acquaintance who pestered him for news about the war.

40, 19. A gazette. An official publication established in 1665 and continued to the present day, giving lists of appointments, promotions, and official reports. In Addison's time it was occupied mostly with foreign news from the armies.

40, 20. Our armies: on the continent. The great war of the Spanish Succession began in 1702 and was not concluded until 1713.

41, 2. Waller. Edmund Waller (1666–1687), was generally credited, in Addison's time, with having done much to introduce smoothness and grace into English verse. Some of his complimentary lyrics, such as Ned Softly admires, have seldom been surpassed in their kind, as the "Go lovely rose" and "Lines to a Girdle."

41, 9. Gothic. The word is generally used in the early eighteenth century as a synonym for rude, inelegant.

41, 10. Quibbles, which are so frequent in the most admired of our English poets: that is, in the poets of the seventeenth century, such as Donne, Herbert, Crashaw, and Cowley.

41, 19. Sonnet. The term is frequently applied in the writings of Addison's time to any short lyric.

42, 8. Roscommon's translation: Wentworth Dillon, fourth Earl of Roscommon, whose translation of Horace's *Art of Poetry* was published in 1680.

SIR ROGER DE COVERLEY IN WESTMINSTER ABBEY. ADDISON: *Spectator, No.* 329

44, 17. (Motto.)

"For we must go
Where Numa and where Ancus went before."
Horace, *Epistles* I, 6.

44, 19. **Sir Roger de Coverley.** The most familiar and delightful of all the characters Steele and Addison have created for us. Perhaps no personage in English fiction is better known. The original conception of the old knight seems to have been Steele's; but Addison developed the character with much more subtle humor, though with a tinge of malicious satire not seen in Steele's more genial picture. This is one of the latest of the Coverley papers; the account of the knight's death followed a few months later.

44, 28. **Baker's Chronicle:** "A chronicle of the Kings of England from the time of the Romans' Government unto the Death of King James. By Sir Richard Baker, 1643."

44, 29. **Sir Andrew Freeport:** the person "of next consideration" to Sir Roger de Coverley in the Spectator Club, introduced in *Spectator*, No. 2.

45, 6. **Widow Trueby's water.** This, and many of the nostrums of that day and of ours, probably owed its efficacy largely to the alcohol they contained. Accounts of the quack medicines of the day may be found in the *Tatler*, No. 224, and in *Spectator*, Nos. 113, 120.

45, 20. **The sickness being at Dantzick:** the plague which raged through Prussia and Lithuania in 1709.

46, 13. **A roll of their best Virginia:** tobacco made up in rolls for smoking.

46, 19. **Sir Cloudesley Shovel.** See note on line 27, page 50.

46, 23. **Dr. Busby.** Headmaster of Westminster School from 1640 to 1695. Like that other famous schoolmaster, Dr. Boyer, headmaster of Christ's Hospital School who used to flog Coleridge and Lamb, a hundred and twenty-five years later, Dr. Busby was proverbially severe in his discipline.

46, 26. **The little chapel on the right hand:** St. Edmund's.

46, 29. **The Lord who had cut off the King of Morocco's head:** Sir Bernard Brocas. The crest in his coat of arms was a Moor's head; but the story referred to in the text is probably legendary.

46, 31. **The statesman Cecil on his knees:** William Cecil, Lord Burleigh, the great Secretary of State to Queen Elizabeth. He is represented as kneeling before the tomb of his wife and daughter.

46, 34. **Martyr . . . who died by the prick of a needle:** Lady Elizabeth Russell, died 1601. She is represented as pointing with her forefinger to a skull at her feet; hence the legend that she died from a prick of a needle.

47, 7. **The two Coronation-chairs.** They stand in the chapel of Edward the Confessor, behind the choir. One is said to have been that of Edward the Confessor; every sovereign of England since Edward has sat in it when crowned. The other was made for Mary, when she and her husband William were jointly crowned king and queen of England, in 1689.

47, 9. The stone . . . brought from Scotland: the "stone of Scone" fabled to be that on which Jacob rested his head at Bethel. After various alleged migrations, it was brought from Scotland to London by Edward I, in 1296.

47, 15. Pay his forfeit: i.e., for sitting down in the chair.

47, 16. Trepanned: more properly spelled trapanned; meaning trapped. It should not be confounded with the verb **trepan, to** remove a piece of the skull.

47, 19. Will Wimble: a whimsical friend of Sir Roger, described charmingly in *Spectator*, No. 109.

47, 22. Edward the Third's sword. This stands between the two Coronation chairs.

47, 24. The Black Prince: eldest son of Edward Third, who died before his father, in 1376. His tomb is not in the abbey, but in the cathedral of Canterbury.

47, 30. Touched for the evil. It was the general belief that the scrofula could be cured by the touch of the royal hand. On this account it was called "the king's evil." The practice of "touching" had fallen into disuse during the reign of William, but was revived by Anne as indicating her legitimate and divine right to the throne. She is said to have "touched" over two hundred people in one day, among them the young Samuel Johnson. But the practice ceased with her.

47, 34. One of our English kings without a head: Henry Fifth. The head, which was of silver, was stolen in the time of Henry Eighth.

REFLECTIONS IN WESTMINSTER ABBEY. ADDISON:
Spectator, No. 26

48, 24. (Motto.) Horace, *Odes*, I, 4, 13–17:
"With equal foot, rich friend, impartial fate
Knocks at the cottage and the palace gate;
Life's span forbids thee to extend thy cares,
And stretch thy hopes beyond thy years;
Night soon will seize, and you must quickly go
To storied ghosts and Pluto's house below."
Trans. by Creech.

49, 19. **In Holy Writ:** *Wisdom of Solomon*, V, 12–13: "Like as when an arrow is shot at a mark it parteth the air, which immediately cometh together again, so that a man cannot know where it went through, even so we in like manner, as soon as we were born began to draw to our end."

50, 14. **The present war:** the war of the Spanish Succession.

50. 18. **Blenheim.** The duke of Marlborough, at the head of the allied armies, had won this "famous victory" over the French, at Blenheim in Bavaria, Aug. 13, 1704.

50, 27. **Sir Cloudesley Shovel:** English admiral. His fleet was wrecked on the shore of the Scilly islands, and he was drowned 1707.

QUERIES AND SUGGESTIONS

1. Examine carefully one of Addison's essays with reference to its plan, structure of paragraphs, sentence form, diction.

2. Point out any examples of carelessness in the writing of Steele that you would not be likely to find in that of Addison.

3. The style of Steele and Addison is sometimes said to have "ease"; what is meant by ease as a quality of style?

4. Write a simple story after the manner of Steele's "Account of a Visit to a Friend."

5. Write a Spectator paper on any incident in your own observation or any fashion or custom of to-day.

6. An Evening in a London coffee-house in the time of Queen Anne.

7. Some Impressions of the character of Richard Steele derived from reading his papers.

8. Some differences in character and temperament between Steele and Addison that you see in the papers you have read.

9. Have you read any recent writing in books or magazines, say anything written within the last thirty years, that reminds you of these essays, either in matter or manner?

10. Do you think that such essays as those in the *Tatler* and *Spectator* would, or would not, be popular to-day? Give the reasons for your opinion.

CHARLES LAMB

The best biography of Charles Lamb is to be read in his essays and letters. No writer takes us more completely into his confidence. The result is. that in spite of all his whimsicality and paradox, no writer is better known, and that, in spite of all his failings, no one is better loved.

The main facts of Lamb's outward life can be briefly stated. The son of a servant of an advocate in the Inner Temple, he got his early training in Christ's Hospital School, which he has described so vividly in two of his essays. Here he first met that "inspired charity boy," Samuel Taylor Coleridge, who was to be his closest life-long friend. He was unable to go on from the school to the university, as his friend Coleridge did, but at the age of seventeen took his place as a clerk in the India House. For thirty-three years he found his daily work there, at "the desk's dull wood," till he was retired by the Company on a pension, in 1825.

The tragedy of his life fell upon him in 1796, when his only sister, Mary, in a temporary fit of insanity, snatched a knife from the table and stabbed her mother to the heart. The old father died shortly thereafter; another brother seems never to have been of much help to any one but himself; and Charles and his sister were left to front life alone. He had been in a mad-house himself for six weeks, some years before; but fortunately never had any return of mental disease. Mary, however, was subject to periods of mental alienation all her days, and it was the sad duty of Lamb to see that she was placed in a hospital, for weeks at a time, at intervals of a few months, all his life long.

Lamb cherished the intimacy of his few old and tried friends, especially Coleridge and the Wordsworths, to whom his most intimate letters are written; and he sought to enliven the loneliness and anxiety of his life by drawing about him a company of newer acquaintances who shared his tastes or tickled his humor. No more interesting group of people could have been found in London than those who used to forgather in Lamb's rooms on his "Wednesday evenings"—Hazlitt, Godwin, Burney, Procter, Hunt, Ayrton, Crabb Robinson, and on some rare occasions, Coleridge himself. There must have been abundance of good talk there; but no talk, we may be sure, more wise or witty than that which fell from the stuttering lips of Lamb himself—sparkling with puns, filled with droll epithet or allusion, passing abruptly from gay to grave, enlivened with light fancy, and all suffused with a gentle and kindly humanity. For Lamb is never to be thought of as that dreary person the professional humorist. "His serious conversation, like his serious writing," said Hazlitt, "is his best. His jests scald like tears; and he probes a question with a play upon words."

On the whole, the impression which the record of Lamb's life leaves upon us is that of quiet, cheerful endurance, almost heroic. He never complained nor quarreled with his lot. It is only now and then in his letters, oftenest to Coleridge or the Wordsworths, that we get some note of weariness or anxiety, and then usually in a hopeful tone. "God tempers the wind to the shorn Lambs," he wrote to Wordsworth once, in mood half humorous and half pathetic. In his latest years, lone and broken in health, the circle of his old companions almost all gone, his painful efforts to maintain in age the cheerful spirits of youth seemed to the rigor of Thomas Carlyle frivolous and unbecoming; but no one who ever really knew him could judge him harshly. The death of Coleridge broke down his spirits. He went about saying to himself, "Coleridge is dead, Coleridge is dead," and a few weeks later he followed his old familiar friend. He died, Dec. 27, 1834.

Lamb's literary career can hardly be said to have begun until he was well on in middle life. In his early years he had published a few short poems and the prose tale of *Rosamund Gray;* he had written a tragedy, *John Woodvil,* which was never acted, and a farce, *Mr. H.,* which was acted and promptly damned. Much more important was the volume of *Specimens of English Dramatic Poets,* published in 1808, which marks the beginning of a new interest in our Elizabethan drama. He had made other occasional contributions to the Reviews; yet the two volumes of his *Complete Works* issued in 1818, which include nearly all he had written up to that date, probably contain little that would have sufficed to keep his name alive. It was not until 1820, when he was nearly forty-five years old, that he really found himself. In that year he sent to the *London Magazine* the first of the Essays over the pseudonym of *Elia.* In 1823 the essays thus far written, twenty-eight in number, were collected and printed in a volume. Eight years later another collection, the *Last Essays of Elia* was published, making fifty in all.

The Elia essays are the most original and intimate series of humorous papers in our literature. They are Charles Lamb talking with us; he puts us in the mood of friendly acquaintance at once. It is not easy to describe such a unique personality as that revealed in these essays, one in which the elements are so subtly and so humorously mingled. We can enumerate certain characteristics of Lamb that constantly appear in his writing—his quaint seventeenth-century diction, his multifarious allusion, his love of paradox and oddity, his dislike of stupid and conventional folk, his humorous application of lofty metaphor and epithet, his constant play of imagination, his moods of grave and serious thought, the momentary gleams of pathos seen through his waggery, his quick appreciation of beauty, the warmth of kindly human feeling underneath all he says. Yet no such analysis can quite explain the charm of these papers. No one of them could by any possibility have been written by any one else than Charles Lamb. We never saw anything else that really reminded us of them.

The three essays included in this volume can give only an inadequate idea of the range of his humor. The first shows him in serene and thoughtful mood, and illustrates admirably that elevated and imaginative diction which his long and loving study of our seventeenth century prose writers—especially Taylor and Browne—had made his natural style. The second is the most familiar of his essays of pure drollery. The third is perhaps the most beautiful paper he ever wrote, a piece of English in simplicity and tenderness quite unsurpassed in the prose of the nineteenth century.

A QUAKERS' MEETING

In his Essays, Lamb is never primarily a jester. His conversation, doubtless, in his brightest hours, was sprinkled thickly with puns—of which he was a very great master, and with all sorts of unexpected quips and odd turns of phrase. It is in his familiar letters that we get some notion of his talk, now sparkling with wit, now droll and waggish, now humorously impudent—talk as Hazlitt said, "like snapdragon." But in the Essays the humor has usually some background of large human interest, and often, as in this essay on *A Quakers' Meeting*, passes insensibly into a tone of grave and serious reflection. There could be no better example, both in manner and matter, of the charm the early seventeenth-century prose writers had for Lamb than this essay, with its stately and solemn imagery and the dignified amplitude of its style. It might have been written by that master whom I think Lamb liked best, Sir Thomas Browne.

Yet in such an essay there is no conscious imitation. On the contrary, Lamb is never more genuinely himself. As he himself says, in the Preface to the *Last Essays of Elia*, his writings "had not been *his*, if they had been other than such; and better it is, that a writer should be natural in a self-pleasing quaintness, than to affect a naturalness (so-called) that should be strange to him."

Two of Lamb's best friends were Quakers, Charles Lloyd and Bernard Barton. And he had at one time at least a passing fancy for a young Quaker girl, Hester Savory, who died in 1803, and on whom Lamb wrote the touching verses beginning—

> "When maidens such as Hester die
>   Their place he may not well supply,
>   Though ye among a thousand try,
>   With vain endeavor."

53. (Motto.) From a dramatic pastoral entitled "Love's Dominion." Richard Flecknoe was a poor poet of the time of Charles II., whom Dryden despised, and satirized in his "Mac-Flecknoe."

53, 23. **Before the winds were made.** The origin of this quotation has not been traced.

54, 2. **Pour wax into the little cells of thy ears.** Ulysses poured wax into the ears of his sailors that they might not hear the songs of the Sirens. See *Odyssey*, Book XII.

54, 10. **Boreas and Cesias and Argestes loud.** See *Paradise Lost*, X, 699.

54, 26. **The Carthusian.** The monks of the Carthusian order— so called because their first seat was at La Chartreuse, in France— are bound to silence.

55, 1. **Zimmerman:** Johann G. von Zimmerman, a Swiss physician, author of a treatise "On Solitude."

55, 5. **Or under hanging mountains,** etc. See Pope, *Ode on St. Cecilia's Day*.

55, 14. **Sands, ignoble things,** etc. See Francis Beaumont (1586–1616), *Lines on the Tombs in Westminster Abbey*.

55, 21. **How reverend is the view of these hushed heads.** This is freely quoted from some lines of a description of York minster in the second act of the drama, *The Mourning Bride*, by Congreve (1670–1729): "How reverend is the face of this tall pile . . . Looking tranquillity." Samuel Johnson once pronounced this passage by Congreve "the finest poetical passage he had ever read."

55, 31. **Fox and Dewsbury:** George Fox (1624–1691), founder of the Society of Friends; William Dewsbury, one of his first preachers.

56, 11. **Penn:** William Penn (1644–1718), founder of the Pennsylvania colony, and most famous of the early Friends.

56, 17. **Sewel's History:** written originally in Dutch, and translated into English, 1722.

56, 25. **James Naylor** (1617–1669): perhaps not quite so mild and amiable a person as Lamb imagined him. He thought himself the reincarnation of Christ, and attempted to ride into Bristol naked because, as he said, Christ had ridden into Jerusalem.

57, 4. **John Woolman:** an American Friend who passed most of his life in New Jersey. His *Journal* has been edited with an admirable introduction by Whittier.

57, 32. **From head to foot equipt in iron mail:** from the poem beginning "Tis said that some have died for love."

58, 16. **The Jocos Risus-que:** "jests and smiles."

Faster than the Loves fled the face of Dis at Enna. It was the classic myth that Proserpine was carried to the lower world by Dis—or Pluto—while she was gathering flowers in the vale of Enna.

58, 23. **Caverns of Trophonius:** one of the Greek oracles, the responses from which were proverbially depressing, making those who consulted it silent or melancholy.

58, 33. **Forty feeding like one:** from Wordsworth's lines *Written in March.*

59, 4. **Their Whitsun-conferences:** "yearly meetings."

59, 7. **The Shining Ones.** "Here they were within sight of the city they were going to; also here met them some of the Inhabitants thereof. For in this land the Shining Ones commonly walked, because it was upon the Borders of Heaven." See Bunyan's *Pilgrim's Progress;* last chapter of Part First.

A Dissertation upon Roast Pig

Note the extreme difference in theme and temper between the preceding essay and this one. Yet there is in both the same vivid imagination, the same wealth of allusion, the same quaint or humorous originality of phrase.

59, 9. **My friend M.:** Thomas Manning, an eccentric and roving genius, who was one of Lamb's most congenial friends. He was in his earlier years a mathematical tutor in Cambridge, where Lamb met him, in 1799. In 1806 he left England and spent over ten years in China and India. He was the first Englishman who ever penetrated to the sacred city of Lhassa in Tartary. It is quite possible that he may have found in China the story on which this essay is based. Lamb's humor is never more irresistible than in his letters to Manning.

59, 13. **Their great Confucius.** Of course this reference to the Chinese philosopher and the statements about the "Chinese manuscript" are all of Lamb's invention.

63, 8. Our Locke: John Locke (1632–1704), author of the famous *Essay Concerning the Human Understanding.*

63, 24. Mundus edibilis: "edible world."

63, 25. Princeps obsoniorum: "chief of dainties."

63, 29. Amor immunditiæ: "love of dirt"; which may be supposed to be the original sin of the race of swine.

63, 32. Præludium: "prelude."

64, 22. Radiant jellies—shooting stars: an allusion to the superstition that a kind of mineral jelly could be found where a shooting star had fallen to the ground.

64, 30. Ere sin could blight or sorrow fade, etc.   See Coleridge's *Epitaph on an Infant.*

65, 33. Tame villatic fowl. See Milton's *Samson Agonistes,* line 1695.

66, 3. Like Lear: "I gave you all."   See *Lear,* Act II, scene 4.

66, 15. Over London bridge: one of Lamb's intentional mystifications; Christ's Hospital School was not over London bridge from his home.

67, 19. St. Omer's: another of Lamb's inventions; St. Omer's is a Jesuit college in France, and of course Lamb was never there.

67, 22. Per flagellationem extremam: "capital punishment by whipping."

DREAM CHILDREN

The most intimate and beautiful of all Lamb's essays.   Here humor passes into pure pathos.   It was written shortly after the death of his brother John, when Lamb felt himself alone in the world with poor Mary.   At such a time his thoughts naturally turned to the memories of his early life, or to revery of all that might have been had not fate denied him the affection of wife or child.   Surely no man loved children better than this jesting old bachelor.

The style, quite unlike that of his other essays, is too sincere and tender to admit any affectations, even that "self-pleasing quaintness" which seems so natural in most of his writing.   In its purity and simplicity it reminds us of the best passages of the Scripture narratives.

68, 5. Their great-grandmother Field. Lamb's grandmother, Mary Field, lived for many years in Blakesware, the manor house of the Plumer family.   For a fuller account of the "great house" and Lamb's early memories of it, see the two essays "Blakesmore in H——shire," and "Mackery End in Hertfordshire."   The great house was not in Norfolk, as Lamb says in this essay, but in Hertfordshire. Another charming picture of Lamb's grandmother is given in one of his earliest poems, "The Grandame."

70, 33. John L.: John Lamb, brother of Charles, who died in October, 1821, only a few weeks before this essay was written. He was a clerk in the South Sea House. For a fuller account of him, read the essay "My Relations," in which Lamb speaks of him as his "cousin, James Elia."

72, 2. I courted the fair Alice W——n. Several references in Lamb's writing point to a girl to whom he might have paid court had not the fatal malady of himself and his sister forbade him all thought of marriage. In his earliest verse, written twenty-five years before this essay, he refers in a tone of tender but hopeless resignation to some "Anna, mild-eyed maid." The character of the heroine of his early story, Rosamund Gray, is evidently suggested by the same person; and years after, in the essay "Mackery End in Hertfordshire," is the portrait of a Beauty with yellow hair, "so like my Alice." The real name of this sweetheart of his boyhood was Ann Simmons. She afterward married one William Bartrum, a London pawnbroker; and thus "the children of Alice call Bartrum father."

Queries and Suggestions

A Quakers' Meeting.

Note in this essay:

1. The effect of half humorous surprise gained in the first paragraphs by the seeming paradox that silence and solitude are intensified by numbers.

2. The striking imagery, noble or beautiful, by which this paradox is illustrated and enforced. Make a detailed study of the imagery in some one paragraph.

3. The effect of the archaic style in which the whole essay is cast. Point out the archaic peculiarities of diction and sentence.

4. The movement and cadence of Lamb's prose in its best passages.

A Dissertation upon Roast Pig.

1. Why does Lamb call his paper a "Dissertation"?

2. Note the ways by which the humorous effects of the narrative part of the paper is heightened.

3. Point out instances of "the humorous application of lofty metaphor and epithet" mentioned on page 319.

4. Point out any other examples of that form of humor which consists in "the sudden juxtaposition of incongruous ideas."

5. Note the effect of archaic forms, especially in the last half of the essay.

6. If you compare this essay with that on *A Quakers' Meeting*, can you see any points of similarity between them, either in temper or in style? And what striking differences?

Dream Children.

1. Point out some striking differences in diction and structure between the style of this essay and that of the other two you have read.

2. Why would the style of the other two be quite inappropriate for this?

3. Mention some passages in this essay that have especially pleased you.

4. What parts of the story are drawn from Lamb's memory, and what parts from his imagination? Show how skillfully the two parts are united.

5. How are the characters of the two children suggested?

6. Show from some passages in this essay that humor and pathos may naturally blend, the one passing insensibly into the other.

7. It is said above that the manner of this essay reminds us of some of the Scripture narratives; can you mention any passages of the Old Testament which suggest such resemblance?

State in a brief essay what you would infer from all three of these essays as to the temperament of Charles Lamb.

WILLIAM HAZLITT

Of the group of English essayists in the early years of the nineteenth century, no one better deserves to be read than William Hazlitt; yet perhaps no one is read less. His fame has been overshadowed by that of Lamb and DeQuincey; it was not until seventy-five years after his death, that we had a complete uniform edition of his writings. Yet he was the ablest and sanest literary critic of his time. He wrote an English that for purity, vigor, and distinction is quite unsurpassed—if, indeed, it be equalled—by any English prose written between 1800 and 1830. And the personality everywhere disclosed in his writings, though his friends doubtless sometimes found it difficult, is one of the most interesting ever put into a book. He loved to write about himself. Four-fifths of his best work is really autobiography. It was not until he was well turned of thirty that he gained any facility with his pen. By that time he had filled his mind with the best things in letters; he had formed his opinions on most subjects, political, religious, and literary; he had gained the few friends and the numerous enemies that were to last him his life-time. For the rest of his days, he had only to draw upon this accumulated stock of memories and principles. Doubtless this is one reason why his work fell into comparative neglect. When a man at thirty years has made up his mind and resolved never to change it, we shall not pay much attention to his verdicts upon whatever happens after that date. We see that his opinions, however interesting, have stiffened into prejudices. It may be admitted that Hazlitt has little to teach us on matters political or historical; but even his prejudices and perversities are entertaining. And there remains the wide personal realm of his reading, memory, and experience, in which his writing is often instructive and always delightful.

William Hazlitt was born in 1778. His father was a dissenting minister, a studious man of simple tastes, and a devoted advocate of civil and religious liberty. When his son William was five years of age, the father took his family to America, hoping to find in the liberal air of the new republic a more congenial field of labor. He gave some lectures in the University of Pennsylvania and for a time preached to a congregation in Hingham, near Boston. But his theology was probably too liberal for the strait Puritan orthodoxy of New England; he failed to secure a call from any parish, and after about a year returned to England. It had been the hope of his father that William Hazlitt would himself become a Unitarian minister; but as the boy grew to manhood, though he shared his father's studious habits and liberal opinions, he showed no inclination to enter his father's profession.

The first noteworthy event in the life of William Hazlitt was the meeting with Coleridge which he has described so vividly in the essay *My First Acquaintance with Poets*. He was then twenty years old, and already had a full set of radical opinions at least in the making. His love of civil and religious liberty inherited from his father, warmed by the ardor of youth, was passing into a genuine enthusiasm. He had sympathized with the revolutionary movement in France, and now looked with eager hope upon the early career of Napoleon as the one man who could bring order out of the chaos of that revolution, the great protagonist in the struggle for an ordered liberty. His literary taste was also well formed; and he had felt a restless dissatisfaction at the failure of his own attempts to put his sentiments into writing. Nor had he yet found among English writers any worthy advocate of the radical cause. The great voices, he had to own, were all on the other side. He had early recognized that incomparably the greatest contemporary master of English prose was Edmund Burke; but Burke in his latest years had become, he thought, the determined foe of public liberty. It can be readily seen why the meeting with Coleridge was such an inspiration. Here at last was a man of philosophic breadth of mind, a genuine lover of liberty, and a consummate master of speech. For those were the days of Coleridge young, full of all high and vague enthusiasms, and eloquent as an angel. Hazlitt at once accepted him as the god of his idolatry; and even in the later years when Coleridge had belied the promise of his youth and gone over to the enemy, Hazlitt still cherished the memory of that early vision, and mourned over Coleridge as an archangel fallen.

Hazlitt's acquaintance with Coleridge doubtless confirmed his determination to become a writer, but it was long before there was much to show for it. He said, later in life, that he had thought for eight years without being able to write a line. His first effort, perhaps encouraged by Coleridge, was in the field of philosophy. He toiled long and hard over a treatise *On the Natural Disinterestedness of the Human Mind*, and succeeded in getting it published in 1805; few people read it then, and nobody reads it now. Hopeless of earning a living by his pen, he decided to follow the profession of an elder brother, who was a portrait painter. For four years he labored to attain excellence in that art, and then, convinced of his inability, threw down his brush. These were not, however, altogether unprofitable years, as we may see from his essay *On the Pleasures of Painting*. They doubtless fostered that accurate observation and quiet reflection so evident in his later work. His home seems to have been with his father in Wem, Shropshire; but he was often in London, and by 1806 he had formed the acquaintance of Charles and Mary Lamb and of Lamb's little company of intimates. In 1808, he committed the indiscretion of marrying a Miss Sarah Stoddard. Miss Stoddard was a very emancipated, unconventional person, whom Heaven had probably not intended to be the wife of any man, certainly not of such a man as William Hazlitt. She had, however, a tiny estate at Winterslow, near Salisbury, and the married couple took up their residence there.

What Hazlitt was doing in those years is not very clear. He seems not to have been writing much. He had published nothing since 1805 except two or three political or philosophical pamphlets and a little treatise on English grammar, in none of which is there any trace of the genius he was so soon to show. But in 1812 the needs of his increasing family forced him to come up to London in search of some regular literary employment.   He accepted a position, first as reporter and then as theatrical critic on the London *Chronicle*, and his dramatic criticism attracted some notice.   It was a little later that he really found himself.   In 1814 he agreed to write for Leigh Hunt's *Examiner* a series of brief essays dealing in the easy manner of Addison with the humors of life and the charms of books.   Hunt himself, just then, was spending his time not unpleasantly in jail, for having printed the year before a very telling libel on the Prince Regent—whereby the circulation of the *Examiner* was notably increased.   In Hazlitt's series of essays, collected two years later under the title of *The Round Table*, his real genius was first disclosed.   They touch a great variety of subjects, books, manners, social customs and follies, with acute observation, and always with a peculiar charm of style. They at once brought Hazlitt into notice as a critic and essayist. His experience with the *Chronicle* had taught him he could write; now he found it easy.   After 1814 he had no difficulty in finding a publisher.   In that year he received his first invitation to con-tribute an article for the *Westminster*, and during the next fifteen years he printed no fewer than nineteen papers in that important periodical.   His writing during the rest of his life, however, was largely in the form of briefer essays, contributed to various papers and magazines, the best of which are collected in the volumes en-titled, *Table Talk*, *The Plain Speaker* and *Sketches and Essays*. In 1818 he gave two courses of public literary lectures, one on *The English Comic Writers* and the other on *English Poetry* from Chaucer to Burns; and the following year, a third course on *The Dramatic Literature of the Age of Elizabeth*.

The remaining years of his life were without noteworthy in-cident.   They were not altogether happy years.   With the down-fall of Napoleon and the rule of the Holy Alliance his hopes for political liberty collapsed.   He had no sympathy for either polit-ical party in England; Whigs and Tories, he felt, under different names were alike foes to the cause of civil liberty.   His old friends, Coleridge, Southey, and Wordsworth, had gone the way of cowards and deserters.   On the other hand, he had little confidence in vague rhapsodists like Shelley, or loud declaimers like Byron. He was dissatisfied with his own career.   The lighter essays on which his fame now mostly rests he never regarded as of much permanent value; while the only two of his books he himself rated highly were just the ones which nobody read or will read—the *Essay on the Disinterestedness of the Human Mind* and the *Life of*

Napoleon—on which he toiled during the last years of his life. His critics, especially *Blackwood* and the *Quarterly*, assailed him with personal abuse which often made him half frenzied with terror and anger. His own temper was moody and difficult. He confesses that he had quarreled more or less with all his friends and shouldn't have liked them so well if he had not. His habits of work were desultory. He had left off reading about the time he began writing; and periods of lonely reflection, alternated with periods of feverish industry. He spent his time mostly in London, but often retired to the Winterslow Hut, a little coaching inn near Salisbury, where much of his latest work was done. Mrs. Hazlitt, whose temperament was neither domestic nor romantic, readily convinced him that their union was a mistake, and accordingly man and wife amicably journeyed to Edinburgh, in 1822, to pass the period of residence there necessary for a divorce under the Scottish law. Hazlitt himself, it must be admitted, was not an exemplary husband. Not long before his divorce, he conceived a violent attachment for a young girl, daughter of a London tailor; and when she, amazed and amused by his extravagant sentiments, very wisely married another admirer, Hazlitt sat down and wrote out the whole story of his passion in a little book, the *Liber Amoris*, which is an astonishing piece of bad taste. Not daunted by his experiences, however, he afterwards married a Mrs. Bridgewater, of whom nothing more is known. Their union was brief. There was a wedding journey to the continent; but Hazlitt seems to have returned alone, and his wife never rejoined him. The last two or three years of his life seem to have been troubled also by financial anxieties. His health, never robust and perhaps impaired by his habit of drinking enormous amounts of strong tea, rapidly declined, and he died in 1830, at the age of fifty-two.

Hazlitt evidently was not formed for society, hardly even for friendship. The combination of unpopular and dogmatic opinions with a sensitive and irritable temperament is not likely to make a man a genial companion. The disappointment of his early political hopes and the alienation of his early friends, the failure of his domestic relations, the violent abuse from his critics, all combined to embitter a nature always shy and self-conscious. He felt himself isolated, and at odds with the world. He was suspicious of everybody. Even Mary Lamb once wished that Hazlitt wouldn't "hate men quite so universally." Yet the few who knew the man well could see that this sensitiveness and suspicion were only the morbid shrinking of a nature really hungry for affection. At heart he loved and coveted all things true and honest and of good report. The best characterization of him is given by the friend who knew him best, Charles Lamb: "I think W. H. to be in his natural and healthy state, one of the wisest and finest spirits breathing; so far from being ashamed of that intimacy which was between us, it is my boast that I was able for so many years to have possessed it entire; and I think I shall go to my grave without finding or expecting such a companion."

But the qualities that made Hazlitt difficult as a friend perhaps made him all the more delightful as a writer. Driven in upon himself, he lived in the realm of memory and speculation, and found there the choicest material for his work. In his controversial writing he is usually vigorous and sometimes angry—his *Letter to William Gifford* is the most scathing piece of invective in the language; but he is never at his best save when in some mood of reminiscence or reflection. His taste is so exacting that the form of his work is sure to be excellent. However familiar, his style is never merely colloquial or vulgar; it has always a certain distinction. He said with truth in his last year, "I have written no commonplace and not a line that licks the dust." Of all the virtues of rhetorical technique he was easily a master. Some of our best modern prose writers—Macaulay, Thackeray, Bagehot, Stevenson—have admired and imitated his style. "We are fine fellows," said Stevenson, "but we can't write like William Hazlitt."

Nor is it chiefly for its manner that the work of Hazlitt deserves admiration. His formal philosophical treatises, his *Life of Napoleon*, and most of his political writing we may dismiss to probable oblivion; but there remains a goodly amount that must last at least another century or two. As a critic he had no equal in his own age, and has had very few since. His criticism is all the better that it is not analytic and formal; it is the record of his own impressions. He tastes the best things in a book with real gusto; and he has the art to make you share his enjoyment. The critic can render us no better service than that. But it is in his personal essays that we shall find his most characteristic work. While they are all filled with the flavor of his own personality, they touch a remarkable variety of subjects. Some of them are in the tone of grave philosophic meditation. Hazlitt inherited from his father a turn for speculation upon the problems of philosophy, and that tendency had been strengthened by long and solitary thinking. In essays like those *On the Feeling of Immortality in Youth, On Personal Identity, Why Distant Objects Please, On the Past and Present,* we have reflection never trite or commonplace, subtle analysis and keen observation enlivened by Hazlitt's peculiar sardonic humor, and every now and then trains of serious thought that slowly rise to the level of solemn, imaginative, impassioned eloquence. To find anything like them we must go back to Jeremy Taylor or Sir Thomas Browne.

But best of all are the intimate autobiographical papers that record his memories of books and men, his hopes and disappointments, his likings and his aversions. These essays are of the nature of soliloquy. He is writing to please himself. He sets down no merely trifling incidents, no idle personal gossip. It is evident that the man's thought and imagination dwell by preference with noble and beautiful things. Even his whims and preversities are usually the utterance of some generous moral feeling in irritation. Nearly all these papers are tinged with a certain melancholy; but the melancholy is not cynical or bitter. The harsher passages of his life, its keener disappointments, are softened by memory into a pensive regret that gives to his writing a sort of lyric quality. In their constant play of imagination, in their sensitiveness to all the intellectual charm of life, in their naïve expression of a most interesting personality, in the perfection of a style easy and spontaneous and yet finished and melodious, these are among the most delightful essays ever written. After reading them we can understand the dying words of Hazlitt, at first thought so strange, "Well, I have had a happy life." The man whose retrospect over life found expression in such essays as these could not have been altogether unhappy.

MY FIRST ACQUAINTANCE WITH POETS

This, perhaps the most delightful essay of personal reminiscence in the language, was written in 1823, twenty-five years after the events which it records.

73, 3. Dreaded name of Demogorgon. See *Paradise Lost*, Book II, lines 964–965. One of the "powers and spirits" surrounding Satan in the nethermost abyss.

73, 4. Coleridge: Coleridge was then twenty-six years of age. He had left the university, Cambridge, in the last days of 1794, without taking a degree. He had formed, and then speedily abandoned, a visionary scheme of emigrating to America and founding an intellectual colony there. In 1796 he had published a thin volume of poems; and his unusual gifts as a talker and a preacher had already begun to attract attention; but his career was as yet undecided.

73, 21. Fluttering the proud Salopians. This is a good example of Hazlitt's habit of free and adapted quotation. Shakespeare wrote:

> "That, like an eagle in a dove-cote, I
> Flutter'd your Volscians in Corioli."
>
> *Coriolanus*, V, vi, 115.

Salopians: the inhabitants of the county of Shropshire, the old name of which was Salop.

73, 25. High-born Hoel's harp. See Gray, *The Bard*, line 28.

74, 14. With Styx nine times round them. See Pope, *Ode for Saint Cecilia's Day*, line 91.

75, 15. Il y a des impressions. From Rousseau's *Confessions:* "There are impressions which no time nor circumstance can efface. Should I live whole ages, the sweet days of my youth could never return to me, nor ever be effaced from my memory."

75, 22. Rose like a steam of rich distilled perfumes: Milton's *Comus*, line 556.

76, 8. As though he should never be old: "Here a shepherd boy, piping as though he should never be old."—Sidney's *Arcadia*, Ch. 2.

76, 14. Such were the notes our once-loved poet sung: opening line of Pope's *Epistle to Oxford*. Pope's "once-loved poet" was Parnell.

76, 27. Jus Divinum: the doctrine of the divine right of kings, which was maintained most strenuously all over Europe in the period of reaction after the French Revolution.

76, 28. Like to that sanguine flower, etc. See Milton's *Lycidas*, line 106.

77, 11. As are the children of yon azure sheen. See Thomson's *Castle of Indolence*, II, stanza 33.

78, 10. Adam Smith (1723–1790), whose *Inquiry into the Nature and Causes of the Wealth of Nations* is the foundation of a new school of political economy.

80, 6. Mary Wollstonecraft. This brilliant woman, the author of the *Vindication of the Rights of Women* (1792), was the wife of William Godwin. She died at the birth of her daughter, Mary, who was afterward the wife of the poet Shelley.

80, 6. Mackintosh: Sir James Mackintosh (1765–1832), an English philosopher and statesman. His *Vindiciæ Gallicæ*, a defence of the French Revolution, was called out by Burke's famous *Reflections on the Revolution in France.*

80, 25. **Tom Wedgewood:** Josiah and Thomas Wedgewood, the famous manufacturers of pottery, were early friends and admirers of Coleridge. It was a gift from them that enabled Coleridge, in 1798–1799, to spend a year in Germany. Thomas Wedgewood died in 1805.

81, 14. **Holcroft:** Thomas Holcroft (1745–1809), an English novelist and playwright. He was a violent liberal, and in 1794 had been tried for high treason, but acquitted.

82, 4. **Deva:** Latin name for the Dee, a river in north Wales.

82, 8. **The Delectable Mountains:** the mountains in Bunyan's *Pilgrim's Progress,* from which one may see the Celestial City.

82, 19. **Cassandra:** the prophetess, a daughter of Priam, enslaved by Agamemnon, and killed by Clytemnestra. Her story is told in the *Agamemnon* of *Aeschylus;* this incident, however, is not found in that play. Perhaps Hazlitt had in mind the play of *Cassandre* by the French dramatist La Calprenède.

82, 29. **Sounding on his way:** Chaucer, Prologue to *Canterbury Tales,* portrait of the Merchant.

83, 11. **Hume:** David Hume (1711–1776), a Scottish philosopher and historian.

83, 12. **South:** Robert South (1634–1716), an eloquent preacher of the English church.

83, 13. **Credat Judæus Appella:** from Horace, *Satires* I, v, 100—

> "Credat Judæus Appella,
>   Non ego"
> "Let the Jew Appella believe it; I will not."

83, 22. **Berkeley:** Bishop George Berkeley (1685–1753), greatest of English idealist philosophers.

83, 24. **Angry with Dr. Johnson:** who said that he confuted Berkeley's denial of the existence of material substance by striking a stone with his foot. The incident is in Boswell's *Life of Johnson* (Hill's edition), Vol. I, p. 471.

83, 29. **Tom Paine.** Thomas Paine (1737–1809) was born in England, but expelled thence for his writings in behalf of the American revolutionists, he came to America in 1776. In 1787 he returned to England. His *Rights of Man* (1791–1792) was the ablest reply to Burke's *Reflections on the Revolution in France.* The reference in the text is probably to his later work, *The Age of Reason,* a defence of deism.

83, 33. Butler: Samuel Butler (1692–1752), English theologian, and ablest opponent of the deistical doctrines prevalent in England in the first half of the eighteenth century.

84, 32. Sidney: Sir Philip Sidney, the pattern English gentleman of the sixteenth century. His series of sonnets, *Astrophel and Stella*, were inspired by his love for Lady Penelope Devereaux.

85, 5. Paley: William Paley (1734–1845), leading representative of the utilitarian theory of ethics, which Coleridge vigorously opposed.

85, 14. Kind and affable: Milton, *Paradise Lost*, VIII, 648–650.

85, 33. Southey's Vision of Judgment: The poem which Southey, as poet laureate, wrote at the death of George Third, lauding the deceased king in most extravagant and really irreverent terms. Upon which Byron, who detested Southey, wrote a poem of the same title, which is perhaps the most scathing and sarcastic parody in the language. Mr. Murray, his London publisher, to whom Byron sent his poem, declined to publish it, fearing a prosecution for libel. "The Bridge-street Junta" was an association formed for the repression of seditious publications; Hazlitt here speaks of Murray sarcastically as its secretary.

86, 32. Tom Jones: the principal novel of Henry Fielding; Hazlitt almost knew it by heart.

87, 1. Paul and Virginia: a famous novel by the French writer Bernardin St. Pierre, issued in 1788.

87, 24. Bridgewater: about eight miles east of Nether Stowey.

87, 26. Camilla: a novel (1796) by Madame d'Arblay (Fanny Burney).

88, 14. Lyrical Ballads. This famous volume made up of poems by Wordsworth and Coleridge, was published in September, 1798, a few weeks after this visit of Hazlitt. It may be said to mark the beginning of a new school of English poetry.

88, 23. Hear the loud stag speak. This quotation has never been located.

89, 17. In spite of pride. See Pope, *Essay on Man*, I, 293:

> "And, spite of Pride, in erring Reason's spite,
> One truth is clear, Whatever is, is Right."

89, 24. While yet the trembling year is unconfirmed: Thomson's *Seasons, Spring*, 18.

89, 27. Of Providence, foreknowledge: Milton, *Paradise Lost*, II, 559–560.

90, 29. Haydon: Benjamin Robert Haydon (1786–1846), a

distinguished though rather too grandiose historical painter. The painting referred to is now in the Catholic cathedral of Cincinnati.

91, 6. Monk Lewis: Matthew Gregory Lewis, English dramatist and novelist; called "Monk" from the title of one of his romances, *Ambrosio, the Monk.*

91, 24. Face was as a book: *Macbeth*, I, v, 63.

92, 14. Tom Poole. Thomas Poole (1765–1837) was a wealthy young radical, engaged in the tanning business, who had become warmly attached to Coleridge, and offered him the cottage at Nether Stowey, in which Coleridge was living at the time of Hazlitt's visit. Mrs. Sandford, his daughter, has written a delightful biography, *Thomas Poole and His Friends*, which contains much information with reference to Coleridge and the Wordsworths in these years.

92, 23. Followed in the chase: *Othello*, II, iii, 370.

92, 34. Followed Coleridge into Germany. Coleridge and Wordsworth spent a year, from the autumn of 1798 to the autumn of 1799 in Germany; Coleridge spending most of the time in Göttingen, Wordsworth in Goslar.

93, 4. Sir Walter Scott's or Mr. Blackwood's . . . at the same table with the king. The reference is probably to a dinner given to George IV, by the magistrates of Edinburgh in 1822. Scott and Blackwood—the founder of *Blackwood's Magazine*—were both very pronounced Tories.

93, 11. Gaspar Poussin: French landscape painter (1613–1675). **Domenichino:** properly Domenico Zampieri, Spanish painter (1581–1641).

94, 5. Giant's Causeway: on the north coast of Ireland.

94, 13. Death of Abel, by Solomon Gessner, a Swiss poet. The *Tod Abels* is, however, in prose.

94, 22. Seasons, by James Thomson, the poem was issued in parts, 1726–1730.

95, 19. Junius: pseudonym of the writer of a famous series of political letters appearing in the London Advertiser from 1768 to 1772. Their authorship has never been certainly determined; but they were probably written by Sir Philip Francis.

95, 25. Caleb Williams: a famous political novel (1794) by William Godwin.

96, 34. Mr. Elliston: Robert William Elliston, a favorite actor in the Drury Lane Theatre.

97, 17. But there is a matter, etc. See Wordsworth's *Hart Leap Well*, lines 95–96.

On Going on a Journey

This very characteristic essay first appeared in the *New Monthly Magazine* for 1822, the first of a series of papers under the heading *Table Talk*.

97, 23. The fields his study, etc. See Bloomfield, *The Farmer's Boy, Spring,* 31.

98, 3. . . . a friend in my retreat. See Cowper, *Retirement,* 742-743.

98, 11. May plume her feathers, etc. From Milton's *Comus,* 378-380.

98, 16. A Tilbury: a two-wheeled carriage without top, called after a London coachmaker of the early nineteenth century.

98, 27. Sunken wrack and sumless treasuries: Shakespeare's *Henry V.,* I, ii, 165.

99, 2. Leave, oh, leave me to my repose: Gray's *The Descent of Odin,* which is a paraphrase of the Icelandic lay *Vegtams kvida.*

99, 5. Very stuff of the conscience: Shakespeare's *Othello,* I, ii, 2.

99, 18. Out upon such half-faced fellowship: Shakespeare's *Henry IV, Part I,* I, iii, 208.

99, 22. Mr. Cobbett: William Cobbett (1762-1835), noted English economist and radical.

99, 27. Sterne: Laurence Sterne (1713-1768), a sentimental novelist of the mid-eighteenth century, with whose writings Hazlitt was very familiar. The remark in the text is from his *Sentimental Journey.*

101, 2. My old friend C ——: Coleridge. See the preceding essay for an account of Coleridge's gift of talk.

101, 6. He talked far above singing. See Beaumont and Fletcher, *Philaster, V,* v: "I did hear you talk far above singing."

101, 15. Here be woods, etc. Fletcher's *Faithful Shepherdess* I, iii, 27-43.

102, 6. L ——: Charles Lamb.

102, 19. Take one's ease at one's inn: Shakespeare's *Henry IV, Part I.,* III, iii, 93.

102, 27. The cups that cheer, but not inebriate: Cowper's *Task,* IV, 39.

102, 31. Sancho: Sancho Panza the squire in the romance of *Don Quixote* by Cervantes. The incident here referred to may be found in Part II, ch. 49.

103, 1. Shandean contemplation: The reference is to Sterne's *Tristram Shandy;* the elder Shandy, "my father," in that singular novel was much given to quaint and sentimental contemplation.

103, 2. Procul, O procul este profani: Vergil's *Aeneid* VI, 258—"Afar, stand afar, ye profane" the regular warning to the uninitiated in religious ceremonies.

103, 23. Unhoused free condition: Shakespeare's *Othello*, I, ii, 26.

103, 26. Lord of one's self, uncumber'd with a name: Dryden, *Epistle to John Driden*, 78: "Lord of yourself, uncumber'd with a wife."

104, 15. St. Neot's: a town near Peterborough.

104, 16. Gribelin's engravings. Simon Gribelin (1661–1733) in 1707 engraved a series of seven plates of the famous cartoons of Raphael which are preserved in Hampton Court palace.

104, 19. Westall: Richard Westall (1765–1836), an English historical painter, specially noted for his designs for the illustration of Bunyan's *Pilgrim's Progress*.

104, 25. Paul and Virginia . . . at Bridgewater. See the essay *On My First Acquaintance with Poets*. The reading of Madame D'Arblay's *Camilla* and Rousseau's *New Eloise* is described in the same essay.

104, 32. St. Preux describes his feelings. The passage may be found in *La Nouvelle Heloise, Partie IV, Lettre* 17.

105, 7. Green upland swells, etc. Coleridge, *Ode to the Departing Year*, VII, 4–6.

105, 20. The beautiful is vanished, etc.: Coleridge, translation of *The Death of Wallenstein*, V, i.

105, 30. Where is he now? In 1822, Coleridge had been for six years living with Dr. Gilman, at Highgate, near London, striving to break the fetters of his bondage to the opium habit. His early political enthusiasms had vanished; his days of poetical inspiration were over; and he was now chiefly interested in philosophical and religious speculations which seemed to Hazlitt barren of any valuable result. Twenty-five years before, in the days of his visit to Nether Stowey, Hazlitt had looked upon Coleridge with almost idolatrous admiration; he always lamented over Coleridge's abandonment of liberal political principles as a kind of treason to all his early ideals. And what was worse, all the world seemed to have made the same surrender—to have become "old and incorrigible."

106, 24. Beyond Hyde Park, says Sir Fopling Flutter, all is a desert. Sir Fopling Flutter is the hero of the comedy *The Man of Mode* by George Etherege (1635–1691). The remark quoted from the play is not made by Sir Fopling Flutter but by Harriet to Dorimant, Act V, ii.

107, 28. Stonhenge: a celebrated prehistoric monument, probably of a religious character, consisting of a circle of stones seventeen in number. It is in Salisbury Plain about eight miles from the city of Salisbury.

107, 33. The mind is its own place: Milton, *Paradise Lost*, I, 254.

108, 2. I once took a party to Oxford. Hazlitt went to Oxford with Charles and Mary Lamb, in the summer of 1810; it is probably this visit to which he refers.

108, 5. With glistering spires and pinnacles adorn'd: Milton, *Paradise Lost*, III, 550.

108, 8. The Bodleian: The famous Bodleian library; **Blenheim:** the seat of the Duke of Marlborough.

108, 30. When I first set my foot on the laughing shores of France. This was in 1802, when he was but twenty-four years old. He was visiting Paris to study in the Louvre.

109, 22. Dr. Johnson remarked. See Boswell's *Life* (Hill's Edition) III, 352.

109, 31. Out of my country and myself I go. This quotation I cannot locate.

ON READING OLD BOOKS

110, 11. Tales of my Landlord. Several of Scott's novels were published in Series under this Title. The first Series, 1861, included *The Black Dwarf* and *Old Mortality;* the second Series, 1818, *Rob Roy* and *The Heart of Midlothian;* the third Series, 1819, *The Bride of Lammermoor* and *A Legend of Montrose.*

110, 13. Lady Morgan: whose maiden name was Sydney Owenson, was the author of a number of Irish stories, in the early nineteenth century, that were very popular in their day.

110, 15. Anastasius: an Eastern romance published anonymously in 1819. It was thought at the time of its appearance to be the work of Byron; but was written by Thomas Hope.

110, 18. Delphine: a novel by Madame de Staël, published in 1802.

110, 26. Andrew Millar: prominent bookseller and publisher of the middle eighteenth century. He published the novels of Fielding and Samuel Johnson's *Dictionary.*

110, 28. Thurloe's State Papers: *A Collection of State Papers,* (7 vols. 1742) by John Thurloe.

110, 29. Sir William Temple's Essays: one of the most interesting early collections of essays, published in 1680 and 1692, Temple was an eminent statesman and scholar in the reign of William and Mary, 1688–1702; but is now perhaps most often remembered as the patron of Jonathan Swift. See Macaulay's interesting essay, *Sir William Temple*.

110, 30. Godfrey Kneller: famous portrait painter (1646–1723).

111, 30. Rifaccimentos: reworking or revision of works of literature.

112, 21. Fortunatus's wishing-cap: a cap which had the power to transport Fortunatus instantly wherever he wished. The legend probably originated at the end of the fifteenth century; a version of it was printed in Augsburg as early as 1509.

112, 25. Bruscambille. See Sterne's *Tristram Shandy*, Book III. ch. 35. The book with which "my father Shandy," solaced himself was probably purely an invention of Sterne's; but Bruscambille was the surname of Deslauriers, a French comic actor of the seventeenth century.

112, 26. Peregrine Pickle (1751), a novel by Tobias Smollett.

112, 27. Tom Jones (1749), the masterpiece of Henry Fielding.

113, 5. The puppets dallying: Shakespeare's *Hamlet III*, 2.

113, 17. Ignorance was bliss: Gray, *On a Distant Prospect of Eton College*, line 10.

113, 32. The Ballantyne Press. James Ballantyne was the publisher of most of the novels and poems of Walter Scott. Scott was himself a silent partner in the concern, and on the failure of Ballantyne assumed the great obligation and virtually killed himself by his heroic efforts to pay it.

113, 34. The Minerva press: a publishing house in Leadenhall Street, London, which in last years of the eighteenth century and the beginning of the nineteenth published many sensational romances.

114, 9. Mrs. Radcliffe's "Romance of the Forest" (1791), one of a number of bugaboo romances by Ann Radcliffe.

114, 11. Sweet in the mouth . . . bitter in the belly. See *Revelation*, X, 9.

114, 13. Gay creatures: Milton's *Comus*, I, 299.

114, 28–31. Major Bath: in Fielding's *Amelia;* **Commodore Trunnion:** in Smollett's *Peregrine Pickle;* **Trim and my Uncle Toby:** in Sterne's *Tristram Shandy;* **Don Quixote and Sancho and Dapple:** in the *Don Quixote* of Cervantes; **Gil Blas and Dame Lorenza Sephora, of Laura and the fair Lucretia:** in the *Gil Blas* of the French novelist Le Sage (1668–1747).

115, 6. O Memory, shield me from the world's poor strife.

These lines appear to be not a quotation, but an original couplet of Hazlitt's.

115, 13. **Chubb's Tracts:** one of the deistical writers of the early eighteenth century. His *Tracts and Posthumous Works* were published, in six volumes, in 1754.

115, 22. **Fate, free-will, fore-knowledge absolute . . . found no end:** Milton's *Paradise Lost*, II, 560.

115, 28. **Would I had never seen.** See Christopher Marlowe (1564–1593): *Dr. Faustus*, scene xix.

115, 29. **Hartley, Hume, Berkeley:** David Hartley (1705–1757); David Hume (1788–1776); George Berkeley (1685–1753): eminent English philosophers of the eighteenth century.

115, 30. **Locke's Essay on the Human Understanding** (1690), the most important philosophical work of the last half of the seventeenth century.

115, 32. **Hobbes** (1588–1679), an English philosopher, whose most important work, the *Leviathan* was issued in 1651.

116, 5. **New Eloise:** Rousseau's famous romance *La Nouvelle Héloise*, published in 1761. The *Héloise* and the *Confessions* of Rousseau were among the books with which Hazlitt was most familiar, and which he is never tired of quoting. The passages here referred to are in Part VI of the "Héloise." The *Social Contract* of Rousseau was published in 1762; the *Confessions*, after his death in 1778. His romance *Emile* (1762) is really a treatise on education.

116, 20. **I have spoken elsewhere:** in an essay "On the Character of Rousseau," *Round Table* No. XXIV.

116, 29. **Sir Fopling Flutter.** See note on line 24, page 106.

117, 8. **Leurre de dupe:** "decoy for a dupe," a phrase from Rousseau's *Confessions* IV, 4.

117, 11. **A Load to sink a navy:** Shakespeare's *Henry VIII*, III, i, 2.

117, 34. **Marcian Colonna is a dainty book:** *Marcian Collonna*, title of a volume of poetry by Barry Cornwall (B. W. Procter). The line is the first of a sonnet by Lamb.

118, 14. **Words, words, words.** Shakespeare's *Hamlet*, II, ii, 194.

118, 19. **The great preacher in the Caledonian chapel:** Edward Irving; an early friend of Thomas Carlyle, and an unsuccessful suitor for the hand of Jane Welsh who afterwards married Carlyle. He went to London as a preacher in 1722, and his eloquence and his peculiar religious pretensions made him for some dozen years one of the most noted figures in London.

118, 23. **As the hart that panteth,** etc.   See Psalm, XLII, 1.

118, 25. **Goethe's Sorrows of Werter and to Schiller's Robbers.**
The *Werther* was finished in 1774 and the *Robbers* in 1782.   "The
Robbers was the first play I ever read, and the effect it produced
upon me was the greatest."   Hazlitt, "Lectures on the Age of
Elizabeth," VIII.

118, 27. **Giving my stock of more,** etc.: Shakespeare's *As You
Like It*, II, i, 48.

119, 2. **My acquaintance with the authors of the Lyrical Ballads.**
See the preceding essay, page 73.

119, 8. **Valentine, Tattle, or Miss Prue:** characters in the play
of *Love for Love* by William Congreve (1670–1729).

119, 13. **Know my cue:** Shakespeare's *Othello*, I, ii, 84.

119, 15. **Intus et in cute:** Persius, *Satires*, III, epilogue:

> "Ego te intus et in cute novi."
> "I knew you intimately and in the skin."

119, 21. **Sir Humphrey Davy** (1778–1829), an eminent English
physicist.

119, 28. **Spectator . . . Tatler:** by Addison and Steele.

119, 30. **Rambler** (1750–1752), edited by Johnson; **Adventurer**
(1752–1754), by John Hawkesworth; **World** (1753–1756), by
Edward Moore; **Connoisseur** (1754–1758), by George Colman and
Bonnel Thornton.   Hazlitt has a valuable lecture on these periodical
essayists in his series *On the Comic Writers*.

120, 5. **Clarissa . . . Clementina . . . Pamela:** the heroines of
Richardson's three novels, *Pamela*, *Clarissa Harlowe*, and *Sir
Charles Grandison*.

120, 6. **With every trick and line:** Shakespeare's *All's Well
That Ends Well*, I, i, 107.

120, 9. **Mackenzie's "Julia Roubigne."**   Henry Mackenzie's
three novels—the two mentioned here and *The Man of the World*
—were published between 1770 and 1780; they were very sentimental and had, for a time, many admirers.

120, 14. **Miss ——:** probably Miss Sarah Walker, for whom
Hazlitt had for a little time a most surprising infatuation, the
record of which he put into a volume, entitled "Liber Amoris."

120, 15. **That ligament, fine as it was:** a phrase from the story
of Le Fevre in Sterne's *Tristram Shandy*, Book VI, ch. x.

120, 19. **Boccaccio:** Giovanni Boccaccio (1313–1375), a celebrated Italian poet and novelist.   The story of the Hawk is from
his principal work, the *Decameron*, a collection of a hundred tales.

A graceful modern version of that story may be read in "The Student's Tale" in Longfellow's *Tales of a Wayside Inn*.

120, 23. I remember, as long ago as the year 1798. This was the year of his visit to Coleridge described in "My First Acquaintance with Poets."

120, 24. Farquhar . . . "Recruiting Officer": George Farquhar (1678–1707), comic dramatist of the Restoration period.

120, 26. At one proud swoop: "At one fell swoop." See Shakespeare's *Macbeth*, IV, iii, 289.

120, 31. With all its giddy raptures: Wordsworth, "Lines above Tintern Abbey."

120, 33. Embalmed with odors: Milton's *Paradise Lost*, II, 843.

121, 9.—His form had not yet lost: *Ibid*, I, 591.

121, 13. Falls flat upon the grunsel edge: *Ibid.*, I, 640.

121, 25. Letter to a Noble Lord. This was Edmund Burke's triumphant and crushing reply to the Duke of Bedford who had charged Burke with subserviency to the government because he had accepted a pension. The "Letter" shows Burke's powers at their height.

121, 30. Junius. See note on line 19, page 95.

122, 4. Like an eagle in a dove cote. See note on line 21, page 73.

122, 16. Essay on Marriage. Wordsworth is not known to have written any such essay. Hazlitt's memory was probably at fault.

122, 29. I regarded the wonders of his pen. Compare the statement in the essay "On My First Acquaintance with Poets," page 73.

123, 17. Lord Clarendon's (1608–1674): *History of the Rebellion and Civil Wars in England*.

123, 24. Froissart's Chronicles: Jean Froissart (1338–1410), French historian and chronicler. **Holinshed and Stowe, and Fuller's "Worthies":** Ralph Holinshed, *Chronicles of England, Scotland and Ireland*, whence Shakespeare drew much of the material for his English historical plays; John Stowe, *Summarie of English Chronicles* (1561), *A Survey of London* (1598); Thomas Fuller, *The History of the Worthies of England* (1662).

123, 26. Beaumont and Fletcher: Francis Beaumont (1586–1616) and John Fletcher (1579–1625) after Shakespeare and Ben Jonson the most prominent of the dramatists of the early seventeenth century. In many of their plays they worked together.

123, 30. Thucydides: the greatest of Greek historians; he wrote between 450 and 401 B. C.

123, 31. Guicciardini: Francesco Guicciardini, an Italian historian (1483–1540).

123, 32. Loves of Persiles and Sigismunda: the last work of Cervantes published 1617; *Galatea* was his first work (1585).

123, 34. Another Yarrow: "Yarrow Unvisited," the first of the three poems by Wordsworth on the Scottish river Yarrow.

QUERIES AND SUGGESTIONS

My First Acquaintance with Poets.

1. How old was Hazlitt when he first met Coleridge?

2. What was it, do you think, in the sermon of Coleridge that so delighted Hazlitt?

3. What traits of Hazlitt's genius can you see in his father as described in the remarkable paragraph, page, 78?

4. Coleridge as a talker.

5. Some other characteristics of Coleridge in his early years, as seen in this paper.

6. What do you gather as to the political and social opinions of Coleridge in this period of his life?

7. What book was Hazlitt himself vainly trying to write at this time?

8. When did Hazlitt visit Coleridge and how long was he on the journey? Does he mention this journey in either of the other essays in this volume?

9. Nether Stowey and Alfoxden as you imagine them.

10. How did Coleridge and Wordsworth happen to be living so near each other at this time? What important poems written by each during this period in their lives?

11. Prosaic appearance and manner of Wordsworth.

12. Describing their walk to Linton, Coleridge says that if he had to choose of the three, Coleridge, Wordsworth and John Chester, for a traveling companion, "it would be John Chester." Why? Illustrate his preference by reference to a later essay.

13. What do you gather from these papers as to Hazlitt's temperament in youth, and his early social and political opinions?

14. Illustrate from this charming paper Hazlitt's imagination, his gift of personal portraiture, the structure and cadence of his sentences.

On Going a Journey.

1. What are some of the reasons why Hazlitt likes to go by himself?

2. Later in the essay he admits that in some cases he has no objections to going "in company with a friend or a party"; when? and why?

3. What would seem to be generally the subject and temper of his reflections when he is alone?

4. Do you think he shows a careful or accurate observation of nature when he is on a journey? Has he the eye of a naturalist?

5. What particular journey does he refer to as taken in 1798?

6. How are Coleridge and Lamb compared in this paper?

7. Can you see any indications in this essay that Hazlitt, though sometimes a very delightful companion, might often be a difficult one, and even a difficult friend?

8. At the close of the paragraph on page 107, Hazlitt says, "To return to the question I have quitted above." What is that "question," and where did he quit it? Do you find here a suggestion as to a criticism upon Hazlitt's style?

On Reading Old Books.

1. Hazlitt says at the beginning of this essay that there are twenty or thirty books he has read over and over again; make out a list of *ten* books that you infer from the three essays read were most familiar to him.

2. What are his reasons for preferring the books he has read before?

3. Why is he inclined to regret his early liking for philosophical literature?

4. He read few poets in his youth because, as he avers, he is "deficient in the faculty of imagination"; do you think he was?

5. Comment upon Hazlitt's curious statement of the conditions of success, in the paragraph on page 117. Do you think the statement just? Do you know any facts in Hazlitt's life that may account for it? And how does it illustrate his temperament?

6. Why does he think himself a better judge of fiction than of poetry?

7. What qualities of Burke's writing—especially in the *Reflections on the Revolution in France*—did he greatly admire? But how did he regard the opinions of that book?

Set down in a brief essay your notion of the man William Hazlitt—his temperament, habits, moods, opinions, prejudices—as you have formed it from the essays in this volume.

THOMAS DE QUINCEY

Thomas De Quincey was born in Manchester, August 15th, 1785, the son of a well-to-do West Indian merchant. The father died when the son Thomas was only five years of age, and the education of the boy was largely directed by his mother. In his boyhood, if we may accept his own account, he showed unusual precocity; he avers that at thirteen he was able to read Greek fluently, and frequently translated the newspaper into that tongue. At a very early age, also, he knew those moods of reverie and dream so characteristic of all his later years. All the children of the De Quincey family—there were eight—seem to have had a morbid intensity of intellect and imagination, combined with a certain willful irresponsibility. Two sisters died in childhood, apparently of some affection of the brain. An elder brother, a singularly brilliant lad, lived for years in a realm of his own imagining, and died when just entering manhood. A younger brother, "Pink," ran away from home to sea, wandered over the globe, and found as strange adventures in the world of reality as his brothers found in the world of dreams.

Thomas De Quincey when he was sixteen was ready for Oxford; but his guardians unwisely insisted on putting him into the Manchester Grammar School. The delicate, dreamy lad, after spending some months with uncongenial teachers and nagging schoolfellows, ran away to Wales, and refused to go back either to home or school. His mother, helpless, gave him a guinea a week and let him wander where he would. At the approach of winter he went up to London. The adventures of that winter of 1802 and 1803 in London, his starving vagabondage in the great city, his strange friendship with Anne of Oxford Street, all the world has read in *The Confessions of an English Opium Eater*, written twenty years later. It is possible that some of the incidents of that story may have been colored in De Quincey's memory by the mist of opium through which he saw them; but without question he passed through experiences of suffering and sympathy such as few young fellows have ever known. He was discovered at last and sent up to Oxford, where he ought to have been a year before. He was nominally in Oxford from 1803 to 1808; though he seems not to have kept terms regularly after 1807. He read voraciously during all that time, especially in philosophy and literature; but his reading was probably fitful and he left the university without taking a degree.

Two things of importance mark this university period. The

first was the formation of the opium habit. It is a mistake to think that the peculiar quality of much of De Quincey's work is due primarily to opium. He was a dreamer from boyhood. His imagination always liked to wander in dim and mysterious regions. But this native tendency was doubtless strengthened after about 1807 by his addiction to opium. It ought to be remembered that he first took the drug to relieve the almost intolerable pains of a malady brought on by the privations of his London winter; and, though he never escaped from the bondage thus invited, he struggled against it all his days, and was seldom absolutely in its power. But of more importance than this first acquaintance with the drug of doom, was his first meeting with Coleridge and the Wordsworths. He had been one of the few readers who recognized the advent of a new poetry in the *Lyrical Ballads* almost ten years before; and it was in 1807 that he first met both the new poets. The papers included in this volume, in which he tells the story of this meeting are among the most interesting passages of his autobiography. That first visit to Wordsworth, in particular, he always accounted a turning point in his career. He declared that the intimate and friendly intercourse with the man whom he had up to that time worshipped only at a distance freed him from morbid shyness and self distrust, and produced a positive "physical change in my nervous system." In 1808, when Wordsworth left his little Dove Cottage in Grasmere, De Quincey, just out of the university, rented it and called it his home for more than twenty years. The little circle of his friends were close about him. Wordsworth was hard by in Grasmere; Wilson, whom he had known in Oxford, was at Ellesmere a few miles south; Southey, with the Coleridge family, was at Keswick, thirteen miles to the north. In 1816, he married the daughter of a farmer in the neighborhood, and indentified himself—so far as such a recluse could do—with the life of the Lake District.

What De Quincey was doing in the dozen years from 1808 to 1820, it is hard to say. "Reading German metaphysics and taking opium," he himself avers, in a familiar passage. Reading, doubtless, for he was always an enormous reader, and he certainly must have turned over a good many pages of German philosophy; yet he could hardly have been called a thorough student of philosophy. His reading, though profound, was always desultory, vagarious; he pursued no consistent lines of study. He had adopted no profession; he seemed to have no vocation. Inheriting a moderate competence, he gave himself up to the life of reading and reverie. Up to 1820, though he had doubtless spoiled a good deal of paper by comments and excerpts, he had not published a line. But the growth of his family forced him to seek some means of increasing his slender annual income. He failed, as might have been expected, in an attempt to edit a local newspaper; but in the summer of 1821 he went up to London, and in September and October of that year published in the "London Magazine," *The Confession of an English Opium Eater*. The one great success of his life had been made suddenly. A new writer had appeared.

Henceforth De Quincey was a contributor to magazines. He remained in London most of the time until 1825, furnishing a number of papers to the "London Magazine" and to "Knight's Quarterly Magazine," and then returned to Grasmere. In 1826, his old friend John Wilson, who since 1817 had been editor of "Blackwood's Magazine," invited him to lend his pen to that periodical; most of his work for the rest of his life was written either for "Blackwood" or for another Edinburgh monthly, "Tait's Magazine." In 1830 he removed with his family to Edinburgh, to be near his publishers; the rest of his life was passed in that city or in the suburban village of Lasswade.

His thirty years of Edinburgh life were without noteworthy external incident. He never had any mastery of practical affairs; but after the death of his wife in 1837, he was affectionately cared for by his daughters. He was a fragile little man, only about five feet in height, with the head of an ancient sage set upon the body of a boy. His withered and wrinkled face, his awkward stoop, his timid and inefficient movements, combined to make him seem a quarter century older than he really was. Morbidly shy and sensitive, absent-minded, he dreaded publicity, and even the ordinary conventions of society were irksome to him. During all the years when he was one of the lions of Edinburgh it was difficult to get sight of him. But when, with a few congenial friends or sometimes in a small company, his tongue was loosened, he would pour forth an amazing stream of talk, varied, brilliant, eloquent. "What wouldn't one give," said Mrs. Carlyle when she had met him one evening, "to have that little man in a box, and take him out now and then to talk." But by choice he lived a recluse with his books and papers, working all day and taking long solitary walks by night. It is a part of the De Quincey tradition that he would occupy one room until he was pushed out of it by the ever accumulating mounds of manuscript which he could not arrange and would not destroy. He published a multitude of articles; but he must have written five times as many as he published. He never freed himself from the opium habit; but after a last period of struggle in 1843-44, he seems to have fixed upon the least daily allowance, and rarely exceeded it. It may be doubted whether this bondage lowered his activity or shortened his life. He himself thought that laudanum had saved him from a tendency to pulmonary disease inherited from his father. The last ten years of his life were passed in a lonely eminence; for he outlived all his early friends, Coleridge, Lamb, Wordsworth, Wilson, Hazlitt, and others half a generation younger. He died in 1859, in his seventy-fifth year.

To estimate the value and rank of De Quincey's work is somewhat difficult. All his writing is miscellaneous and fragmentary. When he writes upon science, history, economics, or any practical subject which demands eyes that open outwards, what he says may be curious or entertaining—indeed, it almost always is—but it is not sure to be true. Nor can it be said that he made any substantial contributions to the literature of philosophy or criticism. His writing, for the most part, is simply his talk put into print, the talk of a secluded, studious man, wide ranging, sometimes profound and sometimes garrulous, but always talk. The truth is, De Quincey never seemed able to hold his mind steadily to one right line of thought or one direct path of narrative. As a result, his more pretentious work never shows the virtues of proportion and completeness. He could not resist the fatal lure of digression.

This habit of mind accounts for the most marked peculiarity of his style. He says, in a very suggestive passage (page 160 of this volume) that in his youth he labored under an embarrassment because he "could not unravel, could not even make perfectly conscious to myself, the secondary thoughts into which a leading thought often radiates; or at least I could not do this with anything like the rapidity requisite for conversation." This ability, which he always coveted, he attained in later life to an astonishing degree. No other English prose writer can so chase a thought into all its ramifications without ever quite losing his way. He prided himself upon this ability. Of the short and simple sentence, he was used to speak with something like contempt. The fault of Lamb's writing, he said, is that it is not "sequacious." His own certainly is. His long sentences wind their way through parentheses and digressions, and yet seldom wander altogether out of control of their main affirmation. He was past master of all forms of what the rhetoricians call "explicit reference."

Now this peculiarity of De Quincey's mental action certainly limits considerably the value of his work.   No philosophic subject can be treated clearly or adequately unless it can be isolated in some degree from its connections.   Life is too short for the discussion of any truth if we must stop to trace its roots and branches in all other truth.   Similarly in his biographical and historical papers, De Quincey is frequently allured into unpardonable divagation. Everything reminds him of something else.   He gives you manifold reasons why something did *not* happen, or manifold reasons that could not account for something that *did* happen.   He fills up his pages with curious and irrelevant fact, sometimes with mere gossip and what Mr. Saintsbury calls "rigmarole," till he is obliged to stop without having told his story after all.   It is true that these papers are well worth the reading—if you have the time. De Quincey is always very full of matter.   Every page will disclose some subtlety of thought or curious felicity of phrase.   His vocabulary is a marvel of richness and precision.   Yet his thinking too seldom has any clear direction or definite conclusion.   He rambles most suggestively, but he doesn't arrive.

But there are two classes of De Quincey's writing in which this vagabond intellectual habit proves no disadvantage, nay sometimes gives an added charm; and it is precisely in these two varieties that his most lasting work is to be found.   In his rambling papers of personal reminiscence, gossip is just what we want; and in the records of his dreaming imagination, tinted more or less by the opium, any definite and ordered method might lessen the sense of mystery and awe which these papers leave with us.   The papers of personal narrative are perhaps the most interesting of all.   It is to De Quincey that we are indebted for the history of the Lake District. Our pictures of the Coleridges, the Wordsworths, and the Southeys would lose half their vivid reality were it not for the gossiping recollections of this sharp-eyed little critic who lets us see them without their singing robes, in their habit as they lived.   While as to the *Confessions* and their sequel, the *Suspiria de Profundis*, they are our best specimens of the literature of waking dream.   De Quincey himself claimed that parts of the *Suspiria*, such as the "dream fugues" following the *Affliction of Childhood* and the *English Mail Coach*, and *Our Ladies of Sorrow* were a new literary form, a kind of impassioned prose or prose-poetry, without precedent in our literature.   Such attempts must always be hazardous, liable to result in a bastard form, neither poetry nor prose, and without the excellences of either.   I do not think that all of the "dream-phantasies" in the *Suspiria* can escape this charge.   They are magniloquent rather than eloquent; their imagination is too evidently labored—De Quincey is "making up" his dream. But in the best portion of the *Suspiria*, the vision of the *Ladies of Sorrow*—included in this volume—he has succeeded in embodying a most august conception in a prose genuinely solemn and stately. These majestic figures are veritable additions to our mythology; shadowy forms that haunt forever the realm of a sorrowing imagination.

MEETING WITH COLERIDGE

De Quincey's account of his first visit to Coleridge and to Wordsworth should be compared with Hazlitt's story of his "First Acquaintance" with the same poets.

125, 6. First edition . . . of the Lyrical Ballads: published in 1798.

125, 20. Professor Wilson: John Wilson, Professor of Moral Philosophy in Edinburgh University, but better known by his pseudonym of "Christopher North" as editor of *Blackwood's Magazine.*

126, 15. Second and enlarged edition: published in 1800.

126, 23. Mr. Southey's Joan of Arc. Southey's first long poem, written when he was in full sympathy with the popular movements in France, was first published in 1796. Coleridge contributed some lines to the second book.

126, 27. Anthology: *English Anthology for* 1799–1800 in 2 volumes, edited by Southey.

126, 29. Poems published under his own name: *Poems on Various Subjects, by S. T. Coleridge, late of Jesus College, Cambridge,* Bristol, 1796.

127, 10. Residing at Malta. Coleridge spent the time from May, 1804 to September 1805 at Malta, whither he had gone in the hope to recover his health. For part of that time he acted as secretary to the Governor, Sir Alexander Ball.

127, 26. Mr. Poole: Thomas Poole, a young man of pronounced radical views who was one of Coleridge's early friends, and in whose cottage at Nether Stowey, Coleridge lived from the beginning of 1797 to the summer of 1798—the period of his intimacy with Wordsworth. See Hazlitt's account of his visit to the two poets at that time.

128, 21. Alfoxden: the house, some three miles distant from Nether Stowey, which Wordsworth occupied.

128, 33. A long residence in France. Wordsworth was in France from November, 1791 to December, 1792; he spent the winter of

1798–99 in Goslar, Germany; his "regular domestication with his sister at Racedown," had been in 1795–97, just before he came to live at Alfoxden near Coleridge.

129, 16. **The Golden Verses:** the *Aureum Pythagoreorum Carmen*, seventy-one verses embodying some principles of the Pythagforean philosophy. They are by an unknown author and date trom the second century B. C. There is no mention of beans in the Golden Verses; but they are forbidden as an article of food in various places in the Pythagorean writings. My colleague, Professor William A. Heidel, refers me to the following instances:

"He bade men abstain from beans for many reasons, sacred as well as natural and having regard to the soul."—Iamblichus: *Life of Pythagoras*, 109.

"He advised men to abstain from beans as they would from human flesh."—Porphyry: *Life of Pythagoras*, 43

A full set of references on the bean superstition among the ancients may be found in Frazer's Edition of *Pausanias*, Vol. IV, p. 240.

A great variety of fanciful reasons have been alleged for this rule forbidding the eating of beans. Who the "German author" here referred to is, I do not know.

130, 30. **Hymn to Chamouni.** Coleridge never explained this flagrant case of plagiarism. The sentiments of the poems and much of its noblest imagery are certainly taken from the poem of Frederica Brun. Coleridge himself was never in the vale of Chamouni.

131, 25. **Bright particular star:** Shakespeare, *All's Well That Ends Well*, Art. I, Sec. 1.

131, 31. **Tormented all the air:** Milton, *Paradise Lost*, VI, 244. The source whence De Quincey thinks it borrowed is probably, *Iliad*, XIII, 673.

131, 33. **A weed of glorious feature.** See Wordsworth's *Beggars*, l. 18.

132, 10. **Fled from his lion ramp:** Milton, *Samson Agonistes*, 136–139.

132, 23. **Shelvocke:** George Shelvocke, author of *A Voyage round the World*, 1719–22. London, 1726; second Edition, 1757.

133, 23. **Schelling:** Friedrich Wilhelm Joseph von Schelling, 1775–1854. There can be no doubt that Coleridge was greatly indebted to the *Natur Philosophie* and the *System der Idealismus* of this famous German philosopher. How far he was himself conscious of his obligations has been matter of dispute ever since this charge was first made by De Quincey. Professor Ferrier, of

Edinburgh University, repeated and enforced the charge in a paper in *Blackwood's Magazine* (Vol. XLVII, 287–289), in which he shows that no less than nineteen pages of Coleridge's work are almost literal translations from Schelling. The daughter of Coleridge, Sara, made a vigorous defence of her father in a paper now usually printed as an Introduction to the *Biographia;* and other students have been ready to acquit Coleridge of the charge of intending to appropriate literally without credit the doctrines of Schelling. The whole question of the indebtedness of Coleridge to his German teachers is a vexed one.   Many passages in his Lectures on Shakespeare certainly show a very close resemblance both in thought and diction to the writings of the great German Shakespeare scholar August Wilhelm von Schlegel. De Quincey's position with reference to the passages in the *Biographia* is curious; he seems first to make the charge of plagiarism unequivocally, and then to excuse it.

134, 1. Fichte: Johann Gottlieb Fichte (1762–1814), eminent philosopher, professor in the universities of Jena and Berlin.

134, 31. Not John Paul: Jean Paul Friedrich Richter (1763–1825), novelist, noted for the romantic luxuriance of his style. De Quincey admired his writing, and was perhaps influenced by it in his own *Suspiria de Profundis.*

135, 28. Milton's account of the rubbish . . . Latin Fathers. "Whatever Time, or the blind hand of blind Chance hath drawn down from of old to this present in her huge drag-net, whether fish or seaweed, shells or shrubs unpicked, unchosen, these are the Fathers."—*Of Prelatical Episcopacy*, 1641.

135, 31. An African Obeah man. *Obi or obeah* is the name of the pretended magic practised by some tribes in Africa and their descendants in America.

138, 10. Bourrienne: Louis Antoine Fauvelet de Bourrienne (1769–1834), private secretary to Napoleon.

139, 34. Chubb, the philosophic writer: Thomas Chubb (1679–1747), a prominent deistical writer.

141, 28. Orellana: a name frequently given in early writings to the Amazon, from its discoverer, Francisco de Orellana.

142, 18. Bishop Berkeley's Siris: the most mature expression of the idealistic philosophy of the philosopher George Berkeley (1685–1753). He was a firm believer in the medicinal value of tar-water; and in this remarkable book follows a curious chain (Siris) of speculation from the effects of the tar-water to the nature of Life and Mind.

143, 2. Hartley: David Hartley (1705–1757), an English materialistic philosopher whose writings had a singular attraction for the early years of Coleridge, though he soon reversed his estimate of them. Hartley explained all mental actions as the result of the vibrations of minute nervous particles, which he called "vibratiuncles."

144, 17. Sir Thomas Browne (1605–1682). In his *Religio Medici*, a noble and eloquent confession of faith, Browne says, "As for those wingy mysteries in divinity, and airy subtleties in religion, which have unhinged the brains of better heads, they never stretched the *pia mater* of mine. Methinks there be not impossibilities enough in religion for an active faith: the deepest mysteries ours contains have not only been illustrated, but maintained by syllogism and the rule of reason. I love to lose myself in a mystery; to pursue my reason to an *O altitudo!*"

144, 28. A Socinian: one who holds the doctrines taught by two Italian theologians of the seventeenth century, Laelius Socinus and Faustus Socinus. Socinians deny the divinity of Christ, though admitting his preëminent character as a teacher, and hold that the sacraments of baptism and the Lord's supper are commemorative merely.

145, 4. Kant: Immanuel Kant (1724–1824), most celebrated of modern German philosophers. De Quincey had given considerable attention to the work of Kant; in a paper published in *Tait's Magazine* about a year after the appearance of these biographical sketches (June, 1836), "On German Studies and Kant in Particular" he attempts a resumê of the more important teachings of Kant. Modern critics, however, have questioned the value of these studies of German philosophy. Most students of Kant would hardly assent to his strictures upon the religious influence of Kant in the long digression given here. Professor Masson's statement is probably a just estimate of De Quincey's Kantian writing: "The accuracy of some of his statements about Kant, and indeed, of his knowledge of Kant, has been called in question of late; but it remains to his credit that in a singularly bleak and vapid period of the native British philosophizing he had contracted such an admiration, all in all, for the great German transcendentalist." *Life of De Quincey*, ch. xii.

145, 10. Gog . . . Magog: two colossal effigies that stand in the Guild hall of London, copies of those placed there in the reign of Henry V. Gog and Magog are mentioned in *Revelation* xx, 8, as nations "in the four quarters of the earth." The origin of the names is obscure.

145, 15. Apollyon: the most terrible enemy of Christian in Bunyan's *Pilgrim's Progress.* In *Revelation* ix, 11, he is called 'the angel of the bottomless pit."

146, 8. John Hunter (1728–1793), noted English surgeon and anatomist.

148, 12. Two milliners from Bath:

> "Coleridge, long before his flighty pen
> Let to the Morning Post its aristocracy;
> When he and Southey, following the same path,
> Espoused two partners (milliners of Bath)."
> *Don Juan* III, stanza 93.

The term "milliner" was often then applied to a woman of loose character—as Byron well knew when he wrote these lines. Southey and Coleridge had married two sisters, the Misses Fricker, of Bristol.

148, 31. Mr. Cottle: Joseph Cottle, a Bristol bookseller, who befriended the early literary efforts of Coleridge, and published the first volume of his poems. Cottle's volume of *Reminiscences* contains much interesting information as to the early life of Coleridge amd Southey.

148, 33. Hannah More (1745–1843), a religious writer whose works for a time enjoyed wide currency; perhaps best remembered by her tract *The Shepherd of Salisbury Plain.* For many years, in the later part of her life she kept a school for young ladies in Bristol, and afterwards at Clifton.

149, 12. Her retirement at Keswick. Mrs. Coleridge passed most of her life after 1807 with her sister, Mrs. Southey at Keswick in the English Lake district.

150, 28. A young lady became a neighbor. The young lady here referred to is Wordsworth's sister, Dorothy, who lived with her brother in 1797–98 at Alfoxden, while Coleridge was living at Nether Stowey, near by. The paragraph that follows is a good specimen of De Quincey's fondness for mere gossip. There is no other reason for thinking that the friendship of Dorothy Wordsworth for the Coleridges was ever trying to the "candour and good temper" of Mrs. Coleridge; and some of the alleged facts cited by De Quincey could have only been known to him through irresponsible tittle-tattle. It was such writing as this that sometimes vexed Wordsworth and the other friends of De Quincey.

152, 18. **Pandora:** in Greek mythology the first woman. In the most familiar form of the myth she is given a box filled with blessings, which she carelessly opened and allowed all the blessings to escape except hope.

153, 24. **Arthur Young** (1741–1820), English traveler and writer on agricultural subjects. His chief work was his *Travels in France*, but De Quincey here seems to allude especially to his *Political Arithmetic*.

153, 31. **A piteous sight it was to see,** etc. De Quincey is quoting from memory and—as he too often does—inaccurately. The lines he quotes do not "come after a description of Coleridge's countenance," and it is pretty certain that they do not refer to Coleridge but to Wordsworth. "There can now be no doubt that in the first four of these *Stanzas*, Wordsworth refers to himself; and that in the last four, he refers to Coleridge."—Knight's edition of *Wordsworth's Poems*, ii, p. 308.

The lines here quoted are the first two of the third stanza.

155, 11. **A service should be rendered to Mr. Coleridge.** In November, 1807, De Quincey sent to Coleridge a gift of three hundred pounds. At that time De Quincey had just come into his inheritance and had for a time plenty of money.

156, 16. **Some continuous sketch of his life.** There follows in De Quincey's paper an extended account of Coleridge's career, omitted in this volume of selections. However interesting, it is not altogether trustworthy. The latest and best biographer of Coleridge says: "The whole article literally bristles with blunders of every description. Even the portions which relate the author's own experience and observation require a large allowance for refraction."—James Dykes Campbell, Introduction to *Poetical Works of Coleridge*, page lxxiii.

MEETING WITH WORDSWORTH

In the last days of December, 1799, after his return from a year's stay in Germany, Wordsworth and his sister Dorothy, took up their residence in the little "Dove Cottage," Grasmere, where they were living at the time of De Quincey's visit.

156, 21. **I have already mentioned:** in his *Oxford Reminiscences*, not included in this volume. See Masson's Edition, II, p. 54.

157, 12. **The ancient hills . . . sequestered glens.** These are all within a few miles of the Grasmere cottage. Windermere and Derwentwater are two lakes, the one in the southern part of the Lake District, the other in the northern.

158, 1. Churchyard amongst the mountains: Books VI and VII of Wordsworth's *Excursion*.

158, 5. Valdarno and Vallombrosa. See Milton's *Paradise Lost*, Book I, lines 290 and 303. Val d'Arno, "the valley of the Arno," in which Florence lies; and Vallombrosa "a shady valley" some fifteen miles distant.

158, 9. Could field or grove, etc. See Wordsworth's *Excursion*, Book VI, lines 806–810.

159, 22. White cottage. "Dove Cottage"—so called because once the Dove and Olive Bough Inn—was the home of Wordsworth from the beginning of 1800 to the summer of 1808; De Quincey occupied it from 1809 to 1830. Some twenty years ago it was bought by lovers of Wordsworth to prevent it from further decay, and presented to the nation; it is now always open to visitors.

160, 7. In early youth I labored. The passage that follows is very suggestive. Later in life De Quincey gained most remarkable power to do just this—to follow out all the "subsidiary thoughts into which one leading thought often radiates," and to "deal with topics in which the understanding combined with deep feelings to suggest mixed and tangled thoughts." It is the most noteworthy peculiarity of his mental action and his literary style.

160, 32. A worldly tone of sentiment in Wordsworth: one of the numerous examples of a strain of petty malice in De Quincey. There is no reason for this charge.

161, 8. Malta. See note on line 10, page 127.

161, 13. Engaged by the Royal Institution to lecture: a course of sixteen lectures on "The Principles of Poetry."

161, 16. Conveying his family to Keswick. In 1880, after his return from a year's stay on the continent, Coleridge leased a house, Greta Hall, in Keswick and removed thither with his family; but he was much away, and in 1803, Robert Southey, coming to visit the Coleridges at Greta Hall, remained there the rest of his life. Coleridge himself was there but seldom after about 1803. Mrs. Coleridge after this visit on which she was escorted by De Quincey, never lived steadily anywhere else.

161, 26. A very interesting family. This passage of purely irrelevant gossip about the Koster family is a good example of De Quincey's divagations.

162, 16. Talavera: a town in Spain where Wellington defeated the French, in 1909.

162, 20. Madame Catalani: Angelica Catalani (1779–1849), a famous Italian singer.

162, 28. **Lady Hamilton** (1761–1815): wife of the English Ambassador at Naples, Sir William Hamilton. She is remembered as the mistress of Lord Nelson, who could never throw off his infatuation for her.

163, 9. **White Moss.** The name indicates that on the top of the hill there was a "moss" or swamp.

164, 4. **Semele:** who prayed to see Jove and was consumed by his lightnings.

164, 33. **Roman nomenclator.** The nomenclator attended the candidate for office in his canvass to name the persons met.

165, 26. **Mrs. Wordsworth.** Wordsworth married, in 1802, his cousin, Mary Hutchinson, whom he had known since they had been school children together.

166, 5. **Mr. Slave-trade Clarkson:** Thomas Clarkson (1762–1846), English Abolitionist, a friend of both Wordsworth and Coleridge.

167, 8. **Like stars of twilight fair:** carelessly quoted; Wordsworth wrote:

> "Her eyes as stars of Twilight fair;
> Like Twilight's, too, her dusky hair."

167, 28. **Her face was of Egyptian brown:** Wordsworth, *Beggars*, line 7: "Her skin was of Egyptian brown."

167, 32. **Wild and startling.** See the references to Dorothy Wordsworth in the *Lines above Tintern Abbey*:

> ". . . and read
> My former pleasures in the shooting lights
> Of thy wild eyes. . . . . . .
> . . . nor catch from thy wild eyes these gleams
> Of past existence."

168, 31. **German charcoal-burners.** Dorothy was with her brother during his year in Germany.

171, 5. **Half-kitchen and half-parlor fire:** the last line of the original version of Wordsworth's sonnet *Personal Talk*. He afterwards altered it—for the worse—so that the last four lines ran:

> "To sit without emotion, hope, or aim,
> In the loved presence of my cottage fire
> And listen to the flapping of the flame,
> Or kettle whispering its faint undersong."

172, 17. **Upon the whole, not a well-made man.** De Quincey's curious liking for half-malicious gossip is seen in these comments on Wordsworth's bad legs, Dorothy's awkward stoop, and Mrs. Wordsworth's "obliquity of vision."

173, 2. **Elegantes formarum spectatrices:** "Elegant critics of beauty"; altered from the *Eunuchus* of Terence, III, 5, 18.

174, 13. **Haydon:** Benjamin Haydon, a noted English historical painter, who was acquainted with Wordsworth, Coleridge, and Lamb. His work was not well appreciated, and in disappointment he committed suicide, in 1846. The picture referred to in the text is now in Cincinnati.

174, 15. **Voltaire:** Francois Marie Arouet (1694–1778), who assumed the name de Voltaire; a famous French poet, dramatist, and critic, well known for his attitude toward historical Christianity. —"Sapping a solemn creed with solemn sneer," as Byron says in *Childe Harold*.

174, 28. **Miss Ferrier:** Susan Ferrier (1782–1854), Scottish novelist and a friend of Walter Scott. Her other novels are *The Inheritance* and *Destiny*.

174, 31. **England is not the land of round faces.** Notice this long excursus for the next two pages suggested by the question whether Wordsworth had a long face.

176, 3. **Irving, the pulpit orator:** Edward Irving (1792–1834), Scottish preacher and friend of Thomas Carlyle, who came up to London, founded a new church with peculiar doctrines and ritual, and was famous for his pulpit eloquence.

177, 2. **Peter's Letters:** *Peter's Letters to His Kinsfolk* (1819), by John Gibson Lockhart, is a series of brilliant and often caustic sketches of men and things in the Edinburgh of that time. Lockhart's most familiar work is his *Life of Sir Walter Scott*. He married Scott's eldest daughter.

177, 21. **The light that never was on land or sea:** from Wordsworth's *Elegiac Stanzas on a Picture of Peele Castle*. There, however, the line runs—

"The light that never was, on sea or land."

178, 14. **Richardson the painter.** "Jonathan Richardson (born about 1665, died 1745) published in 1734 a volume of Explanatory Notes and Remarks on *Paradise Lost*, with a life of Milton containing particulars which Richardson had collected about Milton personally."—Masson's Note.

179, 28. **Those shocks of passion to prepare.** See Wordsworth's *Lament of Mary Queen of Scots*, stanza 6.

180, 4. **That account which the Excursion presents.** The passage referred to is the first three hundred lines of Book First, especially lines 279–300.

180, 19. **A premature expression of old age.** This was more true of De Quincey himself, who was one of the most ancient, dessicated looking of men, though not yet in his sixties.

181, 24. **Lived into his 82nd year:** not quite; he died April 23, 1850, having just entered his 81st year.

182, 31. **Archimedes:** the celebrated geometrician, died 212 B. C. **Apollonius.** Probably De Quincey refers to the Apollonius, surnamed Pergaeus, a famous Greek geometer nearly contemporaneous with Archimedes.

182, 32. **The starry Galileo:** the famous Italian astronomer (1564–1642). The epithet "starry" is from Byron's *Childe Harold*, iv, 34.

183, 9. **The English language.** This foolish prediction as to the influence of "the dreadful republic" upon the spread of the English language, is amusing.

Levana and Our Ladies of Sorrow

In the number of *Blackwood's Magazine* for March, 1845, appeared the first of a projected series of papers by De Quincey which were to bear the collective title, *Suspiria de profundis; being a Sequel to the Confessions of an English opium Eater*. The March number contained an *Introductory Note* on Dreaming and the story of his sister's death with his reveries upon it, which he called *The Affliction of Childhood*. In the April number there were only a few short autobiographic passages; but in June appeared four more papers in the series, *The Palimpsest, The Apparition of the Brocken, Savannh-la-Mar*, and *Levana and Our Ladies of Sorrow*. De Quincey apparently intended to include in his general scheme a very considerable number of these dream-like sketches and narratives, arranging the whole in four groups or Parts; but he never could complete the plan. A long and striking paper of the same character, *The English Mail Coach*, with its accompanying "dream fugues," was probably intended for the series; but it appeared in *Blackwood* for October and December, 1849, without any hint of such intention. Several other fragmentary pieces and the titles for a considerable number more, printed by Mr. Japp in his *Posthumous*

Works of De Quincey indicate the ambitious nature of De Quincey's plan.

Of all these papers, the one printed in this volume, *Levana and Our Ladies of Sorrow* is unquestionably the best. Mr. Masson hardly exaggerates when he calls it "one of the most magnificent pieces of prose in the English or any other language."

186, 7. On the foundation: receiving the income of a scholarship fund.

188, 8. In Rama. See *Jeremiah*, xxxi, 15; *St. Matthew*, ii, 18.

188, 11. Bethlehem . . . when Herod's sword. See *St. Matthew*, ii, 16.

189, 4. Within the bedchamber of the Czar. The Princess Alexandra, daughter of the Czar Nicholas, died in August, 1844.

190, 2. Norfolk Island: in the south Pacific, east of Australia, was through the first half of the nineteenth century a penal settlement for Great Britain.

190, 27. The tents of Shem. See *Genesis*, ix, 27. Shem is traditionally represented as the ancestor of the Semitic races.

191, 3. Cybele: in Greek mythology the daughter of Cronos and mother of the Olympian gods. She was usually represented as wearing a mural crown—that is a crown whose rim is carved in the form of towers.

QUERIES AND SUGGESTIONS

Meeting with Coleridge.

1. From what other essay have you learned something of Mr. Poole and the village of Nether Stowey?

2. On page 136, De Quincey says: "I return to my narrative"; how long before had he left it? Is this characteristic of his method of narrative?

3. Can you see any peculiarities of De Quincey's writing in his long account of the obligations of Coleridge to German writers? What, on the whole, do you understand De Quincey's verdict to be on this charge against Coleridge?

4. The talk of Coleridge, as De Quincey describes it.

5. De Quincey's first impressions of Coleridge compared with Hazlitt's. What was the age of each at his first meeting with Coleridge?

6. The two interviews were about eight years apart; do you see by a comparison of Hazlitt's account with De Quincey's, any evidences of change in Coleridge in these years?

7. Is the paragraph on Kant, page 145, of any value to the narrative?

8. Point out in the paragraphs, pages 149–152, some instances of De Quincey's liking for mere gossip and tittle-tattle.

Meeting with Wordsworth.

1. Notice at the opening of the paper, De Quincey's characteristic analysis, both of the feelings which did *not* prevent an earlier visit to Wordsworth, and of those which did.

2. Show the significance of some statements in the paragraph, page 160, as explaining some of the peculiarities of De Quincey's style.

3. Have the statements about the Kosters page 162, any proper place in De Quincey's narrative?

4. What characteristic excellences of De Quincey's manner in narrative and description can you point out in the next paragraphs, pp. 164–174?

5. On the other hand, do you find in these paragraphs any instances of mere gossip, of no value to his narrative?

6. Do you think Wordsworth was likely to be pleased by De Quincey's account of his personal appearance pp. 171–174.

7. What peculiarity of De Quincey's manner is well illustrated by the paragraph, pp. 174–177?

8. Have the last two paragraphs any justifiable connection with the narrative?

Levana and Our Ladies of Sorrow.

1. This paper is the best example of De Quincey's prose poetry; in what respects, both in subject and in manner, does it resemble poetry? Do you think its effect would have been increased if the same thoughts and imagery had been expressed in verse—if it had been poetry?

2. What phase of De Quincey's genius is strikingly shown in the paper?

Show by reference to particular passages in the essays read, the following peculiarities of De Quincey's writing:

1. His paragraph structure—the arts by which he preserves unity in long and complex paragraphs.

2. His diffuseness, liking to enumerate details, and to pursue a thought into all its ramifications.

3. His inveterate tendency to digression, "divagation."

4. His gift for the analysis of character.

5. The rhythm and melody of his style.

6. His interest in the remote, unusual, unobvious.

7. His excessive egoism.

WILLIAM MAKEPEACE THACKERAY

Shortly before his death Thackeray expressed to his daughter an urgent wish that no formal biography of him should be written. It was characteristic of him to dread alike fulsome praise and unjust blame. His wish has been respected; no detailed account of his life has ever been published. But none is needed. The leonine, warmhearted, generous satirist that his contemporaries knew, still lives for us in all his writings. No author gives a more vivid impression of his personality. He belongs to that small group of writers, like Charles Lamb and Richard Steele, with whom we have always a sense of personal acquaintance. We know the man even better than we know his books.

William Makepeace Thackeray was born in Calcutta, India, in 1811. His father died when Thackeray was only five years old, and shortly after, the boy was sent to England and placed in the Charterhouse school, where he spent six years. He is said not to have enjoyed his stay there; yet he always had a certain fondness for the old school, with its memories of Steele and Addison, and pictures of "Gray Friars" every one remembers in *Pendennis* and the *Newcomes*. In 1829 he was entered at Trinity College, Cambridge. He stayed there, however, only a year, and next year found him in Weimar. Here he lived about a year, learned some German, saw the great Goethe "three times," read Schiller—whom he liked better—spent his money now and then at roulette, idled a good deal, and formed a real liking for the simple society of the "dear little Weimar town." Next year he was back in London again, settled in the Temple chambers reading law. He had decided upon his profession—or thought he had. His experience in the Temple chambers gave him some interesting material for the biography of Arthur Pendennis and George Warrington; but his apprenticeship to the legal profession did not last long. In 1832 he came of age, and finding himself in possession of a comfortable income, bade good-bye to the Temple and the law. The moderate fortune he had inherited he seems rather speedily to have got rid of. Part of it was invested in two short-lived newspapers; something was sunk in an unfortunate Indian bank; and some of it probably was lost at play. At all events, by the beginning of 1834, his pockets were almost empty, and he was studying art in Paris. His art studies, though they soon convinced him that he was never to be an artist, did help to make him an amazingly clever caricaturist, as his illustrations in his own books will show. But they did not put much money in his purse. He had from boyhood a knack at turning a humorous paragraph or writing a copy of satiric verses, and he now tried journalism. As early as that year 1834, he seems to have contributed some brief papers to *Fraser's Magazine,* next year he was Paris correspondent of the *Times,* and between 1836 and 1842 was writing constantly for *Fraser,* the *New Monthly Magazine, Punch,* and other less prominent periodicals. *The Yellowplush Papers,* the *Shabby Genteel Story, Catherine,* and the best of his early works, *The Great Hoggarty Diamond,* all belong to this period.

It was not altogether a careless and Bohemian life. In 1836 he married. Four years afterwards his wife was attacked by a mental illness which soon proved incurable and made it necessary that she should be placed under proper care for the rest of her life. Thus the young husband—not yet thirty—was left with his two little girls, homeless. Many years after, he wrote to a young American friend, "I married at your age, with £400 paid by a newspaper which failed six months afterward, and always love to hear of a young fellow testing his fortune bravely that way. Though my marriage was a wreck, as you know, I would do it over again; for behold Love is the crown and completion of all earthly good."

There were disappointments as well as sorrow in those years from 1840 to 1848. He was working hard. *The Snob Papers* and many of the delightful Ballads appeared in *Punch* in that period; the *Barry Lyndon,* really a little masterpiece, came out in 1844; and he was sending slighter sketches to half a dozen periodicals. Yet he had not got the ear of the public. His contemporary Dickens, in precisely those years, was writing his best novels, and by 1848 England and America were ringing with his plaudits. No one, we may be sure, could feel sorrow or disappointment more keenly than Thackeray. Any one who reads between the lines of his writing at this time may catch underneath all its humor, notes of profound sadness. *The Ballad of Boullibaisse* and *The End of the Play,* for example, are among the most genuinely pathetic of modern poems. A man less courageous or less kindly might have been driven into melancholy or cynicism. As it was, his experience strengthened his resolves, broadened his sympathies, taught him the real good and evil of life, so that when he came to write his great novels he was the most brave, truthful, broad-minded, tender-hearted satirist that ever wrote English.

At last, in 1848, appeared the *Vanity Fair,* and the period of trial and experiment was ended. Here was undoubtedly a great novel; a picture of contemporary society such as had not been given in

England since the days of Henry Fielding. Henceforth Thackeray's position was assured. The great novels followed in rapid succession, *Pendennis* in 1850, *Esmond* in 1852, *The Newcomes* in 1855. While at work upon the *Esmond* he prepared a series of lectures on *The English Humorists*, which he delivered in London in 1851; he repeated them in other English cities, and in the autumn of 1852 came over to America to give them here. They were received so favorably by his American audiences that, three years later, in 1855, he again made a visit to America as a lecturer, this time giving a course upon *The Four Georges*. Some of his admirers have regretted that he spent upon these lectures the time and strength that might have given us more novels; but it may, at all events, be urged that the *English Humorists* are almost perfect models of what a popular literary lecture should be. Perhaps nowhere in equal compass can be found so vivid a picture of the literary life of the early eighteenth century.

Thackeray had been induced to give his *Lectures* largely by the hope to improve his financial condition. His novels had made him widely known, but they had not restored his fortune. He was fond of society, generous, and never very careful in the management of money; but now that his daughters were growing to young womanhood he was almost feverishly anxious to secure a home and competence for them. This anxiety was probably increased sometimes by fear for his own health. A serious illness while he was writing the *Pendennis* had left some permanent weakness which had been aggravated by the strain of travel and public speaking in his lecture tours. This decline of vigor is seen in his next novel, *The Virginians*, 1859, which most readers will pronounce inferior to its predecessors. At the close of that year, 1859, he accepted a liberal offer to assume the editorial control of a new magazine his publishers were to establish. The first number of the *Cornhill Magazine* appeared in January, 1860, and Thackeray continued in charge of it until April, 1862. *Lovel the Widower*, the poorest of all his later works, was printed in the early numbers, followed in the course of the next year by *Philip*. Neither of these novels can be classed among his best. But the series of editorial essays furnished the Magazine month by month under the title of *The Roundabout Papers*, showed him in a new and most congenial rôle. They contain much of his wisest and most wholesome satire, written in his most delightful manner. There is nothing else of the kind quite so good in our literature.

But the care and vexations incident to his editorial work told so heavily upon him and left him so little leisure for any other literary plans, that he felt obliged to resign the position. His fortune had been in good degree repaired. He now leased a large and commodious house, and looked forward to years of quiet life and work at home with his daughters. He was but a little past fifty, and as young at heart as ever; but the labors and vicissitudes of his life had silvered his hair and given him the look of age. For years his friends had spoken of him, half tenderly, as "old Thackeray." He set himself at work upon a new novel, *Denis Duval*, which promised to be as good as the *Esmond*. But it was never finished. In the last weeks of December, 1863, he had been slightly ailing; on Christmas morning he was found dead in his bed.

Thackeray was always essentially a satirist. He loved society, the urbane, conventionalized society of the club and the drawing-room; and he had a quick eye for all its humors and follies. In his earliest writing there is little but mere fun, and indeed, to the end of life he enjoyed—as every healthy man does—the ridiculous phases of the human comedy. Yet from the start his satire has its roots in ethical motive. He was always the foe of all falsehood and pretence; but he laughed at shams because he loved the truth. It was the love of whatsoever was true and pure that kept his satire wholesome and kindly. With the widening knowledge of life which came with his period of struggle and disappointment his satire grew more serious and stern; yet even in the first great novel, *Vanity Fair*, the dominant motive is not so much righteous indignation against falsehood and selfishness as admiration for the unselfish love that can lend nobility and beauty to characters homely like Dobbin, or humble like the Sedleys. *Vanity Fair* is really a putting of the extreme case for love. But in the work of the following years the satire grows more mellow and gentle. The characters we remember are the good women and the honest men—Pendennis and Warrington, and Colonel Newcome, and Ethel and Laura, and the Little Sister. It was love that made all these later novels—the love of Love. Nothing could be more absurdly unjust than the charge of cynicism that sometimes used to be brought against Thackeray. One would think nobody could read his books without finding in them a great force of human sympathy, a love of all things pure and noble, growing deeper all his days. Doubtless the satirist must show us falsehood and meanness as he sees them; but this satirist's laugh was never bitter or cold, and he never really wrote a line of cynicism.

This volume has nothing to do with Thackeray's art as a novelist.

Judged by some modern standards, his novels probably lack definite plot and rapid action. They read more like transcripts of actual ordinary life; and in ordinary life there is not elaborate plot or rapid action. But at all events they have amazing reality, and they introduce us to a company of very genuine men and women. Beatrix Esmond, Becky Sharp, Arthur Pendennis, Philip—these people are as living as Hamlet—or your next door neighbor. Some critics have objected also that Thackeray stops in his story to preach, too often and too long. But some of us think that this only gives verisimilitude to his narrative; and, moreover, Thackeray himself is quite as interesting as any of his people. In this habit, as in some other respects, Thackeray is following one of the greatest masters of fiction, Henry Fielding.

It is only one form of Thackeray's work that can be illustrated in this volume; but this shows him at his very best. The *Roundabout Papers* are the familiar, almost confidential talk of a man who combines the wisdom of years with the buoyancy of youth. Among Thackeray's favorite authors were three great masters of the personal essay, Montaigne—whose *Essays* he says was one of his bedtime books—Joseph Addison, and William Hazlitt; nothing any one of them ever wrote surpasses these *Roundabout Papers* in the charm of personality displayed. In these essays there is humor now caustic and now jovial, but never bitter and never frivolous; sentiment that never sinks to sentimentality; wisdom that never falls into platitude. Above all, along with the old strenuous love of truth, there is that broad humanity, that great-hearted charity, sometimes touched with melancholy, that marks Thackeray's ripest years. Read these papers and you will understand why men older than he, like Thomas Carlyle, and not given to sentimentality, called him "dear old Thackeray." Truth, courage, honor, purity, gentleness—all the virtues of the gentleman; who is there who has preached them more effectively?

It only remains to add that in style the *Roundabout Papers* are models of that most difficult of literary virtues, ease. Thackeray's writing, however familiar, even colloquial, has always a certain urbane distinction, and in its best passages a charm of movement and music which echoes its gracious sentiment.

THE ROUNDABOUT PAPERS

Thackeray was editor of the *Cornhill Magazine* from its first number in January, 1860, to April, 1862. The *Roundabout Papers* were printed monthly as editorials during that period; but he continued to write for the Magazine frequently after he had resigned the editorship, and the last of the *Roundabouts* appeared only a few days before his death.

NIL NISI BONUM

(Title.) NIL NISI BONUM: "Nothing unless Good," i.e., Say nothing unless you can say good things.

193, 1. Sir Walter: Sir Walter Scott's last words to his son-in-law and biographer.

193, 7. The Goldsmith and Gibbon of our time. Goldsmith and Gibbon may be considered the typical essayist and historian of the mid-eighteenth century.

193, 14. The first Ambassador whom the New World of Letters sent to the Old. Irving was Secretary to the American legation in London from 1829 to 1832; it is perhaps this period of official residence to which Thackeray especially refers. But Irving had been in London most of the time from 1815 to 1826, and several of his works—*The Sketch Book*, *Tales of a Traveler*, *Bracebridge Hall*—had been published there, making him generally known to the English public.

194, 8. War had just renewed: the war with England, 1812–1814.

195, 24. His charming little domain: "Sunnyside," at Irvington.

196, 11. He had loved once in his life. He was engaged to be married to Miss Matilda Hoffman of New York, who died in 1809, when only eighteen years of age.

197, 30. Gallant young Bellot: Joseph René Bellot, a lieutenant in the French navy who joined as a volunteer the English expedition sent in search of Sir John Franklin, in 1851, and was lost in an ice crevasse.

198, 12. A place in the senate is straightway offered the young man. Macaulay entered parliament in 1828, when only thirty years of age. "His first speech on the Reform Bill placed him in the front rank of orators."—Morley, *Life of Macaulay*.

198, 20. In the East. Macaulay was in India as legal adviser to the Supreme Council from 1834 to 1837.

198, 28. K. K. Court officials: abbreviation for kaiserlich-königlich (imperial-royal).

198, 29. Napoleon or dating from Schönbrunn. After the victory of Austerlits (Dec. 2, 1805) Napoleon occupied for a time the imperial castle of Schönbrunn, near Vienna, and three weeks later signed there a treaty with Prussia.

199, 18. **Senior wrangler:** in Cambridge university, the student taking first place in the public examination for honors in mathematics.

200, 28. **Domes of Peters and Pauls, Sophia, Pantheon:** Saint Peter's in Rome, Saint Paul's in London, Santa Sophia in Constantinople, the Pantheon in Rome.

200, 30. **That catholic dome in Bloomsbury:** i.e., of the British Museum Library.

201, 12. **Clarissa:** Richardson's principal novel, *Clarissa Harlowe;* it is one of the longest of long novels.

201, 25. **The Athenæum:** Thackeray's favorite club. "My father's club was so much a part of his daily life that it seemed at last to be a part of his home."—Mrs. Thackeray Ritchie, *Biographical Edition of Thackeray*, Vol. XII.

202, 18. **Laus deo:** "Thank God."

De Finibus

(Title.) De Finibus: "Concerning Endings."

203, 3. **When Swift was in love with Stella.** Swift's Journal to Stella, Miss Esther Johnson, written while he was in London and she was in Ireland, is one of the most remarkable and beautiful series of letters in the language.

203, 9. **As some commentator or other has said.** The commentator is Thackeray himself, in his admirable lecture on Swift in the *English Humorists*.

203, 11. **Johnson . . . touching the posts.** "I perceived him at a good distance working along with a peculiar solemnity of deportment, and an awkward sort of measured step. Upon every post as he passed along he deliberately laid his hand; but missing one of them, when he had got some distance, he seemed suddenly to recollect himself, and immediately returning carefully performed the accustomed ceremony, and resumed his former course, not omitting one till he gained the crossing. This, Mr. Sheridan assured me, was his constant practice." See Boswell's *Life of Johnson*, Vol. I, 485 (Hill's Edition).

203, 21. **Pendennis, Clive Newcome, and . . . Philip Firmin:** principal characters in Thackeray's novels, *Pendennis, The Newcomes* and *The Adventures of Philip*. The *Philip* had just been finished when he was writing this paper.

203, 27. **Tamen usque recurro:** "Yet I come back again."

204, 29. **Woolcomb . . . or Twysden:** characters in the *Philip*.

206, 4. Dear little Weimar town. Thackeray went to Weimar in 1831, "for study, or sport, or society," as he says. He always remembered his stay there with pleasure. In a charming letter to George Henry Lewes (included in that author's *Life of Goethe*) he says: "With a five and twenty years' experience since those happy days of which I write, and an acquaintance with an immense variety of human kind, I think I have never seen a society more simple, charitable, courteous, gentlemanlike, than that of the dear little Saxon city where the good Schiller and the great Goethe lived and lie buried."

206, 5. Charming verses which are prefixed to the drama: four stanzas prefixed to the First Part of *Faust*, when it was published in 1808; most of this First Part had been published as a "Fragment" as early as 1790, and some scenes had certainly been written much earlier than that. Hence the tone of half sad reminiscence in the lines. The third stanza, as translated by Bayard Taylor runs thus:

> "They hear no longer these succeeding measures,
> The souls to whom my earliest songs I sang:
> Dispersed the friendly troop with all its pleasures,
> And still, alas! the echoes first that rang!
> I bring the unknown multitude my treasures;
> Their very plaudits give my heart a pang,
> And those beside, whose joy my Song so flattered,
> If still they live, wide through the world are scattered."

207, 4. Lord Palmerston and Mr. Disraeli: Henry John Temple, Viscount Palmerston, 1784–1865, and Benjamin Disraeli, 1804–1881, created Earl of Beaconsfield in 1876, among the most prominent English statesmen of the century. Though each—for the greater part of his career—belonged to the Tory party, their public views were not always in agreement, and in personal taste and temper they were very different.

208, 28. Jacob Faithful: a novel (1834) by Frederick Marryat (1792–1848).

208, 29. Vingt Ans Après: *Twenty Years After*, a novel (1845), by Alexandre Dumas, the elder (1802–1870).

208, 30. Woman in White: by William Wilkie Collins (1824–1889). The novel appeared in 1860.

209, 2. Chevalier d'Artagnan: one of the principal characters in the *Vingt Ans Après*.

209, 15. a la mode le pays de Pole: "After the custom of the Pole," *i.e.*, to give no quarter.

209, 19. Certain Doctor F—— and a certain Mr. T. H——: Doctor Firmin and Thomas Hunt, characters in *Philip*.

210, 18. Dilectissimi fratres: "Dearest brethren."

210, 20. Miserere nobis miseris peccatoribus: "Have mercy upon us miserable sinners."

210, 25. Libera me: "deliver me."

210, 30. Stop in his story and begin to preach. Thackeray certainly does often stop for leisurely chat and comment with his reader upon the persons of his story. But most readers will pronounce these passages among the most delightful in his writing. Fielding had the same habit.

210, 34. Peccavi: "I have sinned."

212, 4. Pythoness on her oracle tripod: the priestess at the oracle of Delphi, who sat upon a tripod placed over the chasm whence the divine afflatus proceeded.

213, 9. Mignon, and Margaret . . . The persons named in this passage are among the immortal characters of fiction. *Mignon* is one of the principal persons in Goethe's *Wilhelm Meister; Margaret* is the heroine in his *Faust; Goetz von Berlichingen* is the hero of his early drama of that name. *Dugald Dalgetty*, from *A Legend of Montrose*, and *Ivanhoe*, of course, are Walter Scott's creations. *Uncas* is the prominent character in Cooper's *Last of the Mohicans*, and *Leatherstocking* is the name applied to Natty Bumpo, who figures in several other of Cooper's tales. *Athos, Porthos, and Aramis* are the *Three Musketeers* of Alexandre Dumas, the elder. *Amelia Booth* is the title character in Fielding's *Amelia*, while *Uncle Toby* is the most delightfully whimsical character in Sterne's *Tristram Shandy*. *Tittlebat Titmouse* is a character in the once famous novel, *Ten Thousand a Year*, by Samuel Warren (1807–1877). *Crummles* is the manager of a very cheap theatrical company in Dicken's *Nicholas Nickleby*. *Gil Blas de Santillane* gives the name to a famous French Romance by Alain René Le Sage (1668–1747). *Roger de Coverley* is the immortal old gentleman of Addison's *Spectator;* and "the greatest of all crazy gentlemen, the Knight of La Mancha" is the *Don Quixote* of Cervantes (1547–1686), who "laughed Spain's chivalry away."

QUERIES AND SUGGESTIONS

Nil nisi Bonum.

1. Why does Thackeray quote at the beginning of this paper the words of Walter Scott, "Be a good man, my dear?"

2. What are the grounds of Thackeray's esteem and admiration for Irving? Does he attempt any estimate of his literary work?

3. And what qualities does he emphasize most in his tribute to Macaulay?

De Finibus.

1. Show by reference to particular passages how this essay exhibits Thackeray's humor, satire, and pathos.

After reading carefully both these essays,

1. Write a brief paper pointing out as well as you can those peculiarities of Thackeray's literary style that give it such *ease* and familiarity—as, for example, the structure and length of his sentences, the nature of his epithets and his allusions, his use of the first-person pronoun, etc.

2. Give in a brief essay the estimate you have formed from these essays of the man, Thackeray,—his temperament, virtues he most admired in others and exemplified in himself, etc.

3. Addison, Lamb, and Thackeray are three great English *humorists*; can you point out any similarities in their character and writing? Any striking differences?

RALPH WALDO EMERSON

Ralph Waldo Emerson, the poet-philosopher of New England, was born in Boston, May 25, 1803. He inherited some of the best blood and brains of America, for his paternal grandfathers for four generations had been Puritan ministers, and most of his immediate maternal ancestry was of the same stock. He was himself intended for the clerical profession. After graduation from Harvard in 1821, and a year or so of not very congenial experience as a school-teacher, he began his studies in divinity, and 1826 was "approbated to preach" by the Middlesex Association of Ministers. He spent a winter in the South for his health—at that period of his life precarious—and after preaching occasionally in various places for another year, was appointed, in 1829, as colleague with Rev. Henry Ware, to the pastorate of the Second Church, Boston. He held this position three years, when differences between himself and the membership of his church as to some of the forms of worship and especially the sacrament of the Lord's Supper, led to his resignation. He continued to preach frequently for the next three or four years, but he never accepted another parish. In truth, his differences with the accepted orthodoxy went much deeper than any mere questions of ritual; he felt that he ought to withdraw from the formal work and office of the ministry. Yet he had by no means ceased to be a preacher; he craved some place for freer utterance than could be offered by any pulpit. This he found in the New England lyceum lecture system, then in its early vigor. From that time for more than thirty years he was a familiar figure before audiences, not only in New England but, as his reputation extended, throughout the middle West. Most of the teaching afterwards to be embodied in his *Essays* was first given to the public from the lecture platform. But up to 1835 he had published nothing.

The decade 1830–1840 was in New England a period of the ferment of thought on almost all subjects. The influence of a new philosophy, mostly derived from Germany through Coleridge and Carlyle, was making itself felt upon young thinking men. The older logical theology was to be widened to make room for intuition and emotion. All sorts of vague ideas upon social reform were in the air, some practical, some visionary. It was in the autumn of 1836 that Mr. Emerson and three other thoughtful young men met in Boston to talk over the state of current opinion on philosophy and religion. The meeting resulted in the informal association of some dozen men and women—George Ripley, Bronson Alcott, Henry Thoreau, James Freeman Clarke, Margaret Fuller, Elizabeth Peabody, and some others—who met occasionally during the next six or eight years, for the discussion of such themes. They came to be called the Transcendental Club—though they never accepted that title—and much of the teaching on philosophical and social matters in the next quarter century really had its rise in the writing and discussions of this group of thinkers. But it was Emerson who in the last half of this decade, first gave striking public expression to the most important of the new ideas. In 1836 he published an epoch-marking little book, *Nature*, which, though often rising to the tone of poetry, is the first pronounced utterance of the new idealism, with its recognition of the claims of sentiment and emotion. Next year, 1837, he delivered before the Phi Beta Kappa Society of Harvard College an Address on *The American Scholar*, which Oliver Wendell Holmes has characterized as our intellectual Declaration of Independence. It was a plea for independent thinking, for freedom of individual belief and action. Finally, in July of 1838, he gave an address before the Senior class of the Cambridge Divinity School in which he claimed for himself and urged upon his hearers the widest liberty of individual belief as a necessary condition of genuine religious life. He frankly abandoned most of the facts of historical Christianity, and flung himself upon the primary spiritual intuitions. The address went beyond the teaching even of the liberal school where it was delivered, and caused immediate and eager controversy.

These utterances placed Emerson at the front of what was vaguely called the Transcendental movement. He had, however, no desire to lead any "movement," or to write a credo for any one else. As he said, later in life, the one subject he had always preached was "the competence of the individual man." He distrusted all organization, all attempts to bind men to associated or uniform action. He joined no party, was chary of espousing any "cause." All his life long, in lectures and essays, he went on teaching large primary truths which the individual must apply to his own conduct as best he can.

Emerson's outward life had no dramatic phases. For many years he usually made a lecture tour every winter, and the returns from these lectures furnished the greater part of the income his frugal life demanded. The first series of the *Essays*—largely made out of the materials used as lectures—appeared in 1841, the second in 1844; other volumes in prose and verse, at intervals of about five years until 1875. In 1834 he had taken up his residence in Concord, at first in his grandfather's "Old Manse"—later made memorable by Hawthorne—but after a few months, in the house just outside the village, where he passed the rest of his days. It is impossible to conceive a better example of plain living and high thinking than his life here for forty years. He was no ascetic. To his neighbors he was a plain citizen, kindly of speech, who dug in his garden and always attended town-meeting. But he had always the serene dignity of one who knows habitually the joy of elevated thought. Hawthorne, who lived hard by, once said, "It was good to meet him in the wood-path or sometimes in our avenue, with that pure intellectual gleam diffusing about his person like the garment of a shining one." As years went by, he came to be regarded with a kind of reverence; for the last ten years of his life he was the most venerable figure among American writers. He died, April 27, 1882.

Matthew Arnold pronounced Emerson's *Essays* "the most important work done in prose in the nineteenth century." To us of this more practical generation this estimate may seem extravagant. If we look for philosophical teaching, we are likely to find Emerson's work obscure or mystical. He seems to mix soul and sense a good deal, and confuses himself with the universe in a way difficult to understand. The truth is, that while Emerson's work is pervaded with a profound spiritual philosophy, he is not in strictness to be called a philosophical writer. He was not a consecutive thinker; he seldom follows out a train of thought. His mind did not work that way. He *perceived* truths directly, one by one; he did not reach them by a process of reasoning. He always preached openness of mind, and never cared much whether the truth of today squared with that of yesterday. Such a man will frame no system of philosophy, and it may prove difficult to decide what are the constant elements in his teaching.

Yet it is, in great part, just this temper of the seer rather than of the philosopher that explains Emerson's power. We wonder sometimes how this plain man on the lecture platform, reading his manuscript with none of the arts of the orator, could hold his audiences in rapt attention. A close linked train of argument they never would have followed for an hour. But one large truth after another rose before them, clad in homely or striking phrase, and they did not stay to connect or relate them. At the end, if they had received no clear teaching, they had been stimulated and enlarged. As Lowell says, in describing the early lectures: "Did they say he was unconnected? So are the stars. If asked what was left, what we carried home, we should not have been careful for an answer. It would have been enough if we had said that something beautiful had passed that way." Now something of the same effect is felt by the reader of one of Emerson's great philosophic essays, like *The Over Soul*. The high truths it contains cannot be confined in clear speech or fitted neatly into a system; it is enough that they expand our minds, quicken our reverence, and make us "feel that we are greater than we know."

But most of Emerson's essays do not move in this high region of speculation. He himself had little care for abstract thinking detached from practice. His philosophy was balanced by a massive common-sense. He was a transcendentalist, but a Yankee transcendentalist. He had the shrewd practical wisdom, the cool self-possession, the touch of rusticity—all the qualities that make up the typical Yankee. It was this side of his character, doubtless, that helped his popularity as a lecturer with plain folk who cared nothing about transcendentalism. This man evidently, whatever his philosophy, was a man of sense. He knew the difference between good work and poor. He knew how to make a little money and keep it. He didn't live in the clouds; he lived in a two-story white house with green blinds, on Concord Street, and he had bought and paid for it. And it is just this balance of qualities that makes Emerson's essays of such permanent and universal value. Most of them are concerned with the general truths of practical life. Their very titles indicate that—*Success, Culture, Wealth, Prudence, Manners, Farming, Works and Days, Domestic Life*. Emerson gave to a volume in which he collected some of the best of his papers the title, *The Conduct of Life;* it is really the theme of all his work—to set forth those truths that enlarge, and refine, and liberalize ordinary life.

Of course even the tyro can criticize the manner of the *Essays*. It is easy to point out that they lack method and consecutiveness. Successive paragraphs sometimes have little obvious connection, and each paragraph falls apart into separate unrelated sentences. Emerson knew that. He once said of his sentences that each one was "an infinitely repellent particle." But, as a compensation, these single sentences are often marvels of terse and pithy wisdom. To fit them together with joints and connections would injure the rounded perfection of each. If you will have his style flowing and "sequacious," you must lose something of its epigrammatic vigor. Emerson's sentences are strong enough to stand alone. They have positiveness and finality. He needs none of the hesitating phrases with which we timidly condition our utterances; his truths are round and certain, as if indeed they had

"Out from the heart of nature rolled."

Moreover, the alleged lack of method in the essays is often rather apparent than real. Careful and sympathetic reading usually shows—as in the essay on *Manners* included in this volume—a unity of theme, an order and advance of thought, rising to an impressive climax at the end.

But, after all, the virtue of any book depends not upon any rhetorical skill, but upon the personality of the man revealed in it. And seldom has a man put himself more wholly into his work than Emerson. His authentic voice speaks from every page. It is the voice of a man calm, optimistic, as having sight of the highest truths, yet full of the wisdom of common life, and urging upon us all, with such pithy originality of phrase and such homely vividness of imagination as none of his contemporaries could command, the virtues of sincerity, courage, self-reliance, independence.

MANNERS

"A lecture with this name had been given by Mr. Emerson in the Boston course on 'The Philosophy of History' in the winter of

1836-37. This essay is the lecture in the course on 'The Times,' given at Tremont Temple in the winter of 1841-42. A year later, and before this essay was published, Mr. Emerson gave in New York five lectures on 'New England,' the third of which treated of 'Manners and Customs of New England.'"—Note in the "Centenary Edition," Vol. III, p. 315.

Some paragraphs in the essay closely resemble passages in the essays *Prudence* and *Aristocracy;* it is probable that the same passages in Mr. Emerson's Note Books may have furnished material for all three essays.

215, 2. Feejee (or Fiji) islanders: inhabitants of a group of islands in the South Pacific, now a dependency of Great Britain. Previous to their conversion to Christianity by Wesleyan missionaries, they were notorious cannibals; at present they are civilized, educated, and have some commerce.

216, 3. Belzoni: Giovanni Battista Belzoni (1778-1823), celebrated Italian traveler and archæologist. His principal work is *A Narrative of Excavations in Egypt and Nubia.*

216, 6. Borgoo: Borgu, or Bussanga, a state in West Central Africa, near the head waters of the Niger.

216, 10. Bornoos: inhabitants of Bornu, a state in the Sudan, Africa.

216, 31. Sir Philip Sidney (1554-1586), English poet, romancer, courtier, soldier—the pattern gentleman of his age.

217, 29. Gentilesse. It is unfortunate that this word is obsolete. It is a favorite word with Chaucer; a familiar definition of gentilesse in his *Wif of Bathes Tale* was included by Emerson in his volume of poetic selections, *Parnassus:*

> "Loke who that is most vertuous alway,
> Privee and apart, and most entendeth ay
> To do the gentil dedes that he can,
> And tak him for the grettest gentil man.
> Crist wol we clayme of him our gentillesse,
> Not of our eldres for hir old richesse."

219, 8. Battle of Lundy's Lane. One of the battles in the War of 1812-14 between England and America, fought July 15, 1814. The force of Emerson's simile is not evident to me.

219, 16. Lord Falkland: Lucius Cary, viscount Falkland (1610?-1643), one of the most scholarly and thoughtful noblemen of the early seventeenth century. He was a friend of constitutional liberty, but when the Civil War broke out, joined the army of the crown and was killed at the battle of Newbury. It was in memory of Falkland that Ben Jonson wrote the beautiful lines beginning

> "It is not growing like a tree
> In bulk, doth make man better be."

See also one of Matthew Arnold's best essays, *Falkland*.

219, 30. **Saladin** (1137-1193): a powerful sultan of Egypt and Syria, the principal foe of the Crusaders in their efforts to capture Jerusalem. He is a principal figure in Walter Scott's *Talisman*. **Sapor:** Sapor II., surnamed "the Great," king of Persia in the fourth century. He greatly extended the bounds of Persia, and successfully defended himself against invasion by the Romans under the emporor Jovian. **The Cid** (about 1040-1099): Ruy, or Rodrigo, Diaz de Rivar, surnamed The Cid, and someitmes El Campeador (the Challenger). A national hero of Spain in the struggle against the Moors. The story of his exploits was put into a romantic Chronicle, within half a century after his death. This Chronicle with other portions of the Cid romance was translated and combined by Robert Southey into his romantic poem *The Chronicle of the Cid*. Mr. Emerson is said to have often read passages from Southey's poem to his children. **Scipio:** Publius Cornelius Scipio, surnamed Africanus Major (about 257-183 B. C.), the greatest Roman general before Julius Caesar. He finally defeated the Carthaginians in the great battle of Zama. **Alexander** (356-323 B. C.), surnamed The Great: son of Philip of Macedon, and conqueror of a large part of the known world of his day. **Pericles** (about 495-429 B .C.): famous Athenian statesman and orator.

220, 12. **Diogenes:** Greek cynic philosopher (about 412-323 B. C.) who according to tradition, lived in a tub; **Socrates:** greatest of Greek philosophers (474-399 B. C.); **Epaminondas** (418-362 B. C.): famous Theban statesman, orator, and general.

220, 16. **Are my contemporaries.** Mr. Edward Cabot Emerson, in the Notes to the Centenary Edition of the *Works* (Vol. III, p. 318) suggests that Emerson's friend Thoreau combined in himself something of the philosophy of Diogenes, the dialectic of Socrates, and the heroic temper of Epaminondas.

221, 6. **Energize.** This intransitive use of the word is not common.

221, 23. **Faubourg St. Germain:** the aristocratic section of Paris.

222, 7. **Mexico:** the scene of the most brilliant conquests of *Cortez*, the greatest Spanish adventurer of the sixteenth century;

Marengo, one of *Napoleon's* most famous victories, June 14, 1808, over the Austrians; **Trafalgar,** perhaps the greatest victory in English naval history, won by *Nelson* over a French and Spanish fleet, October 21, 1805. Nelson was shot, and died in the moment of victory.

222, 26. If . . . two men only were left, etc. Some social reformers in these days seem inclined to forget this truth. The ideal of social reform is the equalization of opportunity, not of position.

223, 34. Send them . . . to Coventry: to ostracize, exclude from society. The phrase was originally a military one, signifying to exclude from the company mess. "This use of the name Coventry is a matter of conjecture."—*Century Dictionary.*

224, 26. Composure, and self-content. This virtue of calm self-reliance is the one on which Emerson is always insisting, and he exemplified it himself in most remarkable degree. Nothing in all his work is more charcateristic than the essay on *Self-Reliance.*

225, 1. He is an underling: *i.e.,* the man who defers to "some eminent person."

225, 9. Vich Ian Vohr with his tail on! In Scott's *Waverley,* Chapter xvi, Evan the follower of McIvor, says to the young Englishman, Edward, "Ah, if you Saxon Duinhe-wassel (English gentlemen) saw but the Chief with his tail on!"

226, 6. Amphitryon: in Greek myth the husband of Alcmene. The use of the name for a host, as here, arises from at incident in the myth, especially as it is expanded by the French dramatist Moliere in his play based upon the Greek story. Jupiter gives a feast to Alcmene, in the absence of her husband, disguising himself as Amphitryon, when the real Amphitryon suddenly appears, and a dispute arises as to which is the real host. The line of Moliere in which it is decided is often quoted: "Le vèritable Amphitryon est l'Amphitryon où l'on dine." "The real Amphitryon is the Amphitryon where one dines"—or, "that gives the feast."

226, 14. Tuileries: the royal palace of the kings of France, begun before the close of the sixteenth century and brought to completion by Louis Fourteenth near the close of the seventeenth. It was burned to the ground by the Paris commune, in 1871.

226, 14. Escurial: a mass of building some thirty miles north of Madrid, Spain, containing a monastery, and the palace, chapel, and mausoleum of the kings of Spain.

226, 30. Voice of the Lord in the garden. See *Genesis,* iii, 8.

227, 4. Madame de Stael: Anne Loise Germaine Necker,

Baroness de Staël (1766–1817), an illustrious French writer, only child of the financier Necker. She early encountered the personal enmity of Napoleon, and when her most famous book, *De l'Allemagne* (Germany) appeared, in 1810, Napoleon ordered the ten thousand copies of the first Paris edition to be destroyed.

227, 13. Montaigne (1533–92): *Michel Eyquem de Montaigne.* The most famous of French essayists, who may almost be said to have originated the personal essay as a distinct literary form. His *Essais* have been frequently translated; the translation to which Emerson refers, including the "Travels," was published in 1842 by William Hazlitt, Jr. son of the essayist.

229, 23. What belongs to coming together. Notice this exact definition of a word by its etymology. The definition of fashion which follows is an excellent example of Emerson's gift of summing up a paragraph in a sentence.

230, 3. The dry light: *i.e.,* the clear intellectual perception unmodified by passion or prejudice.

231, 6. Fox: Charles James Fox (1749–1806), an eminent Liberal statesman and brilliant debater. During the earlier portion of his career, Fox had been in political sympathy and warm personal friendship with his great contemporary Edmund Burke; but Burke's attitude toward the French Revolution alienated them. The famous scene to which Emerson refers occurred in a debate on the Canada bill, May 6, 1791, when Burke, exasperated at what he thought the harshness and injustice of his friend, cried out "I have done my duty at the price of my friend. Our friendship is at an end!"

231, 17. Sheridan: Richard Brinsley Sheridan (1751–1816), a Whig politician, almost equally eminent as an orator and a dramatist and a wit. Both Fox and Sheridan were inveterate gamesters; the "debt of honor" had been contracted at the gaming table.

232, 22. Circe, to her horned company. Circe is represented in the *Odyssey* (Book x.) as dwelling in a pleasant valley, and surrounded by lions and wolves that are tame and obedient. It is not clear where Emerson finds any mention of a "*horned*" company about her.

232, 26. Captain Symmes, from the interior of the earth. John Cleves Symmes, a captain in the United States army, conceived the strange theory that the earth was hollow, and consisted of six or seven concentric spheres, open at the north pole, where entrance to them might be had. Hence the north pole came to be known as "Symmes's hole." He published his theory in 1826.

232, 30. Torre del Greco: a town near Naples, at the foot of Vesuvius.

233, 27. Here lies Sir Jenkin Grout. This epitaph has never been found, and may have been an invention of Emerson.

234, 3. Some friend of Poland; some Philhellene. The breaking up of the kingdom of Poland and its forcible partition between Russia, Prussia, and Austria, in the last part of the eighteenth century, caused a good deal of indignation among friends of political liberty. The term Philhellene was applied to those who assisted the Greeks in their struggle with the Turks for independence.

234, 25. As heaven and earth are fairer far, etc. See Keats, *Hyperion*, Book ii, lines 206–215, 228–229.

236, 19. Robin Hood: the legendary popular hero of the ballads that originated in England during the thirteenth and fourteenth centuries, and that represent the temper of popular resistance to the exactions of the nobility and cloistered clergy.

236, 33. In behalf of Women's Rights. Mr. Emerson was always in favor of granting equal civil and political rights to women wherever they deliberately claim them; he trusted the sense and judgment of woman to determine what she needed. His views on the question may be seen in an *Address* before the Woman's Rights Convention, in Boston, Sept. 20, 1855.

237, 10. The place of muses and of Delphic Sibyls. It was of this paragraph that Oliver Wendell Holmes said: "Emerson speaks of woman in language that seems to pant for rhythm and rime."

237, 21. Hafiz or Firdousi: Shams ed-Din Muhammad, surnamed Hafiz, the greatest of Persian poets, who wrote in the fourteenth century. Abul Kasim Mansur, surnamed Firdusi or Firdausi (Paradise) an epic Persian poet of the tenth century, whose great poem the *Shahnamah* tells the story of Persian kings and heroes from the earliest time to the seventh century. He has been called the Homer of Persia.

Emerson had no knowledge of the oriental languages, but he was attracted to eastern poetry chiefly by its tone of mysticism.

238, 9. Byzantine. This epithet, usually applied to a certain school of architecture, is here probably intended by Emerson to characterize "chivalry or fashion" as irregular, capricious, extravagant.

239, 22. The king of Shiraz . . . the poor Osman. Shiraz was one of the capitals of Persia, the residence of Hafiz. "Osman was the name given by Emerson to the ideal man, subject to the same conditions as himself"—note in Centenary Edition, III, 322.

239, 25. Koran: the sacred book of Mohammedans, the contents of which, it is claimed, were directly revealed to Mohammed.

240, 7. I overheard Jove, one day. This fable, which closes the essay, is of Emerson's own invention.

QUERIES AND SUGGESTIONS

1. After reading carefully this essay, set down as clearly as you can but without special care as to their arrangement, as many as you can remember of the particular truths taught in the essay.

2. Then, with the text before you, make out an analysis of the argument of the whole essay.

3. Show by an examination of several paragraphs that we usually find in Emerson's writing unity in the paragraph, but lack of clear connection between the consecutive sentences.

4. Select from the essay as many as ten brief, pithy sentences, each expressing some important truth in striking manner, and commit them to memory.

5. Explain in your own way what Emerson means by "Power" (p. 218).

6. Interpret, consistently with its context, this sentence: "The intellect relies on memory to make some supplies to face these extemporaneous squadrons." (p. 219.)

7. What, according to Emerson, is the relation between Power, Manners, and Fashion?

8. What does he mean by the statement: "Fashion . . . is virtue gone to seed." (p. 221.)

9. Emerson says (p. 223) and repeats and illustrates the statement in the following paragraphs, that "Fashion rests on reality, and hates nothing so much as pretenders"; how far do you think this true? And do you find any statements later in the essay that seem inconsistent with it?

10. Explain what Emerson means by "deference." (p. 227.)

11. Another requisite of Manners is "a certain degree of taste" (p. 229); how would you define "Taste"?

12. Fashion is again defined (p. 234) as "an attempt to organize beauty of behavior." Is this definition consistent with that given above, in query 8?

13. Yet, says Emerson (p. 235), "elegance comes of no breeding but of birth," and declares in the same paragraph that Shakespeare is "the best-bred man in England in all Christendom"; what does he mean by that?

14. What do you infer from the paragraph (pp. 236–37) that Emerson would say of the later movements "in behalf of Women's Rights"?

15. After all, what seems to be the teaching of Emerson in the last two paragraphs of the essay as to the relative value of "everything that is called fashion and courtesy"?

JAMES RUSSELL LOWELL

In versatility and breadth of culture no American man of letters has surpassed James Russell Lowell. Journalist, editor, reformer, literary critic, poet, university professor, politician, diplomat—he played many parts and played them all well. If he just missed of the highest eminence in any, he failed in none. His breadth of attainment was not gained at the expense of efficiency.

James Russell Lowell was born February 22, 1819. Like Emerson he was of the Brahmin caste of New England, for his father, Rev. Charles Lowell, was a New England parson of the best type. In his early years, Charles Lowell, after graduation from Harvard, had seen something of the great world, studied in Edinburgh, met Wilberforce in London, heard Pitt and Fox and Sheridan in Parliament, and then came home to be minister of the West Church in Boston, and to live on that goodly homestead of Elmwood where his greater son was to spend all his days. In the Elmwood house there was a library of some four thousand volumes, by no means all theological; and when we get our first glimpse of James Russell Lowell he is reading there with his sister Mary. That is the most noteworthy thing in his life for the next twenty years—he is always reading, and reading the great books. In college he permitted himself some neglect of required tasks; but he revels in Milton and Cowley, he has read all Shakespeare, and is making eager acquaintance with Chaucer and the old dramatists. Within two or three years after graduation he is familiar not only with a wide range of English literature, but with the best things in the Greek poets and dramatists. He is laying the foundations of a broad human culture. One other life-long characteristic of the man is evident in the boy, a healthy humor, a certain exuberance of spirits which kept him from pedantry or priggishness. So much reading meant writing. After graduation, in 1838, he read law—though rather unwillingly—and was actually admitted to the bar, but it is not on record that he had any clients; he had always an inclination to live by literature, and by 1840 seems to have decided that to be his only vocation.

Perhaps this decision was confirmed by a friendship Lowell formed in the autumn of 1839. Maria White, the daughter of a farmer in Watertown, Mass., was a girl of singular depth, sensitiveness, and serenity of character. She had been touched by the influence of Emerson, and though quite without any mannish desire for publicity, she shared the new interest in matters social and intellectual so prevalent in New England just then. Lowell saw her often with a group of young people who met for simple forms of social recreation, with music, readings, and discussion, more or less transcendental, of all things. They were engaged by the middle of 1840. The first result of the engagement was a thin volume of poems, *A Year's Life*, of which Maria White is the inspiration and the only theme. Three years later, 1844, Lowell issued another volume of *Poems* with a somewhat wider range of interest. Yet in this volume, too, the most noteworthy thing is that enthusiasm for ethical and social ideals which Maria White had done so much to quicken.

Meantime he seemed settling into the career of a journalist. In 1842 he contributed to the *Boston Miscellany* a series of papers that two years later were collected and published under the title *Conversations on Some of the Old Poets*. In the same year, 1842, he projected a new literary journal to be called *The Pioneer;* it enlisted the services of a very brilliant corps of young contributors—and lived three months. But at the close of 1844 he secured what promised to be a more permanent position, as editor of the *Pennsylvania Freeman,* whereat he married and removed with his bride to Philadelphia. They set up their simple house-keeping in a third story back room, and deemed it a kind of city idyll; Lowell in after life always remembered it with a certain tenderness. But in five months he was back again in his father's house at Elmwood. For the next two years he wrote little except a number of articles contributed to various papers, mostly on the slavery question. He had not yet got the ear of the public.

It was the year 1848 that revealed the range of Lowell's ability and established his reputation. In that year he published three noteworthy volumes of poetry. The *Fable for Critics* is a half satiric estimate of most of the younger writers of that day, run into a verse surprisingly facile and witty. Here Lowell shows for the first time his exuberant high spirits in combination with a remarkable accuracy of critical judgment. The keenness and justice with which this young fellow characterizes the other young fellows—most of them were under forty—is astonishing. The *Fable* has never been adequately appreciated; it is really the best critical survey of contemporary American literature at the middle of the nineteenth century. The *Biglow Papers* were a yet happier inspiration. The first of them, "a sort of squib" as he called it, expressing New England sentiment on the war with Mexico, appeared in the "Boston Courier" for June 17, 1846. As the subsequent papers appeared they excited general attention, and when, in 1848, they were collected into a volume they were at once recognized both in England and in America as the most original and effective political satire this country had produced. First and last, Lowell's best work is in the *Biglow Papers*. Here the whole man speaks. For there was a Parson Wilbur in Lowell, and there was a Hosea Biglow; and both were Yankees. The third volume of that year, *The Vision of Sir Launfal*, if less original, has been more popular, especially with younger readers. It is the type of poem one hopes will always be popular with youth; for it is the embodiment of a high ethical ideal in fresh and charming imagery. Sir Launfal is Lowell himself in the June of his life, half mystic half social reformer, and in love with all things pure and chivalrous. In all Lowell's work up to this time there is an aggressive ethical sentiment, a sort of militant righteousness. "Whenever you hear of a good fight, go to it," said his father to young Philip Sidney; something of this temper is in all of Lowell's writing.

The promise of that year 1848, however, was not immediately fulfilled. The next decade was not a productive period in Lowell's life. Private sorrows in part account for that. In 1853 his wife died. He emerged but slowly from the shadow of this great sorrow, and his friends noticed in him some loss thereafter of the buoyant elasticity of his earlier years. He gave some public lectures, and spent a year in Europe. On his return, in 1856, he resided for a time with his daughter and her governess Miss Dunlop, in the house of his brother-in-law, Dr. Estes Howe. Later in that year he contracted an engagement with Miss Dunlop, who had been an intimate friend of his wife; and they were married in September of 1857.

In 1856 he was elected to the chair of Modern Languages in Harvard College, just vacated by the resignation of Longfellow. This position he held for sixteen years. As a college professor he was unhampered by any academic traditions, and his lectures, though always inspiring to thoughtful men, were often very unconventional. It is more important to note that one product of his literary studies during the long period of his professorship was the series of brilliant critical essays upon which his reputation as a prose writer must chiefly rest. These essays, first published in the *Atlantic Monthly* and *North American Review*, were collected in the volumes *Among My Books*, 1870 and 1876, and *My Study Windows*, 1871.

Before Lowell had been in his professor's chair a year, he had accepted another position even more important. The first number of *The Atlantic Monthly* appeared in November, 1857, under his editorship. He carried the double work of professor and editor only four years; but in that time the *Atlantic* took a foremost place in the periodical literature of England and America. And no wonder; for it included in its early list of contributors almost every writer of eminence in New England—Longfellow, Emerson, Whittier, Holmes, Cabot, Higginson, Sumner, Motley, Mrs. Stowe, and a score of others hardly less prominent. Lowell, although he resigned his editorship in 1861, continued to be one of its most valued contributors. The outburst of patriotic feeling at the beginning of the Civil War stirred in him the old poetic impulse, and his war poems published in the *Atlantic* between 1862 and 1865, the *Washers of the Shroud*, the Second Series of the *Biglow Papers*, and the great Harvard *Commemoration Ode* contain his very noblest work. Nearly all his writing, whether in prose or verse, during this period, was on national themes. From 1863 to 1872, he consented to share with his friend Professor Norton the editorship of the *North American Review*, and although he turned over to his colleague most of the editorial work, he himself contributed to the *Review* a series of vigorous political papers.

As years went by, Lowell found the duties of his college professorship increasingly irksome. They dulled his poetic impulse— "dampened his powder," as he put it. In fact, his poetic work was practically finished with *The Cathedral*, 1869, a poem which shows a wealth of reflection rather than the freshness of imaginative impulse. And, on the other hand, the secluded academic life seemed to remove him from active participation in those public affairs in which he had come to take increasing interest. All through the troubled period of reconstruction that followed the Civil War he followed the course of events with anxiety over what seemed the increasing corruption in our national politics, and was a representative in the National Republican Convention which nominated Mr. Hayes for the presidency. It was not, therefore, a matter of surprise that he should accept the offer by president Hayes of the Mission to Spain in 1877; and yet more natural that, two years and a half later, he should gladly accept the transfer from Spain to England. He took up his official residence in London as American Minister in March, 1880. He had, indeed, some misgivings as to his reception; for in the *Biglow Papers* and in the essay on *A Certain Condescension in Foreigners* he had said some very plain things in criticism of England and the English people; and during the whole period of his English residence he was the strenuous defender of America. But his outspoken frankness did him no harm. He was soon recognized as representing the best culture and the best statesmanship of his country—an ideal scholar-diplomat. Probably no American minister at the court of St. James was ever more generally admired or more highly honored; and his recall was regretted by all classes of Englishmen. After the inauguration of President Cleveland, he resigned his portfolio, and came back to America in June, 1885.

The last years of his life were quiet and lonely. His wife had died in London just before his return. He tried to resume his studies; he gave some public lectures; but his work was really done. A thin volume of verse, mostly reminiscent, *Heartsease and Rue*, 1888, was the only important publication of this closing period. He died, August 12, 1891.

Lowell's reputation as a prose writer must rest principally upon the series of his critical essays in the volumes *Among My Books* and *My Study Windows*. He had two of the first requisites of the literary critic; keen and just appreciation of the best things in letters, and a remarkably catholic taste. It is seldom that a critic can discuss with equal appreciation two such polar opposites as, let us say, Dante and Dryden. Lowell's criticism is not formal or academic; he has no critical yardstick to lay down upon a book. In fact, he cares less for the book than for the man in the book. Such papers as those on Dante, Spenser, Wordsworth, Rousseau, are excellent studies in personality. On the whole, one risks little in saying that these essays form the best body of literary criticism that any American writer has yet produced.

Perhaps, however, all the characteristics of Lowell's manner are best seen in those more personal essays like that included in this volume. Here he is not bound by conformity to any critical principles, and not concerned to render any final estimate. He is simply expressing his personal feelings. He can let himself go. For the merits and defects of Lowell's writing proceed from the same essentials of character. He is always profuse and exuberant. Writing from a full mind, he sometimes seems impatient of the preliminary work of selecting and arranging his matter, with the result that his essay lacks method and is prone to run off into digression. Then his wide reading, at the service of an active imagination, made him the most allusive and one of the most metaphorical of writers. He can seldom resist the lure of a striking analogy or curious example. Moreover, his exuberant humor is often a little too much for his dignity. The sticklers for classic propriety get a good many shocks from his pages. For he was a Yankee, not over respectful of dignities and seldom fearful of putting his reputation for sober sense at the hazard of a joke. Indeed, he is in all ways indifferent to the starched rhetorician, and confesses in one of his poems that he is more a Goth than a Greek. He likes freedom better than precision. He likes the idiomatic word, the quaint allusion, the homely incident.

But all these faults—so far as they are faults—are hardly noticed in such an essay as the *Condescension in Foreigners*. Indeed, most readers will think that in all the essays, faults like these are venial when compared with the substantial merits of Lowell's prose. For they all grow out of that full and hearty personality which gives charm to his writing. Perhaps classic perfection of manner must usually be purchased at some cost of warm and spontaneous personal utterance. At all events, Lowell made no such sacrifice. No prose is more vital, racy, more full of the man. If it now and then seems bookish, that is because Lowell was a bookish man, always ready to fit any scene or action with a parallel from his reading. But he is never pedantic or dry. For he was never the slave of his reading; his first interest was in men. To a most unusual degree he united the temper of the man of the study with the temper of the man of affairs—Hosea Biglow with the college professor. In these essays there are learning, imagination, wit, satire, passion; but all fused in a great personality. To read them is to make acquaintance with one of the wisest and most broadly cultured, and at the same time one of the most genial and homely, of American writers.

ON A CERTAIN CONDESCENSION IN FOREIGNERS

This essay, printed in the *Atlantic Monthly* for January, 1869, was prompted by Lowell's resentment of the attitude of England toward this country during our Civil War. That resentment found pungent expression in the *Biglow Papers* as early as 1862, when England demanded—justly, but with needless arrogance—the surrender of the confederate commissioners, Mason and Slidell, whom Captain

Wilkes of our navy had taken out of the English merchant vessel, Trent. Mr. Lowell's lines express very well the feeling of the North at that time:

"We own the ocean, tu, John:
    You mus'n' take it hard,
Ef we can't think with you, John,
    It's jest your own back yard.
Ole Uncle S. sez he 'I guess,
    Ef *thet's* his claim,' sez he,
'The fencin'-stuff'll cost enough
    To bust up friend J. B.,
Ez wal ez you an' me'!"

"We give the critters back, John,
    Cos Abram thought 'twas right;
It warn't your bullyin' clack, John,
    Provokin' us to fight,
Ole Uncle S. sez he, 'I guess
    We've a hard row,' sez he,
'To hoe jest now; but thet, somehow,
    May happen to J. B.
Ez wal ez you an' me'!"

As the war went on, this feeling of resentment was intensified by the general English sympathy with the South, and especially by the indifference with which the English government seemed to regard the fact that privateers to prey upon American commerce were built, armed and equipped in England, and sailed from English ports.

After the close of the war, the American government made claims upon England for damages by these privateers; and it was while the discussion of these claims was hottest that this paper was written. A treaty, negotiated with Great Britain by our minister, Mr Reverdy Johnson, was rejected by the Senate because it made no adequate provision for the settlement of these claims. In April 1869, Charles Sumner made a famous speech urging extravagant claims upon England for indirect or "consequential" damages. There was great excitement in both countries, and for a time there seemed probability of an open rupture. Mr. Lowell himself dreaded that, and evidently thought that a frank, but good-humored, expression of American feeling would appeal to the English sense of fair play. In May, 1869, he wrote to Mr. Godkin, editor of *The Nation:*

"I wrote the essay you allude to, mainly with the hope of bringing about a better understanding. My heart aches with apprehension as I sit here in my solitude and brood over the present aspect of things between the two countries. We are crowding England into a fight which would be a horrible calamity for both—but worse for us than for them . . . It is not so much of what England *did* as of the *animus* with which she did it that we complain—a matter of sentiment wholly incapable of arbitration. Sumner's speech expressed the feeling of the country very truly, but I fear it was not a wise speech . . . It is a frightful tangle—but let us hope for the best."

242, 12. Twice made the scarlet leaves of October seem stained with blood. Two nephews of Lowell fell in the civil war; James Jackson Lowell, killed at Leesburg, June 30, 1862; Charles Russell Lowell, died of wounds received in the battle of Cedar Mountain, Oct. 20, 1864. See the touching stanzas in the second series of *Biglow Papers*, no. X.

243, 5. Henry Vaughan's Rainbow: Henry Vaughan (1622–1695), one of the most quaint and original minor poets of his century. The poem referred to begins,

> "Still young and fine! but what is still in view
> We slight as old and soil'd, though fresh and new."

243, 24. Collins: William Collins (1721–1759). His "Ode to Evening" is the most noteworthy poem of nature written in England between 1650 and 1750.

243, 26. Dodsley's Collection: Robert Dodsley (1703–1764), London bookseller, published in 1744, *A Select Collection of Old Plays, edited by Thomas Coxeter, 12 Vols.* I have not identified the passage on Solitude referred to.

243, 30. Estate in Gavelkind. "In Great Britain or Ireland an estate which by custom having the force of law is inheritable by all the sons together, and therefore subject to partition instead of going exclusively to the eldest."—*Century Dictionary*.

244, 6. Mrs. Radcliffe's heroes: Ann Radcliffe (1764–1823), author of several very wild romances, of which the most famous is *The Mysteries of Udolpho*.

245, 17. Hatem Tai's tent: Hatem (or Hatim) et Tai, chief of the Arabian tribe of the Tai in the fifth century, famed in Eastern legend for his generosity.

246, 4. Mecklenburg-Schwerin: a grand-duchy in North Germany, forming a part of the German Empire.

246, 12. General Banks: Nathaniel Prentiss Banks (1816–1894). Massachusetts politician, general during the civil war, and member of Congress from Massachusetts 1865–73, 1875–77, 1889–91. He was nicknamed "The Bobbin Boy" because in boyhood he worked in a cotton mill of which his father was superintendent.

246, 22. Buckle doctrine of averages: Henry Thomas Buckle (1821–1862), English historian. His principal book, *A History of Civilization in England* was left unfinished at his death. He held that the exceptional abilities of different individuals balanced each other, producing a general average, which is determined principally by external causes, such as climate, soil, food, etc., so that any particular social phenomena—e.g., suicides—occur with great uniformity in successive years. See especially Chaps. I and IV of Vol. I.

246, 25. Wandering Jew: according to tradition a Jew who refused permission to Christ to sit down when bearing the cross to Golgotha, and who was condemned by Christ to "wander on earth till I return."

247, 9. Gano: Italian form of Ganelon. Character in the *Chanson de Roland*, who betrays Roland to defeat and death; he is the typical traitor in mediæval epic romance.

247, 15. Baden Revolution. The grand-duchy of Baden is situated in the southwest corner of the German empire. The "revolution" referred to is probably that by which the Duchy in 1815 joined the German Confederation.

247, 18. Baden-Baden: chief city of the Duchy of Baden, noted for its medicinal springs, and even more noted, for more than a half century, as the most fashionable gaming center of Europe—hence the "revolutions practised every season" there.

247, 25. Jonathan Wild: a novel (1743) by Henry Fielding. "James Wild distinguished himself on both sides the question in the Civil War, passing from one to t'other, as Heaven seemed to declare itself in favor of either party." Chap. ii.

248, 6. Post hoc ergo propter hoc: "After that, therefore on account of that." The fallacy of assuming that the antecedent of any event is therefore its cause.

248, 29. Pigeon-livered and lack gall. See *Hamlet*, Act. II, line 604.

250, 19. Art thou there, old Truepenny? *Hamlet*, Act. I, sc. v, line 150.

250, 28. Montaigne. See Note on line 13, page 227.

250, 32. Père Bouhours (1628–1702): French Jesuit grammarian and man of letters. His principal work was *Entretiens d'Ariste et d'Eugene.*

250, 33. Si un Allemand peut être bel-esprit: "Whether a German can be a man of letters."

251, 1. Pückler-Muskau: Prince Hermann Ludwig Heinrich von (1785–1871), a German writer of travels in which the satiric temper is often prominent.

251, 3. Chance phrase of gentle Hawthorne: The reference is probably to a passage in *Our Old Home* in which Hawthorne describes in not complimentary terms a typical English dowager as "massive with solid beef and streaky tallow, so that you inevitably think of her as made up of steaks and sirloins." He was obliged to see the unfortunate passage quoted with indignation in a good many English journals.

251, 22. That unexpressive she. "The fair, the chaste, and unexpressive she."—*As You Like It.* Act III, sc. ii, line 10.

252, 10. Laius: king of Thebes. Being warned by an oracle that he would lose his life if his son Oedipus should reach man's estate, Laius gave the child to a herdsman to be destroyed; but the herdsman, moved with pity saved the child alive. Years afterward, Oedipus unwittingly killed his father.

252, 16. Holbein: Hans Holbein (1497–1543), greatest German painter of the early sixteenth century. The "all-but loveliest of Madonnas" is probably that in the gallery at Dresden.

252, 17. Rembrandt: Rembrandt Hermanzoon van Rijn (1607–1669), most famous painter of the Dutch school. The "graceful girl on his knee" is his wife, "Saskia."

252, 19. Rubens: Peter Paul (1577–1640), celebrated Flemish painter. His "abounding goddesses," which are not at all etherial, were said to be mostly copies of his wife Helena Fourment.

252, 24. Riveted with gigantic piles, etc.: from "The Character of Holland," a satire by Andrew Marvell (1621–1678).

252, 32. Motley: John Lothrop Motley (1814–1877), one of the most eminent of American historians. The reference here is to his *Rise of the Dutch Republic.*

253, 27. Atlantis: a mythical island in the Atlantic fabled to have disappeared with all its inhabitants.

254, 2. Who reads a Russian book? The "Edinburgh" had asked "Who reads an American book?"

255, 5. The World's West-End. The West-End is the fashionable residential part of London.

255, 12. **Vere de Vere:**

> "that repose
> Which stamps the caste of Vere de Vere."
> Tennyson's *Lady Clara Vere de Vere.*

255, 30. **Lucifer, Son of the Morning:** properly the Morning Star; but by a mistake in the rendering of a verse of Scripture (*Isaiah*, xiv, 12) applied to Satan.

256, 26. **The Indian mutiny.** The Sepoy or Indian mutiny against the British in India, 1857–58, was marked by the noblest endurance and heroism on the part of the garrisons at Delhi and Lucknow. Men like Sir Henry Havelock and Colin Campbell who defended and relieved Lucknow are in Lowell's thought.

257, 8. **Bloomsbury:** a section of London north of New Oxford street which a century and a half ago seemed likely to be the aristocratic quarter of London, but which has now been mostly given over to a different class—it contains many pensions and boarding houses.

257, 10. **Europa upon his back.** In Greek myth, Jupiter, in love with Europa, took the form of a bull and carried her off upon his back.

258, 1. **Unsexes her with the bravo.** Because "bravo" is the masculine form, instead of "brava," feminine.

258, 6. **Agassiz, Guyot, and Goldwin Smith:** eminent scholars of foreign birth whose work was largely done in America. Jean Louis Rodolphe Agassiz, born and educated in Switzerland, professor of zoology and geology in Harvard University, 1848 to his death in 1873; Arnold Henry Guyot (1807–1884), eminent geographer, born in Switzerland, professor in Princeton from 1855 to his death; Goldwin Smith (1823–1910), English historian and economist who came to America to take the chair of constitutional history in Cornell University at the opening of that institution in 1868, holding the position until 1871, when he removed his residence to Toronto.

258, 17. **Rousseau-tinted spectacles:** Jean Jacques Rousseau (1712–1778), the famous Swiss philosopher, sentimentalist, romancer. His teachings on the origin of society and the basis of government had great influence over Europe and America. The "French officers" may have expected to see in the new American republic something of the charm of a simple and primitive society that Rousseau had assumed in his *Contrat Social.*

258, 24. **Niaiseries of M. Maurice Sand.** Maurice Sand is the pseudonym—inherited from his mother "George Sand"—of Maurice Dudevant, whose "trivialities" on America were published in the "*Revue de Deux Mondes*."

258, 3. Jean Crapaud: nickname for a Frenchman.

259, 3. Gare de l'eau: "Look out for water" (slops).

259, 4. Duvergier d' Hauranne: Prosper (1798–1881): French politician and journalist.

259, 6. Le Français est plutôt indiscret que confiant: "The Frenchman is often indiscreet, seldom confiding."

259, 8. Tant-soit-peu: "just a little."

259, 16. Barnum: Phineas Taylor (1810–1891): great American showman.

260, 18. Mutato nomine, de te: "The name changed, (the fable or the charge applies) to you."

261, 1. L. S.: Leslie Stephen, English man of letters, and a warm friend of Lowell. In the summer of 1868 he paid Lowell a visit, just before this essay was written.

261, 3. Clough: Arthur Hugh (1819–1861), an English poet, who spent a year in America at the invitation of Emerson and formed many friendships here. Lowell's estimate of his poetry hardly seems extravagant to many of his admirers.

261, 5. T. H.: Thomas Hughes, the well-known English author and reformer, author of *Tom Brown's School Days* and *Tom Brown at Oxford*. He lectured in the United States in 1871, and in 1880 founded a "Rugby Colony" of English settlers in Tennessee.

261, 12. British parson, traveling in Newfoundland. I have not identified the reformer.

261, 27. Brocken-specter. The Brocken is the highest peak of the Harz mountains in Germany. The "specter" is a peculiar shadow or mirage which takes the form of a vastly magnified human figure or figures, seen upon the mountain or in the sky.

263, 13. If you tickle us, do we not laugh? See Shakespeare, *Merchant of Venice*, Act iii, sc. 1, line 68.

263, 30. Wilhelmus Conquestor: William the Conqueror, the monarch who achieved the Norman conquest of England, 1066.

263, 34. Carlyle's sneer. Carlyle had spoken with some contempt of the American people before; but the outbreak of the Civil War provoked him to bitter cynicism. The war was, he said, only "the burning out a smoky chimney," a "nigger agony"; and in 1863 he published in *Macmillan's Magazine* a vulgar squib, *Iliad in Nuce* (Iliad in a Nutshell) of which he was himself afterward a little ashamed.

264, 2. The Hohonzollerns: the German imperial family to which Frederick the Great belonged, whose history Carlyle was then (1858-1865) publishing.

264, 22. Leigh Hunt (1784-1859), an English poet and essayist. "More than half Americanized" because Hunt's father had passed his early life in Philadelphia, and had married an American young woman; perhaps also because Hunt all his life showed the meaner side of a "shopkeeper's" nature, without the shopkeeper's thrift.

264, 30. John Hawkwood: a famous Condottiore or free lance of the fourteenth century. He served with distinction in the wars of Edward Third, and later in the century took service in Italy. The allusion to a needle refers to the tradition that in his youth he had been a tailor in London.

264, 34. Cleon into the place of Pericles: i.e., a demagogue in the place of a statesman. Pericles was the great Athenian statesman and orator, leader of the democratic party; at his death, 429 B. C., his place as leader of the party was taken by Cleon, a fluent and shifty man.

265, 7. Porphyro geniti: "born in the purple."

267, 26. A Dana here and there: Charles A. Dana (1819-97) prominent editor and politician. He served as Assistant Secretary of war (1863-65), and when this essay was written, had just begun (1868) his long career as editor of the *New York Sun*.

268, 15. Charing Cross. "I talked of the cheerfulness of Fleet Street . . . 'Why sir' (said Johnson) 'Fleet street has a very animated appearance; but I think the full tide of human existence is at Charing Cross.'"—Boswell's *Johnson*, Vol. ii, p. 337 (Hill's ed.).

268, 18. Doubtless God could, etc. "We may say of angling as Dr. Boteler said of strawberries, 'Doubtless God could have made a better berry, but doubtless God never did.'"—Izaak Walton's *Complete Angler*, Part i, ch. 1.

269, 1. Reverdy Johnson: appointed minister to England in 1868, and negotiated in that year the Johnson-Clarendon treaty, which was rejected by the Senate the following year, on the ground that it made no adequate provision for the payment by England of the claim for damages by the *Alabama* and other Confederate privateers fitted out in English ports. When this essay was a writing, Mr. Johnson was very popular in England—less so in his own country.

269, 6. My Lord, this means war. In September, 1863, Charles Francis Adams, American minister to England, learning that another vessel was about to sail from England as a Confederate war vessel, wrote to Lord Russell, English Foreign Secretary, informing him of the fact, and added, "It would be superfluous in me to point out to your lordship that this is war."

269, 29. **Since 1660, when you married again:** that is, after the Restoration of the monarchy in Charles Second and the emphatic repudiation of republican ideas.

270, 3. **Do, child, go to it grandam,** etc.   See Shakespeare, *King John,* Act. II, scene 1, lines 159–161.

Queries and Suggestions

1. Make out an analysis of this essay that will show its method.

2. Is there any special appropriateness in the beautiful passage of quiet description with which it opens?

3. Show the purpose of the narrative that follows as an introduction to the paper.

4. Is the introductory portion of the essay too long?

5. Is there any explanation for the irritating condescension that foreigners have shown toward America and Americans?

6. Lowell said he wrote this essay with the hope of "bringing about a better understanding" between England and America; do you think it was well calculated to have that effect?

7. Select from the essay at least five excellent examples of satire.

8. Show by an examination of some three or four pages the frequency and range of Lowell's allusions.

9. In the same way show the wealth of imagination in his metaphors.

10. Rewrite in plain language the figurative statements in the last two sentences of the paragraph on page 262.

Do you think these sentences suggest any criticism of Lowell's use of metaphor?

11. Characterize as well as you can the humor of Lowell, to which his writing owes so much of its charm.

12. If you knew nothing else of Lowell's life or work, what traits of his mind and temper could you infer from this essay?

ROBERT LOUIS STEVENSON

Robert Louis Stevenson was a hero and adventurer; but his heroism and adventure were in the realm of the spirit.   Almost the only outward incidents in his life were those brave journeyings about the world, over seas and across continents, to find some place where he could live and work. He was born in Edinburgh, in 1850. His father and grandfather were civil engineers in the Scottish light-house service, hardy men, clear of head and strong of hand, with a strenuous sense of duty. From his mother, the daughter of a Scottish minister, he is said to have inherited his cheerful optimism, along with that ethical interest that made him always something of a preacher. From her, too, he inherited his tendency to pulmonary disease; but she, although always an invalid, outlived both her husband and her son. From early boyhood Stevenson was slight and frail of body, adventurous and imaginative in temper. He had been intended for the profession of his father; but it was evident before the close of his university days that he had neither strength nor inclination for that. He then, at the wish of his father, began the study of law, and after five years passed his examinations, and was called to the Scottish bar. But some of the most gloomy months of his life fell in those years. He knew there could be no satisfaction nor success for him in the law. His one desire was to make of himself a man of letters; but meantime it seemed he must either starve or live on the bounty of his father. Worst of all, his health, always feeble, now broke down altogether, and in the fall of 1873 he was sent to the south of France to save his life. The paper *Ordered South*, printed in *Macmillan's Magazine* the next spring, is a poignant expression of his loneliness and depression. Years afterward, in a note added to this paper when republished, he says in apology for the mood of the writer, "A young man finds himself one too many in the world; he has no calling; no obvious utility; no ties but to his parents, and these he is sure to disregard. I do not think that a proper allowance has been made for the true causes of suffering in youth." But in the course of the winter this hopeless temper passed away; and he never allowed it to return. There is an interval of less than four years between the *Ordered South* and the *Aes Triplex;* the difference in temper between the two is amazing. Before 1878 the young man has regained his courage; he can do stoutly the work of the day; can taste to the full the pleasures of life; and can look with dauntless and defiant cheer into the very face of death.

But this change did not mean any permanent security in his health. The record of the years from 1874 to 1880 is the story of frequent flights, for a considerable portion of every year, to some climate where he could live and breathe—to Paris, Barbizon, Mentone, Switzerland. Yet those years were among the most profitable of his life. He had definitely resolved upon the literary career, and his father no longer discouraged it. His early papers in the magazines had attracted the attention of discriminating readers, and the circle of his acquaintance soon included a number of the most promising young English writers, Sidney Colvin, Edmund Gosse, Leslie Stephen, Andrew Lang, W. T. Henley. During those years he spent much time in France, and the influence of French life and French literature may be seen in the increasing flexibility, point, and precision of his writings. It is the period of the *Inland Voyage*, the *Travels with a Donkey*, and all of those delightful essays afterwards collected in the volume *Virginibus Puerisque*. He was sedulously studying his art; by 1878 he may almost be said to have mastered it. And his mind was ripening as well as his art. It may be questioned whether in matter as well as in manner such an essay as the *Aes Triplex* is not the equal of anything he ever wrote. In its union of the brave confidence of youth with the maturer wisdom of years, and in the easy perfection of its phrase, this is amazingly good prose for a young man of twenty-seven.

It was late in 1876, when staying with the artist colony at Grez near Barbizon, that Stevenson first met Mrs. Osborne, an American lady whose family life had been broken up—by no fault of hers—and who had come to Europe to educate her children. It was a case of love at first sight. Next year Mrs. Osborne returned to California, and in 1879 Stevenson determined to follow. His parents and all his friends thought the acquaintance unfortunate; but opposition and difficulty only spurred his romantic resolve. He took steerage passage in a cheap steamer, crossed the continent in an emigrant train, and in the last days of summer arrived in San Francisco. In the next six months, he lay for weeks at the point of death in a goat ranch in the Coast Mountains; a little recovered, he watched the wild, half-Spanish life in the ranches and the town of Monterey; found some friends in the raw and boisterous life of San Francisco; turned his experience into some very interesting books—and in May, 1880, he married Mrs. Osborne and brought her home to the house of his now relenting and approving father. He had been at grips with death half a dozen times; he had met many varieties of hardship; he had not yet been able to make the great public listen to him. But all this only sent this man out more bravely upon the adventure of life, glad that

> " The world is so full of a number of things!"

And he never doubted his vocation. As he wrote to his friend Henley, when he was living in one room for seventy cents a day, in

San Francisco, "There is something in me worth saying, though I can't find out what it is yet."

He was soon to find out. The *Treasure Island* ran through the winter months of 1881–82 quietly enough in the pages of an obscure magazine; but when it appeared in book form, next year, the public began to discover Stevenson. The reviews pronounced it the best story since Defoe. "Statesmen and judges," says Stevenson's biographer, "became boys again sitting up long after bedtime to read their new book." It was published simultaneously in London and Boston, and pirated everywhere else. Within two years it had been translated even into Spanish and Greek. But neither success nor failure could check Stevenson's tremendous industry. His health was no better. The greater part of the four years following his return from America he was forced to spend in exile at Davos Platz or in the Riviera. Twice he was near death, and always had to live "as if he were walking on eggs." Yet the list of his books written between 1880 and 1886 numbers over sixty titles. One of these papers won instant and startling success. *The Strange Case of Dr. Jekyll and Mr. Hyde*, published in 1886, established his reputation, and still is probably the best known of all his writings.

Stevenson wearied of attempts to "patch up his carcase" by repeated flights to some more genial climate. After a residence in the south of England for two years which resulted only in steady decline of health, he resolved to try at least a year in America. His writings had made him as well known here as in England, and publishers on both sides the Atlantic were clamorous for anything he would write. In August of 1887, taking his wife and mother with him—his father had died the year before—he sailed for New York. The next winter he passed in a health resort in the Adirondacks, while his wife went on to San Francisco to arrange for an extended sea voyage the following summer. In June, 1888, the Stevenson family embarked at San Francisco on a seventy-ton schooner they had chartered, for a cruise in the South Pacific. The cruise lasted three years. To sail thus, month after month, through tropic seas, from one strange island to another, over that unknown side of the world, made life for Stevenson one long romance—"better than any poem." And it seemed probable that here if anywhere he could hope for something like health. He decided not to come back to civilization. In 1891, he chose a hill-side near Apia in the Samoan islands, and here he built his house. He cleared a space of virgin forest, he planted his garden, and after long wandering felt for the first time in his life something of the settled peace of home.

There were three years left him. He resumed his literary work with his old eagerness. The experiences of travel furnished him material for several books and briefer articles, and he turned again hopefully to the field of fiction. He finished *David Balfour*—the sequel of *Kidnapped*—and he began what promised to be his most ambitious novel, *Weir of Hermiston*. But in fact the best work of his life had been done before he left England. He never quite regained the vigor or the magic of his earlier writing. The end came, not as might have been expected after a period of decline, but as he would have wished it, suddenly. Elate, full of enthusiasm, at the close of a long day's work, as he talked with his wife at sundown, he suddenly threw up his hands to his head exclaiming "What's that!" —and never spoke again.

Stevenson's writings are our best modern example of the value of the literary art. He had naturally the quick sense of phrase, the inborn gift of the right word; and he had cultivated it by tireless and exacting practice. His writing covers a very wide range of subjects—fiction, narratives of travel and adventure, biography, literary criticism, personal essays, poetry; but an art so finished touched nothing that it did not adorn. His page is never dull and lead-colored. A narrative that, written by another, would be plodding common-place, sparkles with unexpected felicities of observation, in a diction remarkably precise yet fresh and unstudied.

Yet art alone, however perfect, will hardly suffice to keep any writing from oblivion. It is probably true that more than half of Stevenson's twenty-six volumes are already forgotten. He is most often thought of as a novelist. His novels—or, to speak more accurately, romances—have the one great virtue of action. In a time when the public began to weary of the novel of society with its analysis of characters not worth analyzing, the sort of novel in which nothing happens and there is no reason why anything ever should happen, there was a welcome for these stirring stories where there is always something doing. But besides this sense of constant action, it may be questioned whether these books have any compelling interest. They are not studies of human life as it is. They have many acute and truthful statements of motive and mood, but there are few real men and women in them. They do not add many persons to our acquaintance. The *Treasure Island* is the best of them, because the most convincing. It appeals irresistibly to that boy's love of adventure and fight which no man with any blood in him ever quite outgrows. The *Dr. Jekyll and Mr. Hyde* will live because it presents one of the fatal possibilities of human nature in an allegory startlingly vivid. The story came to Stevenson, it is said, in a dream; it has the uncanny reality of a nightmare.

After all, the most interesting person in all Stevenson's books is Stevenson himself. His character was unusually rich and complex, combining an eager enjoyment of all pleasures of body and mind with a strong ethical sense, and driven by a powerful will. Mr. Henley in the closing lines of his familiar memorial sonnet, attempts to give some notion of the opposite characteristics united in his friend:

> "Buffoon and poet, lover and sensualist,
> A deal of Ariel, just a streak of Puck,
> Much Antony, of Hamlet most of all,
> And something of the Shorter Catechist."

Yet these lines are rather brilliant than true. Surely there was little of Antony in a man who never threw the reins upon the neck of his passions; of Hamlet there was certainly much less in that adventurous spirit who, for all his interest in the mystery of life, was always athirst for action, braved the assaults of outrageous fortune with defiant laughter, and never could have uttered a line of the world-weary, melancholy Dane. Of the "Shorter Catechist" there certainly was something in Stevenson; but it is difficult to conceive in what proportions that dour personage could combine with Marc Antony and Hamlet. If I were to venture a suggestion in Henley's manner, I should say that a union of John Knox and Robert Burns might make a character not unlike that of Robert Louis Stevenson.

In the opinion of many readers, the personality of Stevenson finds best expression in the *Essays*. These papers are his philosophy of life. They were written in that early period when he had conquered his first fears and found that life, in spite of all its hardships, is an extremely good thing. Nowhere does the inner force of his character speak more boldly. The essays are full of his exhilarating, militant optimism. There is no bravado in them; their courage is not the ignorant assurance of untried youth. He does not blink any of the manifold ills of circumstance; but he will not think God's world a place where a man may whimper and whine. These essays are full of his humor, too. Not the humor of the satirist, nor of the frivolous man who deems anything in life may be matter of idle jest; but the brave and helpful humor that finds men and women always interesting, and often issues in that kindly laughter that doeth good like a medicine. The student of literature delights in such essays as

El Dorado and *Aes Triplex* as finished specimens of his art; but they are more than that. They are inspiring studies of the possibilities of life.

EL DORADO

El Dorado: the name of the reputed king of a fabled city of great wealth supposed in the fifteenth and sixteenth centuries, to exist somewhere in South America. In popular usage the name came to be transferred to the city itself, and is used as typical of any object of imaginative search.

271, 22. To have many of these is to be spiritually rich: an admirable expression of the wealth of Stevenson's own nature.

272, 24. Note-books upon Frederick the Great; Thomas Carlyle's last great historical work, finished in 1865. Called here "note-books" probably because of their multifarious detail imperfectly wrought into a flowing narrative.

272, 30. Decline and Fall: The *Decline and Fall of the Roman Empire;* most important historical work in English literature of the eighteenth century, by Edward Gibbon (1737–1794). It was mostly written in Lausanne. Gibbon says in his *Autobiography:* "It was on the day, or rather night, of the 27th of June, 1787. between the hours of eleven and twelve, that I wrote the last lines of the last page, in a summer house in my garden. I took several turns in a *berceau* or covered walk of accacias, which commands a prospect of the country, the lake, and the mountains . . . . . I will not dissemble the first emotions of joy on recovery of my freedom, and perhaps the establishment of my fame. But my pride was soon humbled, and a sober melancholy was spread over my mind by the idea that I had taken an everlasting leave of an old and agreeable companion."

273, 23. Of making books there is no end: Ecclesiastes, xii, 12.

WALKING TOURS

This essay should be compared with Hazlitt's paper *On Going a Journey,* page 97 of this volume, which Stevenson so admired.

276, 20. Christian. In Bunyan's *Pilgrim's Progress,* when Christian "came up with the Cross, his burden loosed from off his shoulders, and fell from off his back . . . then Christian gave three leaps for joy and went out singing."

276, 30. Abudah's chest. The story of Abudah may be found in *Tales of the Genii,* by James Ridley, a collection of stories modeled on the *Arabian Nights.*

281, 14. Says Hazlitt. See the passage in Hazlitt's essay, page 104.

281, 22. Heine's songs: Heinrich Heine (1797–1856), German poet and critic. His *Buch der Lieder* contains many exquisite specimens of German lyric.

281, 22. Tristram Shandy: the masterpiece of that whimsical parson and novelist, Laurence Sterne (1713–1768).

282, 9. Happy thinking:

> "I hae been blythe wi' comrades dear;
> I hae been merry drinking;
> I hae been joyfu' gath'rin gear;
> I hae been happy thinking."
>
>   Burns, "*The Rigs o' Barley.*"

Aes Triplex

This essay was first printed in the *Cornhill Magazine* for April, 1881, and afterwards included, like the other essays of this volume in the *Virginibus Puerisque*. It represents Stevenson's literary style at his very best, and is a most inspiring expression of that valiant cheerfulness which the ·man carried through all his life, though always in the shadow of death.

Aes triplex: "Triple brass." The phrase comes from Horace, *Odes*, Book I, 5, and has often been used as a synonym for courage and endurance.

> "Illi robur et æs triplex
> Circa pectus erat, qui fragilem truci
> Commisit pelago ratem
> Primus."

> "Oak and brass of triple fold
> Encompass'd sure that heart
> Which first made bold
> To the raging sea to trust
> A fragile bark."

283, 31. Thug. The thugs were a society of professed assassins and robbers in India who waylaid and strangled travelers. They were suppressed by the British government before the middle of the last century.

284, 11. Dule (or dool) tree: in Scotland a memorial or mourning tree.

286, 1. The blue-peter might fly at the truck. The blue-peter is a blue flag with a white square in the center hoisted at the mast head as a signal that the ship is ready to sail. The truck is a circular block at the top of a mast, with holes through which the halyards are passed.

286, 27. Balaclava: a small town in the Crimea, the scene of the famous charge of the English "light brigade," commemorated in the familiar poem by Tennyson.

286, 30. Curtius. According to the Roman legend, an earthquake had opened a great chasm in the Forum which the soothsayers said could only be closed by throwing into it the most precious thing in Rome. Curtius, a noble youth, plunged into it, and it closed over him.

287, 4. The Derby: the most fashionable of the English races, held at Epsom on the last Wednesday of May. It is the great English holiday of the spring, and the race is witnessed by thousands. Called after the earl of Derby, who established it in 1780.

287, 6. Caligula: Roman emperor (37–41 A. D.). His savage cruelty and license indicate that he was probably insane. The story here referred to is told by the Roman historian Tacitus.

287, 15. Prætorian. The pretorian guard was the body-guard of the Roman emperors; their commanding officer, or Prefect, came to be one of the most powerful and dreaded persons in the state.

288, 5. Job and Omar Khayyam to Thomas Carlyle or Walt Whitman: all of whom have pondered, though in very different tempers, the meaning of life and the mystery of death. Omar Khayyam was a Persian poet and astronomer of the first part of the twelfth century. His principal work, the *Rubaiyat*, familiar to English readers from the paraphrase made by Edward Fitzgerald, 1859, may be described as a poetic expansion of the motto, "Let us eat and drink, for to-morrow we die."

Walt Whitman (1819–1862), robust, out-of-door American writer, to whom one cannot deny the title of poet, though he had no eye for what most people think beauty and no ear for what most people think poetic form. He often mistakes bigness for greatness; but there are many high and solemn things in his work—and many things neither high nor solemn. Stevenson himself has written, on the whole, perhaps the most just appreciation of Whitman, in the volume of *Familiar Studies*.

288, 17. Permanent Possibility of Sensation. This phrase was used by John Stuart Mill as a definition of Matter, and then, slightly modified, as a definition of Mind. "The Permanent Possibility of feeling, which forms my notion of myself." See Mill's *Examination of the Philosophy of Sir William Hamilton*, Vol. i, chaps. xi, xii.

289, 23. The Commander's statue. The reference is to the story of Don Juan as given in Moliere's play, *Dom Juan ou le Festin de Pierre*. The libertine Don Juan in jest invites to supper the statue of the Commander who was the father of one of his victims; the statue accepts and knocks at Don Juan's door; and the visit later results in the death of the seducer. The incident is often used to illustrate the imminence of some unexpected calamity.

290, 5. A mere bag's end, *as the French say:* "Cul de sac."

290, 17. Our respected lexicographer: Samuel Johnson, who all his life admitted that he dreaded death. Many passages may be found in Boswell's *Life* like the following: "I told him that David Hume said to me, he was no more uneasy to think he should not be after this life, than that he had not been before he began to exist." Johnson: "Sir, if he really thinks so, his perceptions are disturbed, he is mad; if he does not think so, he lies." . . . "To my question, whether we might not fortify our minds for the approach of death, he anwered, in a passion, 'No, Sir, let it alone. . . . A man knows it must be so and submits. It will do him no good to whine.'" Boswell *Life of Johnson* (Hill's Ed.) Vol. II, p. 106.

290, 21. Highland tour: made in 1773, when Johnson was sixty-seven years of age.

291, 29. Mim-mouthed: "Reserved in discourse"; implying affectation of modesty. *Century Dictionary.*

292, 1. A peerage or Westminster Abbey, cried Nelson: Horatio Nelson, England's most famous naval hero, killed in the moment of victory in his great battle of Trafalgar. The famous words quoted here were uttered three years earlier on the eve of the battle of Aboukir Bay.

292, 6. Tread down the nettle danger. See Shakespeare *Henry IV*, Part I, Act ii, sc. 3.

292, 9. His dictionary. Johnson set at work upon his *Dictionary* in 1747, an obscure and struggling author in London; he published it in 1755.

292, 14. Thackeray and Dickens . . . fallen in mid-course. Thackeray left unfinished *Denis Duval*, Dickens left unfinished *The Mystery of Edwin Drood*. Stevenson himself had begun what promised to be his greatest novel, *Weir of Hermiston*, when death met him; he was working upon it, in high spirits, all through the last day of his life.

293, 16. Whom the gods love die young. See Plautus *Bacchides*, Act IV, sc. 7.

293, 24. Trailing with him clouds of glory: from Wordsworth's *Ode on the Intimations of Immortality*, a favorite poem with Stevenson.

The closing lines of this essay seem almost prophetic of Stevenson's last hour. He died as he had wished. He worked in cheerful spirits through the day; at sunset he chatted pleasantly with his wife; at eight o'clock he had gone.

QUERIES AND SUGGESTIONS

El Dorado.

1. State in one clear proposition the subject of this essay.
2. Suggest some other examples of this truth, besides those which Stevenson gives in the essay.
3. In what ways does the essay seem characteristic of Stevenson, and illustrated by the facts of his life?

Walking Tours.

1. Compare this essay with Hazlitt's *On Going a Journey;* what pleasures do both men find in walking?
2. Both men prefer to walk alone; but what are the reasons for the preference in each case?
3. Do you think the after dinner mood of "happy thinking" described on page 282 more characteristic of Stevenson or of Hazlitt?
4. Mention any other points of similarity or of contrast between the two men suggested by a comparison of the two essays. Which essay, on the whole, do you find the more interesting? And why?

Aes Triplex.

1. Make out an analysis of this essay.
2. Show by an examination of a number of passages, the excellence of paragraph structure in the essay.
3. Make a detailed examination of a passage of some length—say the second, third, and fourth paragraphs of the essay—to show the imaginative richness of Stevenson's style, in metaphors, allusions, epithets.
4. What do you understand to be the distinction Stevenson makes in this essay between the "love of life" and the "love of living"?
5. What circumstances in Stevenson's earlier years make this essay especially significant?
6. Write a brief paper showing that Stevenson is at his best in this essay, both as a man and as a writer.